Matter in Mind

A Study of Kant's Transcendental Deduction

Studies in Phenomenology and
Existential Philosophy

Matter in Mind

*A Study of Kant's
Transcendental Deduction*

Richard E. Aquila

Indiana University Press • Bloomington and Indianapolis

Manufactured in the United States of America

Library of Congress Cataloging-in-Publication Data
Aquila, Richard E., 1944–
    Matter in mind.

    (Studies in phenomenology and existential philosophy)
    Includes bibliographical references and index.
    1. Kant, Immanuel, 1724–1804 Kritik der reinen
Vernuft.   2. Knowledge, Theory of-History—18th century.
3. Intuition—History—18th century.   4. Kant, Immanuel,
1724–1804—Contributions in theory of perception.
5. Perception (Philosophy—History—18th century.
6. Transcendentalism—History—18th century.   I. Title.
II. Series.
B2779.A67   1989   121   88-45387
ISBN 0-253-33712-7
1   2   3   4   5   93   92   91   90   89

For Jean

CONTENTS

Preface

This is a study of the Transcendental Deduction in Kant's *Critique of Pure Reason*. The framework of Kant's theory of cognition in that work, and of consciousness generally, is provided by the distinction between matter and form in cognition. The distinction is doubly important for Kant. It is important in the Transcendental Aesthetic, where Kant regards sensation (*Empfindung*) as the material of sensory intuition (*Anschauung*). And it is important in the Transcendental Logic, of which the Deduction is a part, where Kant then regards the latter as material for even higher forming. The higher forming occurs by means of something that Kant calls "synthesis." He claims that it provides the foundation for any act of conceptualization, or for any exercise of understanding, that is directed toward any object of sensory intuition:

> Transcendental Logic, on the other hand, has a manifold of sensibility lying before it *a priori*, presented to it by the transcendental aesthetic, in order to give material to the pure concepts of understanding. . . . But the spontaneity of our thought requires that this manifold first be gone through in a certain way, taken up, and connected, in order that a cognition be made out of it. This act I name synthesis. (A76-7/B102)

Apparently interchangeably, Kant regards the higher forming in question as constitutive of a "unity of consciousness" in regard to the corresponding material:

> Thus the mode in which the manifold of sensible representation (intuition) belongs to one consciousness precedes all cognition of the object, as its intellectual form. . . . (A129)

> Two components of cognition take place *a priori*. 1. Intuitions, 2. Unity of consciousness of the manifold of intuitions (even of empirical intuitions). This unity of consciousness constitutes the form of experience as objective empirical cognition.[1]

A number of additional passages to the effect will be examined throughout this study.

It may seem that Kant is confused in these notions, or perhaps he draws a legitimate distinction in a confusing pair of ways. One might distinguish, for example, between the variety of sensory impingements upon a subject at any moment, and that subject's capacity for a more or less unitary cognitive response to them. That response provides the subject with its own "representation" of a world from which those impingements might have arisen in the first place. We might therefore say that the distinction in question is a distinction between a matter and a form in any experience of a world. But why do we need to distinguish, in addition, between two different levels of experience (or at least of "experience")? One may feel that the distinction of levels, if not arbitrary, could be of purely pragmatic significance. For purely pragmatic purposes, some types of cognitive response will be considered to be less sophisticated, or less cognitively demanding, than others. I argue against this sort of approach, both in interpreting Kant and independently. I argue that any appreciation of the role of understanding in experience requires that we first take seriously the more basic notions of matter and form on the level of mere intuition, where the "form" of the latter needs to be introduced as a primitive in the philosophy of mind. On the level of understanding of what is then "given" in intuition, the basic claims will be two: (a) that concepts are always made out of a certain kind of material, in a sense that is importantly analogous to the way in which sensory intuitions are made out of sensations, and (b) that, at least in the case of concepts other than "categories," the material out of which a concept is made must in its own turn be ingredient as a material in intuitions—in just the sense in which sensations are. (The categories, in this view, could be nothing other than the intellectual forms for the transformation of the given material, precisely in their role as applied to that material.) The additional material is provided by, or by a species of, what Kant calls imagination.

Unfortunately, Kant's choice of the title _imagination_ is misleading, and so is his insistence that its bearer is a kind of intuition in its own right. I argue that his concern is with anticipations and retentions of a sort that I try to characterize. The title _anticipation_ in this context is natural; I speak of _retention_ partly for convenience and partly on account of Kant's own concern with _Reproduktion_ in the first edition. I take that concern, and that version of the Transcendental Deduction, more seriously than is generally the case. However, Chapter Five provides a detailed examination of the second edition Deduction. The notion of anticipation should become clear fairly quickly. The role of retention will finally be made clearer in Chapter Six.

It is important to distinguish between different kinds of anticipation and retention. What we ordinarily associate with these terms is an essentially "conceptual" affair, in the sense of that notion that Kant attempts to elucidate in the Deduction. So construed, to appeal to anticipation and retention as the material of conceptualization would be circular. To highlight a central feature of Kant's theory, I shall occasionally speak of merely "animal" anticipation and retention. The feature that I have in mind concerns Kant's attempt to account for the distinction, but also to account for a kind of harmony, between the purely animal and the distinctively human in consciousness. This aspect of Kant's endeavor is universally acknowledged to be central to his ethics. In his theory of mind and knowledge, it is generally recognized only in his view that "sensation" provides the material of intuition. Its counterpart in the theory of understanding is overlooked. Distinctively human conception and judgment rests on a kind of second, though not necessarily temporally second, forming of a body of material that we might as well regard, though Kant was reluctant to do so in so many words, as constitutive of purely animal conception and judgment. Though there are senses in which it is nonsense to say so, I go so far as to defend a sense in which non-categorial *concepts*, not just conceptions and judgments, are nothing but such formings of "imaginative" matter.

As it happens, while Kant himself comes at least close to saying that imagination provides the material of concepts, he does not, to my knowledge, ever explicitly say that imagination functions as material in intuition. Implausibly, as I have noted, he insists that imagination is always a kind of intuition itself. He even says, at one point, that it is always defined by form, not matter. [2] In addition, Kant sometimes appears to hold that the only relevant distinction between matter and form, on the level of understanding, is such that the former is provided by the *objects* of understanding, not by anything literally ingredient *in* understanding itself. [3] It will be important to see that it is nonetheless necessary to regard a kind of imagination as providing material capable of serving as material in intuitions. Unlike mere "sensations," there will not be a sense in which such material could be *the* material of intuitions. Unlike sensations, it cannot provide the material requisite for the constitution of an intuition (or at least a non-"pure" one) as an intuition in the first place. But that is not the claim that I intend to defend. The suggestion is not that imagination provides the material of intuitions as such. It is rather that, in order to provide the material for a grasp of anything *through* intuitions, imagination must provide something that, at least on those occasions, is as intrinsically ingredient within intuitions as sensations ever are.

The notion of understanding and perceiving "through" a body of material will be crucial throughout this study. I utilize it in connection with a related phenomenological distinction. This is the distinction between the matter and form of a subject's cognitive acts—on the noetic side of cognition—and the intentional correlates of that matter and form in objects or appearances—on the correlative noematic side of cognition. For example, a certain sensory quality apprehended as spread through regions of intuitional space is the intentional correlate of the ingredience of mere sensations in cognition. In Chapter One, I elaborate this claim in a way that avoids objections to similar claims. In Chapter Four, I argue that Kant's doctrine of the "affinity" of appearances embodies his extension of these notions to the relationship between imagination and understanding. The affinity of appearances is the intentional correlate of the imaginative material *through* which those appearances are originally apprehended in experience. These distinctions will also shed some light on some aspects of Kant's account of aesthetic judgment in the *Critique of Judgment*.

In Chapter Six, I extend these notions to Kant's account of self-consciousness. It may seem unwise to have abstracted from such questions up to that point. It is clear that the problem of unity of consciousness, and of self-consciousness, is central to both of the versions of the Deduction. However, it is typical to regard the problem of unity of consciousness in the Deduction in too simplistic a way. It is typical to regard it as a problem concerning the capacity of a single subject for ascribing a set of distinct subjective states to itself. I argue that this problem is secondary to a different one. The overall structure of Kant's reflection is this: (1) Any conceptualization of experience requires the formation of objective con-

cepts out of a body of anticipative and retentive material that is ingredient as material in (would-be) experiences themselves. (2) The intellectual forms that are required for the formation of objective concepts out of the anticipative and retentive
material ingredient in experiences must embody anticipations and retentions,
which need not otherwise have been so embodied, into a structure of anticipations
and retentions concerning the actual and the possible courses of *one's own* experience. (3) One's original self-conception, as of a subject to which a set of distinct
subjective states are ascribable, is derivative from the resulting anticipative and
retentive structure. The preparation for an account of self-consciousness thus requires a prior appreciation of the general problems to which the first of these three
claims refers us.

I argue that the upshot is an account of self-consciousness that is much more
Sartrean than generally realized: the Kantian self is originally self-conscious only
through consciousness of the noematic *correlate*, in the world of appearances, of
its own noetic structuring of experience. Appreciation of this point requires
greater appreciation of a distinction between levels and structures within one's
consciousness of appearances themselves. In an important sense, Kantian consciousness is not in the first instance self-consciousness. It is consciousness of self
only through its consciousness of the world. In Chapter Seven, I finally turn to
consider the more specific bearing of this reading on Kant's attempt to specify
particular "categories" presupposed in this way by both self-consciousness and
consciousness of objects.

In a sense, the doctrine of understanding that I ascribe to Kant is reductionistic.
It is, at least, reductionistic with respect to the existence of *concepts* as quasi-
linguistic terms, supposed to be "applied" to intuitions or to objects, and to be
employed or utilized in judgments. Obviously, my account will not be reductionistic in some other, more obvious ways. For example, I do not reduce concepts to
rules, or to dispositions, or to aspects of functional states. I take more seriously
than all such approaches the role of concepts as aspects of cognitive *acts*. The central idea will be that, apart from legitimate but irrelevant senses in which concepts
may be said to be rules, dispositions, or aspects of functional states, a concept
is an aspect of cognitive activity that needs to be originally *formed* by that activity
on each occasion of its use. It follows that the notion of applying or using a concept
is misleading. The "forms of judgment" that, in the Metaphysical Deduction, Kant
regards as constitutive of relations among the concepts one employs in a judgment
are in the Transcendental Deduction recognized to be essential to the formation
of the concepts employed in any judgment in the first place. The upshot is a way
of acknowledging that "meaning is use." But it is a way that does not suffer from
the usual failings of that truism. In Chapter Three, after a general account of the
distinction between the "application" of concepts to some material (subject) in a
conception or in a judgment, and the sort of "application" of understanding that
forms a concept *out* of some material in the first place, I show how all of these
claims cohere with what may seem to have spoken for a much cruder variety of
reductionism, namely, with Kant's claim that (non-categorial) concepts essentially
are, or "serve as," rules.

Chapter One provides a preliminary clarification of the relevant notions in the Transcendental Aesthetic, needed for our purpose, and a defense of Kant's use of them. In Chapter Two, I offer independent argument for extending the framework along the lines that I have suggested. This chapter relates the issues to current debates in cognitive psychology and to cognate notions in Searle (on non-representational states as co-determinative of intentional content), Husserl (on motivation, association, and the distinction between matter and form in noetic activity), and Croce (on matter and form on the several levels of "spirit"). In an earlier work, I supported my reading of the Aesthetic with a detailed analysis of the text.[4] In Chapter One of the present study, I aim more directly for an independent defense of the framework that I ascribe to Kant. The viability of that framework in a reading of Kant must rest here on the fruitfulness of its extension beyond the Aesthetic. In the earlier work, I also defended in detail a particular variety of "phenomenalistic" reading of Kant's Idealism. I tried to show how that kind of phenomenalism both arises out of the arguments of the Transcendental Aesthetic and avoids the absurdities of more standard formulations of such doctrines. In the final section of Chapter One, I show how the present approach permits a still more satisfactory formulation of Kantian phenomenalism.

Throughout, I do not claim that the views that I attribute to Kant are always clearly and unambiguously put forth by Kant himself. The main proof of my reading will have to lie in the extent to which it helps to explain some of the more notorious confusions and apparent self-contradictions in the Transcendental Deduction. I hope to show that the views in any case ought to be taken seriously.

It is reasonable to hypothesize that Kant's own difficulty with these notions is the main source of the obscurity of the Deduction. He was rightly uncomfortable with his own claim that imaginative matter is by nature intuitional. He was also preoccupied with the role of that matter in the formation of concepts. Therefore, he sometimes obscured the pre-conceptual status of the kind of anticipation and retention that his theory of experience presupposes, and the subordinate role of such material as only the matter of conception. For the same reasons, Kant tended to formulate his claims by appeal—on the noematic side—to categorial structurings of objects or appearances, when he ought to have done so—on the noetic side—by direct appeal to the structuring of anticipations and retentions as cognitive or pre-cognitive states. Finally, Kant may have feared that the approach in question would have the absurd consequence that concepts are a kind of particular item in the mind. I show how these difficulties may be avoided.

Kant's authority has been invoked in support of competing theories of the working of mind. In recent years, Kant's concern with the connection between concepts and "rules" has suggested that his authority might be lent to support purely functionalistic accounts of the mind. Or if purely functionalistic accounts are not possible, then perhaps all we need, beyond Kantian concepts, would be a surd of non-functionalistically reducible sensations, to which those concepts would then constitute one's "response." Sensation, that we share with the animals, would resist a functionalist account. Thought, that we share with computers, would not. I hope that the present study will at least redirect the authority of Kant from a defense of such visions. Insofar as thought involves understanding, it involves the capacity, not simply for responding to some body of material for thought, but rather for the incorporation of that material *into* thought. It is difficult to see how such incorporation could be elucidated in terms of a model of sensory "input" and functionally characterizable "response." The input needs to *become* a response.

A note on references and translations: Throughout, parenthetical references will be made to the *Critique of Pure Reason* by means of the standard (A. . ./B. . .) format. Unless otherwise specified, references to "the *Critique*" will be to this work. In general, I follow Norman Kemp Smith's translation (New York: St. Martin's Press, 1965; reprint of Macmillan's edition of 1929). However, I occasionally modify the translation. (I translate *Erkenntnis* as "cognition" throughout; otherwise, where the departure from Kemp Smith warrants it, I comment to the effect. For this purpose, I have followed the German edition edited by Raymund Schmidt, in the "Philosophische Bibliothek" series [Hamburg: Verlag von Felix Meiner, 1956].) For references to Kant's writings besides the *Critique*, I include parenthetical notations of the form (*xx.yy*): this refers, first, to the volume in the *Akademie-Ausgabe* of Kant's writings; second, to the page in that volume. The various *Reflexionen* to be found in Kant's *Nachlass*, and the various sets of lecture notes to his courses on logic, are designated in a way that should be clear to the reader. I have tried to be careful not to rest my interpretative suggestions on an appeal to notes and reflections from Kant's pre-Critical (or, for that matter, post-Critical) period.

Some of the material in Chapters Four and Six has been drawn, respectively, from my papers "Matter, Form, and Imaginative Association in Sensory Intuition" (in *New Essays on Kant*, ed. Bernard den Ouden and Marcia Moen [New York: Peter Lang, 1987]) and "Self-Consciousness, Self-Determination, and Imagination in Kant" (*Topoi*, 7 [1988], 65–79). I thank the publishers and editors for permission to use the material.

Matter in Mind

A Study of Kant's Transcendental Deduction

Chapter 1

The Framework

I. Introduction

IN THIS chapter I try to develop a general framework that will be fruitful for a study of Kant, but also independently appealing in a study of the mind. In the first of these respects, we must take account of several distinctions that Kant himself draws. But the language in which he draws them is ambiguous. The ambiguity reflects, at least in part, Kant's desire to emphasize a correlation between those aspects of subjective activity through which things are apprehended and those things themselves, and their various aspects, *qua* apprehended (or apprehensible).

This sort of correlation is most likely to be seen by those concerned with the role of "conceptual schemes" in the constitution or determination of objects of cognition. But there is a perfectly defensible, and distinctively Kantian, approach to the problem of "constitution" that goes beyond a conceptual idealism of this sort. To understand it we need to clarify the distinction between matter and form in intuition. Some readings of that distinction are too subjectivistic. This is so, for example, when the immediate objects of intuition are taken to be, or to be "formed" out of, items such as sensations, sense impressions, or "sense data."[1] Other readings are insufficiently subjectivistic. Such, for example, are those for which the relevant distinction is simply between the set of one's most basic *conceptual* formations and some appropriately binding or limiting set of nonconceptual limitations *upon* such formations.[2] Our need is to formulate a sense in which intuitional form is in its own right an irreducible mode of subjective directedness, without regressing to the first type of reading. As we will see, the corresponding "matter" can then only be a kind of subjective material that is not merely somehow binding or limiting, with respect to conceptual acts, but much more internally material *through* which those acts are able to function, and much more literally *ingredient* in them than is generally acknowledged.

II. Some Correlations and Distinctions

We need first to relate the notion of intuition to some more general notions in Kant. It is supposed to be a species of *Vorstellung* (A320/B376-7)—as I shall call it, "representation." But Kant uses both terms in a number of ways. Some-times, the objects of ordinary perception are said to be representations (A30/B45, A114, B147, A492/B520) or intuitions (A163/ B204, B207, A370). And sometimes Kant uses the latter term for a particular aspect, the purely spatiotemporal aspect, of the objects of ordinary perception (B202, B207). In addition, he speaks of space and time as intuitions (A25/B39, A27/B43, B207). But this may all be regarded as derivative from a usage that more directly concerns cognitive states themselves.

In the primary sense of the term, we may say that an ordinary sense percep-tion,[3] not its object or any part or aspect of its object, is an instance of intuition or of intuitional representation. With qualification to be added presently, another example will be any instance of ordinary imagination. These are paradigmatic ex-amples of "representation" for Kant, because (with qualification to be added here too) they are ways of having one's awareness directed toward possible "objects." As such, they represent (or in some way "present") those objects in a state of con-sciousness. However, other sorts of Vorstellungen are not, even with qualification, concrete ways of being directed toward possible objects. Sensations and concepts are examples of this. Obviously, sensations and concepts are not intuitions for Kant. But they are nonetheless representations. The primary reason for this is that, while not themselves ways of being directed toward objects, they are none-theless able to contribute, in an internal way, to ways of being directed toward objects.

A question remains concerning the notion of a purely "internal" contribution to representation. With regard to concepts, that is the main concern of this study. In any event, in addition to eventually clarifying a sense in which sensations and concepts are representations, though neither alone a way in which consciousness is directed toward objects, we may avoid supposing that representations are pecu-liarly subjective objects of consciousness. Indeed, we cannot even suppose that, in every case, they are items or entities in consciousness. Intuitions, in the pri-mary sense, and (with some qualification) sensations, are "states" of a subject, or at least of a potential subject, of consciousness. But concepts are neither states of a possible subject nor peculiar objects. Our task will be to develop a sense in which concepts are nontheless (possible) aspects of consciousness. They will in that case be, as suggested, "representations" in virtue of contributing, in an appro-priately internal way, to the latter's object-directedness.

There may seem to be a number of problems in the proposal to regard intui-tions, in the primary sense, as those states of a subject that are its truly "object-directed" states. The least of them may be that Kant himself defines intuition in terms of the notions of representations that are "singular" and "immediate." I have argued elsewhere that both of these notions amount to nothing other than the internal capacity of certain states to direct a subject, in a sense to be clarified, toward objects.[4] There may seem to be other problems. As we shall see more clearly in the next section, the proposal requires taking seriously the notion of being intuitionally directed toward merely possible objects. It does this because intuitional "form" is an intrinsic aspect of intuitional states. As such, intuitional form does not require the obtaining of any factual, e.g., causal, relations with ac-tual objects.

A further complication concerns abstract thoughts. As distinguished from such genuinely intuitional states as perceptions (and, with qualification, imaginings), these do not always seem to involve a way of being directed toward objects. Or it may seem that they do so at most in a way that is different from what is in question in the case of intuitions. It is hardly clear, in any case, that we could do justice to abstract thoughts by merely relegating them to the class of those things that are at most able to contribute, in an albeit internal manner, to ways in which *other* states might direct one toward objects.

The same might appear to go for instances of mere "belief" or "knowledge." Many people find it useful to regard these as modes of "representation." That Kant himself does so may seem to be entailed by his use of the term *Erkenntnis*. Kemp Smith generally translates it as *knowledge* (in the plural: *modes of knowledge*), when in many cases some other term is preferable, e.g., *judgment* or *cognition*.[5] In any event, one might suppose that belief and knowledge are constituted out of concepts, and concepts are of course representations. Now Kant places particular weight on the connection between concepts and "rules." In some sense he seems virtually to identify the two. But rules are something that one can learn or master. Having done so, one has apparently entered into a more or less enduring subjective "state" that may be said to contain or embody, in a purely internal way, the particular conceptual *abilities* that were in question. These states might then be regarded as representational states. We do not need to pursue this issue now. Later I shall argue that Kant's conception of concepts as rules, or as embodying rules, does not imply anything like this sort of view. It does not involve this sort of dissociation of concepts from the concrete course of ongoing consciousness. In fact, concepts are, in a sense, merely forms or aspects of consciousness itself. If this is so, then we should not presume that mere states of believing and knowing are *ever* representations in the Kantian sense (although they may involve or presuppose representations in that sense, and may also be representations in some other sense).

The question remains concerning occurrently conscious thoughts and judgments in general. Even apart from the question of abstraction, and from that of merely "dispositional" belief or knowledge, it may seem necessary to extend our general approach in order to accommodate them. For example, one might extend the notion of representation so as to include, not simply particular ways of being directed toward objects (perception and imagination), nor merely whatever elements are capable of contributing in an internal way to ways of being thus directed (sensations and concepts), but also modes of consciousness that are in their own turn constituted out of representations in either of the former senses. It may seem obvious that thoughts and judgments, so long as they are occurrent states of consciousness, not mere dispositions or knowledge merely "possessed," must be constituted out of one or the other (or some combination) of intuitions, sensations, and concepts. But in fact, I shall suggest, Kantian "judgments" are themselves *intuitions*. They are intuitions, that is, that have been converted *into* judgments (i.e., into *Erkenntnisse*). The main obstacle must of course lie in the challenge of purely abstract cognition.[6] As it happens, Kant himself does not seem clear in this regard:

Since no representation, save when it is an intuition, is in immediate relation to an object, no concept is ever related to an object immediately, but to some other representation of it, be that other representation an intuition, or itself a concept. Judgment is therefore the mediate cognition of an object, that is, the representation of a representation of it. In every judgment there is a concept which holds [*gilt*] of many representations, and among these also grasps [*begreift*] a given representation that is immediately related to an object. Thus in the judgment, "all bodies are divisible," the concept of the divisible is related to various other concepts; but among these it is here especially related to the concept of body, and this concept again to certain appearances that present themselves to us. These objects, therefore, are mediately represented through the concept of divisibility. Accordingly, all judgments are functions of unity among our representations, since instead of an immediate representation, a higher representation, which grasps [*unter sich begreift*] this one and several others, is used for the cognition of the object, and thereby many possible cognitions are drawn together into one. (A68-9/B93-4)

It is not clear what point Kant is making. But we might suppose him to be suggesting that even the most abstract judgment still demands the embodiment of concepts in intuitional material, at least if it is to be a judgment in any way about "objects." If so, it remains unclear what the form of embodiment needs to be. As we shall see later, the only kind of embodiment that constitutes a genuinely cognitive "response" to an intuition, thus to an object *qua* object of that intuition, is an operation by virtue of which the latter is itself converted into the very judgment in question. It must be an operation by virtue of which the intuition is made an *Erkenntnis* in its own right. Perhaps Kant is suggesting that we take this as our model for judgment generally. (That all judgments are intuitional has in fact been argued by others; I comment on such a case in Chapter Two. The apparent absurdity may in part be removed by recalling that, with qualification, intuition includes "imagination." In addition, nothing prevents the admission of purely abstract "judgments" in some sense at most *related* to the proper Kantian one. I comment on this point in the Conclusion.)

Consider the judgment that all bodies are divisible, as a judgment actually "formed" on some occasion. Kant may be supposing that this judgment involves the imaginative presentation of some possible body or bodies. If it does, then one is of course not merely conceptualizing the latter *as* some possible body or bodies. One must be conceptualizing it as *all* bodies. (There need be no question of error, in virtue of having, in that case, *mistaken* some for all bodies. Taken "in themselves," the objects need really *be* neither some nor all bodies. It is not, after all, a matter of imagining actual bodies. It is more like imagining *possible* bodies and taking them as "representative" of all. The question of "possible objects" will occupy us in the next section.) The full judgment would consist, then, in the "application" of the concept *divisible*, not simply to the concept *body* (or even to the concept *all bodies*), but precisely (and in an appropriately modified sense of the term) to the conceptualized intuition itself. Of course, this would raise problems for Kant's claim that some judgments are purely analytic, hence do not relate concepts to objects at all.[7] In any event, such is the theory of judgment that I shall argue to be implicit in the Transcendental Deduction.

There is an additional ambiguity concerning the notion of consciousness, reflected in Kant's inclination to deny that intuition, apart from concepts, is genuine consciousness at all: it is "blind" without them (A52/B75); without them, "nothing to us" (A120; cf. A112, A119, B132). But while there is an apparently strong inclination to this effect in the *Critique*, the inclination is also contradicted in that work and elsewhere in Kant. It seems clear that unconceptualized intuitions are in some sense still instances of "consciousness," yet is also clear that Kant sees a sense in which consciousness depends on concepts.

If Kant is otherwise right, we could always *stipulate* a sense in which intuitions, even apart from concepts, are modes of consciousness. We could say that they are modes of consciousness, for example, in that they contribute a unique sort of object-directedness to any state in which they are appropriately ingredient. If it is the intuitional dimension in any conscious state that is responsible for its object-directedness as such, then that may be reason enough for conceding that intuitions are themselves instances of "consciousness." Their conceptualization, we might then say, is simply their elevation to a higher *level* of consciousness. In any event, Kant has no particular theory about the kind of consciousness peculiar to intuition as such, over and above his views concerning its role in the constitution of object-directedness.

Kant of course distinguishes between pure and empirical intuition. The latter, I have suggested, includes ordinary sense perception. But ordinary sense perception involves concepts. This may incline us to say that it cannot be an example of empirical intuition. But that would be a mistake. The mistake would rest on supposing that the conceptualization of an intuition involves the attachment of a concept or a judgment to it, or perhaps the imposition of some external structure upon it (or upon it together with others). Again, one of the points of this study is to propose an alternative to this view. Conceptualized intuitions are still intuitions. They are *conceptualized* intuitions by virtue of some internal alteration or elevation, not by virtue of something that is attached to or imposed on them.

Sometimes, what Kant calls "pure" intuition is just a type of imagination, namely, the type that plays a special role in mathematics. But Kant also uses the term in other senses. He uses it for space and time, for example, and for the purely spatiotemporal aspects of objects of intuition. Most crucial for our purposes, he also uses it for a certain structure in our representations *of* any object of intuition, that is, for the pure "form" that is in them.

As a variety of imagination, pure intuition is a kind of imagination that is in a sense *doubly* pure. It is pure because pure intuitions are devoid of sensations (or if they contain sensation, then only inessentially). And they are pure because the concepts in them need to be "pure" (any others occurring inessentially). Like any instance of merely ("purely") imagining something, a pure intuition does not involve sensation in the way that a perception does. In this respect, any instance of it is like an instance of merely imagining a cup of tea, instead of actually seeing one. But there is also a feature of pure intuition that distinguishes it from imagining in general. It may be tempting, from what Kant says, to suppose that it lies in the fact that pure intuition does not involve any concepts at all. (It is of course difficult to see what imagining a cup of tea could be, apart from the employment of concepts.) But this would be wrong. Whatever he might mean by it, Kant sometimes speaks of mathematical concepts as "pure" concepts (A140/B180; cf. A719/B747). What Kant sometimes calls pure intuition is simply that special kind of imagination in which such concepts are "constructed" or represented for the purpose of mathematical cognition (A713ff/ B741ff).

A more difficult issue concerns the connection between pure intuition and what Kant calls the "categories." In fact, Kant sometimes seems to distinguish between two sorts of categories. One sort appears to be so pure as to contain no reference to the conditions of spatiotemporal representation at all, hence to be even more pure than pure intuition: the so-called unschematized categories. Whatever we say about them, there is in any case a problem concerning the schematized categories.

For those who think of concepts as "rules," the relation between categories and pure intuition may seem simple. The pure intuitions in question might just be space or time themselves, or determinate aspects of these; the connection with the categories would simply be that the latter are rules that involve an essential reference to the former. But suppose that concepts, as in our own view, are forms or modes of consciousness, not merely rules (though non-categorial concepts must of course *involve* rules in a way yet to be analyzed). Then how shall we conceive of the relationship between pure intuition and the categories? One suggestion, which I have elaborated elsewhere, is that the schematized categories, if they are concepts at all—not mere forms for the *forming* of concepts out of material in intuition—must be, in a sense, pure intuitional imaginings in their own right, or at least some formal *aspect* of the latter, over and above the pure "form of intuition" that these contain.[8] But it is not clear what sense can ultimately be made of this view. In any event, I shall be concerned with the Kantian "categories" in this study only in their role as forms for the "formation" of concepts.[9]

We are finally ready to return to the notions of matter and form in intuition more generally. The first main point is to be sure that we do not fall prey to a common misinterpretation. It is one that finds some support in Kant's text, but also much to confute it. It is a form of the subjectivistic interpretation that I mentioned earlier. In considering it, it is necessary to comment on another possible source of ambiguity. The ambiguity concerns the notion of sensation (*Empfindung*). It is likely that Kant uses this term in more than one way. In its primary employment, it is used to designate certain sorts of states of the perceiving subject. (The latter notion may of course prove ambiguous too: as between the perceiver as a "thing in itself" and as mere "appearance." In that case, the notion of sensation will be doubly ambiguous.) The crux of the subjectivistic reading is this: that sensations, as states of the subject, are the "matter" or the material of the "appearances" that are the immediate objects of sensory intuition.

Proponents of such a reading might put the point differently. They might put it simply by saying that sensations are the material of sensory intuitions. This is something Kant himself says (e.g., A20-2/B34-5). The question is what he means. As noted, Kant sometimes means by "intuition" what might more properly be said to be the objects of intuition. It does not follow from this that when he speaks of sensation as the material of intuitions he is adopting a form of the subjectivistic view. He might, on those occasions, be speaking of intuitions more properly, namely, as instances (at least when conceptualized) of ordinary sensory experience. In that case, he would only be saying that sensations are the material of ordinary sensory experiences. On the other hand, he might be using the term peculiarly. He might be regarding sensation as the material of objects of consciousness (appearances), but yet not any longer saying that our own subjective states are the material of those objects. The question is additionally complicated by ambiguities in the notion of "appearance."

In one sense of the term, appearances might indeed be regarded as composed of subjective material. This must involve a merely empirical, as opposed to the "transcendental," notion of appearance. In the transcendental sense, even material objects are appearances for Kant. The way these objects in turn *appear* may be said to involve "appearances" in a merely empirical sense (A29-30/B45). Now there is a perfectly legitimate sense in which Kant may speak of such appearances as formed out of sensations. So understood, they would presumably be states, or aspects of states, through which subjects apprehend objects or possible objects. As Kant says, such appearances would only be "changes in the subject" (A29/B45). Unfortunately, he also seems to say something that makes little sense. He gives, as an example of such an appearance, the colors that one perceives in perceiving some object. It is difficult to make sense of the notion that some of the states of a perceiving subject actually are colors. At most, Kant ought to say, they are states through which colors are apprehended.

We may suggest an explanation of such formulations. Two very different things might be meant by appearances, even in the empirical sense, and by the "ways in which" material objects appear. The distinction is a difficult one, and it is not unlikely that Kant occasionally slipped on it. First, appearances in the empirical sense might simply be the intentional correlates of sensory apprehension, considered precisely as such correlates, and hence without regard to their reality as material objects. For the sake of our present discussion, we may call them correlate-appearances. Considered just as such, correlate-appearances are not formed or made out of anything at all. Hence they are not made out of sensations. Nor are they made out of anything else. Considered as mere correlates of the apprehension of them, such talk is simply misplaced.

Now it is crucial to my reading of Kant that it is precisely correlate-appearances that one ordinarily takes to be materially real objects, and is usually right in doing so. (I try to clarify this notion further in the final section of this chapter.) In that case, one must of course take the appearances in question to be formed or made out of something. What one takes them to be formed or made out of is what Kant himself calls either their *Realität* (A166/B207ff) or their *Materie* (A20/B34, B207). Kant thinks of this as whatever it is that really fills some region of space, whenever a material object is filling it. But consider mere correlate-appearances. Even though, just as such, they are not made out of anything, they too can be described in terms of a kind of "filling" of space. They can be described in terms of an at least *apparent* filling of a region of space, for an at least possible object. We may therefore speak, quite legitimately, of the correlate-material of correlate-appearances. To take the most obvious case, perceived colors would be examples of such material. To make the distinction, we need simply distinguish real colors from correlate-colors. The tendency to do so would be all the more powerful, given that mere correlate-material is in effect what one ordinarily takes, and is usually right in doing so, *as* the real colors of real material objects.

Thus we can understand Kant's tendency to regard correlate-appearances as made out of something, even though they are not made out of anything at all. Given that tendency, we can also understand something else. We can understand why, in general, Kant might be inclined to refer to correlate-material as "sensation." It is, after all, only *through* sensation that one apprehends correlate-material in the first place.[10] And it is difficult to see that any other, except a purely technical term, would do better. It does not follow from this that Kant really supposed that correlate-appearances are formed from subjective states. In any case, correlate-appearances are only one of the two things that might be meant by appearances in the empirical sense of the term. It may be Kant's tendency to confuse the two that led him to forget that correlate-material is not a kind of material.

But what could be the point of claiming that ordinary *experiences* have a "material"? To see this, we need to see what Kant contrasts with the latter. We need to see what he means by the "form" of an experience. But here we also encounter ambiguity. Often, what Kant means by the "form of intuition" is not at all an aspect of sensory experiences. Rather, it is an aspect of the objects *of* sensory experience. Still, what does Kant mean by the form of a sensory intuition, when he does in fact take it to be an aspect of a sensory experience?

In one sense, the form of an experience might simply be identified with its object-directed character. In another sense, it can only be identified with an important part of that character. However we choose to put it, we presumably need to allow for the fact that, in some sense or other, the object-directed character of experience is in part determined by concepts. I do not propose to have Kant deny this.

One might suppose that, for a very simple reason, an experience's conceptual content cannot completely exhaust its object-directed character. One might suppose that this is so because the object-directed character of an experience is dependent upon sensation. What I am seeing or hearing does not merely depend on what I take myself, conceptually, to be seeing or hearing. To some extent it also depends on what my sensory state really is, and not on what I take it to be. However, this cannot be the reason why Kant regards conceptual content as at most contributory to object-directed character, and intuitional form as more strictly constitutive of it. This is because Kant excludes mere sensations, as much as he does concepts, from the intuitional form of an experience. Getting clear about the reason for this is a necessary preliminary to getting clear about the object-directed character of experience in the first place.

What we need to appreciate from the start is the importance that Kant attaches to the fact that the very same object might be presented either in a sensory or in a *non*-sensory "experience." That this is indeed a fact, he takes pains to insist at the earliest possible moment in the Aesthetic:

> Thus, if I take away from the representation of a body that which the understanding thinks in regard to it, substance, force, divisibility, etc., and likewise what belongs to sensation, impenetrability, hardness, colour, etc., something still remains over from this empirical intuition, namely, extension and figure. These belong to pure intuition, which, even without any actual object of the senses or of sensation, takes place [*stattfindet*] in the mind *a priori* as a mere form of sensibility. (A20-1/B35)

One might suppose that the only sense in which the very "same object" might be presented in a sensory and in a non-sensory manner is one that is purely conceptual: the object of a thought that we think in connection with an experience, or the object of a judgment, might continue to be the object of the very same thought, or of the very same judgment, even after all of the sensations in question have vanished. But Kant makes it clear that his point is different from this. He makes it clear that the "presence" of the very same object is not a purely conceptual matter at all. Even if the same concepts were employed on two occasions, one of them involving sensation and the other not, the fact that the same object (extension and figure) is in question could not possibly be explained by appeal to those concepts. The reason is this: Those concepts merely serve to *conceptualize*[11] whatever object is in question. Therefore they do not by themselves account for the fact that some object is in question in the first place.

Kant's reasoning turns on a distinction between two kinds of imagination that is independent of his own distinction between pure and empirical intuition. It is the distinction between imagining some (possible) *object*, on the one hand, and merely imagining or supposing that something is (or might be) the case, on the other. Imagining some possible extension or figure, for example, is clearly different from merely imagining or supposing that there is, or that there might somewhere be, a particular extension or figure, or from imagining or supposing anything else about some extension or figure that is not actually imagined on that occasion. It may be that the latter sort of imagining is a purely conceptual matter. The former cannot be. In the former case, one is not simply employing certain concepts, but employing them precisely in thinking about some imagined object. Now obviously there is much more to be said on the question than this.[12] For example, one might attempt to account for the difference between the two sorts of imagining by appealing, not to a primitive intuitional "form" in the more intuitional case, but merely to the presence of special phenomenal qualities, perhaps analogous to sensations, in addition to whatever concepts might be involved. I argue against this suggestion in the next section.

The distinction does not rest on assuming, as Kant may appear to do, that any instance of imagining some extension or figure might actually remain in full-blown consciousness even after the removal of all modes of conceptualization of that extension or figure. Though Kant may be assuming the possibility, his argument does not hinge on the assumption. Kant may very well concede, at this point, that there is no such thing as imagining a triangle or a line of any sort, apart from actually imagining that it is a triangle or a line. (In fact, there is no reason to concede quite this much. One might be said to imagine a triangle or a line, just in case one is imagining something that one would normally be *ex-*

pected to conceptualize as a triangle or as a line. The most one could plausibly claim is that, in order to do the latter, one must be conceptualizing the imagined object in some way or other.) Even if this were conceded, the point would remain that the concepts in question are "object-directed," in any imagining, in a way that is not itself a purely conceptual matter. I do not have a way of defining what I mean by this notion. But as with Kant, it seems to me appropriate to appeal to it precisely as the point of difference between merely imagining or supposing that something is or might be the case, in regard to some possible extension or figure, and imagining or supposing in regard to some actually *imagined* extension or figure. The inability to define the difference may simply reflect its primitive character.

Once we appreciate the difference between imagining an object and merely imagining or supposing that something is or might be the case, then we are in a position to focus on that aspect of a sensory intuition that Kant calls its "form." The latter simply is that non-conceptual aspect of a perceptual experience, even of a hallucinatory one (I won't bother to repeat the qualification throughout), that it is able to share with purely imaginative but non-hallucinatory intuitions.[13] Again, the question does not turn on supposing that it makes sense, apart from the way we actually conceptualize imagined or perceived objects, or may normally be expected to conceptualize them, to talk about the very "same object" being presented in a purely imaginative and also in a sensory experience. Even if concepts are involved in both cases, the fact remains that, in the one case, what we conceptualize in some particular way is presented in a sensory manner, and in the other case it is not. Hence sensation no more than conception, nor a combination of the two, is responsible for the "object-directed character" of the presentations.

The issue regarding the role of sensation, and its connection with object-directedness, is complicated by a further ambiguity concerning both these notions. I said earlier that, in the primary sense, sensations are "states" of perceiving subjects. But Kant sometimes seems to regard such states as purely internal to perceivers, and other times as essentially involving perceptual relations with actually existing objects.[14] In the former sense, but not in the latter, even the sheerest hallucination could be said to involve sensation. In the latter sense, in any event, we would appear to have a sense in which mere sensation is able to determine an "object" for a perceptual state.

It should be clear that this is compatible with what I have said so far. I have not denied that there is a *sense* in which intuitions are "objected-directed" in virtue, or at least partly in virtue, of purely external relations, or even that sensations may be essential to such directedness. What I have said at most implies that actually *taking* any object to *be* an object (imaginary or real), with respect to any intuitional state in fact apprehending it, always involves the (perhaps conceptual) enrichment, or the "conceptualization," of a different sort of object-directedness than sensation provides. (The notion of "taking," and of "conceptualization," will soon become ambiguous as well.) The sort in question is not a matter of one's actually standing in a perceptual relation with objects. Nor is it a matter of being in a "sensory" state, even in the sense in which hallucinations may be said to be so.

Much more, of course, needs to be said. I have so far only been formulating some distinctions. In the next section, I offer an independent defense of them. A thorough discussion will also require additional concern with "objects," and even with the question of an object's "reality." Regarding the latter, I have argued elsewhere that Kant is committed to a kind of phenomenalism, at least with respect to the reality of objects perceivable in space and time. Thus he is committed to a kind of phenomenalism with respect to perceptual "relations" (at least insofar as they are not presumed to involve some unknowable relation with "things in themselves"). I have also tried to show how this particular kind of phenomenalism differs from more objectionable forms of that doctrine. In the final section of this chapter, I attempt a further contribution to this project. But this can only be done once we have expanded our notion of "material" in a sensory intuition even be- yond the two notions of "sensation" so far encountered.

This much not only should give us a preliminary idea of what Kant means by the pure "form of intuition," in what I propose to regard as the primary sense of that term, and why all instances of imagination, and even hallucination, need to involve it. In addition, it should give an idea of the point of Kant's claim that sensations, and sensations alone, are the "matter" of sensory intuitions as such. However, we shall also need to see the sense in which, even though sensation is the matter of (sensory) intuitions as such, some *other* sort of material must be capable of serving as matter in it as well. This, I shall eventually argue, is a kind of material that Kant attributes to "imagination." But it will be in a sense that we have not yet encountered.

In order further to clarify the notion of sensation itself as "matter," it will in any case not suffice to say, as I have so far said, that, while the pure form of intuition constitutes a primitive kind of directedness in a subjective state, sensa- tion is what contributes, on a non-conceptual level, to the specific *way* in which such directedness occurs. We cannot say this, precisely because the same will hold for the "imaginative" material within an intuition. Nor should we say, for example, that sensations constitute that aspect of a sensory intuition whose distinctive "in- tentional correlate" is the presence of some immediately perceivable *quality* in perceived objects: say, their immediately perceivable phenomenal color. We should not say this because it is at the least unclear, despite Kant's own occasional suggestions to the contrary, to what extent such qualities are in fact apprehensible apart from some way in which the subject actually *takes* those qualities.

One might of course always say that the sensory matter of an intuition is that aspect of it that accounts for the fact that its object is presented in a "sensory" manner, and simply take the latter notion as primitive. But Kant himself often attempts to say more. He sometimes tends to do so, for example, by reference to the sorts of alterations that are normally produced in the state of a subject by means of the stimulation of its sense organs, or that are apt to call attention to a subject's sense organs, or at least to its own internal condition.[15] A related sug- gestion that is also close to Kant's own formulations, but perhaps more resistant to counterexample, is this: the distinctively "sensational" matter of any sensory intuition is that aspect of it in virtue of which it is *prima facie* reasonable to take its object to be real.[16] However, in the light of our own conclusions to follow, we might also simply mean this: the specifically "sensational" matter of an intuition is just whatever non-conceptual aspect of it contributes to the way in which its object is presented, but is—unlike any merely "imaginative" material it may contain—unsuited for service as material for the formation of *concepts*.

However we spell it out, nothing stands in the way of presuming that an intuitional state is itself made or "formed" out of whatever happens to serve as its "matter."[17] Its "form" will then be whatever constitutes it as a state by virtue of which an object is apprehended *through* that material, as a potential subject for conceptualization. On the other hand, we might also accommodate the supposition— on some level, Kant's own—that any genuine "apprehension" of objects must always involve at least some degree of conceptualization from the start. The concession, should we make it, does not disturb the general point. In that case, we should say that intuitional "form" is what *would* constitute a state as one by virtue of which something is "apprehended" through a certain body of material—given that the latter, or some appropriate portion of the latter, should *also* happen to serve as material for an act of conceptualization.

III. Primitive Directedness *vs.* Translatable Content in Intuition

The approach that I have begun to develop may seem ontologically objectionable. The difficulty stems from the fact that, according to the account in question, ordinary experience always consists of a series of conceptualizations, or at least of some kind of "takings," of objects that might or might not be, or that might or might not have been, real or actual objects. (A reminder: For convenience and where context assures clarity, I speak both of the conceptualization of intuitions and of the objects that are presented in them.) This is because an intuition's intrinsic directedness—provided by its "form"—is neutral as between imagining or hallucination, on the one hand, and a concrete apprehension of reality, on the other. Indeed, it is neutral as between mere imagining and the apprehension of what one even so much as *takes* to be reality. The latter involves a particular *way* of taking an object, but it does not need to involve a way of taking an object that really exists.

Kant argues, in the "Refutation of Idealism" (B274-9), that a necessary condition of one's capacity for self-cognition is that one's intuition always be related to a real world in some way. But in any particular case, what is conceptualized as a concrete, solid, object in space might still be a purely imaginary or hallucinated extension or figure (B278).[18] This seems to imply that real objects might have been something other than real. And in any case, it rests on the notion of taking things to be real that, in any particular instance, need not be or have been. We may thus appear to be committed to a realm of purely "intentional" objects whose intrinsic being is other than real being.[19]

Two strategies may seem to contain the alternatives for avoiding this commitment. Each may be regarded as attempting to favor one of the two parts of an ordinary intuition. The first may appear to be my own. It posits a primitive directional character or quality in consciousness, in order to account for instances of the primitive object-directedness that I have been trying to capture. Those instances would be provided by determinate occurrences of this primitive determinable character. Since the character is supposed to be a purely intrinsic quality, not a relational property, it would not carry any real commitment to objects of consciousness as such. The variety of apparent objects would merely be the phenomenological or intentional counterpart, and so at best a grammatical reflection, of the possible varieties of that primitive directional character. Obviously, I think that there is something right about this position. But there is something wrong as well.

The second approach does not hold that the assignment of objects to states of consciousness, in the neutral mode that I have been trying to capture, rests on the ascription to consciousness of a variety of primitive object-directed characters or qualities. Instead, it may be regarded as no more than the provision of a variety of "translations," into the language of the ascription in question, of the intentional "contents" of those states. (Independent considerations will call for the distinction between states and their contents.) We need not assume, on this approach, that intentional contents are distinct entities to which intentional states are externally related. We might, for example, regard them as a certain type of instantiable feature of intentional states, or as a variety of types that the latter are capable of "tokening." In any case, the suggestion is this: to say that a certain state represents (or presents) a possible object, in the relevantly neutral sense, is simply to say, or at least to indicate in an appropriately specific manner, that the state in question is translatable, or has a content that is translatable, by means of an appropriately specific expression in whatever language is in fact employed in the provision of that translation.[20]

In an obvious sense, the first of these approaches is more ontologically oriented than the second. But they agree in one respect. They agree that it is possible to acknowledge an object-directedness intrinsic to particular subjective states, without having to assume an ontological commitment to the objects of those states, as entities to which they are related. The commitment to relations with objects, as entities of any sort, would enter only with the eventual inclusion of purely extrinsic factors (e.g., with the inclusion of facts about entities that might be, or might be appropriately related to, things that actually affect one's sense organs). Each of these approaches is inadequate. But each represents a factor that needs to be included in an adequate conception of the kind of directedness that can be intrinsic to subjective states.

The first approach would be, in one way, like a familiar attempt to avoid a commitment to "sense data" in perception. One might, for example, attempt to avoid the commitment by regarding such predicates as *sees a green spot*, when they are not supposed to involve the real existence of anything seen, as expressing no more that a certain way of being "appeared to" sensorily. That strategy is, of course, consistent with a number of views of perceptual judgment. For example, our judgment about the ways of appearing might be construed as implicitly comparative: one is being appeared to "in the way that (or in one of the ways out of a range

of ways that) one is standardly appeared to when. . . ." Or they might simply be
taken to rest on acquaintance with a multitude of primitive phenomenal qualities,
comparable to one another, but not themselves to be defined in ultimately comparative terms. Perhaps most plausibily of all, a combination of the two is in order:
We are acquainted with standard cases of (really) perceiving (real) spots and of perceiving something green. We are *also* capable of discriminating respects in which
such cases agree and differ with respect to aspects of phenomenal quality. That
we could not verbally define such respects need be no objection to the supposition
that our apparent awareness of a primitive mental "directedness" in sensation is,
throughout, merely the awareness of respects in which modes of appearing are
both like and unlike certain standard cases of sensory appearing.

These sorts of elaboration might appear to avoid an immediate objection to the
strategy as originally proposed. What the strategy appears to require is the
construal of primitive directional qualities as, so to speak, indivisible units. For example, one such unit would be involved in apprehending an O as an F, another
is apprehending an O as a G. But insofar as we are dealing with indivisible units,
not relational properties, the strategy would appear to exclude the possibility of
cases in which a single object happens to be apprehended in different ways. So
far as we could say, we would simply be dealing with two completely different
"objects," O-as-F and O-as-G; it would make no sense to inquire whether, in addition to this, the O's are the same or different.[21] All we could ask is whether the
primitive directional qualities are the same or different. And of course they are
different. But as elaborated so as to allow for differential *comparisons* among
phenomenal qualities, or instances of primitive "directedness," the proposal may
appear to avoid at least this difficulty. However, it also seems unlikely that any
such approach could be plausibly extended beyond the purely sensory case: for
example, to the case of merely *imagining* a spot, not to mention that of imagining
or supposing that there is, or might, somewhere be one.

We might try to extend the comparative approach by continuing to appeal to a
standard range of sensory appearings. The purely imaginative cases might then
be handled in terms of our ability to discriminate respects in which other cases
are qualitatively comparable to them, even though they are not themselves sensory in quality. Once again, that these respects are "primitive" in the sense that
we could not verbally *define* them, in a non-circular way, need be no objection
to the supposition that our apparent awareness in either case of primitive mental
directedness is merely that of respects in which a non-sensory state is like and
unlike possible members of a standard range of sensory appearings.

Whatever additional objection may apply to the suggestion, the suggestion is impossible for the following reason: it implies that our awareness of the similarity
between imagining and sensing, apart from whatever corresponds to the specific
terms used describe them (e.g.,*green* or *spot*) is of something purely negative,
namely, of the fact that the imaginative cases do not involve any actual mode of
sensory appearing. Of course, Hume, notoriously, offered a way out of this difficulty. He did it by proposing that there is indeed a discriminable positive element, shared by imagining and sensing, in addition to whatever corresponds to the
particular terms used to describe them. For there is, in his view, some positive

degree of "force and vivacity" in each case; it is simply that it is lower in the case of imagining. But except so far as talk about degrees of force and vivacity is merely another way of talking about primitive mental directedness, the suggestion seems crudely *ad hoc*. In any case, as further discussion will show, the strategy could not possibly explain the essential twofold structure that Kant rightly saw in at least certain mental states, namely, in those in which some content is intentionally directed *toward* some (possible merely imagined) object.

It will be important to see why the second strategy fails in the same respect. The second strategy does not appeal to irreducible ways of appearing or being appeared-to, or to primitive mental directedness. It appeals to a purely functionally defined notion of "content." The latter is simply a term for the fact that a mental state can be regarded as "saying" something or other. The functional significance of this latter notion might then be supposed to lie wholly in what we acknowledge to be acceptable *translations* of what is said. As to the question of an underlying *ground* of translation, should we ask it, the most controversially reductive approach is, of course, one that involves an analysis that is also "functional" in a more narrow sense, namely, in primitive causal terms.[22] Kant's own view might be thought to fall somewhere in between. This is because of his emphasis on concepts, not as states of (nor, apparently, as contents in) minds, but as functions of potential unities with regard to states of mind:

> Whereas all intuitions, as sensible, rest on affections, concepts rest on functions. By 'function' I mean the unity of the act of bringing various representations under one common representation. (A68/B93)

This suggests at least a general sort of "functionalist" approach. Kant also attempts to be more specific regarding what is needed in order to constitute any commonality of conceptual function. It does not appear to have anything to do with commonality of causal role. It rather involves some kind of commonality of normatively binding "rules" for the employment of any concept: "But a concept is always, as regards its form, something universal, which serves as a rule" (A106). From this, the Kantian approach might seem to be a particular instance of the translational approach to content. The suggestion would appear to be that a conscious state "says," for example, that *a* is *F* (or at least in some other way "represents" *a*-as-*F*) just in case it tokens a type, or instantiates a feature, or in general has a content, whose role is governed by just the same rules as govern that of some corresponding item in a language of translation. I shall return, in Chapter Three, to the question of "rules" in Kant.

On a purely formal level, this sort of approach has value. But it can also be misleading. As we shall see, a closer look at precisely *how* concepts are able to serve as "functions of unity" among states of consciousness reveals a dimension of representation that needs to be ingredient in states of consciousness in a way that merely instantiated features, or tokened tokens—and in general translatable "contents" as we have so far been understanding them—are not. Kant himself may have a tendency to blur this issue, on account of his tendency to shift between a more formal and a more material way of looking at concepts. On a purely formal level, we may indeed regard (non-categorial) concepts as a kind of quasi-linguistic term potentially tokenable or instantiable by a manifold of distinct states. As such, a concept provides translatable content to possible states of consciousness simply by virtue of being tokenable or instantiable in accordance with appropriate "rules." When we report the contents of those states—as opposed to theorizing, as we shall be, about what makes them possible in the first place—we are simply not generally interested in what might otherwise be ingredient in them. All the same, conceptual content could not possibly be a matter of merely tokenable or instantiable translatable content. It must rest on something that is more literally ingredient in conceptual states. Conceptualization involves the presence of translatable content, not simply through unifying functions in regard to translatable states as wholes, but through functions that bear on the very *material* out of which those states are formed in the first place.

The suggestions need to remain vague for a while. We must first return to our distinction between what seemed to be incompatible strategies in regard to the intrinsic directedness of consciousness. I want to argue that what we need is an approach that involves elements of both. To show this, I shall consider the case of a certain sort of imagination, namely, the sort that, as I have already suggested, requires appeal to a primitive "form of intuition"—that is, imagining "an object" as opposed to merely imagining that something is or might be the case. To make the point, one might also appeal to sensory intuition. But while it is obvious that such states would involve more than translatable content, they involve so much more that it is difficult to focus on what is truly relevant in them.

An imaginative intuition presumably always exemplifies some conceptual or descriptive content as well. In a perfectly natural sense, one cannot imagine a bowl of soup without in some sense "conceptualizing" what one imagines as soup (or at least without conceptualizing it in a way that would in turn make it reasonable, perhaps under different circumstances, to conceptualize it as soup). But how could one ever *translate* the content of an imaginative intuition? A translating *sentence* seems to be ruled out from the start. In effect, we have already excluded such attempts as "There is, somewhere, a bowl of soup" and "There might, somewhere, be a bowl of soup," and any more specific variations on such attempts. These sorts of translations might be appropriate to imagining that something is or might be the case regarding a bowl of soup. They are not appropriate to imagining that something is or might be the case regarding a bowl of soup that one happens actually to be *imagining*. Of course, we could always appeal to something like "*This* is a bowl of soup, or at least an imaginary one." But that, for obvious reasons, appears to duplicate the problem. (Or perhaps it does not. I argue below against some recent attempts to explicate the notion of "demonstrative content.")

Perhaps we need to consider words or phrases, instead of sentences, in order to capture the content of imaginative intuition.[23] We might consider, for example: "a bowl of soup." But the suggestion is unacceptable. The suggestion implies that the state of imagining a bowl of soup, and in general the state of imagining any *object*, is derivable by mere subtraction from that of imagining that something is the case. Consider the thought that there actually is, or might be, a bowl of soup somewhere. On the suggestion in question, the state of imagining a bowl of soup, at least with respect to its "content," is obtainable by mere subtraction from this one. The only relevant difference would be that the content of imagining a bowl of soup involves only a part of the content that is involved in a case of imagining that there is, or might be, a bowl of soup somewhere. This seems impossible. The former ought to involve more, not less, than the latter.

It might still be possible to appeal to something other than translatable content and yet avoid a reversion to primitive directional qualities. The most likely candidate may seem to be what some people call "raw feels," "phenomenal qualities," or "qualia."[24] Such solutions might introduce a primitive but non-directional feel or quality, in order to account for the additional element in actually imagining some kind of object, as opposed to merely imagining that there is or might be an object of that kind. We might then suppose that the total content of an imaginative state is only a matter of the appropriate (perhaps causal) connection between this phenomenal component and a bit of genuinely translatable mental content. The connection, and neither element alone, would constitute the peculiarly imaginative content in question. The whole of the content might appear to be translatable at first. It might appear to be translatable precisely as "This is a bowl of soup (or an at least imaginary one)." But on the suggestion, what we really have is a connection between a bit of phenomenal quality and a content that is strictly translatable, not as a "statement" to the effect that *this* is a bowl of soup, or even a merely imaginary one, but at most in terms of a non-sentential phrase: "a bowl of soup, or an at least imaginary one."

Just as stated, and apart from its own insistence that the relevant "phenomenal qualities" are non-directional, the suggestion might of course be taken to formulate Kant's own view, and as a way of recognizing primitive directional quality after all, in addition to a mental state's possession of translatable content. How crude we judge the formulation to be would depend on what we suppose to be involved in the "connection" between translatable content and primitive phenomenal quality. If it simply amounts to whatever it takes to embody, in a conscious state, a content that is translatable by means of a particular expression, then there is really no argument. The connection of that content with a particular raw feel, or with a special phenomenal quality, might be regarded as nothing other than its tokening or instantiation by a Kantian *Anschauung*. To put it differently, the need for such a "connection" would be just the need to recognize that a state with a given translatable content is not simply a state that has directional quality in addition to that content. Rather, it is a state in which that content *itself* needs, as it were, to receive the form of directedness in question. This will become clearer later. In any case, the present suggestion is intended very differently. It is intended to rest on a distinction, as well as on an external connection, between two different sorts of subjective states, or at least between two different aspects of a single state. Each is supposed to enjoy an identity of its own and to be in principle describable independently of the other.

The suggestion that two states are involved, or even two distinguishable aspects of a single state, is untenable. This can be seen from the following consideration. If it were really a matter of distinct states, or of distinguishable aspects of a single state, needing to be connected in some way on a particular occasion, then there would be no absurdity in the supposition that any particular translatable content might end up being connected with any primitive phenomenal quality whatsoever, or even with any number of them at once. Consider, for example, the phenomenal quality presumed to be involved in some particular instance of imagining a rose bush. By hypothesis, that quality is what we need to postulate, in order to account for the "plus" enjoyed by actually imagining a rose bush, over and above its merely translatable content. Some presumably rather different quality would need to be postulated in order to account for the "plus" enjoyed in imagining a bowl of soup. And of course we would also need to postulate more specific qualities and differences, in order to account for the different ways there are of imagining such things, so long as these are not explicable by appeal to translatable content alone. But insofar as the postulated qualities are presumed to involve independent states, or independent aspects of states, both with respect to one another and to whatever translatable contents with which they might be connected, there ought to be no absurdity in supposing that those qualities and contents get randomly switched on occasion. We might suppose, for example, that the translatable content that is normally connected with the "feel" of imagining soup is now connected with the feel of imagining a rose bush. But the supposition seems, to the contrary, perfectly absurd.

If we are indeed prepared to countenance "phenomenal qualities" as essential to imagining in the first place, then there of course ought to be some leeway regarding the connection between such qualities and genuinely translatable content. As we might want to put it, although it is also a bit misleading: in anyone's view, a single mental "image" might get variously *taken*. The image taken as a bowl of soup (or an at least imaginary one) might instead have been taken as a bowl of colored water. With appropriate background assumptions, it might even have been taken as a rose bush looking like soup. A certain amount of recombination is possible. Nor does conceding this imply, as it might seem to, that "images" are entities that get conceptually taken in various ways in imagining. Certainly, it would seem odd to suppose that phenomenal *qualities*, as aspects of mental states, are what get so taken.[25] It is not clear what we should finally want to say about such matters. In any event, I introduced the notion of a mental "image" only to make a certain point more graphic. The usage conforms to what many people are inclined to say about imagining. However we spell it out, what is supposed to be captured is just the same as what was supposed to be captured by introducing phenomenal quality in imagining in the first place. In either case, we have to deal with the concession that there is something more to imaginative intuition than the tokening or instantiation of descriptive or conceptual content. Whoever is prepared to concede the point must also concede that there is always leeway in regard to "connecting" whatever elements are then in question. My argument need not deny this. (Whether there is comparable leeway regarding the connection of phenomenal quality with translatable content—or ways of "taking"—in general, not simply with *conceptual* content, remains a point to be reconsidered. I have, for the sake of convenience, so far not distinguished between "taking" and "conceptualizing.")

When it is reformulated in order to capture this concession, my argument is simply that, while the introduction of phenomenal, but intrinsically non-directional, quality ought to allow for a degree of play with respect to its actual connection with translatable content in imagining, a construal of such quality and content in terms of distinct states, or in terms of distinct aspects of states, allows for too much leeway. As we have seen, whatever such quality is involved in imagining a bowl of soup might instead have been involved in imagining a rose bush. But appropriate background assumptions were needed to make this intelligible. One needs to imagine, for example, that a rose bush is "appearing" under circumstances in which it happens to look like soup. By contrast, when phenomenal quality and translatable content are merely distinct states, or distinct aspects of states, no such assumptions are any more appropriate than others. (By a construal in terms of distinct states, or distinct aspects of states, I simply mean the supposition, again, that the ingredience of particular quality and the tokening or instantiation of content constitute a single state only by virtue of being connected *into* that state: for example, by virtue of standing in appropriate causal connection to one another, or perhaps merely by virtue of being instantiated together in that state.)

It will help, in seeing the point, to recall the original motivation of the suggestion. Even though it concedes, in effect, that the translatable content of imagining objects is not in itself a full sentential content, the suggestion may be regarded as resting on a model of content that involves full sentences. What seems to be left out of any purely conceptual content, and seems not to be capturable by our normal means for completing analogous sentences, is what we might call the "referential," or at least the apparently referential, element in imagining. This element would be left out, for example, of any instance of tokening a content that is merely translatable as "a bowl of soup," as opposed to "This is (or might be) a bowl of soup." Though it might be held to capture its strictly conceptual content, the former obviously fails to capture the full content of imagining a bowl of soup. The latter, on the other hand, would seem to capture that content at the cost of re-introducing primitive directional qualities. So to compensate for what appears to be left out, but without running the risk of tolerating primitive directional qualities, one may simply be inclined to postulate the occurrence, among one's subjective states, of a state (or of an aspect of a state) that is in some way a counterpart of—even though obviously not translatable as—the missing demonstrative term. Like the term in the corresponding sentence, the occurrence of that state at least generates the feeling that one is really referring to something. But unlike a correct use of the demonstrative term, it only needs to involve the *feeling* that such usage is correct. Unlike whatever genuinely conceptual content is in question, the counterpart of "this" is not translatable, and *a fortiori* not as *this*.

Now one might of course reply to the argument so far offered that while any such connection of "terms" (content and quality) is indeed logically possible, we can only in fact manage to *effect* certain ones, given certain sets of background assumptions. But that would be *ad hoc*. If phenomenal quality is ever able, together with translatable content, to constitute a single imaginative state, then it ought to be able to do so whenever it is appropriately tied to such content. Consider, again, the linguistic analogy. What we would be talking about, when we are considering such apparently "absurd" connections, would be analogous to the formation of ill-formed sentences. By the same analogy, we ought to expect, on the approach in question, precisely the possibility of generating instances of ill-formed *imagining*. The fact that ill-formed imagining (at least in the sense of ill-formed imaginative "intuition") seems in turn to be unimaginable, undercuts the sentential analogy. (Of course, irrelevantly, one may always imagine *that* various "ill-formed" states of affairs obtain.)

Now as I have already suggested, the concession of a role for "phenomenal quality" in imagining might in fact be nothing other than acknowledgment of the need for a middle position between our two strategies. It might be a way of acknowledging the need for both irreducible directional quality and merely translatable "content" in at least some mental states. But we need to see how to acknowledge the duality without appealing to primitive determinates of a single determinable quality of directedness. To revert again to Kantian terminology, the solution must be to recognize that any kind of translatable content, if it is to be relevant to the directedness of consciousness of the sort that concerns us, must be regarded as the content of a state whose "quality" of directedness is the very *form* of that state. (This, so far as I shall argue, is compatible with regarding that content as also able to serve as the content of states that are mental, and even "directional," but yet not so in the way that intuition is.)

Consider again the case of imagining a bowl of soup (as a bowl of soup). Unlike the approach that proceeds in terms of a determinable directional quality, we cannot construe this as a case in which some subject is in a state possessed of the primitive character "imagining-a-bowl-of-soup" (or even of two distinct characters, one to account for the quality of imagining, the other for requisite specificity). Unlike the approach that proceeds in terms of translatable content, neither can we construe the case as one that merely involves a state possessed of translatable content (or even, additionally, of some primitive phenomenal feel or quality). The case must rather be one in which some content—one translatable, for example, as "a bowl (or at least a possible bowl) of soup"—is ingredient in a state of consciousness precisely by virtue of being ingredient in a special *sort* of state. That is, we must suppose that the content is ingredient in consciousness precisely by *virtue* of its ingredience in a state possessed of primitive directional quality.

Our appeal must be to a primitive quality of directedness, but not to primitive determinate *modes* of such directedness. What we need to concede, in other words, is only that there *are* indeed irreducibly directional states of consciousness. Beyond this, we do not need to acknowledge the existence of a multitude of irreducibly determinate modes of directedness. As I shall argue, in order to account for the specific forms that the directedness in question takes, we need simply appeal, as on the second of our strategies, to the ingredience of purely translatable content *in* a state of that sort. By virtue of this appeal, any recognition of complexity of "structure" in intentional content ought then to remain as available to us as it did not on the first of our strategies, and it ought to be no less available than it was on the second. In any case, the admission of primitive directional quality continues to avoid a commitment to intentional objects as entities. For it is still regarded as an intrinsic quality, not a relational feature of mental states.

We need to modify the second of our strategies as well, beyond merely combining it with the first. As we left it, that strategy was compatible with a number of views as to the notion of translatable content. For example, it was compatible with a narrowly functionalistic view, according to which translatable content, considered in itself, is solely a matter of causal relations in which a state, or some aspect of a state, stands. But I shall now argue—by what is in effect an extension of the argument concerning primitive "feel" in a state—that a mental state's translatable content cannot simply be an *aspect* (or a part) of a state, merely externally connected with its primitive directedness. Rather (adopting once more our Kantian terminology), whatever constitutes translatable content in a state of consciousness must serve as a kind of *material* in a state whose "form" is precisely that of primitive directedness.

The argument concerns the necessity that translatable "content" in a mental state that is primitively object-directed—that is, object-directed in the way that at least imaginative intuition is—must make some difference in how an object (a possibly non-existent one) is apprehended through that state. I do not mean to overstate the point. In the first place, we are still limiting our concern to mental states in which, as in imaginative intuition, there is indeed some difference between translatable content and primitive directional quality as such. In the second place, the point is not intended to imply that translatable content always makes a difference in what one might call the *appearance* of some object present to consciousness. In any event, whatever we might say about states possessed of translatable content, but not of primitive directedness, it would seem to be a condition on any theory of translatable content that it at least account for the fact that translatable content needs to make a difference in how one apprehends an object of consciousness, at least when the object in question is regarded as a "correlate" of that very directedness. My argument will be that this cannot be accommodated by views in which translatable content is, as it were, purely "instantiated" or "tokened" content, and in no further sense *ingredient* in a state whose content it is. We may regard such views as instances of a "formal" approach to content. It should be clear that functionalist approaches, in the narrower sense of the term, will be instances of formal approaches in this sense.

It may seem that a formal approach to content should have no difficulty conceding that translatable content, in a state that is intrinsically object-directed, necessarily affects the way in which one apprehends an object. This may seem to follow from the fact that, even according to a formal approach, content needs to be tokened or instantiated *by* the very state to which that content is ascribable. However, the fact that content is tokened or instantiated by a state at most implies that the latter exhibits a feature that it would otherwise not have exhibited. This implies that the ascribability of content makes a difference to the particular state to which it is ascribable. It does not imply that it makes a difference in how some object is apprehended through that state. It does not imply the latter, even on the assumption that the state is intrinsically object-directed. Even on that assumption, the question remains: Why should the fact that a state, which happens to be object-directed, comes to exhibit a feature that it might otherwise not have exhibited have any bearing on the way in which an object is apprehended through it? Of course, one wants to say that any translatable content instantiated or tokened by a state is a special feature of that state. It is just the sort of feature that does not merely make a difference in the quality of states as states. Instead, it makes a difference in a state's *cognitive* content. But this only restates the problem. How could there be a feature that is special in this way, if it fails to enter into the fabric of an object-directed state, or to rest on something that enters into that state itself, in something more than the sense that it is tokened or instantiated by it?

Apart from something further, what we have so far learned is only that the "content" of a state is a translatable aspect of it. A number of accounts, again, might attempt to explain the ultimate ground of such translatability. But whatever the ultimate ground, the most we are so far offered is this: that a state possessed of primitive directedness is able to come to token, or is able to come to instantiate, an additional feature of a certain special sort, namely, a feature that manages to "say" something that is in some way translatable. In these terms, our question may be posed in the following form: How can the instantiation or tokening of *any* such feature, even when it is instantiated or tokened by an object-directed state, amount to that state *itself* "saying" anything at all, and in particular saying something about its own object?

The answer would be easy if one of the features, as with our first strategy, were merely a determinate form of the other one. It would be easy, for example, if the translatable "content" in a directional state were merely a determinate mode of that state's quality of directedness in the first place. But we have already seen that this is impossible. The primitive directional character of a state is not a determinable quality of which the specific modes of apprehension are determinates. If it were, then all possible modes of apprehending objects would involve equally primitive qualities, and we could not account for the presence of structure in the contents of mental states.

An analogy may be helpful. On the purely formal approach, we may compare the tokening or instantiation of contents by mental states—or at least by those "intuitional" ones to which we are restricting our attention—to the action of inscribing a text on an arrow. An arrow may really happen to point at an object. When it does, then from the fact that something has been inscribed on an arrow, it of course follows that it has been inscribed on a thing that points at an object. But it is clear that this could not explain how the inscribed text might *itself* manage to point at an object, in anything like the original sense of pointing. Furthermore, even if the inscribed text should happen to point at an object, or to be "about" an object, the mere fact of its inscription on an arrow could do nothing to ensure that it must be about the *same* object as the one at which the arrow points. This is because the mere inscription of a text on a surface does not, apart from the purely formal fact of co-presence in it, connect that text with any of the *other* of the features of the surface. It does nothing of the kind, even if, by supposition, pointing at a particular object should also happen to be a feature of that surface. The question still remains: What could possibly constitute the needed connection, between acts of "pointing" at objects and acts of tokening "contentful" texts, short of construing the latter, impossibly, as a determinate mode of the former in the first place?

It is difficult to avoid concluding that the relationship between the contentful "text" in a mental state and the particular instance of primitive directedness in it must indeed be, or at least be explicable in terms of, the relation between "matter" and "form" in a single state. The conceptualization of any object that is intuitively apprehended must be grounded in the presence of something that is *ingredient* in the apprehending state, not merely tokened or instantiated by it. If it were merely tokened or instantiated, then whatever the ultimate ground of the translatability of the content in question, it would remain at most a feature among the features of that state. In whatever sense it might be said to be an "object-directed" content, it would in no way share in the object-directedness of the state as a whole. For this we need to suppose, not simply a primitive form of directedness in certain states, but a form of directedness that directs them *through* a body of material of which those very states are composed.

A generalization of this argument seems to me also to show the inadequacy of certain accounts that do not appeal directly to the translatability of content. Consider, for example, the suggestion that the notion of "demonstrative" content is to be explicated in terms of patterns of a subject's "sensitivity to evidence" for and against the truth of a content.[26] Here, what makes a content demonstrative is not its connection with a bit of phenomenal quality. Rather, it is the fact that it is a content, with regard to the instantiation of which the subject has *sensitivities* that appropriately parallel the pattern of canonical evidence for and against the truth of a (thereby) corresponding possible demonstrative utterance. The problem with this suggestion is that it is perfectly compatible with the instantiation of demonstrative content while unconscious. To rectify it, we would at least need to be more specific about the medium (as it were) *in which* the content in question is instantiated. In particular, we would need to specify that it is instantiated in a state of consciousness. But then the argument above applies: the presence of demonstrative content ought to make some difference in a state precisely *as* a state of consciousness. According to the proposal, demonstrative content would at most be a feature of the state in question, in *addition* to the feature of its being a state of consciousness.[27]

I conclude the section with two comments on points on which I have already touched. First, I have assumed for the sake of argument that genuinely translatable content must always be "conceptual" in form. And once we have distinguished translatable content from purely "phenomenal quality," it may in fact appear difficult to defend any other assumption. However we construe the ingredience of translatable content in consciousness, it may seem impossible to draw a non-arbitrary line between those instances of it that are truly conceptual and those that are not. But the account that I propose to develop also accommodates an important distinction. It allows us to recognize an element of translatable content that—aside from the doctrine of "judgments of perception" as presented in the *Prolegomena* (and on which I comment in detail in Chapter Five)—is below the level of what Kant himself officially regards as conceptual or judgmental. On the other hand, insofar as it is still a question of something more than intuition itself, and the sensations ingredient in it, we might also continue to insist on its judgmental or conceptual nature. What is crucial is simply to see that, so far as we would at most be dealing with some kind of (albeit non-"sensory") material *in* intuition, we would by that very fact still at most be dealing with mere material *for* concepts and judgments, in the official Kantian sense of the latter terms.

We shall find it useful to regard such contents, apart from their actual forming into *Kantian* concepts, as comprising concepts and judgments of a more purely "animal" sort. Obviously, the limits of toleration are vague as regards the acceptability of translations for contents in contexts that are unambiguously human. Those for translating would-be animal contents might seem to be even more so. This may lead to hesitation to acknowledge that translatable contents are ascribable to animals at all, whether or not we regard those contents as conceptual.[28] Alternatively, one may regard the problems of inter-species translation as unusual only in degree with respect to problems involved in the translation of human contents.[29] In any event, there is at least nothing in Kant against the supposition that animals, and human beings too, instantiate contents that are not "conceptual," in the Kantian sense, but are nonetheless *translatable*. One advantage of the present approach is not simply that it permits the distinction, but that it also provides an account of the *relationship* between the two sorts of content in human consciousness: the more primitive is simply material for the more sophisticated.

Our distinctions might also be employed to clarify the notion of phenomenal quality. In the case of a genuinely sensory state, one may of course be inclined to suppose that the presence of such quality is precisely what Kant means to account for by appeal to the ingredience of sensations. By supposition, the "material" of a state of consciousness will always make some difference in the way in which it presents an object (or a would-be object), but not a difference that in turn rests on the way in which the object is conceptualized. By extension, we might suppose that the recognition of such quality in mere imagining would need to postulate some analogue of Kantian sensations. According to the present account, however, there will be no reason to deny that conceptualization itself, through the *material* that is essentially ingredient in it, is perfectly capable of contributing to the "phenomenal quality" or primitive "feel" of a state of consciousness. This is because, again, the material for the formation of concepts "applied" to intuitions must itself be material, as well, *in* those intuitions. As I shall propose, it is constituted out of a body of pre-conceptual anticipations and retentions concerning the course of possible experience. As "material" in intuitional states, the material in question might of course be regarded as analogous to sensations. But the analogy need extend no further. In the case of purely imaginative consciousness, then, it seems reasonable to conclude that phenomenal quality or primitive feel is simply reducible to the general character of directedness itself, together with whatever such material is in question. There is no need for special mental "images," nor for imagistic analogues of sensation of any sort.

This of course requires rethinking the suggestion that mere (Kantian) "sensations" are in fact what account for the phenomenal quality of sensory states themselves. At most they could account for that part of phenomenal quality or feel that is *peculiar* to sensory states—for example, to actually seeing colors as opposed to merely imagining them. But the total phenomenal quality of seeing involves more. Some may insist that it also involves distinctively conceptual elements. Again, the proposed account permits a middle road. It does justice to our inclination to deny that phenomenal quality, in perception, is completely independent of the ways in which perceptions are "taken." Yet it permits a sense in which conceptualization always involves a conceptual response to what is independently accessible, purely phenomenally, in perception. The latter will still be so in the sense that the "application" of concepts always involves some kind of forming of a body of anticipations and retentions ingredient as material in an intuitional state. (The requisite forming need not follow the latter in order of time. In most cases, an initial body of material may be responded to in a single "act" that is *simultaneously* introductive of additional material and appropriately formative.) It seems reasonable to assume that the latter ingredience is what provides the phenomenal quality of conceptualization itself.

An obvious consequence follows from this for the problem of leeway regarding the possible variety of "connection" between particular contents and phenomenal qualities in imagining. It should be clear that, in at least one sense, the present account is required to deny that such leeway exists at all. The ingredience of particular anticipations and retentions in an imaginative intuition simply is, according to the present account, the phenomenal quality of that state. Since that ingredience is at the same time constitutive of a kind of translatable content, it follows that, with respect to that kind, no leeway is possible between phenomenal quality and translatable content. Nevertheless, there is still some leeway to be recognized between the presence of phenomenal quality and the ingredience of genuinely *conceptual* content in an imaginative intuition. Presumably, there ought to be room for recognizing whatever leeway we might have had in mind earlier, in conceding that a given "image" may be conceptualized in various ways (with appropriate background assumptions). The account can recognize this. Any particular set of anticipations and retentions, ingredient in intuitive imagining, may in turn be regarded as potential material for inclusion in a variety of distinct conceptual contents, all regarded as legitimately "applicable" to the intuition in question. All of the points made earlier, in terms of the notion of taking or conceptualizing "images," can be recognized here as well, but without incurring a commitment to images as peculiar objects. The solution is simply to recognize that the anticipative and retentive material in an intuitional state, whether sensory or imaginative, is in turn available as material for, but no more than as material for, whatever acts of conceptualization are also applicable to it.[30]

IV. Objects and Appearances

One may finally say something more about the concept of an "object" and of the related notion of an "appearance." So far, I have attended to object-directedness as an aspect of consciousness itself. Any objects in question were thus considered only with respect to their status as the intentional correlates of the latter. The main endeavor was to see that this did not entail an objectionable ontological commitment. This notion of the objects of consciousness, as correlates of the consciousness of them, will prove crucial in some of the later discussions, most notably concerning association and the "affinity of appearances" (Chapter Four), the two stages of the second-edition Deduction (Chapter Five), and the account of self-consciousness and self-knowledge (Chapter Six). But there must also be a sense in which the objects of consciousness are not, for Kant, mere correlates of the consciousness of them. If there were not such a sense, then there would be no way for him to account for a consciousness of objective reality.

I have argued elsewhere on behalf of a kind of phenomenalist reading of Kant, with respect to the reality of objects of possible knowledge. (One may try to be more tolerant as regards "objects" of suitably abstract conception.)[31] It should be clear that this need not be incompatible with regarding objectively real objects as something more than the correlates of one's immediate consciousness of them. The most obvious way to pursue a phenomenalistic line, compatibly with this concession, would be to regard objectively real objects as a kind of correlate, not of particular states of consciousness, but of a suitably generalized *possible* consciousness. Kant seems to say as much:

> In the *mere concept* of a thing no mark of its existence is to be found. . . . For that the concept precedes the perception signifies the concept's mere possibility; the perception which supplies the *content* [emphasis added] to the concept is the sole mark of actuality. (A225/B272-3)

> That there may be inhabitants in the moon, although no one has ever perceived them, must certainly be admitted. This, however, only means [*aber es bedeutet nur so viel*] that in the possible advance of experience we may encounter them. . . . To call an appearance a real thing prior to our perceiving it, either means that in the advance of experience we must meet with such a perception, or it means nothing at all. (A493/B521)

What may seem impossible is the combination of such an approach, in terms of "possible appearances," and my contention that the apprehension of objective reality involves the apprehension of appearances—i.e., of correlate-appearances—*as* objective realities (not, for example, merely as components into which such realities are reducible). The difficulty may seem to lie in my denial that regarding appearances as "correlates" in the first place requires granting them an independent ontological status. If, apart from having been actually identified as objectively real, appearances need not be supposed to possess any being of their own (not even some kind of "mental" being), then what sense could it make to suppose that they ever *could* be so identified? Denying them an independent ontological status seems precisely to remove the point of speaking of *them* in the first place. If there are no such items to begin with, then how could one possibly take "them" for really existing objects?

To put the point differently, I have argued that talk of appearances merely as candidates *for* objective regard is really just a way of talking about the intrinsic directedness of intuitional states. It may seem to follow from this that it is impossible ever to make a judgment (at least in intuition) about anything *other* than intuitional states. That, of course, contradicts the claim that such judgments can really be about perceivable objects.

It should be clear that this difficulty, if it is one, is not peculiar to judgments concerning the objective reality of appearances. If it has any force at all, it should apply to any sort of attempt to conceptualize appearances. For example, even to take some appearance as of a roughly circular (but perhaps merely hallucinated) shape, whether or not we also take it to be objectively real, will have to involve a judgment that is every bit as "directed" toward that particular appearance as a judgment to the effect that it is in fact objectively real.[32] And yet, it may seem, both sorts of judgment are impossible on the terms laid down. On those terms, there really "is" no appearance to make such a judgment about in the first place.

This would be a serious objection against a purely formal approach to conceptual content. According to that sort of approach, as I have argued, there is no useful sense in which the conceptual content present in a state of consciousness might be regarded as part of the way in which the immediately apprehended object of that state is apprehended. At most, according to such an approach, an object-directed state of consciousness might, in some more or less abstract way, manage to "say" something about *something* or other. Or rather: it might manage to instantiate or token a content that manages to say something. But there is no way that such a state, or its tokened or instantiated content, could be construed as saying something about the very *object* of that particular state of consciousness. At least this would not be possible, so long as the latter is regarded as the intentional correlate of that state's intrinsic directedness, that is, of its intuitional "form" as such.

One of the main advantages of the present approach is precisely that it does account for our ability to conceptualize the immediate objects of consciousness— whether as objectively real things or in some other terms—without requiring that we abandon the insight that the immediate objects of consciousness are intentional correlates of the consciousness of them. It is able to do this because, according to that account, concepts themselves (at least non-categorial ones) are originally *formed* out the very material *through which* one is able to apprehend objects in intuition in the first place. As I shall eventually argue in Chapter Six, what specifically conceptual form adds to any such mode of apprehension is simply a kind of embedding of that same material, by means of the "forms of judgment," in a higher order consciousness of a special sort.

Insofar as the material in question is not merely externally associated with an intuition, but is as much ingredient *in* it as sensations ever could be, when one apprehends appearances through them, then we would at least have an explanation of how concepts might be "applied" to immediately apprehended objects, and how those objects might be conceptually "taken" in this way or that, without having to abandon our notion that the immediate objects of consciousness are intentional correlates of the apprehension of them. The account will be phenomenalistic, because, as suggested, the basic *material* of such conception will be at bottom nothing other than a manifold of anticipations and retentions concerning the course of possible experience. But the account will also be compatible with the recognition of objective reality on the part of at least some intuitional objects. This is so because the corresponding judgments are not *about* one's own intuitions, but are every bit as object-directed as the intuitions to which they are applied.

(Obviously, the suggestion requires that we rethink what is to be meant by "application" of a concept in the first place.) The anticipations in question are, by supposition, anticipations concerning future possible appearances. (The retentions, which we may ignore for now, might be regarded as "anticipations" concerning *past* possible appearances, that is, anticipations of what *might have been* perceived.) But the judgment in question is not reducible to those anticipations. Rather, it is *formed* out of them. In turn, those anticipations are a part of the "material" through which an appearance is apprehended. That is, they are a part of the material through which the form of intuition originally operates in some case. In virtue of this, the judgment in question is precisely *about* that apprehended appearance. According to the account in question, that is just what it *is* for such a judgment to be "about" such an object.[33]

It should also be clear that, according to the account proposed, the fact that immediately apprehended appearances are, as such, the "intentional correlates" of the apprehension of them is compatible with conceding that—*qua* identifiable as objectively real—those appearances have qualities that are different from, and even incompatible with, the qualities that they immediately *appear* to have. We may simply regard this as a case in which the anticipations embodied in the predicated *concept* are anticipations of sets of future possible appearances (relative to various possible conditions for their apprehension) that are not the sorts of appearances that one would normally be led to anticipate, solely on the basis of the "given" appearance—*insofar as the latter is apprehended merely through whatever sensations are in question.* (In one sense, of course, the fact that appearances are apprehended "through" certain anticipations must have some kind of counterpart in those appearances as well, *qua* intentional objects. But all that this shows is that the notion of an intentional object, hence of an intentional "correlate," needs to be considered with respect to more than one level of analysis.)

As for whether a given judgment is also *true* of a given appearance, *qua* objectively real object: according to the proposed account, that would have to be a matter of whether or not the anticipations that the judgment embodies are actually *satisfiable* (or, perhaps, of whether or not they would be, in some eventual "long run," *justified*).[34] In any given instance, some of them are likely to be, and others, not. (Of course, Kant argues, in the "Refutation of Idealism," that at least some of them must be *taken* to be in fact satisfiable. For at least some given appearances must be taken to *be* such objectively real objects.) But that need not pose a problem for our account. It simply requires the ability to characterize the sorts of anticipations that are specifically relevant to the minimal reality of an apprehended object. (In fact, our proposal does not even rule out recognizing one or more senses in which one may be said to apprehend really existing objects quite apart from *any* question as to the anticipations ingredient in apprehension. If one favors a causal theory, for example, one might stipulate that under certain conditions, involving the causal origin of an intuition, that intuition is to count as the perceptual apprehension of a really existing object. But that sort of question is not the one that interests us here.)

There is a final advantage in the proposed account, with respect to the sort of "phenomenalism" that it supports. It allows us to avoid the problem of *circular-*

ity that may appear to affect varieties of phenomenalism. The apparent difficulty is this. Such views seem to demand a phenomenalistic *analysis* of judgments regarding ordinary objects. Such an analysis, presumably, will involve judgments to the effect that certain sorts of perceptions are or would have been obtainable, given satisfaction of the appropriate antecedent conditions. But this leads to circularity, because those latter judgments in turn require phenomenalistic analysis, and the only plausible candidates for it will eventually need to mention material conditions among the "appropriate" conditions originally in question. For example, they will need to mention such things as the sorts of perceptions that would be obtained were one's *eyes* oriented in a particular direction. Thus we will not have succeeded in reducing judgments about objects to judgments about possible perceptions.

The response to this objection is that the proposed account does not propose the possibility (not even in principle) of reducing judgments about material objects to judgments about possible perceptions. According to the proposed account, judgments about material objects are regarded as formed out of *anticipations* (I continue, for the time being, to ignore the role of retentions) concerning possible perceptions. In turn, the anticipations in question must be "conditional" ones: anticipations of possible perceptions relative to the satisfaction of equally anticipable conditions. But this does not imply that those anticipations involve judgments, or even conceptions, in regard to those conditions—or at least not that they do so in the relevant sense of those terms. In the relevant sense of the terms, the proposal maintains that the anticipations in question are merely the material out of which judgments and conceptions proper are *formed*. (Clearly, nothing prevents describing such material as itself involving judgment or conception as well, but in some different sense of the terms.)

It is equally clear that any attempt to give linguistic *expression* to the material in question will require describing *what* is anticipated, and thus will require conceptualizing the latter in some particular way. There is no harm in conceding that this, in turn, requires concepts that are in some way already dependent upon one's conception of material reality. But describing or communicating a set of anticipations, and *forming* them (or having them formed) into modes of conception in the first place are hardly the same thing. So the required appeal to material conceptions does not support a charge of circularity. (As we shall see in Chapter Six, any complete description of the relevantly anticipated "appearances" would require describing those appearances as appearances eventually perceivable by *oneself* as well; but this is compatible with maintaining that one's original self-*concept* is in turn nothing other than the concept of whatever subject of experience is reflected, as an intentional correlate, precisely *in* such anticipated appearances, *qua* anticipated.)

CHAPTER 2

Extending the Framework

I. Introduction

IN CHAPTER ONE I developed a notion of intuition, and of the distinction beween matter and form in intuition, that will serve as the basis of my account of the application of concepts to intuitions. I provided some evidence that the interpretation accords with Kant's intentions in the Aesthetic, but argued that the distinction is independently defensible. I also considered the claim that sensation is the matter of sensory intuition. I argued that this claim is compatible with the view that something else serves as matter in intuition as well. I suggested, but did not try to show, that, at least for Kant, something that we might call "imaginative anticipation and retention" will need to be what serves as such material. It will need to do so in order that it may thereby be available for forming into the concepts that one is said to "apply" to intuitions. Beginning with Chapter Three, I show that this suggestion is not only consonant with Kant's claims in the Logic, but is required in order to make sense of what is otherwise most obscure in it. The present chapter offers additional clarification of the suggestion. Section II does this by relating the view to some issues of concern to philosophers of a more behavioristic or functionalistic stamp. Section III adds some additional points of reference by showing how the proposal relates to some notions developed by other philosophers in three very different philosophical traditions.

II. Conceptual Material and a Subject's Dispositions

Whatever we make of Kant's pronouncements concerning the role of imaginative anticipations and retentions in conception, everyone presumably agrees that, at least *like* a certain sort of anticipation and retention, some of a subject's "dispositional" states are essential to its possession of conceptual abilities. Some readings of Kant go so far as to identify concepts *with* dispositions. As it stands, this runs afoul of Kant's claim that concepts are the "predicates" of possible judgments (A69/B94). This seems to imply that they are not, for example, merely dispositions toward the *making* of judgments. In any event, the question would remain as to the nature of judgments themselves.

The irrelevance of the suggestion in this respect might suggest a variation on the dispositional approach, namely, the view that concepts are multiply instantiable aspects of (possible) representations; that it is in virtue of these aspects that the latter ever are (if intuitional in nature) judgmental with respect to objects (i.e, in virtue of which they ever are *Erkenntnisse*); and that in turn these aspects play their essentially "predicative" role only in virtue of being appropriately *connected* with a subject's dispositions. According to this approach, specification of the relevant dispositions, and the relevant connection, would *ipso facto* clarify the nature of judgment itself. To a certain extent, this is my own proposal. But there are various ways in which the "connection" might be construed.

A purely functionalist approach might seek to establish the connection with a subject's dispositions purely in terms of the "typical causes and effects" of the relevant predicative aspects of mental states.[1] We might propose, for example, that any feature tokenable or instantiable as a "predicate" in some state derives its conceptual status from its purely causal connections with other features tokenable or instantiable in states. Apart from the feeling that this ignores the crucial notion of *consciousness* (e.g., ignores the problem of the very consciousness of the connections in question), this may seem especially plausible as an elucidation of Kant's insistence that concepts are predicates of possible judgments only to the extent that they serve a function of "rule-governed synthesis" among possible representations. The causal connections, in the proposed view, would simply *define* the rules of synthesis. The proposal may also seem plausible because capacities and dispositions may in their own turn seem eventually reducible in terms of the causal powers of internal states of a subject.

The suggestion would, of course, need refining. Any truly conceptual state of a subject—apart, perhaps, from the state of idly having some content "in mind"— always involves additional capacities and dispositions, over and above whatever may be involved in the constitution of a content as such in the first place. Otherwise, there would be no difference between the mere presence of a content in mind, like idle doodling, and what a subject actually happens to be thinking at any moment.[2] But this, it may be claimed, is no problem for a functionalist. The additional capacities and dispositions may be regarded as so many additional "causal powers" of a content, on an occasion of its presence in consciousness, over and above those involved in its constitution as an in principle abstractly presentable content in the first place.

As an interpretation of Kant, there would seem to be an obvious problem in the proposal. For one thing, functionalism appears to get things backward. This is because, for Kant, causes and effects, at least insofar as they are possible objects of knowledge, are essentially governed by systems of causal laws. So according to a functionalist approach, the very idea of conceptual content would have to presuppose the idea of a system of causal laws naturally obtaining. But in Kant's own thinking, the very *idea* that a system of laws naturally obtains seems to be derivative from the idea of a being who is capable of representing determinate sorts of objects in the first place (B164).

To be sure, Kant does not maintain that pure understanding prescribes particular laws. Apparently, it merely prescribes the general form of lawfulness in nature; it is up to the empirical ("impure") understanding to find what the laws are (B165). Nevertheless, it is difficult to see, in Kant's view, how the very *idea* of a nature

that is subject to particular laws can be anything other than the idea of a realm
of appearances that is in some way the correlate of a subject capable of judging
in a certain way, namely, of a subject who is capable of taking certain sequences
of appearances as "necessary." I argue in Chapter Four that the apprehension of
a causal order is in fact based, for Kant, upon an apprehension of the intentional
correlate of one's own anticipations and retentions in experience. If this is so, then
any account that attempts to explicate the notion of representational content in
terms of causal roles will be circular. The relevant concept of causality would already contain an implicit reference to the possibility of representation.

A second consideration concerns Kant's insistence on the "spontaneity" of
acts of the understanding: "the mind's power of producing representations from
itself, the spontaneity of knowledge, should be called the understanding" (A51/
B75; cf. B130, B162n). An act of spontaneity is one that must be regarded as expressing a causality other than according to causal laws. It must be regarded as
expressing a "free" causality, wherein something is determined to occur, but not
simply as a law-governed consequence of antecedently obtaining conditions
(A444-7/B472-5, A533/B561). This is contrary to the kind of causality presumed
to be in question in functionalist accounts of the mind, or at least in functionalist
accounts of a purely causal sort.[3]

Kant develops his notion of spontaneous causality primarily with respect to the
problem of intentionally performed actions. In that case, he specifically attributes
acts of spontaneity to "reason" as distinct from understanding. But the only difference seems to be that acts of the latter are limited to the conceptualization of sensible appearances (and their form). Apart from that, understanding's operations
are as free as those of reason. They are, *qua* acts of the understanding, limited
by nothing other than the nature of understanding itself:

> As a pure spontaneous faculty [reason] is elevated even above understanding. For
> though the latter is also a spontaneous activity and does not, like sense, merely con-
> tain conceptions which arise only when one is affected by things, being passive, it
> nevertheless cannot produce by its activity any other *concepts* [emphasis added]
> than those which serve to bring the sensuous representations under rules, and
> thereby to unite them in one consciousness.[4]

It is difficult to be sure what Kant means by the spontaneity of understanding.
It is particularly difficult in view of the fact that he concedes that all events are
necessitated by causal laws. The only difference is, apparently, that we need to
distinguish two points of view with respect to any event that expresses spontaneity: the same event that is subject to causal laws may also be regarded as expressive of spontaneous causality. It is not clear what the qualification is supposed to
amount to. However, Kant seems to be distinguishing precisely between the conceptual and other aspects of conceptual states, and to be denying that the former
could be determined by causal laws. In the passage just quoted, and as I emphasized in quoting it, he does not simply speak of conceptual states as products of
spontaneity. It is the very concepts that are involved *in* such states that are products of spontaneity. Consider also the following passages:

> Our cognition springs from two fundamental sources of the mind; the first is the capacity of receiving representations (receptivity of impressions), the second is the power of cognizing an object through these representations (spontaneity of concepts). (A50/B74)

> Concepts are based on the spontaneity of thought, sensible intuitions on the receptivity of impressions. (A68/B93)

As we shall see in more detail in subsequent chapters, Kant is serious in proposing that a spontaneous faculty of understanding is responsible for the "production" of concepts themselves, not simply for the production of states or events that embody, token, or instantiate them. So far as I can see, this can only mean that the conceptual dimension of a subjective state cannot be a matter of that state's involvement in some network of typical causes and effects.

This may be thought to read too much into Kant's claims about spontaneity. Perhaps his point is that conceptual states are (or embody) *actions*. If conceptual states are actions, then, analogously to the case of ordinary intentional actions, it would follow that the occurrence of a conceptual state could never be adequately comprehended in terms of the working of causal laws. The point can be granted, it seems, without raising any question concerning the "production" of the very concepts involved in conceptual states. It only concerns their character as "actions," not their specifically representational dimension. But consider the following passage:

> Should one ask whether understanding itself is determined, either in itself *or* [emphasis added] with respect to how it acts or fails to act [*an sich selbst so wohl als in Ansehung dessen was er thut oder unterlässt*], then we must say: there is no possible experience that can show this, because that would always be mere appearance. Understanding is itself no object of sensory intuition.[5]

The point seems to be that the spontaneity of acts of understanding is not simply their spontaneity as actions of some kind. It is their spontaneity precisely as acts of *understanding*. It is difficult to see what this distinction is, if it is not between a spontaneity involved in the factual occurrence of conceptual states on occasions and one involved in the original constitution of their conceptual content. In any case, to the considerations so far adduced, I would simply add the following: If anything like the functionalist view really were Kant's, then it is difficult to see why he found it so difficult to be clear. In particular, it is difficult to see why so much of his effort, and so much apparent confusion, concerned the relationship between "imagination" and conceptual representation. If all that Kant had in mind, in his notion of "spontaneity," were explicable in causal terms, then it ought to have been much easier to have said so.

Apart from interpreting Kant, the approach is independently objectionable. It is not plausible to suppose that the dispositions one ascribes to a subject, in ascribing conceptual states to it, are without circularity reducible to powers for affecting and being affected possessed by those states themselves. A recent example of Stephen Stich's seems to me to make this point, though Stich himself employs the example for a somewhat different purpose.[6] The general point is this: that

whether or not we are prepared to judge that the causal powers of a state of a person (or of some feature of a state of a person) have remained unaltered throughout
an undeniable course of altering the subject's condition depends solely on our judgment concerning the typical causes and effects that this state would continue to
have, given the satisfaction of certain antecedent *conditions.* It does not hinge,
in general, on a judgment as to whether or not the alteration has undercut the very
possibility of those conditions being satisfied in the first place. For example, if a
subject is no longer able to access certain stored memories, then that subject may
be judged to lack a portion of whatever capacities and dispositions are normally
associated with judging that McKinley was assassinated. But that is perfectly compatible with supposing that the "content" originally constitutive of judging that
McKinley was assassinated continues to be such that, were the access in question
regained, then the typical results would continue to follow from the tokening or
instantiation of that content. And it is perfectly compatible with supposing that relevant additional states remain such that, were further conditions satisfied, then that
content would in its turn arise as a typical effect of them. The point is that
there is no reason *in principle* why our judgment concerning alterations in the
"causal powers" of states (or of their features) needs to coincide with our judgment
concerning alterations in the capacities and dispositions ascribable to the subject of those states.

The argument does not rest on supposing that a purely causal approach, in
terms of internal states rather than subjects as wholes, must fail to capture some
special sense of "agent causality." Even if all causality is ultimately state- or event-
causality, the point is that there is no reason in principle why our judgments concerning a subject's capacities and dispositions need to be secondary to judgments
concerning the capacities and dispositions of a subject's internal states. However
we eventually analyze the latter notion, we should always be free to *rule,* in any
particular case, that a subject's capacities and dispositions have undergone impair-
ment, but its internal states have the same "causal powers" as before. Nothing
in the *concept* of a state's causal powers rules that out.

One may object that I am adopting too narrow a conception of the causal powers
attributable to the states of a subject. According to various standards, that may
be. But there is only one way to make the objection work in the present context.
We would have to insist that our judgments concerning the causal powers of
states, at least in cases that involve the ascription of conceptual contents to states,
have got to be brought into *conformity* with our ordinary ascriptions of certain
sorts of capacities and dispositions to the subjects of those states. But that, in effect, would be to concede at least an important part of the point in dispute. The
conclusion would then be unavoidable that, whatever else we may say about the
conceptual states of a subject, they must be states in which a special sort of "material" is essentially ingredient. They must be states in which a sub-set of the very
capacities and dispositions of the subject itself is ingredient, or at least in which
their "categorical basis," as such, is.

Even if it is not the case that the capacities and dispositions of a subject, of
the sort involved in the ascription of conceptual content, are only circularly reducible to the causal powers of *states* of a subject, the argument presented in the

preceding chapter, against a purely "formal" approach, should continue to tell against a specifically functionalist view of content. That argument concerned the need to connect the conceptual content of a state with the object-directed character of that state. Even if we conceded that everything essential to conceptual content, considered just in itself, was capturable by reference to the powers of cognitive states (or of their features), the problem would remain of explaining why such content should ever be regarded as directed toward the objects presented in particular intuitions. According to a functionalist account of conceptual contents, as causally functional features of possible states, what could possibly give us anything more—when those features are in fact tokened by object-directed states—than the case of a text that merely happens to be inscribed on an arrow? The answer, I have argued, is that insofar as contents are directed toward objects, the states that apprehend those objects must do so precisely *through* whatever material is constitutive of the contents themselves. Even if it were the case that such material is describable in causal terms, the fact remains that it is at most the material out of which conceptions may be formed. Its mere tokening or instantiation in would-be cognitive states is not, except in that limited sense, constitutive of the representational content of any state.

In any event, nothing stands in the way, on the alternative that I propose, of equating the basic "material" of conception with various of the dispositions of a subject (or with their categorical basis). Kant's own way of seeing the point is, I have suggested, simply to recognize the role of "anticipations and retentions" as material for the forming of concepts. To this extent, the proposal leans more toward behaviorism than functionalism. But there is also a sense in which it leans more toward the latter. For the proposal also insists that what constitutes conceptual content must be "tokenable or instantiable," not simply within the subject of intuitional states, but as an actual feature *of* those very states. In order to serve as material for predication in intuition (whether sensory or imaginative), it must also serve as material *in* intuition.

III. Some Comparisons

The extension of the Kantian framework of matter and form, which I shall argue is at least implicit in the Transcendental Deduction, yields a view that is both like and unlike some views about the intentionality of consciousness that have been offered by other philosophers. I begin with attention to a philosopher who would in fact reject some essential aspects of that framework. Despite this difference from Kant, the suggestion that I have put in terms of a distinction between matter and form, in both intuition and conception, bears some similarity to Searle's account of the co-determination of content against a non-intentional Background.[7]

Searle accepts the irreducibility of intentional content, as a feature of mental states. But he rejects, in effect, the notion of intuitional directedness that I espoused in Chapter One. Since it is irreducible, Searle does not try to define the notion of intentional content. Rather, he simply characterizes one central *type* of intentional content and suggests that all intentional states either possess an instance of it or else involve more complex structures, the basic components of which are states that possess such content. (Searle also distinguishes the "direction of fit" in which a content may be present and phenomenological "feelings" that may be characteristic of a state. But the latter do not serve as "material" in the way that sensations, for example, do for Kant.) The central case is that in which content "determines" a mental state's "conditions of satisfaction." In the case of belief, for example, it determines the conditions under which the belief would be true; for desire, the conditions under which the desire would be satisfied.

We may concern ourselves primarily with what Searle says about "experiences" (in the technical sense in which he employs that term). For him, experiences have an intrinsic intentional content. Here is what he says about visual experiences:

> . . . the two forms of mental phenomena, belief and visual experience, are intrinsi-
> cally Intentional. Internal to each phenomenon is an Intentional content that deter-
> mines its conditions of satisfaction. The argument that visual experiences are intrin-
> sically Intentional, in sum, is that they have conditions of satisfaction which are
> determined by the content of the experience in exactly the same sense that other
> Intentional states have conditions of satisfaction which are determined by the con-
> tent of the states. (P. 40)

The intentional content of a visual experience is an internal and irreducible feature that "determines" the conditions that would need to be satisfied in order for
that experience not to be hallucinatory. It is important to avoid regarding this notion as trivially obvious. It seems trivial to claim that there are conditions that
need to be satisfied in order for an experience not to be hallucinatory, and that
these conditions have something to do with the internal features of an experience.
But Searle's claim goes beyond this. It says, if I might so put it, that it makes
a difference to an experience *itself* whether or not it is an hallucinatory one. It
is not just that we possess a concept of success or failure, with regard to possible
experiences, and that this *concept* concerns some connection between the internal
features of an experience and the actual state of the world. It is rather that *the experience itself* "has to determine what counts as succeeding" (p. 38). This cannot,
of course, mean that an experience actually *lays claim to being* a veridical experience. That would imply that a belief or judgment needs to be in question; furthermore, Searle maintains that one's beliefs and judgments might in fact contradict
the content of a visual experience (p. 55). But it seems to imply that, in some
sense, an experience at least essentially contains a (non-linguistic [p. 49]) "description" of some possible state of affairs, and a representation (or, as Searle prefers,
a "presentation") of the world *as fitting* the description.[8] However, the notion that
an experience contains descriptions, in a certain "direction of fit," cannot be a
basic notion for Searle. It is itself to be explicated in terms of the fact that experiences contain contents "determining" conditions of satisfaction.

In some ways, Searle's experiences may seem comparable to sensory intuitions
in Kant. But there are differences. First of all, Searle rejects any attempt to elucidate the notion by appeal to a primitive notion of experiential "directedness." To
the contrary, the notion of directedness needs itself to be explicated in terms of
that of a state's conditions of satisfaction (p. 39). The same goes for any other attempt to make sense of the idea of apprehending (possibly non-existent) "inten-

tional objects," whether in the case of mere belief (pp. 16–17), for example, or in that of "imagining" objects (where the intentional content, for Searle, is in effect always reducible to that of merely imagining-that: p. 18). The point is that *whatever* it is that determines experiential "directedness" must be, for Searle, just the same sort of thing that determines the content of, say, a non-experiential belief or desire. It is this, in turn, that needs to be seen as an irreducible aspect of mental states.

According to the Kantian approach, recognition of primitive directedness in at least certain sorts of states—in those that are "intuitional" (i.e., sensory states and certain instances of imaginative awareness) — does not of itself preclude recognition of states that lack such directedness and yet still possess "content." But if there are such states, then, in the view that I shall elaborate, their intentional contents would not be primitive features of those states. Rather, to whatever extent they are anything more than dispositional aspects of those states, they would have to be "constituted" features, that is, features that are in a sense *formed* by mental activity (though not necessarily by "action" in any purposive sense of that term) out of material internal to the states in question. In addition, such material must, at least potentially, be material for intuitionally directed states as well. In the Kantian view, that is, nonintuitional intentional "content," if there really is such a thing,[9] fails on two accounts to be primitive. First, it is essentially "constituted" content. Second, its possibility is parasitical upon that of intuitionally directed content. In any case, I have already rebutted the supposition—in fact, Searle's own—that the recognition of primitive directedness entails commitment to unusual entities (p. 17).

If they are not quite intuitions, in Kant's sense, then it may seem best to regard "experiences" as the upshot of some kind of embodiment, or some kind of "realization,"[10] of *concepts* in the medium of something like Kant's "sensations." But Searle himself is unclear as to the connection between content and "concepts." The most that he seems to say is that intentional content is usually *connected* with, or affected by, one's possession of certain concepts (and, *a fortiori*, by beliefs and judgments that utilize those concepts). In certain cases (e.g., of "seeing-as"),

> . . . one wants to say that a certain conceptual mastery is a precondition of having visual experience; and such cases suggest that the Intentionality of visual perception is tied up in all sorts of complicated ways with other forms of Intentionality such as belief and expectation, and also with our systems of representation, most notably language. Both the Network of Intentional states and the Background of non-representational mental capacities affect perception. (P. 54)

As we shall see more clearly presently, the relation between such states and capacities, on the one hand, and intentional content, on the other hand, is in an important sense an external one for Searle. To be sure, he speaks of such material as "reach[ing] inside the Intentional content to determine" aspects of a state's conditions of satisfaction (P. 66). But all that this can presumably mean is that such material helps in many cases to *determine* a state's conditions of satisfaction. (So even in the case of an actual influence from one's "conceptual masteries," it would not necessarily follow that the relevant intentional content is itself conceptual in

nature. In fact, Searle does not commit himself as regards the need for some minimal extent of such influence.)[11] In any event, even when conceptual masteries help
to determine conditions of satisfaction, it seems to remain the case that intentional
content is an irreducible *feature* of the state whose content it is. So there could
be no sense in which it is itself even partially "formed" out of such masteries in
the first place. (In the view that I am ascribing to Kant, the possibility of an intuition that is lacking in conceptual content cannot be excluded either, though Kant
himself has a tendency—to which he does not consistently adhere—to suppose
that such states must at least be devoid of "consciousness." As for questions concerning the "objects" of such depleted states, the proposal is in fact compatible
with conceding a considerable *indeterminacy*. At most, it would seem we can say,
any answer needs to take the form of the following: The state in question is directed toward some possible region of space/time that *might*, under such-and-such
circumstances, be conceptualized in this way or that.)

Now despite Searle's rejection of primitive object-directedness, his view of the
role of Background material, in the determination of conditions of satisfaction, is
comparable to my suggestion concerning the distinction between matter and form
in the constitution of content. As we have seen, what Searle himself argues is that
at least some contents determine conditions of satisfaction only "against" a Background of non-intentional material:

> An Intentional state only determines its conditions of satisfaction—and thus only
> is the state that it is—given its position in a *Network* of other Intentional states and
> against a *Background* of practices and preintentional assumptions that are neither
> themselves Intentional states nor are they parts of the conditions of satisfaction of
> Intentional states. (P. 19; cf. pp. 54ff, 141ff)

The following are some examples: (1) the "preintentional stance toward the
world" involved in the fact "that I recognize degrees of the hardness of things
as part of 'how things are'"—for example, that one can intend to peel an orange
but not a car, but without having any kind of *belief* that one can do the former
but not the latter (p. 144); (2) the kind of "understanding" that allows one to navi-
gate among the various senses of "open" in "The chairman opened the meeting,"
"The artillery opened fire," and "Bill opened a restaurant," and to reject as nonsense such sentences as "Bill opened the mountain," "Sally opened the grass,"
and "Sam opened the sun" (pp. 145–46); (3) the kinds of "associations" that allow
one to distinguish metaphorical from non-metaphorical language, and to distinguish intentions in metaphor, but which are not formulable in terms of one's grasp
of linguistic rules (p. 149); (4) whatever it is by virtue of which the "expert skier
is flexible and responds differently to different conditions of terrain and snow,"
given that it could not possibly involve either conscious or unconscious consultation of rules or conscious or unconscious calculation of any sort (p. 150). An additional example, inspired by Searle, is the following: (5) the sense in which, at least
ordinarily, one's "habit" of using a desk-top to sit on precludes the very possibility
of certain anticipations, upon entering one's office, yet without there actually
being a *belief* that these anticipations are justified.[12]

As Searle notes, it is difficult to *describe* Background material in a way that does not seem already to entail its structuring as intentional content. Searle himself speaks of the Background as comprising "assumptions," "presuppositions," and "presumptions" (p. 156), and even, as we have seen, "recognition" and "understanding." In most of the examples, as well, it would seem in order to speak of a subject's "expectations" or "anticipations." Searle objects to this terminology (p. 157), though he does speak of "associations." In any event, we need to avoid supposing that what is in question is something that a subject could formulate, even if asked to. And of course, what is in question cannot be "beliefs," in Searle's sense, though they might always be described as beliefs in some other sense. In addition, Searle also describes the Background material as "nonrepresentational" (p. 143). But, of course, Kant need not be limited in this way. For Kant, "representational" (e.g., sensations) states do not always possess intentional content. Searle himself offers no account of the general nature of Background material, although his inclination to describe it by reference to "capacities" and "practices" (p. 156), and in terms of the vocabulary of "knowing-how" (p. 143), may suggest a leaning toward some kind of dispositional approach.

In the view that concerns us, the anticipations and retentions that serve as material in the formation of intentional content, for Kant, must share at least two features with the material in Searle's Background. First, they cannot, on pain of circularity, themselves possess content in the sense in question (though they might in some other). Second, they must nevertheless contribute *to* the content of certain intentional states. Unlike Searle, however, Kant will regard such content as wholly constituted *out* of such material. (At least, this must be the case for a basic set of contents. Once formed, these may in turn provide material for the formation of additional contents. I generally abstract from this complication.)

Apart from the fact that, according to Searle's approach, intentional content is not originally "formed" from the material contained in the Background, the most important difference between the approaches is connected with the issue of primitive directedness. The distinction between matter and form is dependent upon that notion. The matter of an intuition, as we have been considering it, is the set of states *through which* an intuition is directed. That is, it is the set of states that, by virtue of being *ingredient* in an intuition, make some difference in the way in which that intuition is directed. (This is, of course, compatible with conceding that other factors, besides ingredient states, can make a difference in the way in which an intuition is directed. For example, it says nothing about the role of concepts, which are at most formed *out* of ingredient material.)

What the approaches have in common is their recognition that non-intentional states always influence the way in which intentional states are directed. But the problem with Searle's approach, from a Kantian perspective, is that it leaves it entirely mysterious how this could possibly be the case. How are the states in the Background in fact able to "reach inside" an intentional content, in order to bear on its determination of conditions of satisfaction? Searle himself describes the material in question as constituting a part of one's "stance" toward the world. But it would seem unable, in his view, ever to form an actual part of one's *intentional* stance. If it could indeed have an influence upon one's intentional stance, it seems never to be an actual *constituent* of that stance. According to the Kantian alternative, the contrary is the case. This is because, in that view, the material in question is the very material out of which intentional stances are formed in the first place.

While Searle does speak of Background material as "reach[ing] inside" of content, he also puts the point in different terms. Background material, he says, simply "provides a set of enabling conditions that make it possible for particular forms of Intentionality to function" (p. 157). Here, the conditions in question are explicitly causal conditions—though merely enabling, not causally determining, ones (p. 158). Searle's view therefore seems to be this: in an entirely non-causal sense, intentional contents "determine" the conditions of satisfaction for the states whose contents they are; Background material, in turn, has at most a causal influence on which contents are able to *be* the contents of which states in the first place.

Apart from the apparently Cartesian difficulty as to how such material might have an influence on the instantiation of primitive properties of an entirely different order,[13] the proposal involves an implausibly external approach to the relation between intentional content and non-intentional material. Surely, the manifold of one's (non-intentional) "expectations" and "stances" is as much a *constituent* of one's visual experience, say, in skiing, as are the "phenomenal qualities" in which those experiences are "realized" (p. 45). Though they are not reflectively present, nor even such that they might be articulated with effort, they form an integral part of the way in which the skier is *seeing*. In some special and immediately phenomenological sense, the intentional content of a visual experience determines, for Searle, what one sees things "as" (pp. 50-57). Therefore, the expectations and stances in question should be a part of the very content. But in Searle's own view, they cannot be. At most, they could exercise an "enabling" influence on one's ability to see things "as" something or other. The advantage of the Kantian view, in addition to its recognition of primitive intuitional directedness, is precisely that it helps overcome this apparently arbitrary, and troublingly Cartesian, dichotomy. But then, as we have already seen, these two points are really just aspects of one.

Despite these differences between Searle's approach and the one I have said is Kant's, both Searle and Kant take intentional content to involve an irreducibly mental function. In addition, both recognize the role of non-intentional material in the performance of that function. I now want to consider two philosophers whose thought is directly influenced by Kant himself. The first of them is Husserl.[14] For our purpose, the most obvious difference between Husserl and Searle is that the former relies on a primitive notion of intentional directedness (i.e., directedness toward some "object" that may or may not be real). This is, of course, not equivalent to Searle's notion of a mental state's possession of intentional content. That is, it cannot be equated with the notion of an intrinsic character by virtue of which a state has "conditions of satisfaction." In Husserl's view, rather, appeal to primitive directedness would be needed in order to make any sense of Searle's notion of content in the first place. For Searle, as we have seen, the reverse is the case: any useful notion of object-directedness must be explicated in terms of the notion of content.

In the "pregnant" sense of the term *consciousness*, Husserl tells us, the relevant notion of being object-directed is simply that of having "consciousness of something."[15] More explicitly:

> Under intentionality we understand the own peculiarity of mental processes "to be consciousness *of* something". . . . [For example,] a perceiving is a perceiving of something, perhaps a physical thing; a judging is a judging of a predicatively formed affair-complex. . . . In every actional cogito a radiating "regard" is directed from the pure Ego to the "object" of the consciousness-correlate in question. . . . [16]

To be sure, Husserl draws some important distinctions concerning the "something" toward which consciousness is intentionally directed. Apart from the obvious distinction between directedness as such, and directedness toward really existing objects (and obtaining states of affairs), the most important is that between "actional" or "wakeful" directedness and directedness toward what is merely in the *background* of consciousness.[17] It follows from the latter distinction that the (complete) "intentional object" toward which consciousness is directed cannot simply be an object (not even a possible object) in the usual sense of the term. It would seem rather to involve a structure that, in a more or less determinate way, contains a vast number of actual and possible objects. This may seem to constitute a difference from Kant as I have presented him. I shall not be concerned to settle this question, although I do think that my approach to Kant implies that, whether he did so or not, Kant was at least committed to recognizing the notion of an "object" of consciousness in a sense that is broader than that of an object of "intuition" as I have so far characterized that notion. That is, Kant needs to recognize a notion of intuitional directedness that involves more than that of directedness toward possible regions of space and regions of time (and even more than whatever holistic awareness of these latter had already been seen in the Aesthetic).[18]

Husserl introduces the term *noema* in order to indicate the full "object" with both of the qualifications that I have already noted—that is, (a) in abstraction from the question of the reality of the "object" in question, and (b) inclusive of aspects and features, and of whole realms of unexplored possibilities, extending well into the "background" of consciousness as usually understood.[19] On some readings, the noema is not to be understood in such terms at all. Husserl's view is sometimes taken to be more like Searle's: attention to an act's noema is simply attention to a quasi-Fregean meaning-content that determines its intentionality.[20] Perhaps, according to this approach, we might still say that attention to an act's noema is attention to what determines its "object-directedness." But if we do, then we should not regard this as clarificatory of the notion in question. That would get things backward: the very notion of intentional directedness, according to the Fregean approach to Husserl, needs to be explained in terms of that of intentional "content." It is impossible to try to settle this issue here.[21]

The nearest similarity between Husserl's and Kant's approaches to intentionality may seem to concern the relation between intuitional directedness in Kant and that particular structure of the noema that Husserl refers to as its "central point" (or rather, as the central point of its noematic "core"). Husserl speaks of that central point as the "object" or the "determinable X" *in* the noema. He does this despite the fact that, as we have already seen, the noema as a whole is regarded by him as the "intentional object" of consciousness in its own right:

> Each consciousness has its *What* and each means "its" objective something; it is evident that, in the case of each consciousness, we must, essentially speaking, be able to make such a noematic description of "its" objective something, "precisely as it is meant"; we acquire by explication and conceptual comprehension a closed set of formal or material, materially determined or "undetermined" ("emptily" meant) *"predicates"*. . . . The predicates are, however, predicates of *"something,"* and this "something" also belongs, and obviously inseparably, to the core in question; it is the central point of which we spoke above. It is the central point of connection or the "bearer" of the predicates. . . .[22]

It may appear natural to identify the central X with the "referent" of a Kantian intuition (that is, with the "referent" of a Kantian intuitional *state*.) [23] Correspondingly, the act of reference *to*, or the apprehension *of*, the noematic X may seem most naturally equated with Kant's notion of intuitional directedness as such. To put the suggestion differently, the distinction between directedness toward the X and directedness toward it precisely as the "bearer" of certain predicates may seem most naturally equated with Kant's distinction between intuition and predication *in* intuition. However, it is not possible to draw the comparison in quite these terms. This is because Husserl seems to intend the distinction to have general application, therefore not to be limited to what I have taken be distinctively intuitional awareness—sensory awareness and the imagining of objects.

A further difficulty may appear to lie in the fact that, as seems clear from the continuation of the passage just quoted, directedness toward a noematic X is always the intentional correlate of directedness toward an in principle re-identifiable object. Of course, Husserl could not mean to suggest that any object that is so represented must in fact be a re-identifiable piece of reality. In the case of a sensory noema, it might be a mere hallucination, for example. In another sort of case, it might be a purely fictional character, at most re-identifiable in an appropriately imaginary context of discourse. But in either case, the X would seem to be, for Husserl, the intentional correlate of an instance of directedness toward what is at least represented *as* an in principle re-identifiable object. In apparent contrast with this, purely intuitional directedness, for Kant, is neutral with respect to the question whether the "object" in question *is* in fact so represented.[24]

This difficulty need not stand in the way of equating the apprehension of a noematic X with intuitional directedness in Kant. In fact, Husserl himself does not regard the notion of apprehending a "re-identifiable object" as at all incompatible with that of apprehending what is, and even what one takes to be, purely hallucinatory. In the case of sensory apprehension, for example, Husserl distinguishes between "objects" as mere "spatial phantasms" (*Raumphantome*) and as concrete material things; he elaborates at considerable length on the various levels of apprehension wherein the former are finally apprehended *as* (or "constituted" as) the latter. Throughout, the point is that, at each of these levels, we may continue to speak of an appropriately correlative notion of "object-identity."[25]

Suppose one is hallucinating a pink elephant, and takes oneself to be doing so. Without having to regard the object in question as anything more than hallucinatory, we may still speak of its potential re-identifiability. For example, as one attends to the hallucinated animal, it is perfectly in order to suppose that one has observed the animal to move in various ways. In other words, we are entitled to say that *it* has moved, without having to abandon the supposition that it is not a real thing at all. The presence of an *X* in the corresponding noema is presumably the correlate of this possibility. A parallel point could be made in regard to the purely imaginative case.[26]

It seems clear that Kant has little interest in this level of phenomenological description. The level at which he is concerned with the possibility of identifying and re-identifying objects of intuition is precisely that at which those objects are to be identified as real things. All the same, nothing in Kant's view prevents equating the apprehension of the *X* in a Husserlian sensory (or imaginative) noema with Kant's own notion of intuitional directedness as such (that is, with his notion of directedness, considered apart from the real thing-hood of the "object" in question). In fact, Kant's own argument in the "Anticipations of Perception" (A166ff/B207ff) seems to rely on this notion. He tells us, first of all, that the purely "mathematical" categories—which are what is in question there—are concerned merely with the intuition of appearances, not with their *existence* (A160/B199). But the whole point of the argument then is that, despite this limitation, we can imagine any given appearance as remaining the *same*, except for an internal change that Kant takes to be correlative with the possibility of diminishing the presence of sensation in any intuition apprehending it. (At the point of diminution to zero, one would simply be merely *imagining* some possible region of space and no longer sensorily—not even hallucinatorily—apprehending one).

> Appearances, as objects of perception, are not pure, merely formal intuitions, like space and time. . . . [T]hey contain, that is to say, the real of sensation as merely subjective representation, which gives us only the consciousness that the subject is affected, and which we relate to an object in general. Nor from empirical consciousness to pure consciousness a gradual transition is possible, the real in the former [*n.b.*, not "reality" in the usual sense] completely vanishing and a merely formal *a priori* consciousness of the manifold in space and time remaining. (A166/B207-8)

Of course, this consideration could at most permit an equation of intuition, as such, with a special case of the apprehension of the *X* in a Husserlian noema, namely, with the case in which the noema in question is the correlate of sensory or imaginative apprehension. It remains unclear how to construe the *X*-structure in cases other than the sensory or imaginative. It is not sufficient to recall, for example, that we are even then supposed to be concerned with the intentional correlates of modes of *consciousness*, and that—from a phenomenological perspective—*what* one is conscious of is (as a noematic "whole") always supposed to contain some difference correlative with every single difference in the intentional state itself. Given this, and assuming that there is indeed such a thing as a state of consciousness in which one merely *thinks* an object, but is not intuitively directed toward it (not even imaginatively)—the most we could say is that, for

Husserl, there must be some noematic difference correlative with this fact. But that difference could at most be correlative with an element in the *thought that* there somewhere is (or at least might be or have been) an object of a certain sort. Surely, Kant's intuitional directedness is not a special case of this. But then, by the same token, it seems impossible to regard the intuitional *X*-structure, in Husserl's *own* view, as a special case of it either. In light of this difficulty, the more fruitful comparison might therefore be, not between intuitional form in Kant and (the noetic counterpart of) Husserl's intuitional *X*-structure, but rather between the former and (the noetic counterpart of) the whole *noema* in Husserl. In that case, we would simply have to qualify the comparison by noting that Kant himself had a much narrower *conception* than Husserl did concerning the "objective" correlate of intuitional directedness.[27]

We are finally ready to turn to the role of non-intentional elements in the determination of "intentional content." Like Searle, Husserl is emphatic regarding the role of such elements. Unlike Searle, he formulates his account both in terms of the distinction between matter and form in consciousness and in terms of an act/object correlation. Broadening the notion beyond Kant's, Husserl speaks of the ultimately foundational matter as something purely "sensuous." It should be obvious why it is at least similar to sensation as Kant construed it. It is like sensation in that, in whatever way it might come to be related to objects, it is of itself no more intentionally directed than Kantian sensations are. At most, it is material *through* which intentional acts are directed. Correspondingly, that material's ingredience in intentional acts is necessarily reflected in that *toward which* those acts are intentionally directed. It is necessarily reflected in the noematic correlate in precisely the way in which Kant's sensations are reflected in the "matter of appearances."[28]

It is undeniable, I think, that this twofold structure—of matter and form and of act/object correlation—is what Kant had already attempted to establish in the Transcendental Aesthetic. What is in question for us is the possibility of extending it beyond the Aesthetic's account of the role of sensation (in Kant's narrower usage), and of its reflection in the world of appearances correlative with the intuitions containing it. (As we shall see in Chapter Four, the representation of a *world* of appearances—the representation of a "nature"—rests on this extension.) What is in question is the extent to which Kant saw an additional "faculty" as providing a function for the incorporation of additional material—"sensory" in a way, yet both more than sensation and less than intuition—as a necessary condition for the conceptualization of appearances.

Husserl in any case extends Kant's notion of "sensory" material. What is most relevant for our purpose is his inclusion of what he calls "drives" (*Triebe*):

> . . ."*sensation-contents*" such as color-Data, touch-Data and tone-Data, and the like, which we shall no longer confuse with appearing moments of physical things—coloredness, roughness, etc.—which "present themselves" to mental processes by means of those "contents" [but are rather material *through* which those moments are apprehensible]. Likewise the sensuous pleasure, pain and tickle sensations, and so forth, and no doubt also sensuous moments belonging to the sphere of "drives."[29]

The notion of "drives" is crucial, because Husserl connects it with that of a special type of "motivation."[30] The latter concerns the fact that, in apprehending qualities through a body of sensational material, one is always "motivated" in the direction of more or less determinate *progressions* of (possible) apprehension. Now if one is already conceptualizing appearances in some way, then it is of course obvious that one has a "motive" for the anticipation of more or less specific modes of continuing perception (contingent upon the satisfaction of equally anticipable conditions). But what we are concerned with is not the kind of motivation that is a product of already constituted conceptualization. We must be concerned with something pre-conceptual.

Husserl attempts to elucidate this aspect of "sensuous" motivation by connecting it with a class of sensations that Kant in fact ignored, namely, kinaesthetic sensations:

> Looking at an object, I have at the same time a consciousness of the position of my eyes and, in the form of a unique, systematic, unfulfilled horizon, a consciousness of the whole system of possible positions standing freely at my disposal. Further, what is seen in the given position of the eyes is so connected with the whole system, that I can say with evidence: were I to turn the eyes in this or that direction, then these or those visual appearances would accordingly stream by in a particular order. . . .[31]

Such appearances, Husserl says, are "kinaesthetically motivated."[32] The possibility of obtaining them is "carried" by kinaesthetic sensations.[33] Thus "intentional content" is, at least in part, constituted against a background of non-intentional material of precisely the sort that Searle has in mind. But the difference from Searle, and the affinity with Kant, is crucial: the intentional background is no mere Background in Searle's sense. It is part of what intentional acts are *made of.*

As suggested, what is comparable to this is the Kantian notion of imagination in the Deduction. In the Aesthetic, we encounter imagination only as "pure intuition." In the Deduction, imagination needs rather to be the source of those "anticipations and retentions" that are comparable to Husserl's "sensuous" motivations. Unlike imaginative intuitions, these must serve as mere *material* for object-directed acts. (Whatever directedness they possess on their own—and they surely possess *some*—it is neither Husserl's nor Kant's interest to elucidate it.)[34] On the other hand, within the Deduction itself, imagination also appears in a twofold capacity. Sometimes Kant uses the term to stand, not for the pre-intuitional faculty of anticipation and retention, but rather for that of the *embodiment* of the latter, as material in intuition, precisely with respect to their eventual function as material for conception. The terminological shift, I shall argue, is all that there is to Kant's apparent rethinking, between the two editions of the Deduction, of the respective roles of "reproductive" and "productive" imagination.

For the sake of a final, and perhaps surprising, comparison, we may consider a third philosopher, from a third philosophical tradition. Croce is commonly regarded as paradigmatically Hegelian as opposed to Kantian.[35] But in the respects that concern us, we come closer in Croce to the Kantian view than we did even with Husserl. In Husserl we explored, on the noetic side of consciousness, the structure of material *vs.* intentional forming in acts of apprehension (that is, in the apprehension of "objects" *through* the material in question). But Kant makes a twofold distinction on the level of intentional form. He distinguishes between the "forms" of intuition and conceptual understanding. In Husserl, by contrast—apart from some puzzles concerning the notion of the noematic X—there seems to be but a single formative function, involved in any instance of intentionality as such, whether it is purely intuitional or explicitly "conceptualized." Any relevant difference, expressible in terms of the latter distinction, would seem merely to hinge on some difference in the *material* in question. In this respect, Croce is more Kantian than Husserl, and quite clearly un-Hegelian.[36] For he explicitly distinguishes irreducible *forms* of intentionality.

For our present purpose, the following points may be highlighted. First, both Croce and Kant regard intuition as a basic mode of "(re)presentation." Specifically, they regard it as a mode whereby one is directed toward an at least potential object of judgment. Conceptualization, then, is that mode of mentality through which one is able to recognize, with more or less definiteness, the actual (or even possible) character *of* such objects. Importantly, both of these modes of mentality are indifferent with respect to the actual existence of the objects in question.[37]

Second, in addition to insisting that intuitions are intrinsically object-directed, Croce also maintains, like Kant and Husserl, that their directional form can function only to the extent that it incorporates a special kind of material to serve as its vehicle. In early formulations, Croce sees mere "sensations" as providing at least a substantial part of such material. But he later rejects, unlike Kant and (apparently) Husserl, the very idea of a material that is intrinsically devoid of affective and dispositional content.[38]

Third, and as noted, Croce does not simply extend the notion of intentionally formable material. He also distinguishes levels of intentional formation. On each of these levels, the upshot of forming on the preceding level is what provides the relevant material. In this, Croce is simply following Kant's view that, for example, while sensations are the proper material for intuition, intuitions *formed* from sensations are the material for acts of understanding as such.

Our own study may reveal that, in this respect, a more Husserlian approach is preferable: conceptual form can be regarded as operating on intuitional *states* only by operating in respect to some body of material *in* those states, that is, by constituting the apprehension of something through that material. But does this then mean that, in the final analysis, we have no need for more than one basic "form" in regard to such material? Whatever our judgment on this, I hope it will be seen from Chapter Six that there must in any case be some distinction that is legitimately formulable in terms of a distinction between a lower and a higher *level* of intentional directedness. Croce himself proposes a scale with four such levels.[39]

Croce is led, by these views, to some un-Kantian conclusions. I shall not attend to them in detail. Rather, I want to emphasize how all of the thinkers agree on a point of considerable significance. To put the point in the minimalistic terms that Searle favors: "intentional content" is co-determined by non-intentional factors extending well beyond the domain of mere Kantian "sensation." In Husserlian terms, more is of course involved. This is because Husserl requires, in the place of a single notion of intentional content, the twofold structure of matter and form in intentional activity, on the one hand, and the correlation between (noematic) object and intentional act, on the other. The former structure will be our immediate concern in the next chapter, the latter in the one that follows it.

Unsurprisingly, the noesis/noema correlation does not appear in these terms in Croce. (Indeed, Croce's attitude toward Husserl was markedly, even arrogantly, unfriendly.)[40] The point is present in terms that are un-Kantian as well. This is because, unlike Kant, Croce assumes not only that concepts function as form in regard to matter in intuition but also that they can *only* function in that role. This requires rejection of the analytic/synthetic distinction (or rather requires the conclusion, for Croce, that all judgments are really synthetic *a priori*) and, of course, a denial of the possibility of thoughts in regard to what is unimaginable (and indeed unimagined).[41] These are points that need not concern us here. Nor need we be concerned with the apparently, but in fact only apparently, radical divergence from Kant that is embodied in Croce's insistence that there really are no such things as empirical concepts in the first place—that so-called empirical concepts are merely "pseudo-concepts."[42]

Croce's way of expressing the noesis/noema correlation is to be found, in effect, in his claim that, on each of the four levels of mentality (that is, on the four levels of *lo spirito*), intentional "form" does not simply operate with respect to a body of material. Rather, it actually *informs* that material: that is, it somehow *trans*-forms it. The upshot is what Croce calls a synthesis *a priori*. In it, the form in question is strictly inseparable from whatever "object" is in question. This, of course, is the basis of the rejection of purely analytic judgments. The conclusion rests precisely on the claim that the very *object* of judgment is always at least in part shaped by the judgment that one makes of it.

To make any sense of such claims, we need to presume two things. First, and most obvious, we need to presume that the "object" with which Croce is primarily concerned is the immediate object of intuition, considered apart from any question concerning its identification as a part of material nature—that is, considered apart from the sort of identification that is of primary interest to Kant. Material objects, in this sense, are something merely "constructed," and so they are, in Crocean terms, not really perceptible at all, nor even imaginable.[43] This, so far as I can see, involves a merely terminological divergence from Kant. What Croce calls the construction of nature *via* mere "pseudo-concepts" is what Kant regards as an act of conceptualization proper. What remains the case is that, for both of them, such construction needs to rest on some kind of transformation *of a given intuition*, and of the material that an intuition embodies. It is simply that, for Croce, what is of primary importance is the upshot of that transformation with respect to the immediately given *as such*. (As we shall see in Chapter Four, Kant was not unaware of this level of reflection; its recognition is embodied in the obscure doctrine of Transcendental Affinity.)

For Kant, by contrast, what is of central concern is the possibility—indeed the necessity—of the very same (or an appropriately similar) transformation of a *manifold* of intuitions—all of them thereby "conceptualized" as intuitions of one "object." This difference in point of focus is compatible with recognition by both that any relevant anticipation (or "retention") *of* such manifolds, in connection with the conceptualization (or pseudo-conceptualization) of intuitions, must rest on a kind of anticipation that can only be effected from *within any given* intuition. (In Chapter Six we shall see why, strictly speaking, it is in any case not quite a question of a manifold of intuitions transformable in the very *same* way as a given one; at most it is a question of intuitions that are transformable in appropriately related ways. I would suggest that this distinction is in fact what lies beyond Croce's view of the "concepts" in question as mere pseudo-concepts.)

This point should also make it clear that we need to make a second presumption with respect to Croce's rejection of mere analytic judgments in Kant. In addition to presuming a primary concern with the (suitably transformed) given as such, we also need to presume that Croce has in fact shifted, in his concern with what is "given," from the purely noetic to a correlative noematic standpoint. On the purely noetic level, we may speak of "forming" in the sense of an act whereby a certain body of material is embodied in a certain type of intentional *state*. At that level of reflection, we are simply not yet (explicitly) concerned with any kind of transformation with respect to intuitable *objects*. For the latter, we need to shift to a correlative noematic perspective. A number of passages in Croce seem to require a reading precisely in this sense.[44]

It is arguable, in any case, that all of the thinkers whom I have chosen for comparison, agree on one point: that some kind of non-naturalistic "embodiment" of pre-conceptual material, within a truly conceptual state, is an essential part of the "formation" of any conception in the first place. But we have also noticed some differences. Unlike Husserl and Croce, for example, Searle could not put the point explicitly in terms of the notions of matter and form, nor does he combine his insight with a recognition of a noesis/noema correlation. Unlike Husserl and Searle, furthermore—but correspondingly more like Kant—Croce alone attempts to recognize a *distinction* between a genuinely conceptual and a sub-conceptual (although still truly intentional) level of mental "formation." Despite the differences, some of which may in fact be merely terminological, I have introduced these thinkers in order to provide some diversity of perspective, independent of Kant himself, for assessing what might otherwise seem an implausible view of the nature of conception, and of its relation to Kantian intuition.

Chapter 3

Synthesis

I. Introduction

THIS CHAPTER contains a preliminary defense of my reading of the theory of consciousness and concepts developed in the Deduction. It is both broader and narrower in focus than some of the others. In the first respect, I do not limit my attention to Kant's claims and arguments as they are presented in the Deduction. I give equal attention to some sections of the Logic that are preliminary to the Deduction, devote a section to the Schematism chapter, and make relatively free use of Kant's unpublished notes and notes derived from his lectures on logic. As to topics that may seem to be slighted, there is first of all the problem of the relationship between the first and second versions of the Deduction. In the present chapter, I make little use of passages specific to the second-edition Deduction. The second area of neglect concerns the concept of consciousness.

Although I am centrally concerned with Kant's theory of consciousness, I often formulate questions in this and the following two chapters in terms that do not explicitly invoke the concept of consciousness, for example, in terms that involve such notions as those of synthesis and imagination, or of understanding or (synonymously) intellect or conception. One might suppose that there are in fact both conscious and unconscious forms of all these things. In one respect, there is no need to question this. The supposition might be accommodated very easily. It might be accommodated simply by regarding all of these things "dispositionally," or as "faculties." I have no objection to this, so long as it is clear that it is not the same as saying that we need to distinguish conscious and unconscious forms of some single kind of activity or process.

Whatever we say about understanding as a mere disposition or faculty, the activities or processes that are its paradigmatic manifestations are essentially and uniquely conscious for Kant. They are so in a twofold sense. First, they embody a consciousness of objects distinguishable from subjects of experience. Second, they embody a form of consciousness of themselves and of their own subjects as well. In at least these respects, the workings of the imagination are not essentially conscious for Kant. Kant suggests that at least some of them are essentially unconscious (A78/B104, A141/B180-1). One may of course wonder whether he is clear as to *what* is thereby supposed to be essentially unconscious. For example, just how clear is he regarding the relationship between faculties and their workings in the first place? In any event, we shall be concerned with something called "imagination" only to the extent that it provides an essential ingredient in what is paradigmatically conscious in Kantian terms. As I develop the relevant notion of "ingredience," the question is largely semantical whether, viewed in themselves, the workings of the imagination are essentially unconscious or not (and indeed even whether or not they may be regarded as somehow "judgmental"). What remains the case is that denying their status as full-blown consciousness does not entail that they are then essentially hidden with respect to the ordinary course of conscious experience. While all of these issues are raised by Kant's arguments, and while more might be said to anticipate them, considerable preliminaries are in order before we can formulate our questions with regard to the relevant notion of consciousness. In particular, we shall need to await Chapter Six for a discussion of the problem of self-consciousness.[1]

It is obvious that most of the difficulty posed by any reading of the Deduction stems from Kant's attempts to get clear about the connection between imagination and intellect. At the least, its first-edition version appears to suffer from what Jonathan Bennett has called "neurotically inept exposition."[2] Whether this is due, as Bennett suggests, to "sheer terminological confusion," to outright self-contradiction, or to some other cause is uncertain. Apart from specific problems, which I postpone to the next chapter, regarding Kant's attempts to distinguish between "reproductive" and "productive" aspects of imagination—and to draw a corresponding distinction between mere "associations" and a genuine grasp of "affinities" involving the objects of consciousness themselves—the primary source of obscurity lies in Kant's unclarity as to which of the two, or whether both of the faculties, should be regarded as responsible for one or more modes of a necessary "synthesis of the manifold of intuition."

Kant sometimes attributes such synthesis to a pre-conceptual faculty:

> Synthesis in general, as we shall hereafter see, is the mere result of the power of imagination, a blind but indispensable function of the soul, without which we should have no cognition whatsoever, but of which we are scarcely ever conscious. However, to bring this synthesis to *concepts* is a function which belongs to the understanding, and it is through this function of the understanding that we first obtain cognition properly so called. (A78/B103)

The intellectual component in cognition, Kant says, lies in the addition of an intellectual element to what would otherwise remain a purely imaginative synthesis. Apparently, it lies in the contribution of a special kind of unity to that synthesis (A79/B104, A94, A118, A130, A155/B194, A158/B197), or at least of some kind of consciousness of such unity (A103-6, A115-6). This may puzzle us not only in its concession of autonomously synthetic powers to imagination. It may puzzle us in a respect that is generally neglected but that I plan to take seriously. Understanding is needed, Kant says, in order to bring syntheses "to concepts." As we shall see, an adequate interpretation of this, and of the correlative notion of a consciousness of "unity," will eventually require an appeal to something much deeper than our ordinary notions of "applying" or "predicating" or, in general, "employing" concepts. The functions of unity in question will be needed to make sense of the notion of the very *forming* of concepts in the first place.

Elsewhere, Kant appears to attribute synthesis directly to intellect. Perhaps most notably, in his personal copy of the *Critique*, he inserted a correction to the passage from which I just quoted. As emended, it simply says that synthesis in general is "a function of the understanding."[3] In any case, whether or not there is a pre-conceptual faculty of synthesis, and whether or not it has an essential role in conceptualizing intuitions, Kant also attributes some kind of synthesis to concepts in their own right, or at least he insists that any synthesis that is ascribable to imagination also needs to be in "accordance" with, and apparently to be guided by, the understanding (A78/B103, A97, A110-13).[4] The second edition might be supposed to resolve the apparent contradiction. It may appear to do so by maintaining that the relevant sorts of conceptual and imaginative syntheses are really just the same thing considered in two respects:

> It is one and the same spontaneity, which in the one case, under the title of imagination, and in the other case, under the title of understanding, brings combination into the manifold of intuitions. (B162n)

This does not require denying that synthesis is a function of imagination. On the other hand, it is apparently compatible with very different views of the relationship between imagination and understanding. One would reduce the former to the latter from the start; the other, the latter to the former.

To most commentators, though not to all,[5] it seems unlikely that Kant construed understanding as a mere function of imagination. However, the opposite might seem to be the case, at least with respect to the particular sort of imaginative synthesis in question, that is, with respect to whatever sort is presumed essential to the conceptualization of intuition. In the second-edition Deduction, Kant may seem at last to be clear: "This synthesis is an action of the understanding on the sensibility" (B152). Perhaps the same claim can be found, if less explicitly formulated, in the first edition as well: "*The unity of apperception in relation to the synthesis of imagination* is the *understanding*" (A119; Kant's emphases). But it is in fact implausible to suppose that Kant's efforts are reductive in either of these fashions: "Imagination and understanding are two friends," he tells us, "who cannot do without one another"; to be sure, Kant adds, they are friends "who also cannot abide one another."[6]

It is no doubt the tension that is generated by such cognitive pull and push, rather than indecision or confusion, that accounts for much of the difficulty in the Deduction. In any event, I want to defend a reading that is reductive in yet a third way. It is not reductive of either of the "faculties" as such. Both are essentially involved in the "application" of concepts to intuitions. On the other hand, the reading might be regarded as reductive with respect to the very *notion* of applying concepts in the first place. More exactly, it might be said to be reductive with respect to the notion of applying empirical[7] concepts. As the second edition itself seem to affirm, such actions are to be reduced in favor of those of a "pure" intellectual faculty.[8]

As is well known, Heidegger has argued that Kant shifts in his view between the two editions: "In the second edition of the *Critique of Pure Reason* the transcendental imagination . . . is thrust aside and transformed—to the benefit of the understanding. . . . While in the first edition, all synthesis, i.e., synthesis as such, arises from the imagination as a faculty not reducible either to sensiblity or understanding, in the second edition the understanding alone assumes the role of origin for all synthesis."[9] My own reading will agree and disagree with some aspects of Heidegger's. It will disagree with the view that the second edition reverses the position of the first. As regards the first edition, I follow Heidegger in seeing a radical dependence of understanding on imagination. It remains a question as to how specifically to construe that dependence.

II. The Transformation of Intuition

Kant's introduction to the Logic begins with reflection on what empirical concepts "contain." In this regard, he makes what may appear an odd suggestion. First, he repeats the familiar point that intuition is what accounts for the fact that thoughts have a "content," that is, that they are thoughts about "objects." Then he draws an expected distinction between pure and empirical forms of both intuition and conception. The apparently odd suggestion concerns this distinction. What Kant seems to say is that empirical intuitions and concepts are those that contain sensations (*wenn Empfindung . . . darin enthalten ist*). Sensation, in such a case, is said to provide the matter or material (*Materie*) of the cognitions in question (A50/B74). At A95, similarly, Kant distinguishes empirical from *a priori* concepts in virtue of the fact that the former consist of elements of a possible experience (*aus Elementen einer möglichen Erfahrung besteht*). Apart from that, a would-be concept would only amount to the "logical form of [*zu*] a concept, not the concept itself through which something is thought."

It is not clear how concepts might be supposed to contain sensations as, or even as part of, their material. One suggestion is that Kant is speaking loosely when he says this. Shortly after the passage in question, he says that earlier, though he doesn't say where, he had used the term *Materie* for the content (*Inhalt*) of cognition (A59/B83). Now the latter term, in the discussion immediately preceding this observation, seems to be used only in order to designate either the objects of cognition themselves or cognitive relations with those objects.[10] It is not used for anything like the sensations which, in the Aesthetic and elsewhere, are said to provide material for cognition. So by calling sensation the matter of (empirical) concepts, not just the matter of intuitions or empirical cognitions, Kant might be speaking loosely. He might only mean that the ability to experience sensations is an essential element in one's general capacity for relating empirical concepts to their objects.

On the other hand, in the discussion that had immediately preceded A59/B83, Kant seems to have been speaking of *Inhalt* in a rather different sense from the way in which he speaks of *Materie* in the passage that we are considering from A50/B74. (Nor does he use the latter term in the later passage.) In the discussion immediately preceding A59/B83, one could as well have spoken of space and time as part of the content, hence of the "matter," of cognition. The point, in that context, was that a concern with spatiotemporal representation as such (whether pure or empirical) is not a concern that abstracts from "content," since it does not abstract from spatiotemporality; because of this, it is not appropriate for consideration in General Logic. In this sense, space and time *are* a part of cognitive content. At A50/B74, by contrast, the point is to exclude the representations of space and time themselves from the class of representations comprising "material" for cognition. This is because, as in the Aesthetic, the representations of space and time are purely formal. So in the sense relevant in the context, something else is needed, namely, sensations, in order to provide material or content for cognition.

What is striking about the passage at A50/B74 seems to be that Kant is now extending the point about the need for ingredient material beyond the need for a distinction between pure and empirical intuitions. It is now extended so as also to apply to the need for a distinction between pure and empirical *concepts*:

> Both may be either pure or empirical. Empirical, if sensation (which presupposes the actual presence of the object) is contained in it [*darin enthalten*]; but pure, if no sensation is ingredient in it [*beigemischt*]. (A50/B74)

Thus it may be possible to speak in two different senses of the *Materie* of concepts. In one sense, the matter of a concept is the range of objects, or of possible objects, that fall under it. By extension, it may be whatever is transcendentally necessary (including the pure form of intuition) for establishing cognitive relations with objects. In a second sense, the matter of a concept may be something whose actual *ingredience* in a concept is a condition of the establishment of cognitive relations with objects. We already know that, in the second of these senses, or at least in an analogous sense, sensation is the matter of empirical intuitions. The question is whether Kant now supposes that sensations, or something analogous to them, must be regarded as similarly incorporable into empirical conceptions.

If this is Kant's suggestion, then he is suggesting that intuitions, not just judgments, must be capable of receiving judgmental form as a part of their internal structure. It is difficult to see what the upshot of an action of this kind could be, if not the very conversion of intuitions into conceptions. Now where, one might ask, would empirical *concepts* fit into such "conceptions"?[11] One is inclined to suppose that concepts are what we need to apply to intuitions in order to yield a certain sort of cognitive state as an upshot, namely, in order to yield a perceptual judgment as a composite of the two. But Kant now seems to be proposing something different. What he seems to have in mind is the generation of perceptual judgments, not by means of the application of concepts to intuitions, but rather by means of the application of the mere forms of judgment to them. Intuitions, by this means, are turned *into* perceptual judgments; what we call "application" of concepts to the former is just whatever act of understanding is involved in their conversion to the latter. If this is Kant's view, then we can at least see *one* point in the suggestion that sensations need to serve as matter in empirical "conceptions." Certainly, they could at least be said to serve as matter in intuitional *judgments*. And it is Kant himself who insists that "the only use which the understanding can make of these concepts is to judge by means of them" (A68/B93). Still, what of the suggestion that sensations are also matter in empirical *concepts*, not merely in empirical judgments?

Kant speaks in a number of places of intuitive representations becoming concepts. At A76/B102, he refers to a process by which representations are "transformed into concepts": *in Begriffe zu verwandeln*. At A147/B187, he speaks of the categories as "functions of the understanding *for* [*zu*: my emphasis] concepts. At A350, similarly, he says that "consciousness" is that which "makes all representations *into* [*zu*: my emphasis] thoughts": *was alle Vorstellungen zu Gedanken macht*. He does the same in various lectures and Reflections on Logic and elsewhere. Throughout, he takes the central question to be "how representations become concepts . . . thus how it comes about that *repraesentatio singularis* becomes *communis*."[12] We also need to be serious about Kant's claim that "the same function which gives unity to the various representations in a judgment also gives unity to the mere synthesis of various representations in an intuition" (*in einer Anschauung*: A79/B104-5). The function is, of course, that of the "pure understanding," through its forms of judgment or the categories. (Perhaps it would be better to say: through its forms of judgment in their role as the categories.)

Kant attributes to this function of understanding a unity of synthesis that does not merely bear on a manifold of several intuitions, but rather on a manifold contained in a single intuition: *in einer Anschauung*. This is what we ought to expect, if his view is that any act of empirical conceptualization involves the elevation or transformation of intuitions, not by means of a distinct act of "applying" concepts to them, but rather by means of the activation of pure intellectual functions in regard to those intuitions. Were the former what is in question, one might suppose that all determinate content, or at least determinate conceptual content, needs to be "brought" into intuitions by the concepts that are to be predicated of them. In a truistic sense, we may say that this is so on any account. But if the application of concepts is to be constituted by an "application" of pure intellectual functions in the first place, then all determinate conceptual content presupposes a body of material that is autonomously (if not also antecedently) ingredient in intuitions in its own right. This is because the forms of understanding do not differ from case to case.

Another way to put the point is this. If the conceptualization of an intuition, and so predicating something of its object, involves the "application" of something intellectual *to* intuitions, then it could not do so merely by means of a function that is exercised in regard, as it were, to intuitions as units, apart from the question of what those units literally contain. This could not possibly work, so long as we were insisting, with Kant, that the addition in question is of a purely formal sort. If it is of a purely formal sort, then what is bestowed on an intuition, in conceptualizing it, is exactly what is to be bestowed on any other one. All "material" similarity and difference would have to come from the intuitions themselves. But if variation in conceptual content were the upshot of operations on intuitions as units, then it would follow that conceptual content always co-varies with variation in those units. That would of course be absurd. In whatever way our account is "reductive" with respect to predication, we want to be able to suppose that qualitatively different intuitions might be conceptualized by means of the very "same concepts," and that a given intuition might have been conceptualized by any number of different concepts. Clearly, the sameness and difference in question could not stem merely from the application of pure intellectual forms (though of course *some* kind of sameness—a purely formal one—does stem from this). There is only one possible alternative. Intellectual form must be able to yield concrete predication only so far as it somehow applies (but in a different sense from what one usually calls "predication") to a body of material *in* the latter—that is, to a body of material that may remain constant or vary within the formal unity of a given intuition. Such "application," one must suppose, in some way forms a full-blown concept (or at least a "concept in use") precisely *out* of that body of material.

I do not propose that sensations, in the usual Kantian sense, could ever provide such material for formation into concepts. The reason for this is simple: intuitions that contain different sensations, in the usual Kantian sense, remain subject to the very same empirical predications; by the same token, the purely sensational "content" of an intuition does nothing to determine the way in which that intuition is to be conceptualized. Nevertheless, it is implicit in my argument so far that if sensations cannot be formed into empirical concepts, then something importantly analogous to them must be able to be so formed. This latter must be something analogous in the sense that, like mere sensation, it also serves as matter within intuitions themselves.

It may be this that Kant somewhat hesitantly acknowledges in his suggestion that sensations need to serve as matter in empirical concepts. In any case, as we have seen, Kant is at least not hesitant in suggesting that, in some sense or other, empirical conceptualization is an operation by which empirical *intuitions* are themselves converted, if not literally into concepts, then into determinate empirical conceptions. It is difficult to see how to make sense of this, apart from something like the proposal in question.

It may be with respect to their focus on such issues as these, not with respect to their doctrines or even their degree of mere clarity, that the first and the second versions of the Deduction ultimately differ. Certainly, the first appears to inquire more explicitly as to what concepts are in the first place.[13] In a dispositional sense, one may of course say that concepts are nothing other than capacities for judgment, that is, for forming conceptions or cognitions. But Kant himself could not ignore the question, nor should we: What is it to *form* a conception or a cognition? It seems clear, in the light of what I have argued so far, that Kant presumed that an account of this needs to recognize that, in a generally neglected sense, intuitions themselves must provide the very "material" for such formation. In comparison, everything else would be mere "form" in a sense more literally *formative* than generally recognized:

> Experience contains two very dissimilar elements, namely, the *matter* for cognition from the senses, and a certain *form* for the ordering of this matter, from the inner source of pure intuition and thought, which, on occasion of the former, are first brought into action *and yield concepts*. (A86/B118; final emphasis added)

This unity of consciousness (of the connection of our representations) is as much *a priori in us* as the foundation of all concepts as the form of appearance is in us as the foundation of intuitions.[14]

Here a concept is considered only subjectively, not with respect to how it determines an object through a *Merkmal*, but rather with respect to how it can be applied [*bezogen*] to several objects. (Not with respect to how they arise [*entspringen*] as representations, but rather with respect to how given representations become concepts in thinking [*im Denken zu Begriffe werden*]. Only with respect to the form of a concept.)[15]

While this aspect of Kant's theory is not usually noted, Paton, for example, gives it some attention. Unfortunately, he confesses himself not "altogether [to] like the statement that we make concepts (as regards their form) out of given intuitions." His best attempt to clarify the statement leaves him uneasy. He notes that Kant often identifies concepts with the common characters (*Merkmale*) of possible individuals. Having done this, Kant then "looks upon what is common as itself an individual intuition which receives its universality by being referred to many different objects as their 'mark'."[16]

At least frequently, Kant does in fact define the notion of a concept in terms of the fact that concepts represent objects by means of their *Merkmale* (e.g., A19/B33, A320/B377). Sometimes he goes so far as to say that concepts are themselves *Merkmale*. Thus somehow, he seems to say, one and the same item is able to serve both as a possible feature of cognizable objects and also as the representational medium through which those very features are cognized.[17]

This, together with the assumption that empirical concepts are "derived" from experience, may suggest that Kant adheres to a version of the Thomistic theory of abstraction. It seems to imply that, in order to know them, the features (or would-be features) of objects need literally to become ingredient in the faculty of cognition itself. Kant's only advance, if it is one, would seem to lie in the conclusion that, for such to be possible, the objects must be "appearances." But it is Kant himself who gives us pause in regard to any doctrine of abstractionism. He concedes that empirical concepts are always "abstract." Truistically, they at least need to abstract from many of the features of the objects that are known by their means. But at the same time, they are not themselves abstract-*ed* from anything, not even "appearances."[18]

Apart from the qualification, we might still make some sense of the notion that (empirical) concepts are "derived" from experience, in particular from intuitions. For example, we might explicate that notion in terms of the formation of concepts out of a body of material available *in* intuitions. That would allow us to say that the concepts are "derived" from intuitions, and even to understand Kant's inclination to put the point in terms of the converting of the "common characters" of appearances into concepts. But it would do nothing to explain an additional tendency to regard them as intuitions, hence particulars. Indeed, it would do nothing to explain an inclination to regard the common features of appearances as entities of *any* sort. In any case, Kant's spatiotemporal ontology for the world of "appearances" could surely not welcome the presumption of such a status for common features.

I have argued elsewhere that Kant's doctrine of sensible form was specifically designed to replace the notion of sensible features as literally ingredient in the cognitive states through which objects (even as appearances) are perceived.[19] It is difficult to avoid supposing that Kant was equally intent on providing an alternative to the corresponding Scholastic approach to "intelligible" form. To do this, he could not escape the question: What *is* it that one "applies" to an intuition, in order to apprehend the latter's object through some concept? Can a concept be some item or entity, at one's disposal for that purpose—even an item or entity that one has oneself *formed* for the purpose? It seems rather to be the case that (except insofar as we are prepared from the start to identify "concepts," irrelevantly, with capacities or dispositions for certain kinds of activities) concepts must be indistinguishable from, or at best mere aspects of, certain kinds of *activities*, namely, the very activities that one normally calls "applying" concepts in the first place.[20] What gets "applied," in the most basic sense, is simply the activities themselves. Despite my own suggestion that concepts are made out of something, thus despite the apparent concession that, once made, they are entities in their own right, the latter involves a view that we need to avoid.

We cannot abandon the idea that empirical concepts function as a kind of predicate in intuition, and that a concept is therefore in *some* sense an item—perhaps even a quasi-linguistic item—attachable to distinct intuitions or "tokenable" by them. But when we do not ignore some of Kant's own apparently odder suggestions, we obtain a view concerning these notions that is radically different from what the linguistic analogies usually suggest. Again, my own proposal is in a way reductive with respect to concepts. It is reductive with respect to the distinction between concepts and the intuitions that they conceptualize. But it is reductive only in a certain way. It is reductive in the sense that the "predicating" of concepts is an action to be explicated as nothing other than the action of applying something pre-conceptual (though not necessarily pre-intellectual) to certain intuitions (and to a correspondingly ingredient material).

This is obviously not intended to deny that there is such a thing as applying concepts to an intuition. It is only to say that doing so is nothing other than an intuition's elevation, through the elevation of some material in it, to a specifically conceptualized status. The elevating factor is attributable wholly to something "formal." But as Kant himself tells us, the formal factor is just *consciousness itself*, insofar as the latter constitutes "the merely subjective form of all our concepts" (A361). As we shall see more clearly later, thus applied to the problem of the formation of particular cognitions, not merely to the problem of a general unity among manifolds of distinct cognitions, Kant's pronouncements concerning a corresponding "unity of consciousness" take on a significance that is more radical than typically supposed:

> But this unity of possible consciousness also constitutes the form of all cognition of objects, whereby the manifold is thought as belonging to a single object. Thus the

mode in which the manifold of sensible representation (intuition) belongs to one
consciousness precedes all cognition of the object as the intellectual form of such
cognition, and itself constitutes a formal cognition of all objects *a priori*, so far as
they are thought (categories). (A129)[21]

It is at this point that we need to attend to the role of imagination in conception.
Undeniably, it is a role that cannot be played by mere sensations, as Kant himself
usually understands the latter. Sensations, in that sense, could never provide material for concepts in anything like the way in which they provide material for intuitions. To suggest that they can, as we have seen Kant does, could at most serve
to anticipate a fuller account. It anticipates an account according to which something relevantly *like* sensations must be material for concepts. Of course, the
ground of comparison is crucial. But my suggestion is that whatever is needed
to provide material for concepts (that is, for non-"categorial" ones) has got to be
comparable to sensations in the respect that Kant himself often takes to be defini-
tive of sensation in the Aesthetic, namely, in the respect that it is a pre-conceptual
matter for *intuitions*, incorporable within the latter by means of intuitional form.
Sensation, in the narrow sense, cannot provide matter for concepts, not even for
empirical ones. But whatever provides that matter must nevertheless, like sensation, provide it for intuition as well. This is because, as already argued, only in
this way can it be anything relevant to the conceptualization *of* intuition in the
first place.[22] I shall argue that, in Kant's view, something "imaginative" needs to
play this role. In particular, it is sets of imaginative "anticipations and retentions."

III. The Manifold of Intuition

In the present section, I do not specifically argue that the pure forms of understanding are modes or operations of consciousness in regard to imaginative anticipations and retentions. But I prepare the way for that enterprise by commenting
on the ambiguity of the notion of synthesis, and of the corresponding notion of
a manifold of intuition, and by discussing some difficulties that confront other approaches that these notions might seem to allow. In Chapter Five, I discuss some
of the same ambiguities and alternatives, but with specific regard to the second-
edition Deduction. Aside from passing reference to the second edition, I continue
to attend to issues that arise elsewhere.

We may begin by considering Kant's introduction of the notion of synthesis into
the *Critique*. It may in fact appear to exclude the idea that imaginative anticipations and retentions are what provide material for concepts:

> Transcendental logic . . . has lying before it a manifold of sensibility *a priori* pre-
> sented by transcendental aesthetic, in order to provide material [*Stoff*] for the pure
> concepts of understanding. In the absence of this material those concepts would be
> without any content, therefore entirely empty. Now space and time contain a mani-
> fold of pure intuition *a priori*, but at the same time are conditions of the receptivity
> of our mind—conditions under which alone it can receive representations of objects,
> and which therefore must also always affect the concept of these objects. But the
> spontaneity of our thought requires that this manifold first be gone through

[*durchgegangen*] in a certain way, taken up [*aufgenommen*], and connected [*verbunden*], in order that a cognition be made out of it [*um daraus eine Erkenntnis zu machen*]. This act [*Handlung*] I name synthesis.

By *synthesis* in the most general sense, I understand the act of putting different representations together [*zueinander hinzuzutun*], and of grasping what is manifold in them in a cognition [*ihre Mannigfaltigkeit in einer Erkenntnis zu begreifen*]. Such a synthesis is *pure*, if the manifold is not empirical but is given *a priori*, as is the manifold in space and time. Before we can analyze our representations, these must themselves be given, and therefore as regards *content* no concepts can first arise [*entspringen*] by way of analysis. Synthesis of a manifold (be it given empirically or *a priori*) is what first gives rise to a cognition [*bringt zuerst eine Erkenntnis hervor*]. This cognition may indeed, at first, be crude and confused, and therefore in need of analysis. Still the synthesis is that which gathers the elements into cognitions and unites them into a certain content [*die Elemente zu Erkenntnissen sammelt, und zu einem gewissen Inhalte vereinigt*]. . . . (A76-7/B102-3)

It would appear from this that the manifold supposed to be gathered by means of synthesis is either a multiplicity of the parts of space and time or (or possibly in addition) a multiplicity of the appearances of spatiotemporal objects or possible objects. This may seem to follow from the fact that Kant says that the manifold in question is provided by "transcendental aesthetic." He in any case does speak of space and time as containing a manifold. On the other hand, we know from our discussion of the Aesthetic that Kant frequently shifts between reflection on cognition as such and reflection on cognition's intentional correlate. So any talk about pure intuition, or about intuitional form, is bound to be ambiguous.

The form of intuition may be space and time, or the spatiotemporal structure of appearances. But the form of intuition may also be a structure of cognition itself, namely, the structure that accounts, when a cognition is conceptualized, for the latter's object-directedness. In that case, it would simply remain to be seen what the corresponding "manifold" could be. It is in any case not through the very parts of space and time themselves, as opposed to our representations of them, that intuitional form, in the second of these senses, is able to direct spatiotemporal concepts toward objects. Similarly, the empirical manifold that Kant contrasts with a corresponding pure one may be a manifold of spatiotemporal appearances or possible appearances. But it may also be a manifold *through* which appearances are to be apprehended, and in that case it presumably ought to comprise, not appearances themselves, but some variety of representation *of* the latter.

There is a straightforward objection to the idea that conceptual representations are generated by means of synthetic activities directed toward parts of space and time or toward the possible appearances in them. The objection concerns the sense in which the requisite acts of synthesis could possibly manage to get directed toward their presumed targets in the first place, in the absence of already functioning representations able to place those targets before the mind. Assume, for example, that the pure manifold is a manifold of actual and possible regions of space and time. These, we might maintain, are given in a pure intuition, and they are in turn utilized as material for synthesis. But in what sense could one possibly be "given" a manifold of distinct regions in the first place, apart from an at least rudimentary power of discrimination already active? The objection is *a fortiori* applicable with respect to a manifold of actual appearances, or a hypothetical manifold of images of merely possible ones, insofar as the members of those manifolds are supposed to be distinctly apprehensible items, sufficiently present to mind to be the targets of possible synthesizing.[23]

This objection may be thought to reject my own account of the Aesthetic. It may seem to do so because it rejects the idea of a pre-conceptual access to space and time. But it only rejects that idea in a certain sense. My account of the Aesthetic does not entail (nor does it deny) that regions of space and time, or appearances in them, are presentable as objects of intuitional consciousness apart from conceptual functions. What the account entails is only that the application of concepts to space and time, or to appearances in them, requires the ingredience of the concepts in question in irreducibly and uniquely object-directed states. It requires their ingredience in cognitive states whose object-directed character is an internal feature of those states, but is reducible neither to the ingredient concepts or sensations in those states nor to mere relations involving such ingredients. Compatibly with this, one might insist that apprehension of spatiotemporal regions, or of spatiotemporal appearances, as genuinely discriminable items before one's mind, presupposes the presence of concepts in intuition. If it does, then it would of course be difficult to see how the synthesis of a multiplicity of material in either perceived or imagined space or time could be required, as Kant suggests it is, in order to make conception possible in the first place.

If the objection is compatible with my account of the Aesthetic, it may nevertheless appear to be incompatible with my suggestion that imaginative material is what constitutes the matter of concepts. If imaginative anticipations and retentions are what provide that material, then we seem to acknowledge pre-conceptual states that are genuinely object-directed. We therefore seem to concede that the manifolds of appearances that are the *objects* of such states may after all be the original targets of synthesis. In the next section, I distinguish two kinds of anticipation and retention. With respect to one of these kinds, it is clear that anticipation and retention presuppose a capacity for forming representations of anticipated and retained objects or appearances, as discriminable intentional objects. But there is also a kind of anticipation and retention that does not presuppose this capacity. A creature that anticipates and retains in this latter way may be said to anticipate, not merely ("*de re*") with respect to some real object or situation, but with respect to the merely possible appearances of merely possible objects or situations. (As we shall see in Chapter Six, the case of retention requires special treatment.) Merely possible appearances may then be regarded as the "objects" thus anticipated. But it does not follow that the anticipating subject has any such objects "in mind," as a manifold of items potentially targetable by mental operations. In particular, it does not follow that the anticipated appearances are, just as such, the objects of intuitional states in Kant's sense. (Kant claims that imagination is a form of intuition. I consider this difficulty in the next section.)

Furthermore, even if we concede the possibility of purely intuitional "consciousness," the fact that we may speak of anticipated appearances merely on the ground that some creature is in an anticipational *state* permits us to speak of "syntheses" of appearances even where the appearances in question are not objects of such consciousness. In that case, one might say that we are dealing with syntheses directed toward "objects" that are, as such, nothing more than the intentional correlates of the very anticipation of them. So construed, I have no objection to the claim that synthesis is a mental operation in regard to a manifold of objects of consciousness. We need only remember, in that case, that the notion of an intentional correlate is different from what I introduced in connection with the Aesthetic. In that context, even if we were unwilling to concede the possibiltiy of truly pre-conceptual consciousness, we could also speak of the intentional correlates of pre-conceptual intuitional states. We could do so simply by referring to the ways in which such states are in principle eventually conceptualizable. What was important, in that context, was to acknowledge the role of intuitional form. Apart from that, the question whether such form alone puts objects before one's "consciousness" runs the risk of raising an issue that is merely verbal. But if we now also speak of the intentional correlates of anticipation and retention, on the most primitive level of the latter, and if we speak of anticipated and retained appearances as thereby before one's consciousness, then there is no longer any reason to suppose that we are talking about states with intuitional form in the first place. For we would now be talking about nothing more than states that might, along with sensations, be able to serve as material *in* intuition.

It may be Kant's unclarity on this score that accounts for much of the unclarity in the Deduction. This may account in particular for the apparent suggestion that the activities of synthesis are supposed to operate on a body of peculiarly non-objectified "objects" of consciousness. That is, it may account for the suggestion that the body of material for the activities of "pure" synthesis comprises, if not the very parts of space and time themselves, then, even more mysteriously, something that is able to get synthesized *into* the parts of space and time. Likewise, it may account for the suggestion that the body of material for the activities of empirical synthesis comprises, if not full-blown appearances, or even the images of possible appearances, then something that is at most capable of getting synthesized *into* appearances. Since imaginative anticipations and retentions, of the sort needed to develop Kant's theory, cannot plausibly be regarded as intuitions in their own right, and yet since they still appear to have (possible) spaces, times, and appearances as their correlates, Kant must have found it considerably easier to write as if the activities of synthesis operated directly on the latter. Strictly, what he needed to consider was the sense in which the manifold of anticipations and retentions was *itself* subject to synthesis of some kind. But the status of that manifold in the first place, with its mysteriously pre-conceptual yet non-intuitional "representation," must have troubled him. On account of this, it may have seemed easier to formulate the doctrine in question in "noematic" rather than "noetic" terms.

Now there are a number of ways in which syntheses might be supposed to function in cognition. Many of them are objectionable, not on account of regarding the former as already bearing on space, time, and appearances as "objects" (which is, in a sense, permissible), but rather because they construe synthesis as already conceptual in nature. If they do that, then they cannot appeal to synthesis to explain how conception is possible in the first place. In the passage that I quoted, the latter is Kant's aim. He implies that concepts, with respect to their "content," first arise [*entspringen*] *via* synthesis. He also says that synthesis is what "gathers the elements into cognitions and unites them into a certain content [*die Elemente zu Erkenntnissen sammelt, und zu einem gewissen Inhalte vereinigt*]," and that synthesis is what "first gives rise to [*bringt . . . hervor*]" cognitions. Finally, that this is in fact Kant's aim seems confirmed by the passages considered in the previous section. Those passages imply that, analogously to the forms through which sensations are incorporated as matter in intuitions, intellectual forms need to incorporate something as matter in acts of conception. The incorporation takes the form of synthesis. As intellectual as the latter might perhaps be, it would be circular to regard it as specifically conceptual in nature.

As I noted in the first section of this chapter, an account according to which transcendental synthesis is essentially intellectual in nature may consider itself able to regard such synthesis as imaginative as well. The easiest way to develop this notion would be to construe the role of the imagination as in effect a merely potential one. Kant's point may then be taken to be that concepts provide a special awareness of imaginable *possibilities*. One can imagine all sorts of possibilities, but concepts are what, by their very nature, dictate that some of those possibilities are more especially in order than others: for example, the possibility, upon apprehending a given appearance, of proceeding *via* a certain route to the apprehension of another. One can imagine a situation, for example, in which a sow's ear, or the appearance of one, gets transformed into a purse, or at least into the appearance of a purse. But the concept of a sow's ear, one might say, conveys no special anticipation of this particular possibility. In general, we may suggest, any (empirical) concept's identity is constituted in terms of its provision of such rules for imaginative possibilities. To this extent, a concept "synthesizes" the latter.[24]

Obviously, these notions might also be thought adequate to account for the centrality of "rules" in Kant's theory of synthesis: "a concept is always, as regards its form, something universal which serves as a rule" (A106). I shall have more to say about the problem of rules later. For now, we may reflect a bit further on the positions available as to the relationship between rules and synthesis. One might suppose, for example, that synthesis is nothing more than whatever it is that rules *qua* rules "do," namely, dictate or prescribe norms with respect to certain possibilities. Alternatively, but equally intellectualistically, one might take synthesis to be whatever is involved in one's more or less explicit intellectual consciousness or conception *of* such rules. Finally, a less intellectualistic position might attempt to ascribe synthesis directly to imagination itself, not either to rules as such or to a specifically intellectual consciousness of them. It might even attempt to construe the rules as grounded in imagination from the start:

> Imagination by itself could give us only pictures or images, but because one and the same understanding is able to conceive the various principles [*n.b.*] upon which the imagination synthetises [*sic*] the given manifold, the concepts of the understanding are able to give us knowledge of objects.[25]

Though it is unclear what Paton intends by the principles upon which imagination synthesizes, what it is for imagination to synthesize "upon" principles in the first place, and therefore what synthesis itself is supposed to be, it is clear that Paton takes concepts to be, at least in the first instance, concepts of rules.[26] At the theoretical extremities, this leaves us with two positions as to the sense in which imagination might be relevant to the rules in question. It might be presumed to be relevant in the fairly minimal way that I have already indicated, namely, in the sense that the rules in question must have a prescriptive bearing on whatever is in principle imaginable in certain contexts. However, imagination might also be presumed to be relevant in a more active or operational way. It might be supposed, as Paton suggests, that imagination already operates in a rule-like manner and that concepts merely express an intellectual consciousness of that operation. Paton himself seems to waver between these extremes. After all, if imagination really provided only pictures or images, it would be difficult to see what could be involved in its also synthesizing the latter, and in its operating "upon" principles in doing so. By contrast with Paton, in any case, others straightforwardly identify concepts with rules from the start, and they consistently distinguish concepts themselves from one's consciousness or conception of rules.[27]

Strawson has tried to do more justice than this to imagination as an actively ingredient element in its own right. Kant's point, he suggests, is that certain imaginable possibilities are in some way actually brought to mind in conceptualizing appearances. They are brought to mind in such a way as to enter the very apprehension of the latter. Consequently, the manifold of appearances in question is not merely a potentially present one:

> [T]he actual occurrent perception of an enduring object as an object of a certain kind, or as a particular object of that kind, is, as it were, soaked with, or animated by, or infused with . . . the thought of other past or possible perceptions of the same object. . . . Nonactual perceptions are in a sense represented in, alive in, the present perception; just as they are represented, by images, in the image-producing activity of imagination.[28]

This approach comes closer to the sort of view that I want to propose. But despite its attempt to do justice to imagination as an actively ingredient element in experience, it is at bottom intellectualistic. This is because the imaginative content of a given experience is still something that a concept alone is supposed to bring to experience. The only reason for regarding that content as imaginative is that, in an unexplained way, the "thought of other past or possible perceptions" is supposed actually to enter into the given experience, thus not to remain a thought that is merely externally attached to it. I am not objecting that it remains unexplained in what way such thoughts might become ingredient in experiences. I am objecting to the suggestion that the imaginative component is in the first place *imaginative* because of the operation of purely intellectual factors on a manifold of sensibility. Kant himself, as I have noted and as we shall see more clearly later, seems to hold that imagination contributes, not as a mere upshot of conceptualization, but as something that helps to make the latter what it is from the start.

A similar point may apply to Allison's defense of the claim that, even in the second edition, Kant continues to ascribe an essential function to a non-conceptual capacity for imagination, precisely with respect to the latter's ability to project the future and to reproduce the past in any act of conceptualization. So far as I can tell, and despite Allison's aim to the contrary, the only respect in which the allegedly "imaginative" function in the case seems to differ "from the purely intellectual synthesis that occurs in judgment [is] that it is also conditioned by the form of inner sense."[29] This would seem to be compatible with any projection and reproduction in the case merely being a matter of thoughts or judgments, somehow embedded or implicit in conceptual acts. The only distinctively non-conceptual element, and the only apparent "conditioning" by the non-conceptual form of inner sense, would appear to lie in the fact that what is in question as the *objects* of that projection and reproduction are non-conceptual items, namely, potentially apprehensible, or already apprehended, times. But what is needed in order to do justice to the role of imagination is rather some reason for saying that the imagining *of* those items involves more than mere judgments to the effect that there might in fact come to be, or already have been, such things (and also, of course, a sense in which such imagining, though not conceptual, might actually be an ingredient *in* something that is conceptual). After all, one may judge about the future and past, as well as intuitively apprehend them.

The question of synthesis is, of course, inseparable from that of the nature of the "manifold" supposed to be synthesized. Whatever their differences, all of the accounts on which I have commented seem to agree on one point in this regard. They appear to presume that, if a manifold of items is in question as a target for synthesis, then it is a manifold of objects, or of potential objects, of consciousness. In this sense, the accounts all deal with a manifold of items that could not themselves be ingredients in cognitive states. At most, they are items that might be apprehended or represented by means of cognitive states, or by what is ingredient in such states. I have agreed that it is possible to speak in this way of the manifold of intuition. In fact, Kant very often seems to intend a manifold of spatiotemporal appearances, when he speaks of the manifold to be synthesized, although on other occasions he seems to mean something else. But one question still needs to be faced, if we regard the synthesized manifold as a manifold of appearances.

We need to face the question as to how those appearances might be present to consciousness in the first place, in order to be targets of synthesis. Now one answer, again, is easy: we might simply suppose that they are present to consciousness by virtue of being conceived of. The problem is that the answer precludes any appeal to synthesis in an account of what conception itself is. At most it could serve in an account of the logical implications of certain conceptions. The alternative is to be serious in what might seem a paradoxical supposition, namely, that while a manifold of appearances is necessarily apprehended *in* any (empirical) conception, its apprehension must be accomplished precisely *through* some non-conceptual mode of representation. Given this, it is not implausible to speculate that any conceptual apprehension of possible appearances, in the conceptualization of a given appearance, must be accomplished through the ingredience in cognition of some other sort of manifold altogether, namely, through the ingredience in it of manifolds of non-conceptually imaginative anticipations and retentions.[30]

Insofar as a manifold of anticipations and retentions is ingredient in intuition, we may speak of a manifold of objects or appearances as an "intentional correlate" of that ingredience as well. In other words, the notion of synthesis is essentially Janus-faced.[31] It is comprehensible only to the extent that we are able to grasp the correlation between its "noetic" and "noematic" dimensions. This, again, may account for much of the ambiguity in Kant's own treatment of that notion. What Kant describes as our capacity for synthesis may sometimes be nothing other than our capacity for ordinary conceptual dealings with the objects of experience (including spaces and times) and the possible appearances of them. If so, then we need to be concerned with synthesis in some other sense as well. We need to be concerned with synthesis in a sense that allows that function to serve in the constitution of conceptual representation in the first place. The point is to see that this can be accomplished only if an intuitional state can contain, and apprehend objects through, a set of sub-states that satisfy at least two conditions: (1) they must be states of an anticipative/retentive nature, in a sense yet to be clarified; (2) while conceptualization, in a sense yet to be clarified, must consist in the elevation of them (though not necessarily by means of a temporally subsequent act) to a higher level of consciousness, they must be in themselves, in the sense in question, non-conceptual in nature.

A number of passages seem to indicate that the primary notion of the manifold of intuition is that of a manifold actually present in a given intuition, not merely of a manifold (and thereby a merely potential manifold) of distinct intuitions. Consider the following passage:

> The unity of apperception is thus the transcendental ground of the necessary conformity to law of all appearances in one experience. This same unity of apperception in respect to a manifold of representations (*determining it out of a single one* [*es nämlich aus einer einzigen zu bestimmen*]) acts as the rule, and the faculty of these rules is the understanding. (A127; emphasis added)

As it happens, Kemp Smith translates the passage so as to conceal the point in question. He replaces "determining it out of a single one" with "determining it out of a unity." It is difficult to see what the latter could mean. In any event, while Kant most often speaks only of a "manifold of intuition," and sometimes directly of a manifold of distinct intuitions or even appearances, several passages also carry a different emphasis:

> . . . die mannigfaltigen Vorstellungen, die in einer gewissen Anschauung gegeben werden. . . . (B132) . . . das Mannigfaltige einer gegebenen Anschauung. . . . (B137) . . . Vorstellungen in irgendeiner gegebenen Anschauung. . . . (B138) . . . alles in einer Anschauung gegebenen Mannigfaltige in einem Begriff vom Object vereinigt. . . . (B139) . . . Das mannifgaltige in einer sinnlichen Anschauung Gegebene . . . alles Mannigfaltige, sofern es in Einer [*sic*] empirischen Anschauung gegeben ist. . . . (B143) . . . das Mannigfaltige in einer gegebenen Anschauung. . . . (B143) . . . Ein Mannigfaltiges, das in einer Anschauung, die ich die meinige nenne. . . . (B144)

In addition, a number of other passages speak of a manifold in, rather than of, "an intuition," though they perhaps do not so strongly suggest that what is in question is a particular instance of intuition, not simply the totality of, or perhaps a subject's mere capacity for, intuition in general.

Thus two different sorts of manifold might be regarded as providing "material" for synthesis and therefore material for the concepts that one applies to an intuition: a manifold of ingredient sub-states in the intuition itself, and a corresponding manifold of anticipated or retained appearances, as objects or as potential objects of consciousness. Kant himself seems to be operating with two different notions of material in the passage quoted above (A76-7/B102-3). He concludes the passage by saying that it is synthesis that is first required in order for cognition to have any content (*Inhalt*) to begin with. But without any "content," it is difficult to see what sort of material could be available as a target for that synthesis to work on. Now it seems unlikely that Kant only means, by the claim that synthesis is necessary for cognition's possession of content, that synthesis is involved in conception. That is obviously his view. But if it were all that he means, then the synthesized manifold could be regarded merely as the correlate of the act of conception as such. It seems unlikely that this is all that Kant means by saying that synthesis is required for content. For in the same passage he also *distinguishes* between the original "material" for conceptual representations and their contents: in the absence of the manifold of intuition, Kant says, the requisite material (*Stoff*) would be lacking for concepts, and so "those concepts would be without any content (*Inhalt*), therefore entirely empty." The last point presumably means that they would be without any object.

Kemp Smith's translation of the preceding sentence may encourage the supposition that the *Stoff* in question already amounts to "content" in the relevant sense, hence at least to a rudimentary sort of object of consciousness. As he translates the passage, the pre-conceptual manifold of intuition is already "presented . . . *as* material for the concepts of pure understanding," which is necessary lest those concepts lack content. What Kant says is only that the manifold needs to be available *in order that* those concepts have a content. A similar distinction seems to be operative at A95: If an empirical concept did not consist [*besteht*] of "elements of a possible experience," then [*er würde alsdann*] it would have no *Inhalt*, "since no intuition corresponds to it; and intuitions in general, through which objects can be given to us, constitute the field, the whole object, of possible experience." There is no suggestion, in either of these passages, that the manifold of material to be synthesized in a concept, or the elements of experience of which a concept "consists," must be in some way part of that concept's very "content." At least there is no such suggestion, insofar as the content of a concept is regarded as either spaces or times or as any sort of object capable of appearing in the spaces or times to which concepts are applicable.

One might, of course, distinguish notions of content, as well as notions of an "object of consciousness." Surely Kant does not deny that, in some sense or other, non-human animals, and human infants, are exposed in intuition to, and are thereby "conscious" of, a variety of contents, hence a variety of "objects," in at least a minimal sense.[32] So one might always maintain that, by means of synthetic activities in question operating upon purely animal/infantile contents, hence upon purely animal/infantile "objects," the latter are somehow converted into distinctively human ones, thus into objects of distinctively human consciousness. But whatever other difficulties stand in the way of it, reading the passage this way requires supposing that Kant used the term *Inhalt*, in the course of a single page on which that term is crucial, in two radically different ways: at the end of the passage, for the full-blown objects of human understanding; at the beginning, for some rudimentary stuff somehow supposed to have originally *become* those objects, at least with respect to one's own conceptualized consciousness of them. That sort of shift, in Kant's case, might seem notoriously possible. In any event, it would make more sense to suppose that, whatever rudimentary stuff is in question, it is not supposed to be formed into the objects that one eventually discriminates in phenomenal space and time, but rather into instances of one's distinctively human discriminations *of* such objects. That is, the stuff in question is merely certain of the subject's own states, ingredient in a given intuition and precisely *through* which conceptual discrimination needs to be effected.

There is a second point to be drawn from the passage on behalf of this reading. It is that Kant takes pains to distinguish between the fact that space and time themselves may be said to contain a manifold of some sort (presumably, a manifold of sub-regions) and a very different sort of fact about space and time, or rather about our representations of the latter. Space and time contain a manifold, Kant says, "but at the same time [*aber gleichwohl*] belong to the conditions of the receptivity of our mind—conditions under which alone it can receive representations of objects, and which therefore must always affect [*affizieren*] the concept of these objects." Here Kant seems to be distinguishing between what pertains to space and time as such as objects of possible consciousness, on the one hand, and what pertains specifically to our representation *of* space and time, on the other hand. (We shall see the same distinction later, in the second-edition Deduction, when Kant distinguishes between space "as an object" and space taken in some other, but closely related, way: B160n.) He then seems to be saying that it is in the latter of these respects that we are to consider the manifold of pure intuition that space and time "contain," when we consider that manifold in relation to the constitution of conceptual contents. The point would seem to be that some special connection needs to be effected with respect to one's spatiotemporal *representations*, in order that we may eventually be in possession of concepts applicable to spatiotemporal regions (and of course also applicable to the appearances therein). This might be what explains the fact that Kant employs the two notions of (a) some sort of *Stoff* for a concept, on the one hand, and (b) a concept's *Inhalt*, on the other. Possession of the former seems not to be identified with possession of the latter; it is rather a necessary condition of it.

IV. Kinds of Anticipation and Retention

It is time to attend more specifically to what I have been calling imaginative "anticipation and retention." The next chapter will develop the notion in relation to Kant's distinction between productive and reproductive imagination. For the present, I limit my discussion to some preliminary clarification and distinctions. Perhaps the first point to notice is that I have chosen to speak of anticipation and retention rather than to use the English term more immediately suggested by Kant's own single term, *Reproduktion*. This is because Kant does not in fact view "reproduction" in primarily past-oriented terms. Far from it, he means to include all of our ordinary empirical anticipations. This is evident from the fact that his primary effort in regard to that notion is to establish a correlation between "the synthesis of reproduction in imagination" and a natural, anticipable, order of things in the world of appearances:

> It is a merely empirical law, that representations which have often followed or ac-companied one another finally become associated, and so are set in a relation whereby, even in the absence of the object, one of these representations can, in accordance with a fixed rule, bring about a transition of the mind to the other. But this law of reproduction presupposes that appearances are themselves actually sub-ject to such a rule, and that in the manifold of their representations a coexistence or sequence takes place in conformity with certain rules.[33] (A100)

We shall have to postpone examination of whatever reasoning might lie behind the apparent inference in this passage: the inference from one's mere capacity for associative reproduction to the apprehension of an objectively anticipable order among objects. But it is in any event clear that the "transition of the mind" that is here intended is not simply a calling forth, or the bringing before one's mind, of something previously experienced and still retained. It is more a matter of the anticipation of a course of experience that one expects to continue (and to continue to change) at least on the whole as it has.

Kant, I presume, had no very clear theoretical idea as to what the difference might be between a mere calling forth of some possible appearance and the actual anticipation of it (relative to certain equally anticipable circumstances). He seems to suggest that the capacity for genuine anticipation stems mainly from a condi-tioning process on the basis of past experience. That may be why he speaks of "reproduction." Obviously, not all anticipations arise in this way. Some of them are the upshot of more or less conscious inferences, or in any case take the form of perfectly reasonable judgments. But then *judgment* and *inference* are them-selves ambiguous terms. A dog that has been conditioned to anticipate the pres-ence of water or food under certain circumstances may be said to judge (or at least to believe) that water or food is forthcoming under those circumstances, and even to have drawn corresponding inferences. It is difficult to be sure what needs to be involved in such cases. Kant himself would perhaps prefer say that what the dog anticipates is merely sets of possible sensations, or perhaps intuitions, but never genuine objects such as water or food. But the question remains as to what it could be to do even this much. It seems unlikely, in any case, that Kant would seriously have thought that it involved nothing more than the "reproduction" of past sensations or past intuitions.

Some type of dispositional analysis, or a narrowly functionalist account, may seem appealing. If we attempted to pursue them, we would at least need to be clear about one thing. We would need to be clear about the distinction between purely dispositional or functionalist accounts of anticipation and retention, of the sort that needs to be in question here, and such accounts of conceptual acts themselves. We may tend to ignore the distinction, because it is permissible to regard even the most primitive anticipation and retention as constitutive of (correspondingly primitive) "belief" or "judgment." But steering clear of purely verbal issues, we need to remember that the relevant capacity for anticipation/retention is merely supposed to provide "material" for acts that are truly conceptual in Kant's sense. The substantive thesis lies in the claim that, if any sorts of beliefs or judgments can be construed in purely animal/infantile terms, then they at most provide the material for the sort of function that in fact distinguishes us from (other) animals and infants.

As noted, Kant himself suggests a still more primitive view of animal/infantile anticipation and retention. He seems to suggest that it amounts to no more than the reproduction of past sensory states. If he supposed this, then he was wrong. But if he was wrong in this way, it is important to remember that there is nothing in his theory that requires him to be so. And there is no reason why his erring in this way need diminish his main claim: that whatever such primitive doings are, they need to be incorporable in intuitions, not merely externally or mechanically associated with them. They need to do this precisely so that they might in turn (though not necessarily subsequently) be relevant to the conceptualization of intuitions.

Kant himself is prepared to grant that animals are in fact capable of a kind of judgment. They are even capable of a kind of "reflective" judgment, at least with respect to their own intuitions. Now in human beings, the capacity for reflective judgment means the ability to reflect on an intuition, with respect to its susceptibility to some particular mode of conceptualization or other: *zum Behuf eines dadurch möglichen Begriffs*. This is a claim that is essential to Kant's aesthetic theory, as well as to the general connection of that theory with his conception of purposiveness in nature. In particular, the claim involves the notion of a certain sort of suitability or affinity between the work of the mere imagination and that of an at least potential understanding. I return to this issue in the next chapter. For now, the point is simply that a certain sort of reflective judgment also takes place in animals. But:

> however only instinctually, it is not in reference to a concept that is thereby to be attained, but rather to an *inclination* that is in a way thereby to be determined [*nicht in Beziehung auf einen dadurch zu erlangenden Begriff, sondern eine etwa dadurch zu bestimmende Neigung*].[34]

Now while purely animal anticipations and retentions are not true judgments, and involve no conceptual form, in what Kant takes to be a privileged sense of these terms, there is of course no reason to deny that human beings often anticipate and retain in an animal way. In itself, the concession leaves two possibilities. One is that instances of animal anticipation and retention simply occur as a part of a person's condition on an occasion, externally interacting with other subjective states of that person. No doubt this is constantly the case. But something else may also be the case. The other possibility is that instances of animal anticipation and retention actually enter in a more direct way *into* other subjective states, namely, into concepts and judgments of the sort that are distinctively human. The possibil-

ities are not exclusive. At a given moment, one may anticipate and retain in both
sorts of ways. What is important is just that, in another sense, this does not involve
a distinction between two "ways" of anticipating and retaining at all. In both cases,
purely animal anticipations and retentions may be in question. That is, we need
not be talking, in either case, about anticipation and retention in the form of explicitly anticipative or retentive judgments. In the second of the cases, we might
be considering anticipations and retentions merely insofar as they function as material in truly conceptual and judgmental states of some sort. (Even the *latter*
states need not themselves amount to conceptually anticipative or retentive judgments. They might, according to the theory, be ordinary judgments about what
is presently the case. The fact that anticipations and retentions are what constitute
their material no more entails that they are anticipations and retentions in their
own right than the fact that certain intuitions incorporate sensations within themselves entails that they are themselves sensations.)

I have said that Kant often appears to regard anticipation and retention as un-
duly primitive in nature. Other times, he may seem to do the opposite. This is
because he sometimes attributes a transcendental dimension to "reproductive imagination." But we need to note an ambiguity. I said that, in a strict sense, merely
animal imagination, even when it functions as the matter of conceptual acts, does
not in itself involve a distinctively conceptual "way" of anticipating and retaining.
It is by hypothesis still purely animal anticipation and retention. The only difference is that it is now functioning as the basis for distinctively human mentality.
In another sense, however, we are of course concerned with a very different and
a distinctively human "way" of anticipating and retaining. For, while the anticipations and retentions are in themselves purely animal, they are no longer functioning on a purely animal *level*. So if we suppose that Kant is regarding the sort of
imagination now in question with particular concern for this *function*, then it is
understandable that he would tend to regard it as itself a "transcendental" capacity. In this sense, Kant's position would be "functionalistic" with respect to the
more primitive capacity. The problem remains how the function is to be explicated. As we shall see more clearly later, Kant himself appeals to a primitive notion of distinctively intellectual consciousness: imaginative anticipations and retentions serve as material, not merely in intuitions, but in the concepts that one
"applies" to intuitions, to the extent that an appropriate level of one's *consciousness* of that material is embodied in those same intuitions.

The "functionalist" dimension may explain Kant's apparent persistence in regarding imagination as in all cases, implausibly, a type of intuition.[35] In some
cases, anticipations and retentions are indeed types of intuition. In these cases,
one may actually picture or in some way relive (or fore-live) an anticipated or retained situation. In other cases, it does not seem reasonable to adopt this line.
In particular, this does not seem reasonable in the case of those anticipations and
retentions that are merely supposed to provide the material for the employment
of concepts. In any event, we might at least recognize that the notion of imagining
"in intuition" (B151) is ambiguous from the start. In some cases, one may be anticipating and retaining, therefore imagining, "in" intuition, simply in the sense that
one's anticipating and retaining serves as *material* in intuition. Assuming that

Kant's own interest in anticipation and retention is limited to this function, and to what presupposes this function, it is perhaps no wonder that he tended to regard it as intuitional in its own right.

We might also notice this. While it is implausible to suppose that all the possibilities one imaginatively anticipates or retains need actually be present to one's intuitional consciousness, it is perhaps at least arguable that it is only insofar as such material serves as material in conceptual acts, hence in intuitions themselves, that one is ever able to *call forth* the corresponding imaginative possibilities as explicit objects of intuitional consciousness. Once again, it may remain a mystery how animal imagination manages to relate to the future or past in the first place, apart from already constituted concepts to guide it. Perhaps for that reason, Kant declares it to be "a blind but indispensable function of the soul . . . of which we are scarcely ever conscious" (A78/B103), and a function "whose real modes of activity nature is hardly likely ever to allow us to discover" (A141/B181-2). At the same time, though apparently in contradiction to this, it is also understandable that Kant took the function to be one of "intuition."

If we do not adopt some such view as this, regarding the type of anticipation and retention that Kant has in mind in connection with his doctrine of synthesis, then we would have something much more mysterious than what Kant is content to leave us. To see this, we need simply ask what we are in fact to make of the anticipating and retaining that uncontroversially lies within the capacity of lower life. It is difficult to believe that dogs and cats, in anticipating the arrival of water or food, are anticipating these in imaginative "intuition," in any sense that involves the occurrence of distinct acts of imagining what is forthcoming. But having conceded that there is in fact a pervasive type of anticipation and retention, as part of our animal heritage, then it is equally difficult to suppose that these functions have nothing essential to do with human conceptual abilities. Obviously, the latter are not—certainly not for Kant—reducible to the former. (For the functionalist in the narrower, causal sense, if they are not so reducible, then they presumably differ at most in degree of complexity.) But it would be plainly incredible if the one did not at least have something essential to do with the other. Presumably, we still are capable of purely animal anticipation and retention. What would be incredible is the suggestion that such a capacity might stand idly alongside our truly conceptual abilities. Nothing would seem more reasonable than that the more primitive capacity should somehow function as material for the more sophisticated. In any event, if we intend to take seriously Kant's own attempts to apply the notions of matter and form to the faculty of understanding, we need to suppose that, however haltingly, he is aiming at just this view of things.

We need to complicate matters a bit further. I have noted that Kant's own notion of "reproduction" includes both retention and anticipation, and that the latter is what is really given priority in his thinking. At least this is the case with Kant's tendency to couple that notion with "association," and to implicate the latter, in turn, in our capacity for the representation of a reliable order of nature. (At A115, Kant even explicitly distinguishes between mere *Reproduktion* and association.) But Kant may seem to be confused on these matters. For in the context in which he couples reproduction and association, with the latter's primary orientation toward the future, he also ascribes something altogether different to the former. It is something apparently much more primitive and much more obviously oriented toward the past. In particular, Kant seems to regard one and the same "reproductive" capacity as responsible both for anticipation, with respect to a general order of nature, and also for the much more primitive ability simply for the holding in mind of what is immediately past: "the first parts of the line, the antecedent parts of the time period, or the units in the order represented" (A102).

Here as well Kant might of course have noted corresponding future-orientations: for example, the anticipation of immediately upcoming parts of the line in question, or of successive parts of a time period, or of the units in some other sort of progressively unfolding order. All the same, there seems to be a significant difference in the cases. Both might be said to involve anticipating "more of the same," and to do so on the basis of some kind of retention of the way things have already been. But an obvious difference is this: what Kant himself regards as distinctively associative anticipation and retention has nothing in particular to do with what one is in fact anticipating or retaining as immediately upcoming or receding. It has rather to do with things that one is able to anticipate or retain either as able to occur or not to occur (or as able to have occurred or not to have occurred) under certain sets of merely conditional *circumstances*. To put it another way, the ability to anticipate "more of the same" that is involved in the case of mere repetition, while no doubt also necessary for one's ability to apply concepts to objects in experience, seems not to provide an appropriate comparison for the anticipative capacity that Kant suggests is more intrinsically ingredient in the very *concepts* one applies to objects. The point, of course, is that different things (or things that one will eventually be able, conceptually, to regard as different) continue to repeat their behavior, and to behave "in the same way," by behaving in all sorts of different ways. We are only able to experience such similarities and differences, as instances of sameness or repetition, once we have already developed appropriate concepts. Inasmuch as Kant's endeavor is to elucidate the very functioning of the latter, the comparison does not seem appropriate. As for the mere ability to "retain" parts of a sequence, which is what Kant himself calls to our attention, the comparison seems even less appropriate.[36]

The approach that I am suggesting may have the advantage of explaining why Kant appears to lump together two such different kinds of retention and anticipation: one of them seeming to have to do with what is immediately arising or receding, and thereby to have only the most general bearing on the problem of conceptualization, the other exhibiting the opposite characteristic. We can see the common ground more clearly once we have noticed a special feature of the more immediate kind of anticipation and retention. It is a feature that may not seem at all evident in the case of anticipation and retention of the less immediately and more purely "associative" kind. But the point is to see that the cases need to be regarded as agreeing with respect to just this feature. At least they need to do so, so long as the associative capacity is supposed to have a bearing on one's ability to conceptualize intuitions. It is obvious that the cases agree in something. They agree in that both involve anticipation and retention, in connection with ongoing and receding intuition. Kant's attention may have been on something less obvious.

To put it a bit paradoxically, what is noteworthy about the more immediate kind of anticipation and retention is that it could not possibly be regarded as a case of (what we may ordinarily consider) "association" at all. That is, it could not possibly be regarded as a case in which anticipations and retentions manage to get associatively *connected* to an occurrent intuition. It does not matter how "immediately" one may suppose certain anticipations and retentions to have gotten connected to an intuition. The point is that they will be able to contribute to the temporal *structure* of an intuition only to the extent that they actually enter into it. If they did not enter the intuition in question, then we could at most say that, while experiencing the latter and very closely *connected* with it, one also managed to retain something of the immediately receding past, and to anticipate something of the immediately arising future. That would be to say something significant about oneself. But it says nothing about the particular intuition whose structure was presumed in question. It therefore fails to do justice to the fact that an intuition must, in some special way, anticipate and retain in its own right. It fails to do justice to the fact that we do not simply experience special triples of intuitions: one that relates to the immediate past, one that relates to the immediate future, and the two of them joined to a third that, taken on its own, bears on an infinitesimally immediate present. It is an alternative to this sort of approach that Kant appears to be seeking from the very opening of the Deduction.

Consider the account of the synthesis of "apprehension in intuition":

> Every intuition contains in itself a manifold which can be represented as a manifold only in so far as the mind distinguishes the time in the sequence of one impression upon another; for each representation, *in so far as it is contained in a single moment*, can never be anything but absolute unity. In order that unity of intuition may arise out of this manifold (as for example in the representation of space) it must first be run through, and held together. This act I name the *synthesis of apprehension*. (A99)

In this first of several, and apparently conflicting, comments on "apprehension," Kant seems to attribute the latter to intuition as opposed to imagination. He then proceeds to the "synthesis of reproduction," which he finally attributes to imagination as such. It is in the latter context, as we have seen, that he couples reflection on "associative" anticipation and retention with reflection on the phenomenon that he had apparently already included under the heading of "apprehension." At most he now adds the hint of an orientation toward the future as well as the past:

> But if I were always to drop out of thought the preceding representations (the first parts of the line, the antecedent parts of the time period, or the units in the order represented), and did not reproduce them while advancing to those that follow, a complete representation would never be obtained. (A102)

After this, Kant concludes that "the synthesis of apprehension is thus inseparably bound up with the synthesis of reproduction." One might rather wonder what could possibly have distinguished them. I shall return to this point in the next chapter, when I also consider Kant's reformulation at A120-1. Right now our question is whether the kind of anticipation and retention involved in the two sorts of cases is not meant to exhibit more commonality than what is already superficially evident. I have suggested that more is at stake. Kant's repetition of the point that he had already covered, in the treatment of apprehension, must hold the key to it.

What joins the cases of immediate and less apparently immediate anticipation and retention is not simply that they both involve an ability to retain and anticipate. What they need to be seen to share, at least in the context of a concern with the conceptualization of intuitions, is what is most prominent in the apparently more immediate of the cases, but which might seem to be altogether absent from the other. If my suggestions so far have been correct, the point of comparison should be clear. The conceptualization of an intuition, with respect to a given object, does not merely relate that intuition to a manifold of anticipations and retentions concerning that object. To the contrary, we would not in the first place have been conceptualizing a particular *intuition* unless a manifold of anticipations and retentions were, within the structure of that very act, an internal component of the intuition itself.

When that condition is not satisfied, we might still bring something forth that has a regular, perhaps a causal, connection with a genuine conceptual act. For example, we might externally attach, in a law- or a rule-like way, a name or a word or some other symbol (perhaps an "image") to a particular intuition. The name or word or symbol will no doubt be one that we "associate" with the intuition in question, by virtue of certain anticipations and retentions. To this extent, it will have a real connection with some concept, predicable of the given intuition. But the attachment in question would still not be an instance of conceptualizing that intuition. It could at most be a convenient and mechanical substitute for it. This, we may suppose, is the real point of comparison between the apparently merely superficially similar phenomena Kant considers: the internal structuring that is more obviously required for one of them (that is, for the apparently more immediate kind of anticipation and retention, in regard to what is immediately arising and receding) needs to serve as a model for the structure of the other as well (that is, for the case of apparently merely "associative" anticipation and retention).

V. Synthesis and Rules

We have already noted that many of the notions central to Kant's argument are ambiguous. The notions of synthesis and of the manifold of intuition are examples. I discuss them further in Chapter Five, in connection with the second-edition Deduction. In the next chapter, I consider some problems in regard to associative imagination, for which I have prepared the way in the preceding section. In the present section, I return to a notion whose ambiguity was touched on earlier. It raises issues that are more prominent in the first-edition Deduction, but also in a chapter that is common to both editions, "The Schematism of the Pure Concepts of the Understanding." Our question concerns the claim that concepts express "rules," and perhaps even that they are themselves rules. One of the advantages of the proposed approach is that it can help make sense of some ambiguities surrounding this point as well.

Kant says that "a concept is always, as regards its form, something universal, which serves as a rule" (A106). In fact, understanding may even be defined as the "faculty of rules" (A126): "Sensibility gives us forms (of intuition), but understanding gives us rules" (A126). Fascination with analogies between mental and linguistic representation has generated considerable interest in this aspect of Kant's thought. But it is not easy to see what Kant's point really is. Kant insists that concepts are essentially "predicates of possible judgments" (A69/B94). We might therefore regard concepts as analogous to linguistic predicates. Accordingly, we might take Kant's position to be that systems of rules are what confer an original meaning on such predicates as predicates. If so, then the rules presumably prescribe, relative to possible sets of circumstances, the various possible intuitions to which those predicates paradigmatically (though of course not exclusively) attach. The privileged set of intuitions would be the manifold of intuitions that are synthesized by a concept: a concept "can be a rule for intuitions only insofar as it represents in any given appearances the necessary reproduction of their manifold, and thereby the synthetic unity in our consciousness of them. The concept of body, in the perception of something outside us, necessitates the representation of extension, and therewith representations of impenetrability, shape, etc." (A106). But there is an obvious problem in all this. It contradicts the presumption from which we began, namely, that concepts are, or serve as, rules of some sort. The view that we end up with is, quite to the contrary, that concepts are merely governed by, or in some way essentially "subject" to, rules.

Kant's position appears to be contradictory. It demands that concepts be predicates of possible judgments, but it also demands that they be the sources of rules that confer meaning on those predicates in the first place. We might try to avoid the difficulty by distinguishing two senses of *concept*. But that postpones the difficulty. The question remains as to what, outside of a concept *qua* predicate, could possibly confer a specific predicative status upon a term. To say that what does it is also a "concept," but this time a concept *qua* rule for predication, rather than a predicate itself, only names the problem. To say that what does it is a quasi-linguistic conceptual "system" does no better. In any event, any source of the rules, outside of the concepts for which they are presumed to be rules, would seem to threaten Kant's own insistence on the autonomy and spontaneity of understanding as a faculty. As I argued in Chapter Two, what may be the main alternative, namely, appeal to a causal system of some kind, is particularly deficient in this regard.

Kant may be taken to speak to this problem in the eleven-page chapter that, according to Heidegger, "forms the heart of the whole work.³⁷ Heidegger's enthusiasm is not universally shared. The main points of difficulty seem to be two. First, there is the difficulty that, by raising the question, Kant must be supposing, absurdly, that a concept can be something apart from the rules for its use or application in the first place, the question then being: What in fact constitutes those rules?³⁸ The second difficulty concerns Kant's attempt to reply to the difficulty. (Kant does not put it, in the case of empirical concepts, in terms of reply to a difficulty; his main concern in the chapter is with a corresponding question concerning the categories.) The reply appeals to a relationship between concepts and their "schemata," a relationship that is somehow supposed to mediate the former's application. The objection is simple. Kant's description of the schemata of empirical concepts (and of any non-categorial ones, hence including pure mathematical concepts) seems to equate schemata with rules for the use of concepts in the first place. Thus the purported solution either restates the problem or, by suggesting that schemata are a "third thing" altogether, generates an infinite regress.[39]

Pippin sums up the general problem this way:

> Some way (usually attributed mysteriously to the imagination) must be found for thinking of a rule in terms of the content of experience. We don't, that is, simply encounter [apart from conceptualization] lists of *Merkmale* in experience, calling for or warranting the application of this rule and not that. Neither do we, especially in such empirical cases, merely impose a conceptual unity on a manifold. We have to understand the use of a rule in terms of the content of empirical judgment, and this poses a problem, since the rule is not a representative [conceptual?] entity. It merely stipulates universal conditions for the recognition and connection of sensible intuitions. But—and now the problem—in *applying* such a rule, we must formulate a "schematic" representation of all these markers as a whole in order to use the rule to distinguish sensible contents. The *Merkmale* of the concept dog are "imagined" together "universally" (*allgemein*) in order to use the concept, or to "connect" it with sensible particulars, "images."[40]

The difficulty, I take it, is this: If the rules for concepts are not themselves conceptions (presumably, conceptions regarding the paradigmatically possible application of concepts to intuitions), or if they are not at least "representative entities" of some kind, then they are unable to provide guidance for the application of the concepts for which they are supposed to provide rules in the first place. But, of course, the rules in question could not already be, without circularity, conceptions, and it is difficult to see what other sorts of representations they could be. To put the problem in still other terms: For a case of real conceptualization, as opposed to a purely causally grounded "response" to intuitions, it must be precisely one's *grasp* of the intuitions in question that accounts for the specific modes in which one conceptualizes the latter. But that seems impossible according to Kant's approach, since it seems to make rules for the use of concepts superfluous; one's immediate "grasp" should already suffice.[41]

Despite his apparent identification of non-categorial concepts with rules of some kind in the Deduction, Kant does appear to regard the "schemata" of these concepts as rules as well. In particular, he appears to regard them as rules for the application of the concepts in question. Of a pure mathematical concept, for example, the schema—"in itself always a product of imagination"—is the "representation of a universal procedure of imagination in providing an image for a concept" (A140/B179-80). It signifies (*bedeutet*: Kemp Smith says it *is*) "a rule of synthesis of imagination" (A141/B180). Regarding an empirical concept, similarly, Kant says both that the schema to which the former stands "in immediate relation" is a rule, and also that it "signifies [*bedeutet*] a rule" (A141/B180). In either case, schematism is "an art concealed in the depths of the human soul, whose real modes of activity nature is hardly likely ever to allow us to discover, and to have open to our gaze" (A141/B181).[42]

Kant appears to proceed from here to attribute sensible schematization in general to "pure *a priori* imagination":

> [T]he *schema* of sensible concepts, such as of figures in space, is a product and, as it were, a monogram, of pure *a priori* imagination, through which, and in accordance with which, images themselves first become possible. These images can be connected with the concept only by means of the schema to which they belong [*welches sie bezeichnen*]. (A141-2/B181)

This may seem to contradict what Kant had said earlier. He had earlier said, at least regarding the schemata of pure sensible concepts, that they "can exist no where but in thought [*in Gedanken*]" (A141/B180). Now he seems to say that they exist in the imagination. (The later passage is in any case not perfectly clear. Kant's example involves concepts "such as of figures in space." Is it meant to apply only to pure sensible concepts, not to sensible concepts generally, including all empirical ones?)[43]

All of this, according to the suggested approach, makes perfectly good sense. In particular, it is understandable why Kant should identify concepts with rules of some sort, and yet also why he should see the need to distinguish them from rules. And it is understandable why Kant should say that schemata are to be found only in thought, and yet also why he attributes them to the imagination. The apparent contradiction reflects what might be regarded as the paradoxical nature of concepts themselves. In a way, concepts can be nothing other than the rules for their own application. The air of paradox diminishes when we elaborate the notion in the terms that I have suggested. The point would then be this: that what concepts are *made out of* is nothing other than what serves to indicate, relative to circumstance, the manifold of the intuitions to which those concepts are (paradigmatically) applicable. As a multiply instantiable aspect of possible cognitions, a given concept is paradigmatically applicable to many intuitions. So we need to ask: What specifies the relevant intuitions, relative to particular circumstances? What provides one with the needed "grasp" of those intuitions in the first place? The simple answer is that what does this is our grasp of the *rules* for a concept. A deeper suggestion, and one that avoids the problems so far encountered, is that this is accomplished precisely by means of the anticipation/retention structure of conception itself.

This is compatible with conceding that it is only as an ingredient *in* some conceptual structure that a manifold of anticipations and retentions can be dignified with the title of a set of "rules" in the first place. In itself, such a manifold could at most provide the anticipation and retention of possible intuitions. As such, it might therefore succeed in indicating a manifold of intuitions to which some particular concept is paradigmatically applicable. But it cannot indicate those intuitions precisely *as* intuitions to which some concept is applicable. In this view, the anticipation and retention of a set of intuitions, as those to which a single concept is applicable, is rather constituted by the incorporation of those anticipations and retentions in a higher form of consciousness. What sort of item or entity is the concept thereby in question? In the proposed view, it is not an item or entity at all. Nor is it what may therefore appear to be the most likely alternative: a mere disposition of some kind. It is simply a mode *of consciousness itself*, or at least of possible consciousness. That is, it is simply an aspect of consciousness, regarded as an aspect potentially instantiable in any number of states of consciousness. The anticipations and retentions in question indicate this manifold (or at least a paradigmatically representative portion of it).

An additional complication is needed to elaborate this view. As we shall see more clearly later, it does not suffice, for the formation of conceptual contents, that just any set of anticipations and retentions get embodied as material in some structure of higher order. In order for such a structure to qualify as conceptual in form, it must include anticipations and retentions of a special sort. It must include anticipations and retentions that are *themselves* of a higher order. In particular, it must include not only anticipations and retentions of possible intuitions, relative to various circumstances, but also anticipations and retentions of intuitions *to which those anticipations and retentions are paradigmatically appropriate.*

I return to this complication in Chapter Six. For now, we should at least have a sense in which (non-categorial) concepts can be both nothing other than, and yet also more than, systems of "rules." They are systems of rules in the sense that they are wholly *made* out of nothing other than what are in effect rules for their own application. But by the same token, they are also more than rules. They are the very "predicates" on whose application those rules are supposed to bear. What distinguishes a concept from the rules for its "use" is, of course, just the form of consciousness that distinguishes it from its own matter. According to alternative accounts, as we have seen, the situation is very different. There, the systems of rules that are presumed to constitute the significance of predicates *qua* predicates (or whatever sorts of systems are presumed to do this) are by their nature external to those predicates themselves. Such, for example, are the causes and effects to which functionalists need to appeal. Even if, on the functionalist's account, the typicality of certain causes and effects is internal to some term's status as predicative in nature, the very *fact* of such typicality is not part of the very being of that term in the first place. It is an external fact about it. According to the present account, if predication is to be possible, then a certain set of a subject's anticipations and retentions needs to be incorporated into the very "term" (that is, into the very aspect of consciousness) on whose predicative status that set is supposed to bear.

On at least three occasions, Kemp Smith blurs this point. That is, he obscures Kant's suggestion that something within a conceptual state *qua* conceptual, but not unambiguously identifiable with a concept itself, pre-conceptually represents or indicates the manifold of possible intuitions to which a concept is supposed to be applicable. Kant says, for example, that a sensible concept is necessarily connected, in an *a priori* and imaginative manner, with the manifold of "images" to which that concept applies "only by means of the schema that indicates" those images (*nur immer vermittelst des Schema, welches sie bezeichnet*). Kemp Smith instead translates: "only by means of the schema to which they belong" (A142/B181). This substitutes the vaguer notion of images "belonging" to a schema for Kant's own notion that those images need to be "indicated," thus in some way present to mind, by means of a concept's schema. The substitution, of course, avoids any question as to what could in fact provide such "indication," short of concepts themselves.

Two related passages in the first-edition Deduction are also mishandled. In both of them, Kant calls explicit attention to the anticipational structure of consciousness. In the first of them, Kant is moving from his treatment of the synthesis of imaginative "reproduction" to his treatment of the synthesis of "recognition in a concept":

> If we were not conscious that what we think is the same as what we thought a moment before . . . in its present state a new representation . . . would not in any way belong to the act whereby it was to have been gradually generated [*wodurch sie nach und nach hat erzeugt werden sollen*]. (A103)

Kemp Smith translates: the new representation "would not in any way belong to the act whereby it was to *be* [my emphasis] gradually generated." Kant's own formulation seems designed to suggest that the possible "generation" of additional representations, from a given one that was originally subject to some mode of predication, must be regarded as already foreshadowed *in* the given representation, independently of (though perhaps not antecedently to) the act of predication as such.[44] A similar alteration occurs at A105. Kemp Smith substitutes "if the intuition cannot be generated in accordance with a rule" for "if the intuition cannot *have been* [my emphasis] generated in accordance with a rule" (*nach einer Regel hat hervorgebracht werden können*).

All of this has been meant to apply to non-categorial concepts. But it is worth noting how the approach might extend to fit Kant's treatment of the relationship between categories and their schemata. I have argued elsewhere for an account of the latter and will not repeat it here. Others have also argued for one or the other of the following propositions: either that the schemata of the categories are pure intuitions or else that they are pure intuitions "determined" with respect to one or more of the pure judgmental or intellectual forms. In any case, the most plausible view, consonant with the approach that I have proposed, is both that the schemata of categories are pure intuitions *and* that the categories themselves, to the extent they are concepts, not mere forms, can be nothing but those very schemata. That is, they can be nothing but those schemata—considered precisely insofar as the latter have been appropriately *informed* ("determined") by the forms in question. Thus categorial concepts, like any others, can only be characterized by a way in which some intuitional "material" is elevated through embodiment in a state whose form is that of the forms of judgment. The difference is in the material. The material of the categories can only be pure intuition as such, that is, intuition as a *whole* considered with respect to its form *qua* intuition. By contrast, the material of empirical concepts is not intuition as such, but manifolds of the sorts of anticipations and retentions that are embodiable in their own turn *in* intuition. In any event, on account of the common structure, and despite the difference in "matter," we may agree with Heidegger: "*All* conceptual representation *is* essentially schematism."[45]

The point can be clarified by relating it to some views similar to my own, at least regarding the categories and their schemata. Gram, for example, also takes transcendental schemata to be various pure intuitions. On the other hand, he sees those schemata as at most relating to the *categories* by way of "falling under" them.[46] In this respect, it might seem that my view ought to more in accord with Allison's. Allison criticizes Gram for failing to recognize that pure intuitions are themselves conceptually "determinable." Because of the latter fact, transcendental schemata are to be regarded not simply as intuitions able to "fall under" concepts, but rather as intellectually "determined" intuitions in their own right.[47]

Allison's approach seems to be like the one that I have proposed. This is because according to that approach, and at least in the categorial case, conceptual "determinations" need to enter into intuitions themselves and not to remain merely externally connectable with them. Thus Allison appears to presuppose a more phenomenological approach, while Gram's is more purely logical: "Although Kant, of course, begins with the radical separation of sensibility and understanding, intuition and concept, the very heart of his account of knowledge consists in the claim that any cognition of an object involves both elements."[48] But it is not clear to what extent my own point is in fact comparable to Allison's. We can see the difficulty by putting the issue in explicitly noetic terms—that is, by focusing explicitly on intuitions and conceptions as "representational states."[49] In these terms, if we are really regarding a category's schema as both intuitional and conceptual—if we are really regarding it as a pure intuition "determined" by conceptual form—then it is difficult to see how a category's schema is supposed to be distinguished from a category itself. So "determined," the schema in question would seem to be a pure mode of representation, both intuitional and conceptual in nature. So it would seem to be identical at least with a "schematized" category.[50] But Allison explicitly *distinguishes* the schemata of the categories from the corresponding categories themselves. The latter, "as rules for the transcendental synthesis of the imagination, serve to determine time. . . . [T]he schema is in each case the product of such determination."[51] In contrast to both these approaches, I take the schemata to be relevantly "determined" by the pure forms of judgment, and the corresponding categorial concepts simply to *be* the resultant schemata/intuitions, viewed as so determined.[52]

From the point of view of their status as already formed categories—that is, as concepts—it will still make perfectly good sense to regard the categories as concepts that, in their own turn, are also able to "determine" intuitions. Indeed, to assure that this makes sense is just the point of Kant's concern with schematism in the first place, as the actual "procedure of understanding with these schemata [*das Verfahren des Verstandes mit diesen Schematen*]" (A140/B179). His concern is to show how the categories, though in a sense nothing more than the pure forms of judgment, are yet not mere forms for the relating of terms internal to judgments. Rather, they are able to "subsume" objects, to be "homogenous" with concrete representations of the latter, and consequently really to "contain something which is represented" in the latter (A137/B176). My own interest is not in the specifically categorial dimension of the subsumptions in question. It is rather in the *Verfahren des Verstandes* by which *any* conceptual content needs to be constituted or formed. But so far as I can see, the relevant *Verfahren*, in the case of categories, must be a procedure by which categorial concepts, like any others, are constituted out of a certain type of material.

Kant's own primary interest in the Schematism chapter is, of course, to show how, by virtue of being formed out of pure intuition, a category is formed out of something that is in its own turn embodiable, and necessarily so, in the intuitive representations of sensible objects. According to that account, any act of empirical conceptualization *is* necessarily an act of categorial determination. For it is always an act in which intellectual form is "applied" to a state whose form is already that of pure intuition. In the case of empirical concepts, by contrast, the corresponding question had already been answered in the Deduction: the fact that their material is simply anticipations and retentions already *explains* why empirical concepts are embodiable in sensible intuition.

In order to appreciate these points, we simply need to recall throughout that the "formation" of a concept in any particular case is nothing distinct from a particular act of conceptualization. Thus concepts, in the relevant sense, are not items or entities that might, for example, be the mere *products* of any kind of action, nor any kind of "possession" somehow internal to a subject. If they were, then we would indeed have a problem explaining their connection with the subject's occurrent grasp, in any act of conceptualization, of the actually operative "rules" for the use of the item on that occasion. (Of course, the question of rules, for obvious reasons, only arises in the case of empirical concepts in the first place.) To be sure, there is nothing in principle wrong in speaking of "concepts" as a kind of possession. As we have seen, perhaps we may even identify them with certain dispositions of a person. But if we do, then we will at most be speaking of dispositions in regard to the very *formation* of concepts—in the *other* sense of the term. The issue, it should be clear, is not a merely terminological one.

Chapter 4

Production, Reproduction, and Affinity

I. Introduction

IN THE preceding chapter, I distinguished between the imaginative synthesis involved in the "anticipation and retention" of immediately upcoming and receding appearances and the kind of anticipation and retention involved in what we may more naturally call the "association" of appearances. The latter, under the title *Reproduktion* in Kant, may appear more readily to lend itself to Kant's own interest in the possibility of a representation of an order of natural objects. This is because "association" is in effect what provides the material for the formation of concepts of objects in the first place. In the context of the Deduction, the importance of the other, more apparently immediate, anticipation and retention is best seen as an effort toward a more adequate notion of the relevant *form* of (embodiment of) anticipation and retention in concepts (or at least in "conceptions") of objects. In any event, it is in his treatment of what we more ordinarily regard as imaginative "association" that Kant attempts to establish a direct connection with our capacity for representing an anticipable order of nature. In this chapter, I try to clarify some of the issues that are involved in this attempt.

It is clear that a relevantly Kantian connection between our capacity for association and for the representation of an anticipable order of nature needs to have some bearing on the problem of conceptual representation in particular. In this regard, we can at the very least say, for example, that a being incapable of even the more immediate anticipation and retention will be unable to apply, or even to develop, any empirical concepts. In itself, the point is fairly trivial. But what is remarkable is that, in certain passages, Kant appears to consider it a significant start toward some very strong conclusions. He does this at A100 as well as in a (supposedly) more systematic presentation of the same material at A119-23. These are the passages on which mainly I want to concentrate. In at least the first of them, Kant is often thought to be confused. I want to argue that in both cases he is attempting to present an essential but a generally neglected aspect of his theory.

It is in the second of the passages in question that Kant also distinguishes between productive and reproductive imagination and ascribes an *a priori* and a transcendental status to the former. Earlier, he had ascribed an *a priori* status to reproduction (A102); now he refuses it on the ground that this "rests on empirical conditions" (A118; cf. A121). In addition, Kant expands upon the notion of an objective order within the world of appearances, supposedly already presupposed by our merely empirical ability to associate. He refers to this order as the "affinity" of appearances (A122-3; cf. A113), and he attributes it to the transcendental capacity of imagination itself. (He also distinguishes, at A114, between a transcendental and an empirical affinity.) But later he also seems to attribute the affinity of appearances to a distinctively intellectual capacity. There are at least two ways in which he might be supposed to waver on this. He might be shifting, on the one hand, between an attribution of affinity to the faculty of imagination (whether productive or also reproductive) and an attribution of affinity to a more intellectual faculty altogether. On the other hand, Kant might be consistent in regarding affinity as the product of imagination and simply be wavering with respect to the question whether imagination, or at least a genuinely productive version of that faculty, is not itself already something intellectual. We may also be charitable if we speak of mere "wavering." It is more common to accuse Kant of blatant self-contradiction.[1]

To get clear regarding affinity, and regarding the issue of productive and reproductive imagination, it is crucial to distinguish between the question of an anticipable order in the world of appearances, as some sort of "ground" of the associability of the latter, and the question of an essential structure internal to ordinary empirical apprehension. In the light of this distinction, Kant's ascription of a transcendental status to productive imagination may seem to foreshadow a disturbingly mysterious doctrine. Even the ascription of such a status to merely reproductive imagination might seem to be less problematic. Kant's point at A100-102 might then simply be that it is a necessary condition of the apprehension of appearances, or at least of any conceptualized apprehension of appearances, that the apprehending subject anticipate and retain instances of other possible apprehensions as well. In this sense, even merely reproductive imagination (or at least an imagination that is not mysteriously productive) may easily count as a "transcendental" faculty. The concession would rest on a perfectly harmless notion of the transcendental. But unless Kant is guilty of self-contradiction, his subsequent claim that only productive imagination is genuinely transcendental would seem to involve a much less modest notion. Here, Kant appears to invite our tolerance, not simply of ordinary anticipation and retention, internal and perhaps essential to any experience of anticipable order, but rather of something responsible for generating such an order to begin with. The "transcendental" may now seem to be much more than a necessary condition of experience. In itself, the latter might be boringly ordinary, something of which we detect countless examples in the course of everyday experience: ordinary anticipations and retentions, for example. But how could we detect the very activities supposed to have been responsible for generating the very order of phenomenal nature itself?[2]

We have seen that reproductive imagination might be in one sense transcendental, or at least possessed of a transcendental dimension, while in another sense not. This is a way of accounting for Kant's apparent contradiction. But the price to pay would be high. It requires the supposition that, in contrast to the faculty of merely reproductive imagination, Kant presumed the existence of a mysterious faculty of productive imagination, responsible for generating the manifold of appearances in the first place. Only once generated, it seems, could the reproductive faculty undertake its course of anticipating and retaining.

A second approach is possible. According to this approach, there need be no question as to whether or not, and in what sense, reproductive or productive imagination is transcendental. Rather we simply ask: In what sense is reproductive imagination itself something *productive* (and not simply reproductive but "transcendental")? By now it should be clear what I mean by the suggestion. We have already seen that, fairly trivially, anticipation and retention are necessary conditions of experience, and therefore transcendental in that sense. What we need to see, very untrivially, is that they are also able fully to *serve* as conditions of experience only to the extent that they are incorporable as material *within* particular experiences, that is, within empirical intuitions. Only thereby can they be material for the acts that conceptualize appearances.

To the extent that imaginative material is ingredient in intuitions, the world of appearances is apprehended *through* that material. That is, it is apprehended through that material in a sense analogous to that in which appearances are apprehended through "sensations." This is a special sense. It involves the notion of an *aspect* of appearances that necessarily corresponds to, and that is an intentional correlate of, the specific character of the material in question. The latter is, of course, just our ordinary anticipations and retentions. Their correlate could then be nothing other than a corresponding order apprehensible in the world of appearances. In this way, reproductive imagination is indeed productive as well. And it is productive in a sense that is much more substantial than what we have so far granted in conceding it to be "transcendental." (At the same time, to whatever extent the suggestion may favor some brand of "phenomenalism," it will in any case favor no supposition of the manufacture of objects out of subjective material.) The main lines of my interpretation will be laid out in the next section. In the final section, I apply them in order to clarify distinctions among several concepts of affinity, as well as some related concepts in the *Critique of Judgment*.

II. From Association to Affinity

We are ready to take a more detailed look at Kant's discussion of association at A100-102. The main line of argument also reappears at A120-3, in explicit connection with the notion of productive imagination. The argument is puzzling. In it, Kant tries to show that one's mere possession of a capacity for associative reproduction presupposes that appearances themselves (*die Erscheinungen selbst*) are subject to rules that correspond to one's modes of association. It will be helpful to divide the passage into two parts:

[A] It is a merely empirical law, that representations which have often followed or accompanied one another finally become associated, and so are set in a relation whereby, even in the absence of the object, one of these representations can, in accordance with a fixed rule, bring about a transition of the mind to the other. [B] But this law of reproduction presupposes that appearances are themselves actually subject to such a rule, and that in the manifold of their representations a coexistence or sequence takes place in conformity with certain rules. (A100)

It is not immediately clear what [B] is meant to assert. That "appearances are themselves" subject to rules might mean that phenomenal realities (real objects in space and time) are subject to rules. Or it might only mean, more weakly, that all experiences of phenomenal realities are subject to rules. In that case, perhaps the claim might simply be that reproduction "presupposes" an order among appearances themselves, in the sense that the former could only *arise* in consequence of regularities among experiences in the first place. This may seem confirmed by the sentence that immediately follows: "Otherwise our empirical imagination would never find opportunity for exercise appropriate to its powers, and so would remain concealed within the mind as a dead and to us unknown faculty."

The most obvious problem with this reading concerns the strength of the alleged presupposition. If Kant is aiming at the conclusion that appearances *necessarily* are rule-bound, then the argument seems irrelevant. Now in [A], Kant in fact speaks of a "merely empirical" law, for which in [B] he purports to provide a ground in appearances. In addition, the second paragraph of the section begins with what appears its intended conclusion: "There must therefore be something which, as the *a priori* ground of a necessary synthetic unity of appearances, makes this very reproduction [*selbst diese Reproduktion*] possible" (A101). So one might well conclude that Kant is seeking a ground, internal to appearances themselves, that is causally necessary for the original formation of reproductive associations. But surely, there is nothing incoherent in the idea that we develop patterns of association that are not in any way causally derived from corresponding perceptual regularities.

Furthermore, a closer look at the argument seems to make it clear that Kant in any case *assumes* from the start, at least for the sake of argument, that associations indeed always derive from a corresponding order in appearances. Premise [A] seems to incorporate that assumption. [B] then attempts to add, as a stronger conclusion, not (or at least not simply) that associations *necessarily* derive from regularities in appearances, but that appearances are themselves necessarily *subject* to the regularities already presumed in [A] to be in question. In other words, [A] seems already to suppose that there needs to be some regularity or other among appearances, in order that associations be possible in the first place. Much more strongly, [B] then appears to conclude that whatever regularities are in question must really be *more* than "regularities." For they must be such that, given the particular facts of association, appearances *must* be subject to them (and not merely to some regularity or other).[3]

Similar difficulties arise in regard to the supposedly (cf. A98, 115) more systematic exposition at A120-3. Again, after covering the ground corresponding to a mere synthesis of "apprehension," Kant introduces the notion of empirical reproduction. He makes it clear, once more, that the latter is already involved in the former. It is involved to the extent that the retention of passing experiences is a necessary condition even for the experience of single images (A121). The discussion of associative reproduction then proceeds to draw a distinction that was not so explicit earlier. It distinguishes two senses in which one might speak of the ground (*Grund*) of associative reproduction. Kant calls one of these grounds the "empirical ground" of reproduction. Somewhat confusingly, he also refers to that ground as the "association of representations" itself:

> If, however, representations reproduced one another in any order, just as they happened to come together, this would not lead to any determinate connection of them, but only to accidental collocations; and so would not give rise to any cognition. Their reproduction must, therefore, conform to a rule, in accordance with which a representation connects in the imagination with some one representation in preference to another. This subjective and *empirical* ground of reproduction according to rules is what is called the *association* of representations. (A121)

Kant does seem to argue, not merely to assert, in this passage that associative reproduction needs some kind of "grounding" in an order of appearances. But at the very least, that argument seems premature. It merely presupposes what Kant is aware needs yet to be argued, namely, that objective "cognition" is necessary in the first place. Apart from this, no transcendental consideration is evident in the argument. Kant will of course argue, eventually, that it is a necessary condition of experience that we retain and associate appearances. He will also argue that it is necessary that objects exhibit an order such that our perceptions of them also, in general, exhibit a *corresponding* order. All of these propositions involve transcendental considerations, and from them it of course follows that it is necessary for experience that appearances contain an order that is at least sufficient for the derivation of corresponding anticipations and retentions. In any case, whether prematurely or not, no such considerations justify the assertion that, by their very nature, imaginative associations must in fact be "grounded" in that order. That appears to involve, once again, an assumption on Kant's part regarding mere causal origins.

If there is an interesting argument concerning the notion of "grounding," at this point, it must rather concern the notion of an "objective"—but also *non-causal*—ground of imaginative association. This is, of course, just Kant's move, again, from whatever order is represented in our imaginative associations—*however* the latter happen to be generated or derived (but assuming that they are in fact "empirically" grounded)—to a corresponding order in the realm of objects. Here is the passage:

> Now if this unity of association had not also an objective ground which makes it impossible that appearances should be apprehended by the imagination otherwise than under the condition of a possible synthetic unity of this apprehension, it would be entirely accidental that appearances should fit into a connected whole of human knowledge. For even though we should have the power of associating perceptions, it would remain entirely undetermined and accidental whether they would themselves be associable; and should they not be associable, there might exist a multitude of perceptions, and indeed an entire sensibility, in which much empirical conscious-

ness would arise in my mind, but in a state of separation, and without belonging
to a consciousness of myself. (A121-2)

This passage introduces a factor that Kant had held in abeyance in his earlier,
less "systematic" discussion. There he had at most implied that some kind of associability of perceptions is a necessary condition of the employment of empirical
concepts, and perhaps even of their development in the first place. After that,
in his account of "recognition in a concept," he connected the relevant notion of
concept with that of a necessary unity of self-consciousness. In the later passage,
he streamlines the treatment by indicating from the start that imaginative association is in some way a necessary condition for a unity of self-consciousness. But
what interests us now is not this aspect of the argument. Our concern is not
yet with the thesis that imaginative association is a necessary condition of
self-consciousness, nor even with the thesis that the latter itself presupposes
some kind of order among appearances. Our concern is rather with the claim
that some such order is quite *directly* a necessary condition of imaginative association as such. What is the point of insisting, not simply that an orderly world
is non-causally necessary for a "unity of consciousness," but that it is—equally
non-causally—necessary for the very occurrence of *association* as such?

It seems unlikely that Kant would consider it important to establish that imaginative associations need to "correspond" to a worldy order, merely for the sake
of having an account of where those associations *come* from in the first place. Nor
should he, at least at the present point, be concerned to establish the fact, even
in order to provide a ground for the eventual "origin" of objective concepts or
cognitions. (Apart from unclarity as to how either concern involves transcendental
issues, even to assume the relevance of the second would be question-begging.)
What I suggest is that Kant had a different notion in mind, with regard to the
way in which associations need to "correspond" to a worldly order. This notion,
as argued, needs to bear on the very *nature* of the relevant sort of association,
not merely on the question either of its causal antecedents or of its logical presupposition by understanding. What reflection on that nature reveals is an important
sense in which, even if the relevant order *is* in fact presupposed by understanding,
it must be regarded as more than a *correlate* of the activity of understanding.[4]

If Kant did not intend something like this, then it is difficult to see why he
should be so centrally concerned with the problem of merely imaginative association. If he were concerned only to establish that a necessary condition of the relevant sort of "unity of consciousness" is that appearances be subject to conceptualization, and that this in turn implies that they exhibit a regular order, there would
be no reason for him to consider the nature of imaginative association as such.
Naturally, if he could establish the truth of these claims, then he would be able
to establish the transcendental necessity that appearances exhibit an order that
"corresponds" to the order represented by imaginative association. But that would
be anti-climactic with respect to the main point. And it would not, of course,
explain why the argument begins precisely with a consideration of imaginative
association.

On the other hand, we need to concede that Kant is in fact not merely concerned with imaginative association *simpliciter*. If he were, then it would indeed be difficult to establish a connection with the corresponding transcendental reflections. What we must assume is that Kant means to deal from the start with that particular *form* of association that is—or will at least eventually be—required as a foundation for understanding, hence for any relevant sort of unity of consciousness. In effect, in other words, we may read Kant's arguments precisely as attempts to distinguish the two "types" of imaginative association. (That would explain why the argument begins with mere association, and also why it appears to *confuse* the question of association with questions that properly arise only at a later stage of reflection.)

We ought not to forget that association *simpliciter* is a rather primitive business. Non-human animals, for example, ought to be as capable of it as they are of most kinds of sensation. Kant, as we have already seen, concedes that they are. But just on that basis, Kant could not hope to establish any interesting conclusion concerning the world "as it appears" to such creatures. One might, of course, argue that such creatures at least live in a world that is able to provide a sufficient (causal) basis for their imaginative associations, hence in a world that itself exhibits a generally corresponding order. But that sort of argument would be possible only after the demand for universal causality had already been established. Even then, the conclusion could be no more than a plausible hypothesis. More important, unless it could be established that causal relations only obtain among appearances, not among things considered "in themselves," there would not even be anything in such an argument to bear precisely on what concerns Kant in the first place, namely, on the question of an order in the world as it *appears*. For all that would have been done, we might have merely succeeded in supporting the hypothesis of an order internal to things in themselves.

Consider again Kant's conclusion regarding the "objective ground" of association. Here is how he describes that ground: It is a "ground which makes it impossible that appearances should be apprehended *by the imagination* otherwise than under the condition of a possible synthetic unity of this apprehension" (emphasis added). Now we know why Kant introduces the unity of apprehension at this point. This is because he holds, and he will independently argue, that it is necessary for unity of consciousness that our conceptualizations represent a corresponding unity as obtaining among the objects (appearances) of which one is conscious. But what is striking, from the perspective of this reflection, is that Kant does not then simply conclude that, corresponding to one's capacity for imaginative association, there is an objective "ground which makes it impossible that appearances should be apprehended by the *understanding* otherwise than under the condition of a possible synthetic unity of this apprehension." As it is, Kant does not merely say that the order demanded by the relevant unity of consciousness, and to which imaginative associations at least generally correspond (and indeed, on the basis in question, why require more than a merely *general* correspondence?), must be an order that is intellectually apprehensible. Instead, he says that the order needs to be apprehended *by the imagination*.

We need, then, to distinguish two levels of reflection in Kant's arguments. These might be seen as resting, respectively, on a more and a less concrete notion of the kind of "correspondence" that is supposed to be in question, between an order of things as represented in one's imaginative associations and an order internal to the world of appearances itself. Both of them bear on the conclusion that some worldy order must correspond to the order that is represented in imaginative association. But only one of them rests on considerations that bear on the particular nature of the latter. The other rests on considerations more specifically concerning self-consciousness and understanding.

It is from the standpoint of the second of these levels that Kant can maintain the following:

> This objective ground of all association of appearances I entitle their *affinity*. It is nowhere to be found save in the principle of the unity of apperception, in respect (*in Ansehung*) of all cognition which is to belong to me. According to this principle all appearances, without exception, must so enter the mind or be apprehended, that they conform to the unity of apperception. Without synthetic unity in their connection, this would be impossible; and such synthetic unity is itself, therefore, objectively necessary. (A122)

But it is from the standpoint of the first level that Kant is also required to say that pure apperception is something that needs to be "*added* [emphasis added] to pure imagination, in order to render its function intellectual" in the first place (A124).

It is obvious, both in the first- and in the second-edition Deduction, that Kant sees the faculty of understanding as capable of functioning only through the faculty of imagination. Notoriously, he is not successful in making it clear what the connection is supposed to be. This may be what accounts for the fact that the discussions of imagination that we have so far been considering seem to conflate two entirely distinct lines of consideration. These two lines, and their uneasy mingling, are also evident in the argument at A100-102. There Kant proceeds as well to connect the question of imaginative association with that of empirical concepts. But he does not do it as explicitly as later, nor in explicit connection with the problem of unitary consciousness:

> If cinnabar were sometimes red, sometimes black, sometimes light, sometimes heavy, if a man changed sometimes into this and sometimes into that animal form, if the country on the longest day were sometimes covered with fruit, sometimes with ice and snow, my empirical imagination would never find opportunity when representing red colour to bring to mind heavy cinnabar. Nor could there be an empirical synthesis of reproduction, if a certain name were sometimes given to this, sometimes to that object, or were one and the same thing named sometimes in one way, sometimes in another, independently of any rule to which appearances are themselves subject. (A100-101)

From these reflections, Kant thinks he has shown that imaginative association needs "grounding" in a "necessary synthetic unity of appearances." At this particular point, again, it remains unclear what the necessity is supposed to involve. At most it would seem to be relative. The unity in question would be necessary *for* the possibility of association itself, which in turn is necessary for the employment of empirical concepts. In any case, Kant proceeds to suppose that this unity must—*in its own turn*—have an *a priori* ground. This, he finally claims, can only lie in the phenomenal nature of appearances:

> What that something is we soon discover, when we reflect that appearances are not things in themselves, but are the mere play of our representations, and in the end reduce to determinations of inner sense. (A101)

There are a number of puzzles here, besides the general difficulty inherent in any attempt to move directly from imaginative association to an actual order among appearances. For one thing, Kant might appear to beg important questions in the move.[5] For example, he might appear to beg the question whether appearances need to be sufficiently regular to allow for the development of material-object concepts in the first place. Apart from this, the point about "names" appears trivial, irrelevant, or confused. And the point about "determinations of inner sense" is obscure. I shall return to some of these points later on. In any case, what may seem a merely question-begging appeal to empirical concepts must be, once again, just a harmless matter of anticipating the further course of Kant's own argument. What is important is not to suppose that this exhausts Kant's point.

No doubt, in the passage in question, Kant is anticipating the transcendental necessity that we develop empirical concepts that are reasonably well connected with the regular course of experience. But this accounts for only one part of Kant's reasoning in the passage in question. In addition, Kant also argues, on the basis of nothing more than our mere ability to *associate*, that the world must exhibit an order that is correlative to the associations in question. If Kant's point is only that the world must exhibit an order correlative to our ability to *conceptualize* it, then he is surely guilty of severe overstatement. Imaginative associations are in some way necessary for the formation of empirical concepts. It would seem a dull joke to argue, just on that basis, that the world must therefore exhibit an order that is correlative to imaginative associations. So the question remains what the point really is, given that Kant has not yet argued for the necessity of objective concepts in the first place. Whatever it is, it has got to reflect more than so obvious a connection between the employment of empirical concepts and one's capacity for imaginative association.[6]

I have proposed that Kant's point is to argue that whatever sort of worldly order one may establish as transcendentally necessary—that is, establish as necessary for the very possibility of a unitary consciousness—it must not be an order that is merely a correlate of the conceptualization of experience, hence only indirectly a correlate of imaginative association. Now in a way, this may seem obvious. Obviously, whatever causal order is reflected in the conceptualization of experience cannot reflect concepts alone. For it must surely have emerged out of some sort of *encounter* between our general capacity for conceptualization and the particular course of experience. The latter concerns the specific detail of the sensations or intuitions available. It is presumably this that in turn is reflected in the associations that we eventually manage to develop. But that is precisely the difficulty. The difficulty is to make sense of the notion of such "encounters." We may be tempted to adopt too simplistic an approach to the notion. In particular, we may be tempted to consider it a matter of merely external *connections* between sensations or intuitions as "stimuli," on the one hand, and whatever conceptual "responses" these are able to elicit, on the other.

The farthest we may be inclined to go, in overcoming the notion of a merely external connection between intuitions and sensations, on the one hand, and our conceptual responses to them, is to rely on a vague picture of the latter as somehow "imposing" an order on the former. But what could this mean? At least part of it is, no doubt, that one's conceptual responses manage to generate the *conception* of a generally orderly world, and a commitment to its reality on the whole. That world is then, in its own turn, represented—and perhaps necessarily so—as containing at least enough order to have *accounted* for the corresponding order of experience in the first place. But the question would still remain: To what extent would such a "representation" ever amount to any real *awareness* of the world as containing an order? Everything we have so far been told is compatible with holding that one is "aware" of that order in a purely conceptual sense: the only qualification being that the conception in question has been "stimulated" in a certain way.

Now I have already argued, in the first chapter, that immediate (intuitional) awareness cannot be grounded in purely external connections between sensory and conceptual elements. It cannot merely involve the capacity of one's sensory intuitions to "stimulate" appropriate judgments or conceptions regarding reality (or would-be reality). It must rather involve the embodiment of judgments and conceptions *in* one's very intuitions. In the earlier discussion, we were of course only considering the general problem of one's intuitive awareness of "objects." In effect, what we are now discovering is that Kant's solution to that problem, in terms of the role of imaginative associations in intuition, at the same time provides the solution to an additional problem, namely, to the problem of one's awareness of a whole *world* of objects. Kant himself does not put the issue in quite these terms. In any event, the central issue is now precisely that of accounting for the possibility of awareness, not simply of objects, but of a natural *order* of objects.

One may see more plausibility in the view that one's "awareness" of an order of nature, as a set of regularities to which objects are subject, is a purely conceptual matter than in the corresponding claim regarding awareness of those objects themselves. Naturally, there is no denying that, in either case, the relevant conceptions and commitments arise in "response" to sensory input. But one may be more inclined, in one of the cases, to concede that, however they arise, what they *are* is only conceptions and commitments.

Few people are prepared to deny that we really and directly "see" concrete objects. Indeed, even those who hold that what we really see is something altogether different—for example, sense data, or even aspects of our own sensory states—will still be happy to concede that we see material objects. They will simply inform us that "seeing" such objects *is* nothing more than judging or believing or conceiving in certain ways, in response to certain sensations. But while few may be comfortable denying that we see material objects, and holding that our apprehension of them is a purely conceptual matter, it may be tempting to suppose it a purely conceptual accomplishment that we "see" an order of nature. We might simply suppose that the latter involves the fact that regularities among the *objects* that we see has somehow stimulated development of an appropriate "conceptual scheme." What we are discovering, now, is how such a position is excluded by Kant's account of our apprehension of objects in the first place.

To summarize, then, with regard to the arguments that Kant himself gives us: We need to distinguish two levels of reasoning. One of these—perhaps the most prominent—directly concerns conditions for the employment of empirical concepts. Thus it ultimately concerns conditions for an appropriate "unity of consciousness." But it rests on no particular conception of the nature of *imagination*, and it rests on only the most abstract view of the latter's relation to the faculty of understanding. On this level, the most that we could say is that the ability to form imaginative associations is a necessary condition of the ability to form concepts. Likewise, it is a condition of the latter that objects themselves exhibit an order that "corresponds," as something objective, to mere associations. These are, of course, significant conclusions, although, at this stage in the argument, the second of them emerges prematurely. In particular, the "corresponding" order in question in the second conclusion is just the order of nature itself—regarded as a correlate of the *conceptualization* of nature (which Kant has, of course, not yet argued to be necessary).

The second level presupposes a more specific notion of the role of imaginative association. More precisely, it rests on a notion of the special *sort* of association that is (or will be eventually) required to play a role in the conceptualization of experience.[7] What the second level of reasoning adds is this: that any imaginative associations that are to be *relevant* to the formation of concepts must satisfy an additional condition, beyond their merely (causally) grounded *connection* with intuitions and conceptions, on the one hand, and with a real order of nature, on the other, and beyond the mere (logical) fact that associations are, in general, necessary for conception. What is needed, of coure, is that specific associations actually become *ingredient* in the intuitions to which they are "connected." So long as they are not, then they are not in a position to serve as material for the formation of any concepts.

The crux of Kant's argument may then be seen as lying in the conclusion that he draws from these reflections. What it amounts to, as I have already suggested, is this: that whatever sort of *world* may be correlative with the understanding's grasp of things, hence with whatever "unity of consciousness" will eventually be in question, must be a world that is perceivable in the first place precisely through a manifold of imaginative associations. To put the point in other words, the very "order of nature" must be a *perceptible aspect* of the world of appearances. This must be so, according to the proposed reasoning, simply because appearances themselves—at least *qua* candidates for conceptualization—need to be apprehended *through* associations in a way that is analogous to their apprehension through mere "sensations" in the first place. This of course goes well beyond the conclusion that associations are necessary for the formation of concepts, and that they must in turn be causally connected with the order of nature represented by means of those concepts.

Kant's distinction between the objective and the empirical "grounds" of association, as well as his notion of "affinity," might now be interpreted in accordance
with this reading. The empirical ground of association is simply whatever causal
relations in fact happens to *connect* one's associations with a corresponding actual
order of nature. As we have seen, Kant either takes it for granted, at this stage
of the argument, that there must be such a grounding, or else he takes this to
follow from an argument (concerning necessary conditions of conceptualization)
that he could only be anticipating at this point. As for the "objective" ground of
association: it is simply a non-causal—but equally non-*logical*—relation of intentional *correlation*. In particular, it is the relation of intentional correlation that
"connects" the order of associations, to the extent that they are actually ingredient
in perceptions themselves, with the order of nature apprehended *through* those
perceptions. The "affinity" of appearances, finally, may be regarded as the corresponding intentional correlate. That is, it may be regarded as what corresponds,
in appearances, *to* the associations through which those appearances are apprehended. (In the next section, we shall need to distinguish several notions of
affinity.)

Apart from whatever more general help this analysis may offer, in an analysis
of the arguments in question, it may also help with an odd turn of phrase at A100
(although it is one altered by Kemp Smith in translation). There Kant claims, as
we saw, that the objective basis for association must lie among appearances themselves, in such a way that "in the manifold *of their representations* a coexistence
or sequence takes place in conformity" with rules. Now were Kant merely arguing
that the imaginative representation of regularities among appearances must be in
some way based upon regularities detectable in appearances themselves, then
why would he immediately blur the very *distinction* in question (namely, between
the realms of imaginative representation, as such, and of appearances thereby
represented) by substituting for a reference to the order inherent in the latter, a
reference to the order inherent in our representations *of* the latter? What Kant
actually says would seem more easily to fit our own reflections. After all, what
we in the first place want to distinguish from the level of (mere) imaginative association is itself just a special *way* of associating, hence indeed a kind of "representation": the kind that is internal to sensory intuitions. Only from here, as its
intentional correlate, do we finally arrive, in the argument in question, at the actually perceptible order of appearances themselves.

This reading requires that we consider Kant's notion of the "manifold" of appearances, and of intuitions, along the lines that I suggested in the preceding
chapter. In the present context, for example, it may seem that the primary distinction is that between associations as such and regularities detectable among a manifold of appearances and intuitions. But if by empirical imagination Kant means
the mere ability to "bring to mind" a manifold of items associated with a given
appearance, then there is another distinction to consider. For we still need to
distinguish that general ability from the more specific capacity for apprehending appearances that, in an important sense, "contain" a manifold of additional
appearances from the start, that is, as a correlate of the anticipations and re-

tentions in their apprehension. In this case, we would not be dealing with a manifold of distinct appearances or intuitions, but rather with a manifold in any *particular* one.

Kant himself emphasizes, in both the earlier and the later presentation, that all appearances do contain a manifold. But he may be thought to be dealing only with what I have called the more "immediate" sort of imaginative association, that is, with anticipation and retention of what is immediately upcoming or receding. It may be easier to suppose that this is so in the earlier passage. There Kant speaks of the manifold within any single intuition in connection with the "synthesis of apprehension." He does not explicitly attribute it to imagination, but to intuition itself, and he reserves the treatment of "reproduction" for a separately numbered section. Though he then reintroduces the more immediate kind of anticipation and retention, and concedes that it, too, involves reproduction, he does not appear to suggest that, like the more immediate kind, what we more usually regard as associative reproduction involves a manifold *in* any given intuition, not merely relations among distinct ones.

In this respect, the later treatment seems different. Kant begins, at A120, by observing that "every [single] appearance contains a manifold," and by attributing to the imagination that special sort of apprehension that is involved in its incorporation into a single image *(Bild)*.[8] He also (A121) indicates that this requires the reproduction of bygone perceptions (just as it presumably requires the anticipation of others). His language may suggest, at this point, concern with the case of merely immediate anticipation and retention. One might then expect him to do two things: to introduce the other sort of anticipation and retention as well, and to indicate that, corresponding to the latter, we represent not only "images," but the very world of appearances as itself objectively ordered. What may at first seem amazing is that Kant instead claims that whatever it is he has already introduced *already* supports that notion. This can only indicate that, at least with respect to the prospect of conceptualizing appearances, even apparently external associations must be as internal to the appearances in question, or at least to their apprehension, as the parts of an image to the image itself, or the parts of an ongoing sequence to that sequence.

The point might also be seen in a later passage, on which I commented earlier. Kemp Smith translates it this way:

> The unity of apperception is thus the transcendental ground of the necessary conformity to law of all appearances in one experience. This same unity of apperception in respect to a manifold of representations (*determining it out of a unity*) acts as the rule, and the faculty of these rules is the understanding. (A127; emphasis added)

We are, of course, not concerned here with the notion of a rule as such. But consider the emphasized passage. As noted earlier, what the original says is that the unity of apperception, in respect to a manifold of representations (*in Ansehung eines Mannigfaltigen von Vorstellungen*), involves, or even in some sense is, the capacity *es nämlich aus einer einzigen zu bestimmen*: "out of" a *single* representation.

The proposed reading may also make sense of a turn of phrase in the argument at A100-101. There Kant says, again, that if cinnabar did not behave in a sufficiently regular way, then the imagination would lack the "opportunity when representing red *colour* to bring to mind heavy *cinnabar*" (emphases added). One might have supposed his point to be more adequately served by observing that imagination would lack the opportunity, when perceiving a certain color—that is, a particular "appearance"—to bring to mind other *appearances*. Indeed, in what way does mere imagination, at least of the relatively primitive sort that must concern us at this point, even manage to bring objects to mind at all, as opposed to a manifold of possible appearances of objects, that is, a manifold that only the understanding may ultimately succeed in *taking* as objects (or at least as the appearances of them)? But suppose that, in Kant's view, conceptualizing appearances as objects (for example, conceptualizing intuitively apprehended colors as cinnabar) essentially involves the elevation, to properly conceptual level, of a manifold of imaginative associations that are themselves internal to the very *apprehension* of those appearances. In that case, Kant could insist, the regular behavior of cinnabar must indeed have been discoverable in the color of cinnabar itself, that is, in any intuited patch of color that is conceptualizable as cinnabar. This would no longer be the obvious, and in any case merely empirical, claim that neither imaginative associations nor empirical concepts could develop in the first place, apart from regularities among appearances.

Finally, this reading allows us to account for Kant's claim that his argument rests on conceding that appearances "are not things in themselves, but are the mere play of our representations, and in the end reduce to determinations of inner sense" (A101). According to the account that I have proposed, the affinity of appearances is, at least as we are so far concerned with it, the intentional correlate of our apprehension of appearances, insofar as the latter contains a manifold of imaginative anticipations and retentions. But this notion was itself derived from an analysis of the apprehension of appearances themselves. Thus with respect at least to this level of reflection, appearances must be regarded precisely as intentional correlates of the apprehension of them. On another level, obviously, appearances will need to be regarded as more than this. The latter occurs when we begin to consider that some appearances, although apprehended, might not be anything real. Of course, Kant thinks he can argue, although has not yet done so, that it is necessary for experience that, at least in general, one take the things that appear in experience to be real, and to have real features that occasionally conflict with what they appear to have. The distinction in question will in any case concern us in the next section.

III. Kinds of Affinity

At A113-4, Kant distinguishes between merely empirical and transcendental affinity. In the same passage, at A113, he also refers to affinity in general—thus apparently including the empirical—as "the ground of the possibility of the association of the manifold, *so far as it lies in the object*" (emphasis added). From this it of course follows that even merely empirical affinity is something "objective," or at least something that "lies in the object." It is therefore not, for example, to be equated with association itself. Neither, presumably, is it to be equated with the merely empirical *ground* of association. The latter seems to involve a purely causal notion, and Kant does not call it "affinity" at all. At A121, as we have seen, he explicitly distinguishes it from affinity. In any case, we now appear to face a distinction between two sorts of "affinitative" grounds of association, both of them "in the object":

> The ground of the possibility of the association of the manifold, so far as it lies in the object, is named the *affinity* of the manifold. I therefore ask, how are we to make comprehensible to ourselves the thoroughgoing affinity of appearances (through which they stand, and *must* stand, under unchanging laws)?
>
> On my principles it is easily explicable. All possible appearances, as representations, belong to the totality of a possible self-consciousness. . . . The representation of a universal condition according to which a certain manifold can be posited in uniform fashion is called a *rule*, and, when it *must* be so posited, a *law*. Thus all appearances stand in thoroughgoing connection according to necessary laws, and therefore in a transcendental affinity, of which the empirical is a mere consequence. (A113-4)

Kant is, of course, ultimately concerned with the possibility of representing a real order of nature. As should be equally clear, any such representation needs to be grounded in something more than affinity as I have so far characterized that notion. At the same time, we might appreciate why Kant puts the distinction precisely in terms of distinction between two *kinds* of "affinity." According to the account proposed, a representation of affinity in objects, in the full-blown sense that must ultimately be in question, requires nothing more than a kind of *enrichment* of the affinity in appearances so far considered, that is, of the affinity that is a mere intentional correlate of imaginative association.

Representation of an order of nature obviously requires more than the ingredience of imaginative associations in intuition. It requires an intellectual capacity that imagination cannot provide, namely, a capacity for incorporating associations into distinct empirical *concepts*. Only once this has been accomplished is the correlate of imaginative apprehension, with its order of what might so far be considered mere "regularities," elevated to the status of that *lawful* order that is the correlate of a truly intellectual mode of representation. We have so far abstracted from this level of representation. As we have seen, Kant himself did not always keep the levels distinct in his own thinking. But the distinction may help in the interpretation of some additional passages.

It may, for example, be precisely a transition between these two sorts of "order"—from a realm of imaginatively apprehended regularities to one of intellectually represented *law*—that Kant has in mind in the following formulation:

> That the affinity of appearances, and with it [*mit ihr*] association, and through this in turn [*durch diese endlich*] reproduction according to laws [*nach Gesetzen*], and so [*folglich*] experience itself, should only be possible by means of this transcendental function of imagination, is indeed strange, but is none the less an obvious consequence of the preceding argument. For without this transcendental function no concepts of objects would come together into an experience. (A123)

Kant proceeds to note that something still needs to be "added to pure imagination," namely, pure apperception, "in order to render its function intellectual" (A124). Apart from the latter, apprehension of the affinity in question—though it involves the apprehension of something *internal to appearances themselves* (which are thereby represented as *an sich assoziabel*), and therefore involves the apprehension of something that is in its own way "objective" (A122)—still falls short of the apprehension of a truly law-governed realm, and therefore of a *truly* "objective" realm.

We may also note that Kant seems to regard affinity in this passage as somehow more intimately *one* with association itself (*mit ihr*) than with the corresponding order of nature (*durch diese endlich*). In this case, the affinity in question must be the imaginative affinity that I discussed in the preceding section. I have argued that there is an important sense in which it constitutes an "order of nature," even though there is another sense in which it does not. How, in any case, does it relate both to "transcendental affinity" and to "empirical affinity"? Transcendental affinity, I suggest, is just the order of nature considered precisely *as* an order of nature, hence, in Kant's view, considered as a correlate of the understanding's conceptualization of appearances. *Empirical affinity is that same order.* But it is that order considered as the correlate of mere "apprehension," that is, considered as a correlate of intuition, insofar as the latter is not purely conceptual, but has ingredient in itself a set of imaginative anticipations and retentions suitable *for* the understanding's conceptualization of appearances in the first place.

I have already tried to make it clear how both of these sorts, or aspects, of affinity—both that of the fully objective order of nature and that of "nature" as a correlate of imaginative apprehension—do indeed involve an order that is represented "in objects." The only remaining puzzle is to make sense of the claim that the latter is a "consequence" of the former (A114). But that, I think, can now be simply put. The point is that the only *reason* for expecting imaginative associations ever in fact to become *ingredient* in intuitions themselves, not to remain merely mechanically or externally "associated" with them—and thus the only reason for ever considering a merely empirical affinity in the first place—is precisely in *order* that intuitions might be subject to conceptualization, and so precisely in order that a genuinely transcendental affinity might ultimately be in question. As Kant himself puts it, though productive imagination needs to have something "added" to it, in order to render its function intellectual, it nevertheless—or rather just for that reason—appears to *aim* at the very possibility of having that something added (*zu ihrer Absicht hat* [A123-4]; imagination considered insofar as it *bloss auf die ursprünglich synthetische Einheit . . . geht* [B151]).

Paton adopts a very different approach to the claim that the empirical is a "consequence" of transcendental affinity. Transcendental affinity, in his view, is the general lawfulness of nature, insofar as it is demanded by the categories. By contrast with transcendental affinity, empirical affinity is the particular *instance* of this lawfulness, as it is in fact to be found in nature. The former is a consequence of the latter, simply in that it is a particular instance of the latter.[9] However, this suggestion seems odd. It seems odd in view of Kant's insistence that, while empirical laws are "special determinations" of pure laws of the understanding, they are precisely not "derivable from them" (A127; cf. B165). If they are not "derivable" from them, it seems odd to say they are "consequences" of them.

In my view, transcendental affinity is, in a sense, empirical affinity as well. It is simply the latter considered as elevated, and necessarily so, to a truly intellectual level. This proposal at least has the advantage of explaining Kant's tendency to fail to distinguish the two. Put differently, it helps to explain his tendency to conflate the two levels of reflection that I distinguished in my earlier analysis of his arguments. Once again: Compatible with this kind of "identification" of the two affinities in question, empirical affinity may said to be a "consequence" of transcendental affinity, simply in that the only possible *ground* for associations ever finding their way into intuitions in the first place, as opposed to remaining merely externally attached to (or "associated" with) them, is precisely in order to render transcendental affinity *possible*, that is, to render possible a conceptually accessible order of nature.

With regard to the question of "grounding," in any case, and in view of the difference between the present approach and the one that Paton proposes, it is not surprising that Paton is led, but that we need not be, to see the only possible reason or ground that Kant himself might be likely to offer, as a reason or ground for empirical affinity, as a reason or ground that arises from an independent order of *things in themselves*.[10] If something like this is indeed the ultimate "ground" of empirical affinity, then why didn't Kant say that empirical affinity is a consequence of *it*, instead of saying that it is a consequence of transcendental affinity? In fact, as Paton himself understands the notion, empirical affinity ought not to *be* any more a consequence of transcendental affinity than it is of an independent order of things in themselves.

Apart from the discussion of affinity in the first-edition Deduction, Kant also uses the term in different ways in other contexts. Though there is presumably a close connection among these notions, it is important to be clear how they differ. This is especially so in view of their inevitable relevance to an assessment of the first *Critique* in relation to the overall development of Kant's thought. Apart from our explicit concern with the notion of affinity, it will therefore be useful to comment briefly on some of the more general issues raised by the distinction between "reflective judgment," as it is treated in the third *Critique*, and the general problem of "understanding," as Kant had already analyzed it.

Two of the additional passages that speak of "affinity" occur in connection with Kant's treatment of the Ideas of Reason in the Transcendental Dialectic (A572/B600, A657/B685ff). Another of them occurs in the "First Introduction" to the *Critique of Judgment*. (By contrast with all three of these passages, the A766/B794 discussion of Hume's confusion between affinity and association enters directly into the ambit of the argument in the Deduction as we have already examined it.)[11] In the "First Introduction," the connection with the question of "purposiveness" in nature is prominent. The latter is apparently something that, for better or worse, was neglected in the analysis of the concept of nature in the first *Critique*. In the passages from the Dialectic, a similar point is at issue. The passages suggest a question concerning the extent to which Kant's analysis of the faculty of understanding in the Deduction, and of its allegedly "constitutive" demands upon any experience of nature, might stand in need of correction or augmentation in terms of an autonomously "regulative" faculty of reason.

It is often claimed that, in moving from the level of mere understanding to that of transcendental reason, and then on to the principle of autonomous "judgment" in the third *Critique*, Kant achieves successively more adequate points of view. Gradually, it may seem, he overcomes a narrow favoritism, on behalf of the mere understanding, that typified the first *Critique*. Whatever one's attitude toward this claim, and apart from the precise use of the terms in various contexts,[12] it does seem clear that there is some important connection between the third *Critique*'s treatment of the "purposiveness" of nature, with respect to our efforts to comprehend it, and the first *Critique*'s treatment of the objective "affinity" of appearances. But it is important to be clear what the connection really is. It does not, so far as I can see, indicate any need on Kant's part to withdraw from the position elaborated in the Deduction.

While it seems to me a bit overstated to claim that the concept of transcendental purposiveness is already present under the title of "transcendental affinity" in the Deduction,[13] in a certain sense we can concede that it is so. But in an important respect, the ground of comparison has nothing to do with reflective judgment at all. It concerns an issue that arises on a level below that of judgment proper. With regard to the connection between "purposiveness" and affinity, as we have been considering the latter, the most important comparison seems to me in fact to lie only in a very specific aspect of the third *Critique*. What we need to attend to is Kant's treatment of *aesthetic* judgment. To see the point of comparison, however, we also need to appreciate the sense in which the latter is not a kind of "judgment" at all for Kant—at least in the usual sense of that term. It is rather a unique kind of intuition. Finally, and just for that reason, we need to appreciate the extent to which the originally suggested allusion to Kant's comments on "affinity" in the Dialectic are misleading.

There is no doubt a connection between the regulative demands of reason, as they are treated in the Dialectic, and the transcendental principle of (reflective) judgment in the third *Critique*. But the point is that our awareness of the former is, as such, of a purely rational kind. It is the awareness of a purely rational demand. It is not a matter of perception or intuition. Indeed, even our awareness of the purposiveness of nature, as it is explained in the third *Critique*, is only in one special *case* a matter for actual perception. It is so only in the special case of a truly *aesthetic* grasp of the purposiveness of nature.[14] On the other hand, I do not, of course, claim that the apprehension of affinity, as it functions in the Deduction, is itself a form of aesthetic apprehension. The latter is essentially mediated by a feeling of pleasure or displeasure. No such mediation is in question in regard to the apprehension of affinity in the Transcendental Deduction. Despite this difference, we can appreciate the sense in which the issues are connected by reflecting more deeply on the nature of aesthetic apprehension.

It is tempting to regard aesthetic apprehension, as Kant conceives it, as a complex involving three factors. First of all, Kant speaks of a special relationship that obtains, at least on certain occasions, between the faculties of imagination and understanding. I shall take the liberty of putting the point in terms of the notions that I have so far developed in this chapter. In these terms, the relationship concerns the suitability of the former as provider of "material" for eventual formation into concepts by the latter. This is not a relationship that obtains in virtue of the latter's actual formation of a concept. An aesthetic judgment, Kant says, is *nicht auf Begriffe gegründet*.[15] The relationship in question is one that obtains simply in virtue of the fact that the corresponding material is *suitable* for the formation of a concept. Kant refers to this suitability as an "agreement" (*Angemessenheit, Einstimmung, Proportion, Übereinstimmung, Zusammenstimmung*) or "harmony" between the faculties of imagination and understanding.[16] Significantly, he also refers to that suitability in terms of a corresponding harmony between the harmony of the faculties themselves and apprehended *objects*.[17]

The harmony or suitability in question is only the first of the three elements involved in any instance of aesthetic apprehension. The second is a feeling of pleasure of some kind. (I ignore the case of disharmony, hence of a corresponding displeasure.) More specifically, the pleasure is of a kind that Kant seems to describe as having been produced (*bewirkt, gewirkt, zur Folge haben*) precisely *by* the relevant harmony of the cognitive faculties.[18] Finally, there is, it seems, the element of "judgment" proper. On one reading of Kant, it is through the specific office of this third element that the others in an aesthetic judgment become its elements in the first place: the aesthetic judgment is a judgment *about* a certain feeling of pleasure, namely, a judgment to the effect that a certain feeling of pleasure has been produced by nothing other than the harmonious working of the appropriate cognitive faculties.

On this reading, we cannot appreciate the connection between aesthetic apprehension and the apprehension of affinity. The latter, I have argued, is the apprehension of an order of things through the ingredience, in intuitions themselves, of an imaginative material that is suitable for the "application" of empirical concepts to the objects of intuitions. That same order, we have seen, can also be represented conceptually. But the point of the doctrine of affinity, as Kant treats it in the Transcendental Deduction, is to make clear that a prior (though not necessarily temporally prior) condition for the conceptual representation of any order in nature is a special kind of preconceptual representation of that same order. Clearly, this does not mean that the apprehension of affinity is simply to be equated with that of aesthetic apprehension. What is missing, at the very least, is the demand that, in aesthetic judgment, the order in question be apprehended with the right sort of pleasure. Despite that difference, we should be able to notice an important similarity.

Like properly aesthetic apprehension, the apprehension of the affinity of appearances can be regarded in two ways. It can be regarded as an apprehension of two different kinds of harmony or fittingness. First of all, as the apprehension of an order in nature, the apprehension in question must involve the awareness of some kind of "affinity," or of some kind of fittingness, that the very elements of nature have *for each other*. But it might also be said to involve the awareness of a very different kind of affinity. In apprehending any such affinity among objects of perception, one may also be said to apprehend an affinity that their internally perceptible order has for *us*. In a sense, after all, what one is apprehending is simply an intentional correlate of imagination. That is to say, what one is apprehending is a correlate of the actual ingredience in one's own *intuition* of one's own imagination, namely, its ingredience in that special mode that is demanded, but not sufficient, for the "application" of concepts to intuitions in the first place. Thus there is a sense in which the apprehension of the order of nature in question (or at least the apprehension of what is in principle conceptualizable *as* an order of nature) is also the apprehension of a harmony or fittingness, not only of the things that are encompassed within nature's own bounds, but of the order of nature itself, with respect to the working of one's own cognitive faculties. In that sense, the apprehension of the affinity of appearances is as much an apprehension of a purposiveness in nature as truly aesthetic apprehension. The only difference would be that the purposiveness in question is not apprehended with that special pleasure that is characteristic of aesthetic apprehension.

This parallel would fail in the view of aesthetic judgment that I have so far sketched. In that view, aesthetic "apprehension" might amount to two different things, but in neither case would it be comparable to the apprehension of affinity as I have presented it. First of all, aesthetic apprehension might simply be the experience of a pleasurable sensation that is in fact caused by the harmonious interplay of one's cognitive faculties in the apprehension of appearances. In that case, we would have two elements in relation: an apprehension of appearances and a feeling of pleasure, caused in a certain way. But there would be no sense in which one has apprehended, precisely *through* that pleasure, a harmonious or purposive aspect of appearances themselves. In a sense, perhaps, one may be said to have apprehended, "through" that pleasure, a certain kind of purposiveness. At least, one will have gotten a feeling that is *caused* by the purposive interplay of one's own faculties. But the fact would remain that the object of that feeling —if we may speak of an "object" in a case that is constituted by purely causal relations—is not an aspect of appearances. It is just something internal to oneself. This seems to run counter to Kant's own view of aesthetic apprehension.[19]

The second alternative fares no better. According to the approach in question, the second thing that we might mean by aesthetic apprehension is just aesthetic "judgment" proper. But aesthetic judgment would then be importantly distinct from the element of apprehension "with pleasure." The latter is just a feeling of pleasure *caused* in a certain way. The former is a judgment to the effect that the feeling is in fact so caused. No such judgment (being purely intellectual) —any more than the feeling itself (regarded as mere effect)—is comparable to a genuine apprehension of some order in the world of appearances. That is why, according to the approach in question, aesthetic apprehension would not be comparable to the apprehension of affinity as I have construed it. So far as I understand it, it is also why that approach is inadequate to Kant's own view of aesthetic apprehension.

I have argued in detail elsewhere against this approach to Kant's account of aesthetic judgment.[20] I will indicate the main considerations here, and then draw the connection with our problem concerning affinity. The first consideration is that Kant aims at a number of identifications of elements that the account in question is constrained to regard as distinct. First of all, Kant persistently tends to speak as if an aesthetic judgment is not at all distinct from the feeling of pleasure that, according to the account in question, that judgment is supposedly about. More specifically, though it may seem oddly, Kant appears to regard feelings of aesthetic pleasure as if they themselves served as the very *predicates* of aesthetic judgments.[21] That is the first point. The second point is that Kant seems to speak, not simply of an aesthetic pleasure as if it were itself the predicate through which an object of aesthetic appreciation is apprehended in the first place, but also as if that pleasure were not distinct from the very harmony of the faculties that is supposed, according to the account I am criticizing, to be its cause.[22]

It is not absurd to suppose that cognitive activity and the establishment of appropriate relations among cognitive factors are not merely capable of generating pleasurable sensations, but *are* themselves pleasurable "sensations," at least on certain occasions. Kant himself describes pleasure in general (or at least any pleasure that one takes in some representation) in a way that seems to regard it as indistinguishable from the representation in which that pleasure is taken:

> Pleasure is a state of the mind in which a representation is in harmony with itself as ground [*mit sich selbst zusammenstimmt als Grund*], either in order merely to maintain that ground [*diesen bloss selbst zu erhalten*] (because the state of mutually supporting mental powers in a representation maintains itself), or in order to produce its object. In the first case, the judgment regarding the given representation is an aesthetic judgment of reflection.[23]

The approach that I am proposing is suited to recognize this point as well as the others. This is because it is based on an analogy between the role that sensations play in intuitions and the role of imagination, at least insofar as the latter is relevant to (hence in "harmony" with) the faculty of understanding, hence relevant to the possibility of intuitions being subject to conceptualization in the first place. This is not to say that, according to my approach, the ingredience of imaginative material in an intuition, in a way that is favorable to the eventual conceptualization of the latter, is *ipso facto* a pleasure of any sort. It is at most to say that the ingredience of imaginative material in an intuition is the sort of thing that *could* be a pleasure on some occasion. In general, and quite apart from the case of specifically aesthetic pleasure, the sensations ingredient in an intuition might or might not be pleasurable. But when they are, there is no reason to suppose that their pleasurable feeling is, strictly speaking, a distinct state from those very sensations themselves. It simply *is* those sensations, now become pleasures. The same, we must now conclude, goes for the purely imaginative material in an intuition.

I have already argued for important analogies between the imaginative material in an intuition and what one is more usually inclined to regard as the "sensations" in them. I now suggest that we continue to take the analogy seriously. I suggest that we suppose that, at least on certain occasions, the imaginative material in an intuition is so well suited to the application of a concept to that intuition—quite apart from the question as to what concepts, if any, are in fact applied to it—that the material in question becomes an actual *pleasure* in the intuition. When it does, then it comes to serve as a kind of "predicate" in intuition. In the preceding section

I argued, in effect, that the ingredience of mere imaginative material in an intuition already serves as a kind of (pre-conceptual) "predicate" in its own right. It does so simply in the sense that the appearances that are apprehended *through* that material are necessarily apprehended as characterized in a certain way; they are necessarily apprehended as part of an order of nature (or of what is in principle conceptualizable as nature). That aesthetic pleasures are able to function as predicates in intuition may thus now be seen as no more than an extension of Kant's account of affinity in the Deduction.

Now let us return to the more general problem of the relationship between the first and the third *Critique*. This concerns us, beyond the specific problem of aesthetic judgment, with the general problem of the relation between "reflective" judgment, in the third *Critique*, and the kind of purely "determining" judgment in regard to which the analysis of judgment was pursued in the Deduction of the first. As I have already indicated, it should not be surprising to find a connection, quite apart from the problem of aesthetic judgment, between Kant's concern with affinity in the first and with the problem of reflective judgment in the third *Critique*. For the latter is simply the problem of "getting" from intuitions, and whatever they contain, to the actual formation of empirical concepts applicable to those intuitions. That, it seems, was nothing other than the problem of the Transcendental Deduction as well. But it is important to appreciate the extent to which, though related, the problems confronted in the two works are also distinct.

The transcendental principle of reflective judgment concerns the guidelines that need to be followed in the formation of concepts that are able to bear on the actual course of experience as we find it. In this regard, Kant argues that we need to postulate a systematic whole, within which the various laws of nature will form, among themselves, an intelligible system.[24] It appears to be precisely the intelligible character of this holistic system that Kant then refers to, in the "First Introduction" to the *Critique of Judgment*, as the "affinity of particular laws under more general ones."[25] Now in the first *Critique*, Kant had of course argued that there need to be laws of nature, and that we must regard every single event as occurring in accordance with those laws, even if we have no idea as to what they actually are. In addition to this, the idea of systematic interrelation also arose in the first *Critique*. But it seems primarily to have been the idea of a systematic interrelation of the various *parts* of nature, as it is treated in the Transcendental Dialectic of that work. What is new, or at least more prominent, in the third *Critique* is the idea of a systematic interrelation of the various laws of nature themselves.[26] In particular, Kant now seems to be maintaining that a necessary condition for any experience of nature at all—that is, a condition that is every bit as necessary as the causal principle of the first *Critique*—is the condition that nature be represented, not simply as conforming to laws, but also as conforming to whatever more systematic demands we need to make in endeavoring to discover what those laws really are.

This new demand may seem not merely to enlarge the problematic of the first *Critique*. It may seem to threaten one of its central claims, namely, that the faculty of understanding is alone the source of "constitutive" demands regarding the experience of nature. But to resolve the difficulty, we simply need to distinguish two "constitutive" problems. The problem of the Transcendental Deduction, I have argued, is that of constituting concepts, just as such, out of the sort of material that is independently available, apart from that actual constitution, among the internal ingredients in intuitions themselves. Now we have considered only one side of this problem. We have not been concerned with the particular factors that need to be involved precisely in elevating that sort of material to the status of genuinely conceptual representation. We shall see, in Chapter Six, that Kant regards this question as one that concerns the structure of a particular mode of "consciousness." In virtue of the consciousness in question, one's imaginative anticipations and retentions will be in an appropriate way transformed, or at least appropriately "structured" in consciousness. At least one part of this structuring will entail that they are now to be regarded as anticipations and retentions of certain possible courses of experience as *necessary* courses of experience (relative to sets of antecedent conditions, themselves represented as at least possible). This much, I take it, is already meant to be established in the first *Critique*, on the basis of an analysis of the faculty of understanding as such.

Now this is obviously very closely related to what Kant regards as a necessary function of "reflective judgment" in the third *Critique*. The connection, as I see it, is this. It is that the basic functions of understanding that Kant regards as essential to the constitution of conceptual consciousness as such suffice only to accomplish one part of what is necessary for genuine *knowledge* regarding the objects thereby conceptualized. [27] This is the accomplishment that is reflected in the earlier work's argument that the conceptualization of particular intuitions necessarily involves the *representation* of certain courses of experience as necessary ones (relative to sets of conditions that are anticipated and retained as themselves at least possible). Obviously, whatever "representation" of necessities are sufficient for the conceptualization of an intuition, as such, will not suffice for a genuine assessment of the cognitive value of that act of conceptualization. It could not possibly do so, to the extent that it abstracts from any question as to what the particular laws might *be*, with respect to which represented necessities obtain. Rightly or wrongly (I do not propose to discuss it), it is specifically the latter problem that is held, in the third *Critique*, to require a transcendental principle that had not previously been discovered, and to require holistic considerations so far ignored.

We may concede that what remains, as a problem for "reflective judgment," involves a principle that is as much "constitutively" necessary as that of understanding as such, as considered in the Deduction. But it does not follow that Kant had been mistaken in supposing that the powers of understanding, as considered in the Deduction, were sufficient for the problem there at hand. Whether we say that its powers are "constitutive" or not, it should be clear that the principle of reflective judgment aims at the "constitution" of something in addition to what had been of primary concern earlier. As I have suggested, and despite the impression that Kant himself may give in some formulations, we can only presume that the later principle does not aim merely at constituting concepts as such, but rather at constituting instances of concrete empirical knowledge. [28] For the latter, as we have noted, we need to go beyond the mere representation of certain anticipable and retainable courses of experience as necessary. We need, in addition, to arrive at a conception of the particular laws by *virtue* of which those courses of experience may be necessary. This in turn requires more than the imaginative representation, internally to the conceptualization of an appearance in intuition, of further appearances whose intuitions are in their own turn obtainable, and necessarily so, from the given one (or— emphasizing "retention"—from which the given one was itself obtainable). In addition, it is arguable, it requires a more or less specific conceptualization of those *further* appearances as objects in relation to the given one. If it did not involve the conceptualization of additional objects, as objects in relation to the given one, and not merely the imaginative representation of further "appearances," then the original act of conceptualization could not have contained any real *understanding* of whatever sort of "necessity" might in fact have been represented in the first place. This in turn, it is arguable, involves holistic considerations that were ignored in the first *Critique*.

Whether or not Kant was justified in demanding a transcendental supplement to the work of understanding to account for them, these considerations may at least help us get clear concerning the place of the systematic and holistic elements introduced both in the Transcendental Dialectic and in the *Critique of Judgment*. They should make it clear why we should not have expected to find that supplement earlier, and why its absence indicates no defect in Kant's procedure. Certainly, we can see why Kant should feel that the problems involved in any attempt at achieving a conceptual representation of the whole of nature, at least in terms of the representation of a system of natural laws, are problems that arise only in regard to the problem of knowledge as such. The first *Critique* was not unconcerned with that problem. But it is clear that it did not attempt to uncover more than certain of the necessary conditions of knowledge. In particular, it was primarily concerned to uncover, in the Transcendental Deduction, only the conditions sufficient for the conceptualization of intuitions. To put the point another way, the Deduction was concerned only with the nature of a *concept*, and with the general concept of a concept's "application" to intuition. The problem of reflective judgment arises in the context of a different problem.

To sum up: We have, in effect, discovered that the notion of "reflective judgment" is ambiguous. In one sense, it is already a notion that was in question in the first *Critique*, but not under that title. (It was in question precisely in the problem of "getting" from the mere material for the formation of concepts to their actual formation.) In another sense, it raises a problem neglected in the first *Critique*, but it offers a solution that is in no way incompatible with the theory presented earlier. In any case, looking at the matter in the terms that I have been proposing in this chapter, we may conclude that the transcendental principle of reflective judgment in no way indicates a diminishment of the uniquely "constitutive" powers of understanding. We should also be clear that what Kant specifically *calls* the lawful "affinity" of nature, in the "First Introduction" to the third *Critique*, is not quite the same thing as the kind of "affinity" already considered in the Transcendental Deduction. The latter involves an "order of nature" whose representability rests on the faculty of imagination, and it is at most a necessary condition of the conceptualization of objects. The former, though resting on the latter, involves a representation of a purely conceptual sort. For this reason, finally, while Kant's additional comments on affinity in the Dialectic of Pure Reason, and even his treatment of the Ideas of Reason generally, may well be inseparable from his later development of the problem of reflective judgment, they too are oriented toward a problem that is legitimately distinguishable from the problem that concerns us.

Chapter 5

The Second-Edition Deduction

I. Introduction

SO FAR our attention has been mainly directed toward the first-edition Deduction. In Chapter Three, I observed that the later version, perhaps even more than the first, seems clear in regarding the primary notion of conceptual "synthesis" as involving a "manifold of representations" that are in some way ingredient in intuitions themselves. It seems clear, in other words, that we are not there concerned with a synthesis of representations that are merely externally connectible, by means of concepts, to *additional* representations. (As we shall see more clearly later, we are not, for example, merely concerned with representations that are connectible in virtue of being "ascribable" to a common subject.) Appropriately construed, the point can be used to support the reading of Kant that I have proposed. But I have yet to defend it in terms specific to the second-edition Deduction.

Whether or not, as often suggested, the second edition departs from the first, it seems plainly to attribute transcendental synthesis to the faculty of intellect alone. Thus it appears to degrade reproduction, and imaginative association, to contingent psychological factors. When it is regarded transcendentally, or "productively," imaginative syntheses seem to be nothing other than instances of the understanding itself at work upon a manifold of intuition. This provides an obvious challenge for our reading of the Deduction.

The present chapter will not exhaust our consideration of the issues raised in the second-edition Deduction. In the next, I focus on the problem of synthesis in both versions of the Deduction, with specific attention to the notions of consciousness, unity of consciousness, and self-consciousness. For the present, we may speak more generally of synthesis and of unity of synthesis without considering these other notions in detail. This may seem unwise, since these notions are obviously crucial to the Deduction. In particular, one is often inclined to formulate the central problem of the Deduction in terms of a problem concerning the "ascribability" of manifolds of states of consciousness to subjects. To a certain extent, I do not disagree with this. I agree that Kant's central argument for the necessity of applying categories to objects is that applying them is necessary for self-consciousness, in particular for consciousness of oneself as an individual to whom representations are "ascribable." I shall argue later, however, that most readings go wrong in their neglect of synthesis as an irreducible form of one's consciousness of *appearances themselves*—that is, of *objects*.[1]

In the second section of this chapter, I try to show that the issue is complicated by some ambiguities that must have been difficult for Kant himself to resolve. One of them bears on a shift made possible by a notion that I have taken to be central to Kant's entire enterprise, namely, by the notion that objects of possible cognition, *qua* objects of *possible* cognition, may always be considered as intentional correlates of the apprehension of them. Another ambiguity may account more specifically for the impression that, at least in the second edition, conceptual "synthesis" involves purely intellectual functions. The ambiguity that accounts for the impression will be the same ambiguity that, as we saw in Chapter Three, accounts for Kant's hesitation as to whether concepts are "rules" or merely embody or contain rules.

I postpone, until the fourth section, a consideration of the overall structure of Kant's argument in the Deduction, in particular its division into two stages. I then suggest that the relationship between stages be read as involving a transition from synthesis regarded "noetically"—that is, as an operation applied to a manifold of anticipations and retentions, ingredient in intuitions—to synthesis regarded "noematically"—as the intentional *correlate* of such operations. (As we shall see, there is a second, derivative logical inference that might also be intended: from the correlate of the mere apprehension of appearances—taken without regard to any questions of *reality*—to the correlate of that same apprehension, taken as the real world of nature.) Our discussion will also benefit from a reconsideration of Kant's distinction between judgments of "perception" and of "experience" in the *Prolegomena*. Far from rejecting the distinction in the Deduction, it is precisely what is needed, in that terminology or another, for a grasp of the latter's structure.

II. The Ambiguity of Synthesis

We have already seen the possibility of two points of view concerning concepts and the syntheses they involve. On one of them, we are concerned with concepts as a kind of "term," already at our disposal, and available for "application" to intuitions. In that case, we can only ask what sort of "synthesis" is involved in that application, insofar as it concerns the relating of a given intuition to others (or, alternatively, insofar as it concerns the relating of one correlative appearance to others). Construed in this way, we are likely to regard synthesis purely intellectually. For we are likely to regard it purely in terms of actually (however explicitly) *conceived* connections among (possible) intuitions or appearances—or at least in terms of connections that one is logically committed to representing conceptually—in any instance of concept-application. In that case, the "transcendental" structures of synthesis might simply be regarded as the most general and necessary *ways* in which one is able to think about things (insofar as one is required to do so in terms of relations among appearances).

The second point of view is very different. It considers how concepts are "possible" in the first place, in a sense that does not merely bear on their logical implications, nor on the logical implications of their application to objects. Instead, it considers what concepts, hence conceptual acts, *are* as such. From this point of view, we may of course continue to focus on what Kant himself regards as purely "intellectual." The distinctively conceptual dimension in any conceptualized intuition is indeed constituted by the "application" to it of a purely intellectual function. The question is how to regard that function. Obviously, we cannot regard it in terms of the application of already available concepts to objects, that is, on the model of predication. I shall argue that we must rather be concerned with the "application" of a special function of *consciousness* that, while not in itself conceptual (at least in any ordinary sense), suffices for the original constitution of a concept in intuition. (Specifically, it must suffice for the constituting of a concept out of a manifold of material to be found *within* the intuition in question.)

It may be misleading to speak of the "application" of anything at all in this case. In any case, however such functions may otherwise be described, they must function by constituting some kind of unity with respect to a manifold of material ingredient in intuitions themselves:

> *Understanding* is, to use general terms, the faculty of *cognitions*. This consists in the determinate relation of given representations to an object; and an *object* is that in the concept of which the manifold of a given intuition [*das Mannigfaltige einer gegebenen Anschauung*] is *united*. (B137)

To be sure, shortly later Kant also says that the relevant problem of unity is one that concerns the "ascribability" of a manifold of distinct representations to a subject:

> This proposition . . . says no more than that all *my* representations in any given intuition [*in ingendeiner gegebenen Anschauung*] must be subject to that condition under which alone I can ascribe them to the identical self as *my* representations, and so can comprehend them as synthetically combined in one apperception through the general expression, '*I think.*' (B138)

But whatever we make of the connection between unifying a manifold in a single intuition, and ascribing distinct intuitions to subjects, the fact remains that the former is depicted, at least in these passages, as an operation with respect to manifolds within single intuitions.

However we provide the details, a number of other passages make the same general point:

> The transcendental unity of apperception is that unity through which all the manifold given in an intuition [*alles in einer Anschauung gegebene Mannigfaltige*] is united into [n.b.] a concept of the object. (B139)
> The manifold given in a sensible intuition [*Das mannigfaltige in einer sinnlichen Anschauung Gegebene*] is necessarily subject to the original synthetic unity of apperception. . . . All the manifold, therefore, so far as it is given in a single empirical intuition [*sofern es in Einer empirischen Anschauung gegeben ist*], is *determined* in respect of one of the logical functions of judgment, through which it is brought to one consciousness. (B143)
> A manifold, contained in an intuition which I call mine [*das in einer Anschauung, die ich die meinige nenne, enthalten ist*], is represented through the synthesis of

understanding as belonging to the *necessary* unity of self-consciousness; and this
is effected by means of the category. (B144)

Of course, all these passages are neutral as to what the basic material *is* that
needs to be combined within single intuitions. In this regard, Kant may seem to
hold a different view from the one that I have proposed. For example, he illustrates the claim "that all the manifold of intuition should be subject to conditions
of the original synthetic unity of apperception" by reference to some kind of manifold contained *in space and time themselves*:

> Space and time, and all their parts, are *intuitions*, and are, therefore, with the mani-
> fold which they contain, singular representations (*vide* the Transcendental Aes-
> thetic). Consequently they are not mere concepts through which one and the same
> consciousness is found to be contained in a number of representations. On the con-
> trary, through them many representations are found to be contained in one repre-
> sentation, and in the consciousness of that representation; and they are thus compos-
> ite. The unity of that consciousness is therefore synthetic and yet is also original.
> The *singularity* of such intuitions is important in the application (*vide* §25). (B136n)

There is a similar passage in a footnote to §26 as well. (It is generally assumed
that Kant meant to refer ahead to this passage, not to §25.) The later section is
the one that is in fact supposed to provide the second of the two "stages" of the
Deduction as a whole. This has led to the supposition that the transition between
the stages is simply a transition from the need for a purely intellectual synthesis
in any instance of cognition as such to the need for the application of such synthesis to perception in particular, in order to generate spatiotemporal unities as *objects* of the latter.[2] How an intellectual synthesis might in fact account for the unity
of intuitively apprehended space and time, as opposed to the unity of space and
time in mere thoughts and judgments[3]—and what sort of "manifold" that synthesis could be applied to, in order to yield such results[4]—remain unanswered questions. In both passages, in any event, Kant seems to focus on synthesis in regard
to the manifold of sub-regions in an intuitively apprehensible region of space or
of time. Other accounts might postulate yet other "material" as well.[5]

One might suppose that *Empfindung* is meant to satisfy this need. It is at least
something sub-intuitional. But it cannot satisfy the need now in question. Its role,
in Kant, is to account for the fact that objects are presented in intuition in irreducibly sensory manners. Other things being equal, it accounts for the fact, for example, that a region of space is seen as filled with a certain color, and is not (whether
correctly or not) merely imagined or thought to be so. But what we are now considering is functions required for the conceptualization of objects. This cannot be
sensation, because we are capable of conceptualizing objects in pure *imagination*.
It cannot be sensation for another reason as well. Sensation cannot account for
the temporal dimension in sensory apprehension. To be sure, sensations belong
to our "inner" condition; to that extent, they are "temporal." But the ingredience
of sensation in an intuition is not what confers a temporal dimension on an *object*
of intuition. Apart from whatever temporal concepts might be in question for the
purpose, it is the temporal *form* of intuition that does that. (Of course, it is essential that the relevant concepts specifically *bear* on that form. But this is accommo-

dated through the role Kant assigns to anticipation and retention in the structure of conception itself.)

Kant indeed suggests that ordinary objects, or at least the "appearances" of them, are somehow formed through the synthesis of an unusual kind of material, unavailable to ordinary awareness. But this may be due to no more than a tendency to shift between the standpoint of cognitive states and the intentional correlates of them. In any event, the proposed account requires nothing more strange than anticipations and retentions as the basic material for synthesis. Of course, these are at most material on the "noetic" side of consciousness. Something needs to "correspond" to them on the noematic side as well. But there is no reason to suppose that, whatever this is, ordinary appearances are *made* out of it, in anything like the sense in which cognitive states might be made out anticipations and retentions. To the extent that we are dealing with mere intentional correlates, the supposition would be nonsense.

Now we may look at the second of the passages to which I earlier referred. It is the footnote to a passage almost identical to the note to B136. Beyond raising the issues on which I have been commenting so far, it might be considered a difficulty for my original reading of the Aesthetic, thus for extending that reading into the Deduction:

> Space, represented as object (as we are required to do in geometry), contains more than mere form of intuition; it also contains *combination* [*Zusammenfassung*] of the manifold, given according to the form of sensibility, into an intuitive representation, so that the form of intuition gives only a manifold, the formal intuition gives unity of representation. In the Aesthetic I have treated this unity as belonging merely to sensibility, simply in order to emphasize that it precedes any concept, although, as a matter of fact, it presupposes a synthesis which does not belong to the senses but through which all concepts of space and time first become possible. For since by its means (in that the understanding determines the sensibility) space and time are first given as intuitions, the unity of this *a priori* intuition belongs to space and time, and not to the concept of the understanding. (B160n)

In the Aesthetic, Kant argued that our ability to apprehend regions of space and time—whether through sensory apprehension of identifiable regions, apprehended as filled with matter, or merely through the imagining of would-be regions—requires a pre-intellectual intuitional "form" in the cognitive states involved. Presumably, the apprehension of such regions amounts to the apprehension of particulars or individuals of a sort. In one sense, it would therefore involve a distinctive "unity" that concepts cannot provide. At the very least, it would do so because it involves the apprehension *of* unities, namely, the apprehension of the particulars in question. But Kant now says that the form of intuition "gives only a manifold." What does this mean? It may seem to imply that the original demand for "intuitional" form could not of itself have been a demand for a special function of "unity." At most, it will have amounted to the demand for an extra-conceptual sensible "context" into which concepts and judgments might first *introduce* any real unity in the first place.

As before, the question would remain as to the nature of the "material" contained in such contexts. Apart from that, it is important to be clear what the passage in fact admits and excludes. In particular, even if Kant is granting that an unorganized manifold is all that intuition has of itself to offer,[6] it is clear that it is neither empirical *concepts* nor any others to which he attributes the eventual responsibility for unity. The responsibility is unambiguously attributed to the faculty of understanding, insofar as the latter is able to "determine" sensibility. But despite this, Kant says, the unity in question is one that "precedes any concept." In addition, Kant says, it "belongs to space and time."

It is not clear what these claims can mean, if the unity in question does not stem from intuition itself. Allison offers a suggestion:

> [T]his cryptic remark can be taken to express the view that the intuited unity of space and time is distinct from the conceptual unity that is imposed upon representations in a judgment. . . . In the case of a judgment the unity belongs to the pure concept of the understanding, whereas in the case of the intuition it belongs to the intuited content.[7]

Presumably, the "intuited content" is an intuitively apprehended space or time. It is obvious that *its* unity is not like the unity in a judgment or a concept. The point should have been too obvious to have needed stating in the first place. To be sure, Kant had devoted a separately numbered argument, in the Aesthetic, to distinguishing the way in which a concept contains representations "under" itself from the way in which an intuition contains representations (B40). But in both cases, I suggest, what Kant is trying to tell us must rather concern the structure, not of "intuitions" in the sense of *objects* of intuition, but of intuitional states as such.

It is obvious that the unity of a spatiotemporal region is different from the unity "in" a concept or a judgment. Even Leibniz—whom one might naturally take as Kant's foil in this case— could grant the point. At most, Leibniz might claim, the unity of a spatiotemporal region is the intentional *correlate* of the unity embodied in a concept or a judgment.[8] What is not obvious is not this, but rather the distinction between structure internal to intuited *objects* and structure internal to intuitional states themselves (insofar as the latter are in fact conceded to have an autonomously functioning structure). Kant plainly states, after all, that the unity in question "belongs to space and time" precisely in order to illustrate his claim that the unity is involved in an *act* by which the understanding "determines the sensibility."

Now, Kant often speaks of the understanding, or of concepts, as "determining" objects or appearances. In that case, he presumably means that those objects or appearances are (at least "problematically") subsumed, in intuition, under particular predicates. But this could not be the sense in which understanding determines *sensibility*. The latter concerns an "effect" of some sort on a subject's internal condition, not merely the intentional *correlate* of such effects with respect to objects. In any event, however the relevant unification is supposed to be effected, the suggestion that it forms intuited *objects* (or even mere "appearances" of objects), out of manifolds of some material, could not help to make any sense of Kant's theory.

It leaves us doubly mystified: as to what the unification in question involves and as to what the manifolds themselves are composed of.

In addition, Kant says that the act of unification is one "through which all concepts of space and time first become possible." So he specifically sees that act, not as accounting (or at least not only, or not directly, as accounting) for the unity of intuited objects or "contents," but rather for the constitution of one's concepts *of* objects. In whatever manner we take "intuited contents" to be generable out of manifolds, it is impossible to suppose anything like that to be relevant to the generation *of concepts themselves*.

There is another difficulty in the passage. Again, as to the claim that "the form of intuition gives only a manifold": we would need to suppose that, as so far explained, Kant must be putting his point in an extremely odd manner. Why should he say that the *form* of intuition gives only a manifold? Why not simply say that intuition itself does so? If his point really is that intuition provides unorganized material for understanding to unify, then why should Kant say that the *form* of intuition is what provides that material?

One might suppose that Kant only means that intuition, by its very *nature*, is what provides the unorganized manifold. But it is surely clear that, throughout the *Critique*, the notion of intuitional "form" plays a weightier role than this. Indeed, in the passage that we are examining, Kant explicitly contrasts the mere form of intuition with full-blown "formal" intuition. It would be an uncharacteristic pun, if by the first he just meant intuition itself. In addition, it is not the case that, in Kant's view, intuition by its very *nature* is what "gives" the appropriate material. If the material is "sensations," the point should be obvious from the start. For there is a purely imaginative kind of intuition, as well as what involves sensations. But even if the relevant material is presumed to be autonomously imaginative, the point would be the same. It is not intuition *as such* that requires the ingredience of such material: the requirement stems from the demand that intuitions be conceptualized. If it is not intuition as such that requires the material to be given, then it is difficult to see why Kant should claim that the very "form" of intuition is what "gives" it.

Perhaps another suggestion is this: We might take Kant to be saying, not that intuition as such "gives" only a manifold, but that *space and time* do so. The understanding is then needed in order to synthesize this manifold. But that is not possible either. Of course, we might always take it as no more than the claim that full-blown cognition presupposes some kind of "synthesis" of spaces and times, and of appearances in space and time. But the question remains why Kant should say that space and time *themselves* are what "give" the items thereby to be synthesized. If anything "gives" the manifold in question, it could hardly be space and time. That would require taking space and time as things existing in themselves. At most, it seems, we should say that they *contain* whatever manifold is in question.

Certainly, this was a point on which Kant had insisted in the Aesthetic: that spaces and times necessarily contain smaller spaces and times. But Kant could not, of course, be saying that the mere containment of spaces and times within larger spaces and times is what provides the understanding with its original material for synthesis. A central doctrine of the Aesthetic is precisely that our original *access* to the parts of space and time is by means of the introduction of "limitations" into the latter (A25/B39). So while space and time necessarily contain a manifold, and while it is a manifold that the understanding will eventually need to synthesize, it makes no sense to suppose that the manifold is one that is originally *given*, as material for such synthesis, simply in virtue of being contained in that very space and time. Any relevant synthesis of the parts of space and time, however necessary it may be, must be the upshot of a more fundamental kind of synthesis.

So we need a very different explanation of Kant's claim that the manifold of intuition is given by the "form" of intuition. The explanation, I suggest, is that Kant wants to emphasize— obviously—the eventual role of the former in acts of conceptualization as such, and that—less obviously—any manifold of material that actually plays such a role in the first place must be supposed to enter *into* intuitions, in a sense that can be formulated only in terms of the notions of matter and form so far presupposed. Kant's suggestion that the "form" of intuition is what "gives" the material in question may simply be a way of saying that, in operating on intuitions, so as actually to conceptualize the latter, understanding cannot operate merely in regard to a manifold of *distinct* intuitions. Nor can it operate merely in regard to a manifold of some other, perhaps sensory or even autonomously imaginative, material. Rather, it must operate on a manifold that is appropriately contained *within* intuitions. That the latter condition is satisfied might well be put by saying that we need to be dealing, not simply with something that is "given in" intuition, but with something that is given through the very *form* of intuition. (It should be equally clear, of course, how the proposal applies to a second claim that we have encountered in this passage, namely, that the material in question is not only given through the "form" of intuition, but is a material "through which concepts of space and time first become possible.")

There is an obvious shift of focus between the Aesthetic and the Analytic. The latter is concerned with the possibility of conceptualization as such. This suffices to account for at least a good part of the apparent "departure" from the Aesthetic. Another factor may also contribute. For the purposes of the Aesthetic, there was no harm in considering the pure "form of intuition" as such as correlative (on the noetic side) with space and time as "objects" in their own right. As we saw in Chapter One, there is a point to such formulations, even if we concede, as Kant does in the present passage, that intellectual functions are *also* needed in order for space and time, and for regions and appearances in them, actually to be *given* as "objects." Apart from what may be verbal quibbles concerning the latter term, the substantive point is the same: whether or not, apart from concepts, intuitions give "objects," conceptual acts are required to operate, not merely on this or that material, nor even on manifolds of specifically imaginative material, in order to generate awareness of objects. They need rather to operate on manifolds of material that are ingredient in the appropriate way in intuitional states.

Whether a state *is* in fact an intuitional state is determined neither by the nature of the material ingredient in it nor by the operations upon it. If the latter are indeed required for a true apprehension of "objects," it remains the case that those operations could never of themselves determine that their target material is at the same time material *through which* an object is to be apprehended in intuition. It is not implausible to suppose that it is the difficulty of these notions, and of the choice of terminology for conveying them—together with the general shift of focus between the Aesthetic and the Analytic—that accounts for Kant's apparent uncertainty as to whether transcendental synthesis is merely a direct application of understanding to intuitions or whether it does not also essentially involve an independently imaginative component.[9]

On this account, there is a sense in which neither "conceptual" syntheses nor "unities" of synthesis are purely intellectual. That is, there is a sense other than the one that is already obvious: that conceptual syntheses or unities of synthesis are always "responses" to, or based on responses to, concrete sensory or imaginative conditions. Depending on what one takes to be the internal structure of "response," concession of the latter may or may not be sufficient. One advantage of the proposed view is that it in any case uncovers an ambiguity in the concession. Accordingly, it can help us to see the ambiguity in the question whether "conceptual" synthesis indeed involves an "imaginative" dimension.[10] Kant, for example, says the following:

> This synthesis of the manifold of sensible intuition, which is possible and necessary *a priori*, may be entitled *figurative* [*figürlich*] (synthesis speciosa). . . . But the figurative synthesis, if it be directed merely to the original synthetic unity of apperception, that is, to the transcendental unity which is thought in the categories, must, in order to be distinguished from the merely intellectual combination [*Verbindung*], be called the *transcendental synthesis of imagination*. . . . But inasmuch as its synthesis is an expression of spontaneity, which is determinative and not, like sense, determinable merely, and which is therefore able to determine sense *a priori* in respect of its form in accordance with the unity of apperception, imagination is to that extent a faculty which determines sensibility *a priori*; and its synthesis of intuitions, conforming as it does to the *categories*, must be the transcendental synthesis of *imagination*. This synthesis is an action [*Wirkung*] of the understanding on the sensibility. (B151-2)

Spontaneity is, of course, officially attributed to the understanding (cf. A51/B75). As a mode of intuition (B151), imagination is apparently not in the sense in question "spontaneous." But in this passage, Kant ascribes imaginative synthesis to a faculty of spontaneity. A page later, he also claims that what "determines" sensibility—as he had already maintained imaginative synthesis does—is always the understanding:

> Thus the understanding, under the title of a *transcendental synthesis of imagination*, performs this act upon the *passive* subject . . . (B153). . . . which is possible only through the consciousness of the determination of the manifold by the transcendental action [*Handlung*] of imagination (synthetic influence of the understanding upon inner sense), which I have entitled figurative synthesis (B154).

Unsurprisingly, Kant draws a conclusion regarding the very capacity for a "synthesis of apprehension." In the first edition, this level of synthesis, or this aspect of synthesis, had been explicitly distinguished both from that of reproductive imagination and from the synthesis of recognition in a concept. Kant now ascribes it to the exercise of an intellectual faculty:

> In this manner it is proved that the synthesis of apprehension, which is empirical, must necessarily be in conformity with the synthesis of apperception, which is intellectual and is contained in the category completely *a priori*. It is one and the same spontaneity, which in the one case, under the title of imagination, and in the other case, under the title of understanding, brings combination [*Verbindung*] into the manifold of intuition. (B162n)

This is certainly compatible with preserving some autonomy for imagination, and not having to reduce it to the work of understanding. For example, to claim that *transcendental* imagination is an action of understanding is compatible with supposing that empirically "reproductive" imagination *also* provides an essential element in conceptualization. As we have already seen, however, a concession of the sort is ambiguous. It might, on the one hand, mean something that nobody would think to deny, namely, that acts of empirical conceptualization essentially "refer" to empirically reproducible possibilities, or in some way involve conceptions or judgments regarding them. On the other hand, it might mean something more interesting. It is in any case compatible with the passages in question to claim that even "reproductive" imagination is much more literally ingredient *in* any act of conception as such. The passages are compatible with maintaining that, to the extent that concepts are *themselves* an element in intuitive apprehension (and do not merely embellish the latter through attachment of quasi-linguistic "terms" of some kind), acts of conception as such—and so, in a sense, the corresponding "concepts"—must actually be *made* out of imaginative material.

It is possible to hold that, in a certain sense, conceptual syntheses are, as such, purely "intellectual," and also to hold that empirical concepts are nothing but imaginative material, intellectually transformed or elevated. (To say the latter, of course, is just to say that, in another sense, conceptual syntheses are *not* as such purely intellectual.) Obviously, there must be something that is purely intellectual in Kant's view. For there must at least be the functions needed for the embodiment of imaginative material, not merely in intuitions, but in concrete concepts in action. This is something purely formal and purely intellectual. But it is only a matter of terminology whether we limit our notion of "transcendental synthesis," or of transcendental *Verbindung*, to this formal element as such or instead consider it specifically in its role in regard to imaginative material. Certainly, to the extent that empirical concepts embody anticipations and retentions, it is at least permissible to say that they embody imaginative "syntheses"—beyond whatever intellectual functions of *Verbindung* are in them. What the latter can at most add is a special kind of *unity* of the former:

> But the concept of combination includes, besides the concept of the manifold and of its synthesis, also [*noch*] the concept of the unity of the manifold. Combination is representation of the *synthetic* unity of the manifold.[11]

An analogy may help. We might say that the difference depends on whether we are oriented toward the animate "body" of a concept as such or rather toward its animating "soul." What is important to see, in these terms, is just that Kant's understanding of the connection between the relevant souls and bodies, or between the form and the matter of concepts, is more like Aristotle's and less like Plato's notion of such relationships. The Platonic model may seem to be suggested by Kemp Smith's translation of the passage quoted from B152. Kemp Smith interprets Kant as saying there that conceptual synthesis is an "action" of the understanding on sensibility. But perhaps he meant only to suggest that it is the *effect* of some action.[12] Kant's choice of the noun (*Wirkung*) allows for either. In any event, Kant seems to prefer a different term altogether when he specifically wants to express the idea of an action in such cases. Thus at A57/B81, he refers to the pure concepts of understanding as *Handlungen* of pure thought.[13]

If the distinction between matter and form in conception were a distinction between two distinct items or sorts of items—only externally related or at most related in that one of them "refers" to the other—then, despite whatever imaginative "dimension" might be conceded to conception, any relevant synthesis literally internal to conceptual acts, as such, might indeed be unambiguously ascribed to a faculty of pure understanding. And sometimes Kant appears to adopt this approach. But other times he attributes synthesis to an imaginative capacity that is distinct from understanding; the latter is merely responsible for the unity of the former's synthesis. Where the relationship is indeed one of matter to form, it is not surprising that the upshot is thus ambiguously describable. For in that case, it would be as proper to say that conceptual syntheses *are* anticipations and retentions as it would be to say that sensory intuitions (at least in abstraction from their conceptual components) are manifolds of sensations. In a sense, a sensory intuition *is*, as such, only sensations. It is sensations appropriately "animated." Analogously, the conceptual syntheses introducible *into* sensory intuitions are just a certain portion of the latter's ingredient anticipations and retentions. They *are* the latter—appropriately "animated." (A non-sensory intuition can of course have no *other* ingredient, in the relevant sense.)

It may seem to be only in the first edition, or perhaps more prominently there, that Kant credits imagination with the primary role of "synthesis" in conception, and understanding only with the "unity" of that synthesis.[14] But if not in the same terms, the second edition makes the same point. Kant says, for example, that he would call all intellectual combination (*Verbindung*) a form of "synthesis"— except for the fact that "the concept of combination includes, besides the concept of the manifold and of its synthesis, also the concept of the unity of the manifold." In particular, "combination is the representation of the *synthetic* unity of the manifold" (B130; Kant's emphasis). Thus the thoroughgoing identity of apperception, far from being identical with a synthesis of representations, "contains" (*enthält*) such a synthesis and is only possible through the consciousness of that synthesis (B133), or at least through the consciousness of its possibility (B134); "it is imagination that connects (*verknüpft*) the manifold of sensible intuition; and imagination is dependent for the unity of its intellectual synthesis upon the understanding, and for the manifoldness of its apprehension upon sensibility" (B164).

The specific issues raised by appeal to a "consciousness" of synthesis need to be postponed to the next chapter. Until then, we must also postpone a full understanding of the "unity" Kant has in mind. But two comments may still be made about these passages. First, we may note the ambiguity in Kant's reference to "the unity of its [that is, of imagination's] intellectual synthesis." We might, of course, take the point to be that, *qua* transcendentally imaginative, imaginative synthesis is a function of the intellect. But the genitive might also be read as the *objective* genitive: imagination depends on the intellect for the unity of whatever intellectual synthesis is directed *toward* itself. This in turn is compatible with two positions. It is compatible with holding that imagination is responsible for no synthesis at all. But it is also compatible with holding that it is responsible for some type of synthesis, but just not for a distinctively intellectual type of synthesis. (The latter reading is viable even if the genitive is possessive.) In any event, it would be a quibble to claim that, apart from the intellect, imagination is responsible for no synthesis at all, in view of Kant's concession that it is at least responsible for some kind of *Verknüpfung*, and of his hesitation in identifying intellectual *Verbindung* with synthesis precisely because every instance of the former must always *include* the latter.

The second point is this. Kant says that the "manifoldness" of imaginative apprehension stems from sensibility. This may seem to imply that it does not stem from imagination itself, and thus it may seem to contradict the suggestion that conceptual syntheses unify imaginative anticipations and retentions. It might even seem to imply that conceptual syntheses unify mere sensations. But we need to remember that, to the extent that it is an ingredient in intuitions, imaginative material is indeed analogous to sensations. We need only remember, in addition, that to the extent that such material is also embodied in *concepts*, "applied" to intuitions, it is responsible for connecting, thus responsible for "synthesizing," a given intuition with a manifold of other possible (past and future) ones. No purely intellectual function does that on its own. In any particular context, Kant might be focusing on one or the other of these aspects of the transcendental function of imagination. Each is essential to the latter's contribution to conception.

However we finally elaborate the notion, the unity of consciousness required with respect to the "manifold contained in an intuition which I call mine" always includes in itself (*in sich schliesst*) a synthesis of the manifold given in that intuition (B144 and note). In turn, the "whole power" of understanding, in any such unity of consciousness, consists "in the act whereby it brings the synthesis of a manifold . . . to the unity of apperception" (B145). This act, Kant tells us, is effected by means of the categories, or by means of the "pure forms" of understanding. Thus, in the first instance (though not necessarily first in temporal order), the understanding does not unify a manifold in virtue of applying empirical *concepts* to it. Whatever original unity it introduces is something much purer than this. In that this unity is partly constitutive of concepts in the first place, applying concepts to intuitions could at most be the upshot of (though not necessarily temporally subsequent to) the presence of such a unity in intuition. Any determinate conceptual "content" is only the upshot of the "imposition" of a correspondingly indeterminate form. We shall have to do more to clarify what such "imposition" involves. But we need at least to be clear that, in any case, what the unity in question is supposed to unify is not in the first instance manifolds of distinct intuitions.

It is rather manifolds of a certain material *in* intuitions. It is only *through* unification of the latter that the understanding is able to unify the former, in any sense that could be said to involve the "application" or "predication" of concepts.

That any truly conceptual synthesis presupposes a pre-conceptually synthetic consciousness of some kind, seems also to be what Kant is arguing in the following passage:

> The analytical unity of consciousness belongs to all general concepts, as such. If, for instance, I think red in general, I thereby represent to myself a property which (as a characteristic [*als Merkmal*]) can be found in something, or can be combined with other representations; that is, only by means of a presupposed [*vorausgedachten*] possible synthetic unity can I represent to myself the analytic unity. . . . Consequently [a representation which is to be thought as common to different representations] must previously be thought [*vorher gedacht*] in synthetic unity with other (though, it may be, only possible) representations, before I can think in it the analytic unity of consciousness, which makes it a *conceptus communis*. (B133n)

In other words, the employment of concepts as *Merkmale* (or as representative of *Merkmale*) cannot by itself constitute, because it is in its own turn constituted by, the consciousness of connections among possible intuitions. Presumably, it is constituted by a consciousness of connections between a given candidate for predication in the first place, and a manifold of other possible candidates. This in turn requires that one be "given," internally to intuitions themselves, a manifold of anticipations or retentions *of* other possible ones.[15] (The specifically anticipative dimension of that "constitutive" consciousness might provide a harmless explanation of Kant's claim, at B134, that the synthetic unity of the manifold is given *a priori* [*a priori gegeben*: contrast Kemp Smith's "generated *a priori*"]. The point need simply be that it is *anticipatively* "given.")

That the unity originally constituted by intellectual functions is not in the first instance a unity of *Merkmale* is suggested by Kant's choice of comparison in the case. He refers to his discussion of "qualitative" unity in §12. In every instance of cognition, Kant had said in that section, "there is *unity* of concept, which may be entitled *qualitative unity*, so far as we think by it only the unity in the combination of the manifold of our cognitions; as, for example, the unity of the theme in a play, a speech, or a story" (B114). By contrast to the mere unification of *Merkmale* in a concept, in a subject of predication, or even in a merely *represented* subject of predication,[16] Kant's suggestion appears to involve the unity that a set of items enjoys (the components of a play, a speech, or a story) by virtue of their all representing—indeed, their all being *made* to represent—a common subject matter. That is very different from their all representing (not to mention their being, or even their possibly being) the predicates of a common subject. As we shall see more clearly later, it is also more like the sort of unification that needs to be "imposed" on anticipations and retentions, in order that they be truly embodied in acts of conception. Those anticipations and retentions need to be "unified" in two respects. They of course need to be unified by virtue of being one and all ingredient in a particular intuition. But they also need to be unified by virtue of being (taken to be) anticipations and retentions regarding a *common subject*, represented *through* an intuition.

The other examples of synthesis Kant offers make it difficult to construe that notion in terms of the unification of *Merkmale*. For example, he offers the case in which, in thinking of some line, one "draws it in thought" (B154; cf. B162 ["I draw as it were the outline of the house"], A102, A162-3/B203). The parts of a line that one "synthesizes," when drawing it in thought, are surely very different from the *Merkmale* of a line. Of course, it may be difficult to see why Kant should say that drawing a line in thought is a necessary condition for thinking it in the first place. One might suggest that, in saying it, Kant must indeed have something in mind like the unification of *Merkmale*, and simply puts it badly. But I have, in effect, already suggested an alternative, in commenting on Kant's more general claim concerning the need for synthesis in the apprehension of space as an "object" (B160n). It is simply that the capacity for conceptualizing figures as lines (which we may take to be, in Kant's view, at least a necessary condition for "thinking of" lines in the first place), presupposes the capacity for giving special expression[17] to a set of *anticipations* regarding the possibility of drawing lines. Specifically, it presupposes the capacity for giving "expression" to certain anticipations, by means of the latter's very *ingredience* in an act of (at least) imaginative intuition. This notion of line-drawing anticipation, not simply as expressible in conceptual acts, but as embodied in intuition, was no doubt a difficult notion for Kant to convey. It is not implausible to suppose that he sometimes overstated it. The point is not that we need to *draw* a line, not even in thought, in order to have it in mind. But there does need to be much *more* "in mind"—having to do with the act of drawing—than the mere ability to "think" in some way or other.

III. Judgments of Perception and Experience

We have yet to consider the overall structure of the second-edition Deduction. In the next section, I argue that it rests on the distinction, drawn in §§18—20 of the *Prolegomena*, between judgments of perception and of experience. In §19 of the Deduction, Kant appears to imply that he had been mistaken in drawing that distinction, at least in terms of a distinction between two kinds of "judgments." My own view is that, while in strict Kantian terms, they are not judgments at all, Kant had an important point in treating judgments of perception as judgments. The relevant points in the *Prolegomena* account are in any case four.

First, a judgment of perception involves nothing more than some kind of "connection" of representations in a perceiver's perceptual state:

> Empirical judgments, so far as they have objective validity, are *judgments of experience*, but those which are only subjectively valid I name mere *judgments of perception*. The latter require no pure concept of the understanding, but only the logical connection of perception in a thinking subject. (P. 298) [A judgment of this sort] only expresses a relation of two sensations to the same subject, that is, myself, and that only in my present state of perception [*nur in meinem diesmaligen Zustande der Wahrnehmung*]. . . . [I] do nothing but refer two of my sensations to each other. (P. 299) The foundation is [*Zum Grunde liegt*] the intuition of which I become

conscious, that is, perception (*perceptio*), which pertains merely to the senses. But in the next place, there is judging (which belongs only to the understanding). But this judging may be twofold: first, I may merely compare perceptions and connect them in a consciousness of my state [*in einem Bewusstsein meines Zustandes*]. . . . The first judgment is merely a connection of perceptions in my mental state [*bloss Verknüpfung der Wahrnehmungen in meinem Gemütszustande*], without reference to the object. (P. 300)[18]

Second, a judgment of experience can only be generated *from* a corresponding judgment of perception. The former is what the latter *becomes*, when it is appropriately "determined" by the logical forms of judgment:

All our judgments are at first [*zuerst*] mere judgments of perception; they hold good only for us (that is, for our subject), and we do not till afterward [*nur hintennach*] give them a new reference (to an object) and desire that they shall always hold good for us and in the same way for everybody else; for when a judgment agrees with an object, all judgments concerning the same object must likewise agree among themselves, and thus the objective validity of the judgment of experience signifies nothing else than its necessary universal validity. (P. 298)

According to Kant, however, there are also two kinds of judgments of perception. One of them cannot—not even through adding pure concepts (*nicht solche Warhnehmungsurteile. . .die jemals Erfahrungsurteile werden könnten, wenn man auch einen Verstandesbegriff hinzu täte*)—ever become a judgment of experience. The other, of course, can: *Wahrnehmungsurteile, die durch hinzugesetzten Verstandesbegriff Erfahrungsurteile werden* (p. 299n). The distinction relates to Kant's distinction between primary and secondary qualities and need not detain us.[19] The point remains that a judgment of experience always involves some operation in regard to a judgment of perception:

For instance, when I say the air is elastic, this judgment is as yet [*zunächst*] a judgment of perception only; I do nothing but refer two of my sensations to each other. But if I would have it called a judgment of experience, I require this connection to stand under a condition which makes it universally valid. (P. 299)

Before, therefore, a judgment of experience can come from a judgment of perception [*ehe aus einem Wahrnehmungsurteil ein Urteil der Erfahrung werden kann*], it is requisite that the perception should be subsumed under some such concept of the understanding. . . . The judgment that air is elastic becomes universally valid and thereby finally [*dadurch allererst*] a judgment of experience. . . . (Pp. 300-1)

Third, Kant describes the requisite "operation" as an operation on perceptions or intuitions themselves. Judgments of perception are *themselves* perceptions:[20]

[A]ll empirical judgments are not judgments of experience; but, besides the empirical, and in general besides what is given to sensuous intuition, special concepts must be superadded—concepts which have their origin wholly *a priori* in the pure understanding, and under which every perception must be first of all subsumed and then by their means changed [*verwandelt*] into experience. (P. 298)

Quite another judgment therefore is required before perception can become experi-

ence [*ehe aus Wahrnehmung Erfahrung werden kann*]. The given intuition must
be subsumed under a concept which determines the form of judging in general relatively to the intuition . . . , which does nothing but determine for an intuition the
general way in which *it* [emphasis added] can serve for judgments [*zu Urteilen
dienen kann*] . . . . [I]t is requisite that the perception be subsumed under some
such concept of the understanding. (P. 300)

The fourth point bears on the particular way in which the forms of judgment
are supposed to "determine" perceptions, and thus convert them into judgments
of experience. They do this, Kant says, by determining and converting, not simply
perceptions themselves, but the very connections *among* perceptions that constitute judgments of perception:

[W]hen through the concept of the understanding the connection of the representations, which it gives to our sensibility, is determined as universally valid, the object
is determined through this relation, and the judgment is objective. . . . But if I would
have it called a judgment of experience, I require this connection to stand under
a condition which makes it universally valid. I desire therefore that I and everybody
else should always connect necessarily the same perceptions under the same circumstances. (P. 299)

But this judging may be twofold: first, I may merely compare perceptions and connect them in a consciousness of my state; or, secondly, I may connect them in a
consciousness in general [*in einem Bewusstsein überhaupt*] . . . [which] connects
empirical consciousness of intuition in consciousness in general [*in einem
Bewusstsein überhaupt*]. (P. 300)

Putting the points together, Kant appears to describe the relationship between
judgments of perception and experience in terms of two different ways in which
perceptions might be "connected," in particular connected *within a given perception.*

There is a way, very different from my own, in which one might attempt to
put these points together. One might suggest that the difference between judgments of perception and experience is that the former involve judgments about
the subject itself, and how things merely seem or appear, while the latter involve
judgments as to how things really are.[21] According to this approach, we do not
take Kant at his word, in his claim that judgments of experience need to be *formed*
out of judgments of perception (not to mention out of perceptions). But perhaps
we might do better with his claim that judgments of experience objectively "determine," not simply perceptions, but subjective connections *among* perceptions,
and indeed that they determine the very connections involved in judgments of
perception. We might simply take the claim to be that a judgment of perception
is a judgment *about* certain connections among perceptions—namely, a judgment
as to how they actually connect in one's experience—while a judgment of experience is a judgment about the way in which they necessarily connect in anyone's
experience.

Apart from slighting Kant's own suggestion that the subjective connections thereby "determined" are those that actually *constitute* judgments of perception—as opposed to being connections that judgments of perception merely *refer* to—we would have to pay a price for this reading. For it would now follow that judgments of experience are not about objects. Instead, they would be about perceptions. Kant says a number of things that seem to imply just this. These are, of course, the things that suggest a phenomenalist reading of Kant. In Chapter Two, I tried to show how the kind of phenomenalism entailed by such pronouncements is in fact compatible with denying that judgments of experience are about perceptions. Putting that issue aside, there is an additional difficulty, in the proposed reading, concerning judgments of perception. The reading is incompatible with Kant's insistence that judgments of perception do not involve "forms of judgment." As I shall propose, it is possible to see why Kant should regard judgments of perception as "judgments," even if they do not involve the forms of judgment. Obviously, they could not be judgments in the official Kantian sense. But it is hardly plausible to suppose that Kant forgot this. On the reading so far suggested, it is in any case impossible to see why Kant should insist that judgments of perception do not involve categories.

A second proposal avoids this final problem. According to it, judgments of perception are merely associations of perceptions—as opposed to judgments *about* associations of perceptions.[22] There is ample reason to suppose that the "connections" involved in judgments of perception are indeed associations:

> But if I would have it called a judgment of experience, I require *this connection* [emphasis added] to stand under a condition which makes it universally valid. I will [*will*] therefore that I and everybody else should always connect necessarily the same perceptions under the same circumstances. (P. 299)

"This connection" can only be a certain pattern of associations. Were it not, then it would be difficult to see how one could ever demand, in the conversion to judgments of experience, that this very *same* connection be universalized. What would there be, in that case, that might happen to obtain peculiarly in me, or in anyone else in particular, but that also might be subjected to the *demand* that it obtain universally? In addition, having already excluded the possibility that the relevant sort of "connection" of perceptions is only a judgment *about* a connection of perceptions, how could the reference to "circumstances" be relevant? We could only be talking, it seems, about patterns of association, insofar as they are, as they always are, relative to circumstances.

Consider also the following:

> If all our synthetical judgments are analyzed so far as they are objectively valid, it will be found that they never consist of mere intuitions connected only (as is commonly believed) by comparison into a judgment; but that they would be impossible were not a pure concept of the understanding superadded to the concepts abstracted from intuition, under which concept these latter are subsumed. (P. 301)

Admittedly, one may wonder how, prior to subsumption under pure concepts, any sorts of concepts are "abstractable" in the first place. But then, that would be no more problematic than Kant's suggestion that judgments themselves are possible in such a case. Contrary to Kant's official terminology, we might simply need to distinguish (as he does) between different notions of a "concept" and a "judgment." Terminology aside, there is no reason for that to pose a problem for Kant. What we should note is rather the following.

Kant says that it is commonly believed that judgments of experience "consist of mere intuitions connected only. . .by comparison into a judgment." That is, it is commonly believed that objective judgments are reducible to judgments of perception. But who could Kant really be thinking might believe such a thing, not to mention embrace it as an item of common opinion? To whom could it possibly seem evident that judgments about objects are no more than subjective "connections" among perceptions (as opposed to being judgments *about* such connections—which in any case surely cannot be supposed a matter of common opinion)? Kant's terminology suggests Hume: that the "connection" in question involves "comparison" is mentioned three times in the course of §20. It is in fact not unreasonable to take Hume to hold, not that judgments about objects are really judgments about perceptions, or even about associations of perceptions, but rather that such judgments are *themselves* associations. Habits of association might naturally be presumed to arise from a kind of "comparison" (of cases repeated in experience). In addition, Kant consistently describes Hume as having substituted mere "habit" for judgment; he does not simply describe him as erring with regard to the *objects* of judgment (p. 258).[23] So it does seem reasonable to conclude that judgments of perception are mere associations of perceptions.

But some problems still remain. First, the suggestion that judgments of perception are mere associations of perceptions does not explain why Kant should call judgments of perception a kind of "judgment." Second, it does not explain how judgments of perception could ever become judgments of experience, nor why all judgments of experience must "first" be judgments of perception. Third, it does not explain how the logical functions that convert the one to the other can be functions exercised with respect to given *perceptions*: associations *of* perceptions seem to be one thing, perceptions themselves another.

I think that we can avoid these problems. The proposal is simply this: that judgments of perception are associations of perceptions—but only so far as such associations are ingredient in *given* perceptions, as a kind of material for the apprehension of appearances. Such ingredience does not really amount to "judgment," nor to the employment of empirical concepts, nor to the apprehension of "objects," in the strict usages that Kant tends to favor. But it is understandable why Kant nevertheless suggests that such ingredience of associations amounts to a kind of judgment. In a sense, it does indeed amount to a kind of "predication" with respect to appearances. For insofar as appearances are apprehended *through* associations, and the latter are not merely externally attached to (or "associated" with) the intuitions through which appearances are apprehended, the correlative appearances must be apprehended as *correlatively characterized*. This is what I argued in the last chapter.

The point holds, we should note, even if we refuse to admit that, apart from conceptualization, appearances are ever "apprehended" to begin with. Even with that restriction, it remains the case that it is a necessary condition for any such apprehension that the apprehension be formed from material ingredient in intuitions. Once again, the way the correlative object is "characterized," *through* such an act, is not solely a function of something intellectual. It is equally a function of the purely associative *material* on which the former operates.

Apart from its bearing on the Deduction, one upshot of this approach is that it allows us to confirm at least part of a suggestion made by Beck in regard to the distinction in question. It concerns the relation between the distinction and Kant's theory of "judgments of taste." In this respect, Beck suggests, "the *Critique of Judgment* seems to have grown out of the doctrines of the *Prolegomena* which were rejected in the second edition of the *Critique of Pure Reason*."[24] Apart from the question of the *Prolegomena*'s relationship to the *Critique*, my account suggests a rather different ground of comparison. According to Beck's proposal, judgments of taste may be regarded as standing to judgments of "agreeableness" in a relation analogous to that in which judgments of experience stand to those of perception. In both cases, the second term of the relation is something purely subjective. Because of that, something needs to be "superadded" to it, in order to yield an instance of objective judgment. In the case of judgments of perception, what needs to be added is subsumption under the categories. What gets thereby subsumed, Beck suggests, is a merely "intuitive image" (and so an item that was really not any kind of "judgment" to begin with). Analogously, what is added to a judgment of agreeableness, to make it a judgment of taste, is subsumption "under the understanding as the *faculty* of concepts in general." (What gets thereby subsumed, apparently, is also a "faculty," namely, that of imagination.)[25]

Beck does not make it clear how what Kant describes as the "harmony" of imagination and understanding, essential to a judgment of taste, can be comparable to a case of subsumption. Certainly, it is difficult to see how "subsumption" under a *faculty* can be significantly comparable to the subsumption of something under concepts or predicates. In addition, it is not, of course, the case that a judgment of agreeableness could ever be transformed *into* a judgment of taste for Kant. (But strictly speaking, Beck presumably takes this lack of analogy to apply as well to the *Prolegomena* distinction.) In any event, Kant himself says that in a judgment of taste it is a non-conceptualized *pleasure in* some relation between the faculties that is supposed to function in a way analogous to the functioning of a predicate in judgment, but without the need for actual conceptualization. This provided the basis, in Chapter Four, for a comparison between judgments of taste and a perception of "affinity" in nature. As we by now have seen, it also provides a basis for comparison between judgments of taste and judgments of "perception." (Obviously, the analogy is compatible with an additional disanalogy, to which Beck also calls our attention: judgments of perception are not "objective," while judgments of taste are. The difference simply reflects the fact that it is purely contingent factors that determine what human beings can associate with what. In Kant's view, at least, it is not purely contingent factors that determine that human beings take pleasure in the harmonious workings of their faculties.)

IV. The Structure of the Deduction

I have dwelt on the *Prolegomena* distinction for the following two reasons. First, I disagree with those who hold that §19— culmination of the Deduction's first stage—rejects that distinction. Second, independent evidence, from throughout the Deduction, supports the view that its structure turns on a shift in perspective (from the noetic to the noematic), the point of which could only be seen if judgments of experience are nothing but judgments of perception, as I have interpreted them, transformed by means of the forms of judgment *into* judgments of experience. As I shall argue, the Deduction turns from a conclusion regarding unification within *intuitions*, required for their transformation into judgments of experience, to a conclusion, in its second stage, regarding a correlative structure among the objects *of* intuitions.

The problem of the Deduction's stages was made the focus of particular recent attention by Henrich. Henrich maintains that the key lies in the fact that §20 terminates the Deduction's first stage with a restricted conclusion: "All the manifold, therefore, so far as it is given in a single [*sofern es in Einer*] empirical intuition, is *determined* in respect of one of the logical functions of judgment, and is thereby brought to a consciousness in general [*zu einem Bewusstsein überhaupt*]" (B143). Thus the first stage infers the need for categories as a condition for a sub-class of logically possible representations, namely, of appropriately "unified" ones. Culminating in §26, the second then extends the conclusion to sensory intuition generally, and to its objects. It does this on the basis of the fact that sensory intuition is representation in space and time, and, as the Aesthetic has already argued, space and time necessarily involve a "unity" of representation. According to Henrich, in other words, the ultimate aim of the Deduction is to exclude "the possibility of a merely partial ability of the understanding to establish unity in the sensible representations." It does so, he suggests, on the ground that "we do in fact have unitary representations of space and time and therefore can also unify all representations of sense."[26]

The main objections to Henrich appear to be three. I am in agreement at least with the first; the others conceal an ambiguity to which both Henrich and opponents may be victim. The first objection is that the text fails to support the claim that, by the end of §20, Kant had not yet concluded that the categories apply to sensible intuition generally.[27]

We need to be careful in formulating the second objection. What is sound in it is this: that the mere concession of whatever unity was available from the Aesthetic does not in fact suffice for the purposes of the Deduction.[28] The objection may give the impression that, according to Henrich, it is *sensibility* that provides the unity to which the Deduction then appeals. But to the contrary, his own claim is that the unity of space and time, laid down as necessary in the Aesthetic, is a product of understanding.[29]

If the unity in question is a product of understanding, then the question of course remains as to how the Aesthetic, confined to sensibility, could have been entitled to introduce it. But this is a question that Henrich himself regards as legitimate. The apparent difficulty is merely indicative of the "synthetic" method employed by Kant in the *Critique*.[30] Alternatively, I would propose, we might simply have distinguished between two kinds of "unity" from the start. In any case, this point also relates to the third of the objections against Henrich. The objection is that it is plainly *unintelligible*, for Kant, to suppose that intuitions might lack a unity of their manifold. But if it is unintelligible, then so is Henrich's suggestion concerning the distinction of stages.[31]

On the account that I have proposed, the Aesthetic argues for a pre-intellectual "unity" in intuition. It does this by arguing that a preconceptual "form of intuition"—internal to (would-be) cognitive states themselves—is necessary for the employment of concepts in the apprehension of any possible *instances* of concepts. (As I have argued, it is, strictly speaking, compatible with this to deny that the form in question is *sufficient* for such apprehension, at least as a mode of full-blown "consciousness.") This is what we examined in Chapter One. Now it might appear that Kant rejects this position in the Deduction. For he there claims that the very "unity of space and time" is a product of understanding. But I have argued that this claim, as intended in the Deduction, does not in fact contradict my reading of the Aesthetic.[32] What concerns us now must in any case be a notion of "unity" that had not been in question in the Aesthetic at all.

In a way, my suggestion concerning the Deduction's stages will be similar to some others. Certainly, a number of readings take it that the Deduction's first stage regards the categories as necessary for a certain sort of unity, while its second concludes that the categories are necessary for a "correlative" unity involving sensible *objects*. So far as I can tell, however, the view that Kant's inference is from one kind of unity to a correlative kind of unity generally involves supposing that the first requires a purely logical or judgmental kind of unity. Validly or not, the second stage then demands application of this kind of unity to the manifold of intuition.[33] In a way, I do not disagree. But if the unity in question in the first stage is supposed to be purely "logical," then it cannot be so in any ordinary sense, certainly not in the sense that is generally assumed. In particular, it must be a unity formed out of a manifold of sensible material. Insofar as the material, though "sensible," is distinct from mere *sensation*, we might perhaps still say that the corresponding unity is purely "logical," but only in a misleading sense.

In the following passage Kant states what has been done, in the Deduction's first stage, and what remains to be done in order to complete the Deduction:

> Thus in the above proposition a beginning is made of a *deduction* of the pure concepts of understanding, in which, since the categories have their source in the understanding alone, *independently of sensibility*, I must still abstract from the mode in which the manifold for an empirical intuition is given, and must direct attention solely to the unity which, in terms of the category, by means of the understanding, enters into the intuition. In what follows (cf. §26) it will be shown, from the mode in which the empirical intuition is given in sensibility, that its unity is no other than that which the category (according to §20) prescribes to the manifold of a given intuition in general. Only thus, by demonstration of the a priori validity of the categories in respect of all objects of our senses, will the purpose of the deduction be fully attained. (B144-5)

The contrast between what the categories prescribe "to the manifold of a given intuition in general" and what they prescribe with respect to "the mode in which the empirical intuition is given in sensibility," may suggest that the operative distinction is between a general case and its specific application: for example, from sensible intuition in general to distinctively human (spatiotemporal) inituition.[34] (Kant himself points out, in the sentence that follows this passage, that the first stage had at least been concerned with sensible intuition specifically.) But there is ample evidence that the first stage was, if not already explicitly directed toward spatiotemporal intuition, at least regarded by Kant as merely trivially applicable to the latter.

We have already examined a passage, from the Deduction's first stage, that specifically *applies* Kant's reasoning to the case of the manifold of spatiotemporal intuition. The passage was from a footnote to §17. It ended with an anticipatory reference to the second stage as well (actually to §25, but presumably intending §26). Kemp Smith translates the reference in the following way: "The *singularity* of such [spatiotemporal] intuitions is found to have important consequences (*vide* §25)" (B136n). I deliberately translated that sentence in a much more awkward way. Kant himself says that the singularity in question is *wichtig in der Anwendung* ("important in [the] application"). I shall later suggest how the phrase may be read in support of my approach. The question remains as to exactly *what* can be merely anticipatory about the reference to spatiotemporal manifolds, at this point, and about the question of "application."

In at least one respect, I agree that the point of the second stage can be *put*, as Kant puts it, in terms of a problem concerning the "manifold given in spatiotemporal intuition." But this is only if we mean by the latter: the manifold of portions of space and time themselves, together with the manifold of possible spatiotemporal "appearances," insofar as these may be regarded as genuine "objects" of awareness. It is with one or with both of these that the footnote in question is concerned. There, for example, Kant specifically discusses space and time as "objects." In addition, in the section to which the note is attached (§17), he is concerned with a distinction between space as an "object" and space—or something that he *calls* space—taken in some other way altogether. Whatever exactly he means by the latter, he puts it by referring to space as a "form." I have already suggested what this distinction must involve. It is a distinction between space itself, and the spatial structure of objects appearing in it, and the intuitional form internal to representations *of* space. What Kant calls "space," taken as a form, is not space at all in the present context. It is simply the form of spatial intuition as such. A closer look confirms this:

> Thus the mere form of outer sensible intuition, space$_1$, is not yet a cognition [*noch gar keine Erkenntnis*]; it supplies only the manifold of intuition *a priori* for a possible cognition. To know anything in space$_2$ (for instance, a line), I must *draw* it, and thus synthetically bring into being a determinate combination of the given manifold, so that the unity of this act is at the same time the unity of consciousness (in the concept of a line); and it is through this unity of consciousness that an object (a determinate space$_2$) is first cognized. (B137-8; subscripts added)

Kant makes a point of saying that "space," as a form, is not yet a cognition. This alone makes it clear that he is using the term *space* (indicated by means of the first subscript) in a technical way. In any ordinary sense, it would be absurd to suppose that space ever is or could become a cognition. As I did in an earlier discussion of a related passage, I therefore conclude that Kant means by "the mere form of outer sensible intuition, space," not space at all, or even spatial form as such, but the irreducibly intuitional form of our representations, or would-be representations, *of* space (or of spatial form as such).

It might seem more natural to conclude that Kant simply means that the mere form of intuition is not in itself a proper object of cognition. But that would be mistaken. In Kant's own view, space and spatial form are as proper an object of cognition as anything else. To be sure, insofar as space and spatial form have not yet been *conceptualized*, they are not full-blown objects of cognition. But that is not a point that concerns the "form" of intuition specifically. It applies as well to "appearances," and to anything that we might regard as mere "matter" in intuition. In any case, the question would still remain: what could be the point of saying that, while space is not yet an object of cognition, it provides a manifold that needs to be synthesized, in order for it actually to *become* an object of cognition? In what sense could space, insofar as it is not an object of cognition, provide or contain any sort of manifold at all? The suggestion threatens to return us to some of the more objectionable readings already rejected.

A more plausible reading will simply assume that Kant is intending to distinguish, in §17, between two very different sorts of manifold and two different sorts of unifying structure. He is distinguishing, on the one hand, between a unifying structure that needs to be "applied" to a manifold internal to spatial *representations* and a structure that needs to be regarded as (thereby) applying to manifolds in space as an object. The latter must depend on the former. A necessary condition for apprehending space, or objects in space—*as objects*—must be the establishment of some kind of unity within cognitive states themselves. In the section in question, Kant emphasizes the latter dimension several times. First, in the passage that I have quoted, he directly refers to the unity of the "act" of cognition (which he also calls unity of "consciousness"). Second, he equates the unity of the act of cognition with a unity within one's very *concepts* of space or of objects—not with a unity internal to space or to objects themselves. In both cases, this sort of unity is a necessary condition for a truly cognitive apprehension of space as an object. A similar distinction, and the same conclusion, is drawn just before the passage that we have been examining:

> *Understanding* is, to use general terms, *the faculty of cognitions*. These consist in the determinate relation of given representations to an object. An *object*, however, is that in the concept of which the manifold of a given intuition is *united*. . . . Consequently it is the unity of consciousness that alone constitutes [*ausmacht*] the relation of representations to an object. . . . (B137)

This reading would make it clear what is and what is not merely anticipatory about the footnote to §17. What is anticipatory is its reference to a structure internal to space itself (and time) as object of cognition. What is not anticipatory is its reference to spatiotemporal "intuition" as such. (To be sure, in most sections of the Deduction, Kant speaks of a manifold of sensible intuition in general, and does not consider spatiotemporal intuition at all. But this, I take it, only indicates that he regards the more specific application as following merely trivially from the general proposition. A triviality of this kind could not be what defines the distinction of stages.) In addition, this reading would make more literal sense of the conclusion to the footnote in question. Kant's point would then be, not simply that the "singularity" of space and time, as objects of cognition, will have an important "consequence" when we eventually reach §26. The point would be, more specifically, that the consequence itself turns on the question of the application (*Anwendung*) of cognitive structures to objects.[35]

As noted, something like this has been suggested, in at least a general way, by a number of commentators. But there is a difference. Typically, when the distinction between the Deduction's stages is taken to rest on a distinction between structures internal to cognition and structures involving objects, the first stage is taken to be merely concerned with structures internal to *thoughts* about objects, or to mere concepts or judgments. In a way, this restriction does of course characterize the Deduction's first stage. But what is crucial is to recognize the fact while also acknowledging another. What we need to see is that the first stage, with its demand for "unity of consciousness" in thoughts and concepts, already presupposes a doctrine regarding the unification of sensible manifolds. In particular, it presupposes a doctrine regarding the unification of manifolds within spatiotemporal intuitions themselves.

One way to combine the points might be thought to lie in a suggestion rejected earlier.[36] We might suppose that the requisite unity, internal to any concept that is truly applicable to objects, is a unity established by means of the conversion of intuitively apprehended features or "impressions" into *Merkmale*, and thereby into concepts. In my view, the requisite unity is of course established by means of the unification of a very different sort of material, namely, imaginative associations. Apart from the intrinsic intelligibility of it, at least one advantage of that alternative should be obvious. It will allow us to see the point of Kant's own treatment of judgments of perception and experience. That distinction, as we shall see, is the key to Kant's argument in §§18–19 of the Deduction. An examination of these sections reveals that the Deduction's first stage rests precisely on the demand for conversion of the former sort of "judgment" into the latter. But in that case, only one task could possibly remain for the Deduction's second stage. The second stage must proceed to conclude that, whatever structures are essentially involved *in* that conversion must in turn be mirrored in the objects of experience themselves.[37]

Now let us return to the beginning of the Deduction. What we need to note, first of all, is that the section (§15) begins squarely from the noetic perspective. That is, it begins from the perspective of the structure of cognitive states or acts, as opposed to that of objects or appearances (or even of potential objects or appearances). The noetic perspective is evident from Kant's characterization of the "manifold" that stands in original need of unification through understanding.

He describes it, namely, as a manifold that concerns nothing more "than the mode in which the subject is affected":

> The manifold of representations can be given in an intuition [*in einer Anschauung*] which is purely sensible, that is, nothing but receptivity; and the form of this intuition can lie *a priori* in our faculty of representation, without being anything more than the mode in which the subject is affected. But the combination [*Verbindung*] (*conjunctio*) of any manifold [*eines Mannigfaltigen überhaupt*] can never come to us through the senses, and cannot, therefore, be already contained in the pure form of sensible intuition. . . . For it is an act of spontaneity . . . understanding. (B129)

The noetic perspective might also be evident from the fact that the manifold in question is said to be contained within a single intuition (*in einer Anschauung*). Although the latter phrase is ambiguous, we have at least seen that the Deduction as a whole is in fact dominated by the notion of the unification of manifolds within single intuitions. And we have seen that the notion is specifically operative in §17.

I have of course already argued that we can make sense of the demand for unification within single "intuitions," when the latter are regarded as instances of cognitive or potentially cognitive states or acts. It is much more difficult to make sense of the demand, when it is construed as bearing on a manifold supposed to be ingredient in appearances themselves, or in intuitable regions of space. That is why, in the latter case, one is more apt to emphasize—despite Kant's suggestions to the contrary—the need for some kind of unification among *distinct* intuitions. In any case, Kant himself does not explicitly characterize the items comprising the manifold. Eventually, through an examination of §§18–19, I shall provide additional reason for holding that it can consist only of imaginative anticipations and retentions. For now, we must be content with the fact that Kant simply begins, in §15, with the claim that the manifold in intuition needs to be unified intellectually.

Why does the manifold in intuition need to be unified intellectually? The following would seem to be Kant's only reason for saying so:

> To this act the general title 'synthesis' may be assigned, in order to indicate at the same time [*um dadurch zugleich*] that we cannot represent to ourselves anything as combined in the object which we have not ourselves previously combined, and that of all representations *combination* is the only one which cannot be given through objects. (B130)

Kant may appear merely to be saying that a necessary condition for the awareness (representation) of relations among objects is that the understanding somehow combines those objects, or at least their appearances, *qua* objects of representation. But depending on what we had already packed into the notion of "awareness," that might be trivially true. As it stands, it seems in fact merely to amount to the claim that any truly conceptual awareness of relations among objects is dependent upon conceptualizations *of* those objects. A much more significant claim would be the one that I have proposed: that a necessary condition for the awareness of relations among objects needs to lie in the effecting of combination within the very cognitive acts or states *through which they are to become* objects of representation in the first place. It is precisely this, I suggest, that is indicated by Kant's use of the phrase *um dadurch zugleich* in the passage. (Kemp Smith simply has Kant say that we indicate by the title of *synthesis* that we cannot represent anything as combined in the object "which we have not ourselves previously combined." What Kant himself says, again, is that the title in question is meant *at the same time* to indicate this truth.) The formulation seems to imply a comparsion. If so, it is presumably a comparison between synthesis, as a combination of something "in the object" itself, and some other, correlative kind of synthesis. On my own reading of the Deduction's stages, it would then be the reference to the former that is merely anticipatory in the context of §15.

Now if we do not in fact take the "synthesis" in question to involve, in the first instance, some kind of combining internal to objects, or appearances, themselves, then it may appear that the real beginning of the Deduction is postponed to §16. And this, of course, is where a problem concerning "ascription" first arises. It arises in the claim that "it must be possible for the 'I think' to accompany all my representations" (B131). Here, at least, our focus seems more univocally to be on cognitive states or acts in their own right, or at least on would-be cognitive states or acts, as opposed to their objects or would-be objects. But what exactly is the problem? At the very least, it may seem clear that it is not what I have suggested it is. For it appears to be a problem that concerns some kind of a synthesis of a manifold of distinct intuitions, not a synthesis involving manifolds ingredient in *single* intuitions. In particular, it appears to be a problem concerning the conditions under which a manifold of distinct intuitions are (representable as) one and all "ascribable" to a single subject, namely, oneself. I do not, of course, propose to deny the centrality of this problem for the Deduction. But—though it may seem implausible to say it—we need to continue to postpone (until the next chapter) our detailed examination of that problem.

What is crucial to see, long before we turn to the problem of "ascription" for its own sake, is that a problem concerning the ascription of representations, in regard to a potential manifold of *distinct* representations, arises directly out of the demand for a certain kind of unification within single intuitions. Suppose that the manifold for the latter is in fact a manifold of anticipations and retentions. Even a non-human animal, we have granted, is able to "anticipate" the approach of possible appearances, and to "retain" other ones. But Kant's point, in the present context, might simply be taken to be this: that while it is necessary for the formation of a truly cognitive act or state that appearances be somehow anticipated and retained, it is not *sufficient* that they be anticipated and retained on a purely animal level. Instead, they need to be appropriately "combined" or connected *in* the very (and what would otherwise remain the *mere*) process of anticipating and retaining them. In particular, the appearances in question need to be combined or connected in at least the following way: they need to be anticipated and retained precisely *as* appearances of which one may *oneself* eventually come to obtain intuitions (or—to emphasize "retention"[38] —as appearances of which one might already have obtained intuitions). It is this notion that we need to examine in detail in the next chapter.

Whatever else in cognition may require "(self-)ascription," with regard to a manifold of distinct intuitions ascribable to single subjects, the conceptualization of intuitions calls for a structure of self-ascription *within any single intuition*. For, as we have already seen at length, it is only anticipations and retentions within a given intuition that could be relevant to *that* intuition's status as subject to conceptualization in the first place. Thus the present account can indeed explain the centrality of the problem of self-ascription, without abandoning the suggestion—in evidence throughout the Deduction—that the central problem concerns the *Verbindung* of manifolds internal to any given intuition. In other words, it is precisely the suggestion most prominent in the first-edition Deduction—that the manifold in question is a manifold of anticipations and retentions—that in fact permits the connection between these *two* undeniably central notions in the Deduction. But then, why was Kant so vague? If the relevant manifold, within single intuitions, is indeed a manifold as down-to-earth as that of ordinary "anticipations and retentions," why not just have said so?

The reasons for Kant's vagueness may be three. The first is something that I already indicated in Chapter Three. We may suppose that Kant was himself unclear regarding the very *status* of anticipations and retentions as "representations." If so, then it would have been natural for him to have tried to avoid the issue altogether, and to have focused instead, as we have seen he does, on questions of "synthesis" regarding objects or appearances directly. Given the correlation between noetic and noematic perspectives, there is indeed, in a way, nothing wrong with doing just this. The second reason for Kant's vagueness may be that he feared that the Deduction would otherwise appear objectionably psychologistic. For example, Kant may have found it difficult to explain exactly *how* cognitions could be "formed" out of something as subjective as anticipations and retentions—without reducing them to a variety of mental "particular," namely, to particular bundles of associations in individual subjects. But it should be clear to us that the danger is avoidable. Finally, the third reason for Kant's vagueness may be that he wanted to state his argument in a way that was applicable to sensible intuition generally (B145), and from there let it (trivially) apply to spatiotemporal intuition in particular. (This, of course, is not to offer that trivial application as the key to the two stages of the Deduction.) In fact, Kant does seems to say, although some consider it carelessness, that the combination of a sensible manifold, whether pure or merely empirical, is indeed an instance of a more general kind of *Verbindung*, applicable to manifolds that might not even be sensible at all (B130)[39] In that case, Kant could not appeal to "anticipation and retention," in anything like the sense in which we are familiar with these things. In any case, our own examination of §§18-19 will eventually provide independent support for the claim that Kant regards (non-categorial) concepts as one and all, in a being whose intuition is at least temporal in form, "formed" out of manifolds of that very being's anticipations and retentions.

The question of Kant's actual argument remains. *Where* does Kant argue—or at least *what* is the argument—that conceptualization of an intuition requires the combination of a manifold in that intuition? If §16 does not contain the argument—but rather, as I have suggested, merely an entailment of its conclusion—then §15 ought to have contained the argument directly. As we shall see more clearly in our examination of §19, the answer is simply that, only by means of actually *forming* any concept, can the understanding be said to "employ" any concept in the first place. But §15, I suggest, had in its own way already made the point. It had made it in its famous observation that "where the understanding has not previously combined, it cannot dissolve, since only as having been combined *by the understanding* can anything that allows of analysis be given to the faculty of representation" (B130).

What is crucial is that Kant here *assumes* that understanding can do nothing other than provide some kind of intellectual "form" for given material. The point is also repeated in the next section: Understanding "is *nothing but* [emphasis added] the faculty of combining *a priori*, and of bringing the manifold of given representations under the unity of apperception" (B135). The point, I think, is generally not taken sufficiently seriously. Taken seriously enough, the needed conclusion follows directly from it. For if the understanding can *only* provide form for given material, then the relevant material needs to be available, and actually ingredient, in every intuition to which any concept is actually "applied." Naturally, there may appear to be an alternative to the conclusion. The apparent alternative would be to suppose that the understanding functions by directly "combining" a manifold of *distinct* intuitions: a given one, subject to whatever conceptualization is in question, "together" with a manifold of others to which the given one is thereby regarded as appropriately related. But the argument, against that alternative, would presumably be this: that all that we could possibly *mean*, by the latter "combination," is just the fact that a manifold of intuitions (or, correlatively, of intuitable appearances) have been subsumed under a particular concept or concepts. That would presume, impossibly, the legitimacy of appealing to the notion of "subsuming" under concepts, as an *explanans*, in the first place—when it is that very notion that the Deduction proposes to explicate in terms of the notion of "combination."

Thus Kant's central assumption, in the Deduction's first stage— enunciated, at least implicitly, in §15—is that the "application" of concepts to objects (or appearances) can in its own turn be nothing other than an "application" *of the very faculty of understanding itself*. For nothing else is given to the understanding to "apply" to objects—not even concepts! But this, taken strictly, entails that nothing is given for the understanding to "apply," beyond its own intrinsic ability to combine some body of material *into* concepts in the first place. Obviously, this requires a notion of combination that cannot be borrowed from an already operative notion of applying, or subsuming under, concepts. In turn, this requires a notion of the combination of a manifold that is internal to intuitions themselves. For the only sense in which the understanding could "combine" *distinct* intuitions is precisely by conceptualizing given intuitions *as* combined with distinct ones, that is, by "applying" already constituted concepts to them.

As I argued in Chapter Three, this position was already implicit in Kant's treatment of the nature of understanding as a "faculty," in the sections prior to the Transcendental Deduction itself. Quite apart from what we have already seen in the first-edition Deduction, it is therefore not arbitrary to read the position "into"

§15. The relative obscurity of the latter may be supposed simply to stem from Kant's refusal to characterize the nature of the manifold that is supposed to be available to understanding for combination into concepts. But once again, what can in any case be seen in §15—and throughout the Deduction—is that the *need* for some such combination lies precisely in the fact that the latter is supposed, in the first instance, to be constitutive of any cognitive state or act as such, out of the constituents of such would-be acts or states, and not to be constitutive of objects or appearances out of constituents of the latter. Surely—in itself as well as in the light of the first edition—no other material is a plausible candidate for this sort of constitution, besides imaginative anticipations and retentions, so far as these are actually ingredient in intuition.

Unfortunately (it may seem), Kant is emphatic that mere "associations" have nothing to do with his project in the Deduction:

> Insofar as imagination is spontaneity, I sometimes also entitle it the *productive* imagination, to distinguish it from the *reproductive* imagination, whose synthesis is entirely subject to empirical laws, namely, of association, and which therefore contributes nothing to the explanation of the possibility of cognition *a priori*. The reproductive synthesis falls within the domain, not of transcendental philosophy, but of psychology. (B152)

I have sometimes spoken of anticipations and retentions as "associations." This passage may therefore appear incompatible with the proposed interpretation.

This is the section (§24), partly examined earlier, in which Kant draws a distinction between *synthesis intellectualis* and *synthesis speciosa*, or "figurative" synthesis. The former is purely intellectual, the latter involves a *Wirkung* of understanding on sensibility: "As figurative, it is distinguished from the intellectual synthesis, which is carried out by the understanding alone, without the aid of the imagination." As I have read Kant's distinction, the purely "intellectual" synthesis consists in whatever operations are required in order to form a conception out of a manifold of material potentially ingredient in a given intuition, and thus required in order to conceptualize any intuition at all. This is provided by the Kantian "forms of judgment," supposedly already enumerated in the Metaphysical Deduction (§9), and considered in abstraction from their role as actually formative of conceptions. By contrast, I take it that *synthesis speciosa* is just those *same* forms—but now regarded as actually "applied" to a manifold of sensibility, that is, as actually formative of a conception out of a manifold of material in intuition. Kant also calls the "figurative" synthesis the "transcendental synthesis of imagination" (B151). It is imaginative, I propose, precisely because its *material* is essentially imaginative.

In this same passage, as we have now seen, Kant in turn equates "productive" imagination with the "transcendental synthesis" in question. From this it would follow that what I have called the mere *material* in transcendental synthesis, hence in "figurative" synthesis, could not be provided by the productive imagination in its own right. It would likewise seem to follow that, if there is indeed a distinction between imaginative material and intellectual form, *internal to productive imagination itself*, then the relevant material could be provided only by *reproductive* imagination. But then Kant plainly says, in the passage just quoted, that the synthesis of merely reproductive imagination "contributes nothing to the explanation of the possibility of cognition *a priori*." This may seem to contradict my proposal. But it does not. The claim that productive or figurative synthesis does, but merely reproductive synthesis does not, contribute to cognition *a priori* is perfectly compatible with the view that reproductive synthesis (that is, anticipations and retentions) contributes to cognition precisely by virtue of being *converted*, by means of *synthesis intellectualis, into* instances of "figurative" synthesis.

We are finally ready to turn, then, to §§18–19, that is, to the sections that correspond to Kant's discussion of the conversion of judgments of perception into judgments of experience in the *Prolegomena*. The first of these sections distinguishes between an "objective" and a merely "empirical," or a merely subjectively valid, "unity of consciousness." It begins with the claim that objective unity is that by which "all the manifold given in an intuition [*in einer Anschauung*] is united into a concept [*in einen Begriff*]" (B139).

Again, the notion of some kind of manifold, capable of ingredience in particular intuitions, but also susceptible of formation into concepts predicable *of* intuitions, is central to my own reading. But it is often underestimated in a reading of this passage.[40] Kemp Smith, for example, obscures the suggestion by translating "into a concept" as "in a concept." Ignoring this distinction, as well as the reference to the containment of manifolds in single intuitions, one might suppose Kant's point simply to be that any concept necessarily *represents* a manifold of possible intuitions in "connection" with a given one. That would, of course, formulate a Kantian claim. But Kant's own formulation appears to suggest something deeper.

Kant does not in fact describe the empirical "unity of consciousness," in §18, in exactly the same terms that he had used to describe judgments of perception in the *Prolegomena*. But this is only because he is not entirely consistent in §18. What I have argued, regarding the *Prolegomena*, is that "judgments of perception" are intuitions in which anticipations and retentions are ingredient in a special way. They are ingredient, that is, in such a way as to provide potential *material* for the "judgments of experience" into which they may eventually be converted. Now often, Kant refers to anticipations and retentions, in connection with given intuitions, as mere "associations" in regard to those intuitions. Conformably with this usage, Kant thus also says, in the present passage, that the empirical "unity of consciousness" is constituted "through association of representations" (B140). This, at least, conforms with the suggestion that the distinction Kant is attempting to draw, between empirical and objective consciousness, is indeed just the familiar distinction between judgments of perception and the objective judgments containing them as mere material. On the other hand, in the same passage, Kant also speaks of the empirical unity of consciousness in rather different terms. For he sometimes seems to regard it, not as the kind of "unity" that is involved in the mere anticipation and retention of possible intuitions, in connection with a given one, but as nothing distinct from the actual *course* of intuition itself: "Whether I can become *empirically* conscious of the manifold as simultaneous or successive depends on circumstances or empirical conditions" (B139).

Kant may simply be wavering between two different contrasts: between the kind of unity represented by means of objective judgments and a mere "unity" of representations in a single course of experience, on the one hand, and between the kind of unity represented by means of objective judgments and a mere unity of association, on the other. Or, tying the two distinctions a bit more closely together, we might simply suppose that Kant is contrasting the kind of unity represented by means of objective judgments with two very different kinds of "association." In the one case, he might be contrasting it with the phenomenon of anticipation and retention as such; in the other case, he might be contrasting it with the phenomenon of actually "having in mind" what *is* anticipated and retained. This might simply reflect Kant's own uncertainty as to the nature of the former in the first place. But whatever Kant's uncertainty, he surely did not suppose that anyone ran the risk of confusing objective judgments themselves with the streaming of actual consciousness, or with instances of the mere togetherness of items in a stream of consciousness. Even Hume, after all, tried to make it clear that the crucial factor is not the fact of mere togetherness in a stream of consciousness, but that the items in question are together *because "associated."* In any event, the phenomenon of anticipation and retention is clearly central to Kant's concern in §18. This is evident, for example, from his appeal to the case of verbal association: "To one man, for instance, a certain word suggests one thing, to another some other thing" (B140).

A puzzle remains in the section. Kant says that the empirical unity of consciousness is "merely derived from the [objective unity] under given conditions *in concreto*" (B140). This is the claim that he illustrates by means of the example of verbal association. The claim may seem to pose a problem for any of the plausible alternatives: whether empirical unity is regarded as the actual course of consciousness, as the course of consciousness as it is merely anticipated and retained, or even, finally, as anticipations and retentions themselves. But we might explain Kant's point in the following way. In themselves, anticipations and retentions might be merely externally (perhaps causally) *connected* with certain of a subject's intuitional states (analogously to the connectibility of particular associations with particular words). On the other hand, those same anticipations and retentions might be actually connected *in* those states so as to constitute at least a "judgment of perception." Now, in the latter case, there could be only one reason why anticipations and retentions *should* be so connected in intuition. The reason could only be that they might then provide material for eventual judgments of experience. The latter, we may presume, are what directly constitute the "objective unity of consciousness." So it would indeed follow that the merely empirical unity of consciousness is "derived" from the objective unity "under given conditions *in concreto*." The explanation simply parallels the one that I gave earlier of a corresponding claim concerning the "derivation" of empirical from transcendental "affinity."

Now let us turn to §19. Here it is clearly "association," again, that is supposed to provide the appropriate contrast with judgments of experience:

> I find that a judgment is nothing but the manner in which given cognitions are brought to the objective unity of apperception. This is what is intended by the copula 'is'. It is employed to distinguish the objective unity of given representations from the subjective. . . . Only in this way does there arise *out of this relation* [emphasis added] a *judgment*, that is, a relation which is *objectively valid*, and so can be adequately distinguished from a relation *of the same representations* [emphasis added] that would have only subjective validity—as when they are connected according to laws of association. In the latter case, all that I could say would be, 'If I support a body, I feel an impression of weight'; I could not say, 'It, the body, is heavy'. Thus to say 'The body is heavy' is not merely to state that the two representations have always been conjoined in my perception, however often that perception be repeated; what we are asserting is they are combined *in the object*, no matter what the state of the subject may be. (B141-2)

It may be objected that Kant is confused in this passage, inasmuch as he attempts to illustrate pre-objective associations by reference to full-blown *judgments*, that is, by reference to judgments that clearly refer to objects (for example, to bodies), and even to oneself.[41] But then no one could illustrate associations of the relevant sort without doing just that. What we should presume to be important, in Kant's attempts, is just that what they are *supposed* to illustrate is neither a type of objective judgment (in the relevant sense) nor the mere phenomenon of the actual togetherness of representations in a stream of consciousness. What is in question is at most supposed to be the *anticipation* of representations. Naturally, such anticipations could not possibly be described apart from the employment of concepts that are, in the relevant sense, "objective." But that does not imply that they are in themselves dependent upon concepts (in the relevant sense). Indeed, it is perfectly compatible with supposing that they are the mere material for the forming of any concepts in the first place.

Only the view that associations, of the intended minimal sort, are what provide the original material for the formation of concepts can make sense of Kant's claims in this passage. For only that view can make sense of the claim that an objective judgment first arises "out of" *the very relation* that is constitutive of an instance of association. And only that view can make sense of the claim that an objective judgment involves an objective relationship *among the very same representations* that a purely associative "judgment" connects in a merely subjective manner:

> Dadurch allein wird *aus diesem Verhältnisse* [emphasis added] ein Urteil, d.i. ein Verhältnis, das objektiv gültig ist, und sich von dem Verhältnisse *eben derselben Vorstellungen* [emphasis added], worin bloss subjektive Gültigkeit wäre.

One normally, of course, thinks of judgments as originally formed out of concepts, somehow placed in relation to one another. That in fact might be said to be Kant's own "official" view. But the fact is that he begins the section precisely with the question as to what such a relation is supposed to "consist" of in the first place: *worin dieses Verhältnis bestehe*. Kant then proceeds to equate this question with a question as to the real force of the copula. This may suggest that he is merely inquiring as to what any judgment *asserts*, in virtue of the connection between the concepts that it contains. But the subsequent discussion is notably silent on this particular point. Kant does not in fact proceed to tell us what judgments have, in general, to *say* about objects, in particular about the objects that they are supposed to be about. Rather, he refers only to the function of judgments as somehow unificatory with respect to one's *representations* of objects. At one point he also refers, not to mere representations, but to "cognitions": "a judgment is nothing but the manner in which given cognitions are brought to the objective unity of apperception" (B141).

This last phrase may suggest that Kant is indeed intending to talk about the bringing of various *concepts* to a "unity of apperception." But the subsequent discussion makes this reading impossible. For it becomes clear that Kant is at most talking about a bringing to the objective unity of consciousness of the very *same* representations that, in any particular instance, might well instead have constituted a purely subjective unity of consciousness. It could not be (objective) concepts that Kant is talking about here. Indeed, in the very heading to the section, Kant seems almost plainly to tell us that concepts need to be originally *formed* precisely by means of whatever structures are about to be introduced to the reader:

> The logical form of all judgments consists in the objective unity of apperception *of the concepts* [emphasis added] which they contain.

It should be clear that the point does not require denying that the "forms of judgment" are constitutive of relations among concepts. To deny the latter would be to reject the Metaphysical Deduction. What I am arguing is simply that the Transcendental Deduction has a more fundamental aim, namely, to argue that, in every instance, the intellectual operations that *are* constitutive of relations among concepts must at the same time be formative of the very concepts thereby related. While the "forms of judgment" essentially constitute unities among concepts, this can only be a (necessary) upshot of their constituting concepts themselves, as actively functioning elements in cognition. (Attention to the notion of cognitive "activity" is crucial in this reading. There are obviously many ways the term *concept* might be used. When it is used, for example, to stand for something that one is merely supposed to be able to "possess," and then on occasion to "use," then concepts might turn out to be any number of things: perhaps even mere dispositions of certain sorts.) As Kant puts it elsewhere, "a judgment of experience is that (*perception* [emphasis added]) out of which a *concept* [emphasis added] of the object arises [*entspringt*]."[42]

Although the following passage, from the *Metaphysical First Principles of Natural Science*, does not speak specifically of "concepts," but rather of "cognitions," it seems to confirm this reading:

> [T]he categories, which are thought, are nothing but mere forms of judgments insofar as these forms are applied to intuitions (which with us are always sensible only), and that by such application our intuitions first of all obtain objects *and become cognitions* [emphasis added]. . . . [A]s to *how* experience is possible by means of these

categories, and only by means of them . . . can be solved almost by a single conclusion from the precisely determined definition of a judgment in general (an act by which given representations *first become cognitions* [emphasis added] of an object.[43]

The point, it should be clear, is not simply to apply cognitions or judgments *to* intuitions. In that case, the former might most naturally be regarded as originally formed through the combination of something called "concepts." In turn, the judgments thereby formed would presumably at most *refer* to (or be in some way "about") the intuitions in question. But Kant's point is, of course, that the latter need to be turned *into* cognitions or judgments in their own right. This, I have argued, could only be done by converting some material *within* intuitions into the very concepts "available" for judgment *about* them in the first place. In any case, as Kant informs us in the continuation of the passage just quoted: he will "take the earliest opportunity" to make all of this clear to the reader. Presumably, he meant to do so in the second-edition Deduction. The improvement, he tells us, is only to concern "the manner of the presentation and not the ground of explanation."

We might briefly notice the same point by returning to §17, in connection with a passage on which I have already commented:

To know anything in space (for instance, a line), I must *draw* it . . . so that the unity of this act is at the same time the unity of consciousness (as in the concept of a line); and it is through this unity of consciousness that an object (a determinate space) is first cognized. (B137-8)

I have already emphasized the fact that the unity of consciousness of which Kant is speaking is a unity supposed to be internal to the act of cognition itself. What we need now only notice, in addition, is that the unity in question is not described as a unity among concepts. It is rather said to be a unity *within* any concept as such, "as in the concept of a line." The same, we saw, might be supposed to be Kant's point in the notoriously difficult footnote to B160. An intellectual synthesis is there said to be required for the mere apprehension of space and time, or of spaces and times, as objects. But it is also a synthesis, Kant says, that "belongs to space and time" themselves, not to concepts. Quite to the contrary of the latter, it is a synthesis through which "concepts of space and time first become possible." Such a synthesis *can* "belong to space and time," I have argued, only to the extent that it is an operation required for the very forming, out of a manifold ingredient in spatiotemporal *intuitions*, of whatever concepts might be regarded as "applicable" to intuitions.

We are finally ready to return to the question of the Deduction's two stages. So far we have seen some reason for saying that, apart from occasional glimpses ahead, the first stage adopts a purely noetic approach to cognition. Its emphasis, that is, is on the need for combinations of manifolds within (would-be) cognitions themselves. Accordingly, any question that concerns the relevant "application" of categorial structures must so far be limited to the question of their "application" to intuitions as opposed to intuitable *objects*. But the term *intuition* is of course ambiguous. Most notoriously, it is ambiguous as between representations and objects represented. For this reason, the heading of §20, and its text, may simply leave us unclear whether the manifold that is so far said to be "subject" to the categories is supposed to be merely a manifold within would-be cognitions, or rather (or perhaps in addition) within appearances as (would-be) objects:

> All sensible intuitions are subject to the categories, as conditions under which alone their manifold can come together into one consciousness. . . . All the manifold, therefore, so far as it is given in a single [*Einer*] empirical intuition, is *determined* in respect of one of the logical functions of judgment, and is thereby brought to a consciousness in general [*zu einem Bewusstsein überhaupt*]. Now the *categories* are just these functions of judgment, insofar as they are employed in determination of the manifold of a given intuition. (B143)

If the conclusion is in fact meant to be drawn with respect to objects, then it is at least surprising that Kant should speak so vaguely of "intuition." Certainly, in any case, the emphasis on combination in (or even "into") a subject's *consciousness* suggests the noetic aspect. The same goes for Kant's reference, in the section that follows, to the "manifold contained in an intuition which I call mine" (B144). And it of course goes for §16 as well, the section that introduces the problem of "the original synthetic unity of apperception" in the first place. What is particularly *mine*, or in principle "ascribable" to me, could hardly be intuitions *qua* objects. It could only be intuitions *qua* representations *of* objects.

The specific concern with the applicability of categories to objects enters with §22: "The category has no other use for the cognition of things than its application to objects of experience" (B146). But the point, in that context, is so far merely limitative, since it has not yet been explicitly stated that the categories necessarily apply to objects at all. The question of limitation is also the subject of §23. It concerns the restriction of categories to sensible intuition, and the purely negative character of any conception (at least by us) of a non-sensible faculty of intuition.

The first of these two sections had simply begun with the distinction between thinking and cognizing. For the latter, Kant says, we require intuition. It might seem that this is what provides the key to the Deduction's stages. For it might be taken to suggest that the first stage concerns a purely "logical" notion of an object (mere "thinking"), while the second concerns, for the first time, the notion of a genuine object of cognition. But we have already seen that the first stage is in fact already concerned with the unification of manifolds within sensible intuitions, and even specifically spatiotemporal ones. So if the Deduction's structure is indeed to turn on a distinction between what is merely thought and what is genuinely cognized, then the former must at least involve "objects" that are in the first place "thinkable" only *through* the very act of unifying manifolds in intuition.

It is perhaps possible, at least on one level, to read the Deduction as turning, in its second stage, from a concern with one kind of "object" to another. And if we do, then of course we need to suppose that the first stage had only dealt with objects in a certain kind of abstraction. But apart from the fact that this kind of distinction would be less fundamental than another (namely, than the distinction between the stages as concerned with noetic and with noematic "unification," respectively), it would be misleading to put the point by saying that the first stage had dealt with objects only *qua* objects of "thought." If we say it, we cannot mean to deny that it had dealt with objects precisely as apprehensible through the unification of manifolds within intuitional states. What we must mean is simply that the first stage had only been dealing with objects regarded in abstraction from their *reality*. If any "objects" at all could be said to be in question in the first stage, then they would not yet constitute a real world of nature. At most, they would merely be the intentional correlates of the very act of apprehending them. In these terms, the second stage might then be regarded as arguing that the categories are indeed applicable to the real world of nature. But in a very important sense, this would hardly mean that the first had been concerned with objects of a purely "logical" sort.

If we did distinguish the stages in this way, then it might seem that we would be committed to supposing that the first could only have legitimated the application of the *mathematical* categories to objects. For Kant tells us that only the dynamical categories concern actual existence (A160/B199; cf. A178/B220). But the conclusion does not follow. The first stage may not yet have concerned the applicability of categories to nature. But it may nonetheless have argued that any truly cognitive apprehension of a *would-be* nature presupposes the application, to the (would-be) cognitions in question, of all of the forms of judgment. Even the apprehension of mere illusions as illusions, for example, might arguably require the representation of at least a manifold of *possible* situations in which the apprehended "objects" might not have been illusory at all. (We need to remember that, by "cognition," we are concerned with what may also be an instance of *mis*cognition.)

In any case, I do not propose to adopt this approach to the Deduction's stages. It could perhaps be done. But this way of drawing the distinction, in terms of a distinction between kinds of objects, would at best be parasitical upon another. So far as it relies on the notion of noetic/noematic "correlation," it would simply fail to emphasize a more *fundamental* inference that Kant first needs to draw. It is the latter to which I now turn.

After the discussion of *synthesis intellectualis* and *synthesis speciosa*, in §24, and of self-consciousness in the appendix to that section and in the section that follows, §26 finally informs us:

> We have now to explain the possibility of knowing *a priori*, by means of *categories*, whatever objects may *present themselves to our senses* [Kant's emphasis] . . . in respect of the laws of their combination, and so, as it were, of prescribing laws to nature, and even of making nature possible. (B159)

We have seen that it is tempting to locate Kant's emphasis, in this passage, in a question regarding the objects that present themselves to *our* senses in particular. But by now we should see that a natural reading is the alternative that I have proposed. We have so far been concerned, Kant tells us, with the necessary structures in one's *apprehension* of objects, insofar as apprehensions are cognitive (or at least would-be cognitive) states; we have now to be concerned with objects as such, that is, with the things that "present themselves" *to* apprehension. This distinction seems to be confirmed by what Kant had said in the sentence preceding the one just quoted:

> In the *metaphysical deduction* the *a priori* origin of the categories has been proved through their complete agreement with the general logical functions of thought; in the *transcendental deduction* we have shown their possibility as *a priori* cognitions of objects of an intuition in general (cf. §§20, 21). We have now to explain. . . .

In other words, the first stage had demonstrated the necessity of application of the categories to *cognitions* of objects; the second must demonstrate—in a different but correlative sense of the term—the necessity of their "application" to objects.

It is the final paragraphs of §26 that then specifically formulate Kant's points in terms, not simply of the application of categories to "intuitions," or to cognitions or would-be cognitions of objects, but rather to appearances themselves, and "to nature, the sum of all appearances" (B163). The general question that then arises—as to how it is that *objects* should necessarily conform to anyone's concepts at all—then provides the topic of §27. The concluding "brief outline," finally, summarizes the whole:

> It is the presentation of the pure concepts of the understanding, and therewith of all theoretical cognition *a priori*, as principles of the possibility of experience; of these, however, as the *determination* of *appearances* [emphasis added] in space and time in general [Stage Two],—and finally, this as *following* [emphasis added] from the principle of the *original* synthetic unity of apperception, *as the form of the understanding* [Stage One; emphasis added] in relation to space and time as original forms of sensibility. (B168-9)

In §21, Kant also describes the relationship between the stages. In the preceding section, he says:

> . . . beginning is made of a *deduction* of the pure concepts of understanding; and in this deduction . . . I must *abstract from the mode in which the manifold for an empirical intuition is given* [emphasis added], and must direct attention solely to the unity which, in terms of the category, and by means of the understanding, enters into the intuition. In what follows (cf. §26) it will be shown, *from* [Stage One; emphasis added] the mode in which the empirical intuition is given in sensibility, that its unity is no other than that which the category (according to §20) prescribes to the manifold of a given intuition in general. Only thus, by demonstration of the *a priori* validity of the categories in respect of all *objects* [Stage Two; emphasis added] of our senses, will the purpose of the deduction be fully attained. (B144-5)

Once again, Kant's reference to the "mode in which the manifold for an empirical intuition is given" may suggest that he is now to be concerned with the special features of human sensibility. And B160 (with its footnote), as we know, in fact specifically considers the problem of space and time as objects (although this was also anticipated in §17 and its footnote). But an alternative reading is clearly available, with respect to Kant's reference to the "mode in which" objects are "given." On that reading, Kant is for the first time to be concerned with the mode in which any kind of manifold is to be given as a real object to which forms of understanding are applicable. Thus the emphasis is on a "given" manifold, and the consequent need for its unity, that is no longer a "given" manifold in the sense that was first in question. Rather, any relevant unification with respect to what is "given" to our senses is now to be regarded as a unification with respect to objects themselves, not merely with respect to a body of material (potentially) available for formation into cognitions. (It is independently evident that Kant was comfortable speaking of the "given" in both of these ways. Sensations, for example, are "given" for Kant, and so are the "appearances" apprehended *through* sensations.) This, it should be clear, is perfectly compatible with seeing the *logic* of the transition as lying in the fact that the relevant "objects"—even when those objects are taken to be altogether (empirically) *real*—are merely the intentional "correlates" of (possible) cognition.

We might also note that §17, which we have already seen to anticipate §26's attention to the distinction between space and time as "forms" (aspects of cognition) and as "objects," had itself been content merely to draw the relevant *distinction* (between cognition and object). That is, it did not itself explicitly *conclude* that the forms of understanding, just by virtue of their "applicability" to the manifold in cognitive states, must also be "applicable" to possible objects of such states. Rather, at least in the passage already examined, any relevant unification is still regarded as unification with respect to a manifold internal to the act of cognition itself. Here is Kant's own more general formulation in the same section:

> *Understanding* is, to use general terms, the faculty of *cognitions*. These consist in the determinate relation of given representation to an object; and an *object* is that in the concept of which the manifold of a given intuition is *united*. Now all unification of representations demands unity of consciousness in the synthesis of them. Consequently it is the unity of consciousness that alone constitutes the relation of representations to an object, and therefore their objective validity and the fact that they are cognitions; and upon it therefore rests the very possibility of the understanding. (B137)

Obviously, Kant does not suppose that, on the basis of this, any considerable *effort* will in fact be required for finally completing the Deduction, that is, for moving from the structure of cognition to the structure of correlative "reality." As it happens, the completion requires only a page plus a footnote in §26.

In §26, the following is the first step in Kant's explanation of why the categories necessarily apply to objects:

> [1] First of all, I may draw attention to the fact that by *synthesis* of *apprehension* I understand that combination of the manifold *in* [emphasis added] an empirical intuition, whereby perception, that is, empirical consciousness *of* [emphasis added] the intuition (as appearance), is possible. (B160)

In this passage, Kant calls attention to, or at least plays upon, the ambiguity of *intuition*. On the one hand, we have been concerned with "intuition" as a kind of cognitive state (or would-be cognitive state). But on the other hand, we have thereby also been concerned—although it has so far not been emphasized—with "intuitions" in the sense of the "appearances" that are the (would-be) objects *of* the former. Presupposing this distinction, the passage then summarizes the Deduction's first stage: the apprehension of appearances, to the extent that it is cognitive, requires combination of a manifold *in* that apprehension. (Kant does not bother to repeat that the forms needed for this, at least in their "application" to the manifold, are nothing other than the categories of understanding; §20 had made that clear.)

The second step is this:

> [2] In the representations of space and time we have *forms* of outer and inner sensible intuition *a priori*; and to these the synthesis of apprehension of the manifold of *appearance* [emphasis added] must always conform, because in no other way can the synthesis take place at all. (B160)

Following this observation, Kant proceeds, as we have seen, to elaborate on the distinction between the mere "form" of spatiotemporal intuition and space and time as objects of intuition.

I have, of course, already argued that, here and in the corresponding portion of §17, Kant's references to the "forms" of intuition are not intended as references to space and time themselves, nor even to the spatiotemporal forms of appearances. Rather, they are intended as references to the intrinsic intuitional forms in one's apprehension *of* (possible) spaces, times, and appearances. Read in this way, [2] then simply serves the dual function of reminding us (a) that "apprehension," except when it is "pure," is always apprehension through a body of appropriate *material* and (b) that objects as "appearances" are the necessary *correlates* of such apprehension. Though we have not so far been explicitly concerned with the notion of correlation, we are now to be concerned precisely with these correlates, and with the spatiotemporal "forms" that are apprehensible in *them*.

This noted, the final inference is indeed an effortless one:

> Thus the *unity of the synthesis* of the manifold, without or within us, and consequently also a *combination* to which everything that is to be represented as determined in space or in time must conform, is given *a priori* as the condition of the synthesis of all *apprehension*—not indeed in, but with these intuitions. . . .[1] the categories are conditions of the possibility of experience, and are therefore [3] also [*auch*] valid *a priori* for all objects of experience. (B161)

In his translation of this passage, Kemp Smith eliminates Kant's use of *auch* in the last sentence. This, of course, obscures the crucial *inference* from the applicability of categories as conditions of all possible experience (Stage One: premise [1] above) to their "applicability," in what must be a merely correlative sense, to all of possible objects of experience (Stage Two: conclusion [3] above). The inference is mediated by a single consideration, namely, the one presented in premise [2].

The Kantian "forms of judgment," available to us from the Metaphysical Deduction, are the forms intended to serve the relevant function of unification in sensibility. As I have argued at length, but primarily on the basis of an examination of §§18-19, and of Kant's distinction between judgments of perception and experience, their function is therefore to unify bodies of "associations" internal to intuitional states. Regarded precisely *as* so functioning, the same forms are of course what Kant calls the "categories." In one sense, therefore, the Deduction's first stage had already demonstrated the necessary "applicability" of categories to sensibility. But at that stage, the manifold in question was simply within (would-be) cognitive states themselves. Completion of the Deduction required an inference to their correlative application to *objects*. The inference, we have seen is almost effortlessly accomplished. But that is what we ought to have expected, if the objects in question are indeed to be regarded as mere "correlates" of their very apprehension in the first place. And that, as Kant informs us , in his general "Observation" on the first stage (§21), is precisely how objects are to be regarded: "Now *things in space and time* are given only insofar as they are perceptions (that is, representations accompanied by sensation)" (B147).

Chapter 6

Self-Consciousness

I. Introduction

SO FAR I have supported the claim that Kant regards empirical concepts as composed of an imaginative material that functions as an essential ingredient in the very experiences of which those concepts are predicated. The imaginative material is a manifold of anticipations and retentions, although Kant often adopts a more noematic perspective. When he does so, he tends to suggest that the most basic material for conceptual synthesis is rather a manifold of possible "appearances," or perhaps even the parts of space and time themselves. In any case, we have not yet carefully examined the sense in which imaginative material is to be regarded as subject to the imposition of "forms," by virtue of which it is finally embodied in full-blown concepts. To this extent, we still fall short of what Kant regards as full-blown "consciousness."

The forms in question can only be what Kant calls "forms of judgment"—the ones that he identifies, in the Metaphysical Deduction, on the basis of an examination of the "logical function of the understanding in judgments" (A70/B95). As we saw in the preceding chapter, this implies that the forms of judgment cannot be mere forms for the connecting of *concepts* into judgments. In the privileged case (if there are indeed others) of judgments of intuition, they can involve nothing other than "that form which the understanding is able to impart to representations"—that is, to intuitions—themselves (A56/B80):

> The same function which gives unity to the various representations in a judgment also gives unity to the mere synthesis of various representations in an intuition. . . .
> The same understanding, through the same operations by which in concepts, by means of analytical unity, it produced the logical form of a judgment, also introduces a transcendental content into its representations, by means of the synthetic unity of the manifold in intuition in general. (A79/B104-5)[1]

The upshot, we have seen, is not simply the constitution of a judgment. It is the original formation of a concept for "use" in a judgment.

But how are we to understand this type of "constitution"? How can Kant suppose that a body of material, potentially ingredient in an intuition,[2] is able to become ingredient in a predicative "term" that one merely "applies" to that intuition among others? Kant's view appears to be that *consciousness itself* is the form required for the purpose:

> [C]onsciousness in itself is not a representation distinguishing a particular object, but a form of representation in general, so far as it is to be entitled cognition; for of it alone can I say that I am thereby thinking something. (A346/B404)

> [T]he merely subjective form of all our concepts [is] consciousness. (A361)

More specifically, what is in question is some special kind of *unity* of consciousness:

> The word 'concept' might of itself suggest this remark. For this unitary consciousness is what combines the manifold, successively intuited, and thereby also reproduced, into one representation. (A103)

> This thoroughgoing synthetic unity of perceptions is indeed the form of experience; it is nothing else than the synthetic unity of appearances in accordance with concepts. (A110)

> But this unity of possible consciousness [of objects as appearances] also constitutes the form of all cognition of objects. . . . [T]he mode in which the manifold of sensible representation (intuition) belongs to one consciousness precedes all cognition of the object as the intellectual form of such cognition, and itself constitutes a formal cognition of all objects *a priori*, so far as they are thought (categories). (A129)

> [Categories] are nothing but forms of thought, which contain the merely logical faculty of uniting *a priori* in one consciousness the manifold given in intuition. (B305)

> This unity of consciousness (of the connection of our representations) is as much *in us a priori* as the foundation of all concepts, as the form of appearance is as the foundation of intuitions.[3]

> A judgment is the representation of the unity of consciousness of various representations or the representation of their relation, *so far as they constitute a concept*.[4]

In other words, full-blown "consciousness" and the relevant "unity" of it are not simply the upshot of conceptualization. They are what constitute concepts in the first place.

It is also clear that Kant regards the relevant unity of consciousness as inseparable from "self"-consciousness. The link appears to lie in his claim that the requisite unity of consciousness does not involve a consciousness of objects, or appearances, *simpliciter*, but of something that he calls the *synthesis* of appearances:

> The original and necessary consciousness of the identity of the self is thus at the same time a consciousness of an equally necessary unity of the synthesis of all appearances according to concepts. . . . (A108)

Assuming that synthesis involves mental activity, the suggestion may seem helpful. It may seem implausible to reduce self-consciousness to the consciousness of a "unity" (or even possible unity) among objects or appearances. But it may not seem implausible to reduce it to the consciousness of some kind of mental activity (or possible activity). For example, self-consciousness might be supposed reducible to a consciousness of the possibility of appropriately justified "self-ascription." However, I shall try to take Kant more literally in his own suggestion that original self-consciousness is consciousness of oneself directly *in* one's consciousness of objects or appearances.

It is important to be clear that the suggestion would not contradict Kant's insistence, *contra* Leibniz and Wolff, that the difference between intuition and conception is not reducible to a difference in the clarity of one's consciousness of objects (cf. A43/B60-1). This is because, according to suggestion, the relevant consciousness of objects or appearances is itself to be explicated in terms of a mode of coming to consciousness *of one's own imaginative condition*, insofar as the latter is embodied in intuitions. In other words, any relevant difference in the "clarity" of one's consciousness of objects or appearances is itself to be explicated in terms of an irreducible relationship (of intentional correlation) *between* a certain mode of consciousness of objects and a mode of self-consciousness. To that extent, one might say both that the distinction between intuition and conception, hence original self-consciousness, is explicable directly in terms of a consciousness of objects or appearances and that it is explicable—only apparently to the contrary—in terms of a function whereby one is originally conscious of portions of one's own imaginative condition. (The latter suggestion might then help make sense of Kant's account of empirical concepts in terms of "abstraction.")[5]

It is Kant himself who says that any truly cognitive apprehension does not merely *entail*, nor is it merely entailed by, some mode of self-consciousness. Rather, it is originally *constituted* through the effecting of the latter, and indeed through the effecting, thereby, of some special mode of "clarity" in consciousness:

> All our cognition has a *twofold* reference: *first* a reference to the *object*, *second* a reference to the *subject*. In the first respect it is referred to *representation*, in the second to *consciousness*, the general condition of all cognition in general.—(Strictly, consciousness is a representation that another representation is in me.) . . . Variation in the form of cognition *rests on* [emphasis added] a condition that accompanies all cognition, on *consciousness*. If I am conscious of the representation: then it is *clear*; if I am not conscious of it, *obscure*. . . . *Since consciousness is the essential condition of logical form in all cognition*, logic can only be concerned with clear, not with obscure representations.[6]

This is not the only passage in which Kant equates consciousness (of objects) with the mere "clarity" of representations to their subject.[7] The only way to avoid the apparent implausibility in this is, I suggest, to develop a sense in which the latter is not, as the claim might suggest, a consciousness of representations as *distinct* from a consciousness of ordinary objects or appearances. Rather, it must be a consciousness that is constituted *in* one's consciousness of objects or appearances in the first place.

However we spell it out, it is the primary aim of the Deduction to establish at least a necessary connection between a more "subjective" (and so regarding one's own states?) and a more "objective" (and so regarding objects or possible objects?) notion of what needs to get "synthesized," in order to constitute a truly cognitive consciousness of objects or appearances. In these terms, the strongest form of such an endeavor might then appear to be the one that attempts to show that each of these is a necessary condition of the other. For example, we might try to show that the ability to be conscious of oneself as a subject is a necessary condition of the ability to recognize (or misrecognize) objects, and that the latter is also a necessary condition of the former. Correspondingly, a weaker approach in one direction, but stronger in the other, might attempt to show that at least the ability to achieve verifiable *knowledge* of oneself, as a subject, is a necessary condition of the ability to recognize or misrecognize objects, and that the latter is also a necessary condition of the former. Or reversing the permutations: perhaps the ability to be merely conscious of oneself as a subject is a necessary condition of the ability to achieve a verifiable knowledge of objects, and—more significantly—perhaps the latter is also necessary for the former. Whatever the variation, Kant's contribution might be supposed to lie in the establishment of an external, albeit logical, connection between "consciousness" of self and of objects or their aspects.[8] I want to suggest that he is aiming at a much closer connection.

II. Consciousness and Concept Formation

When we consider what we mean by consciousness, in particular by the consciousness of "objects," then it is worth bearing in mind that we are considering something of which it has only in fact been recently permissible to speak, in either philosophical or ordinary English. The situation has been similar in French. In the traditions of Locke and Descartes, philosophical usage has only gradually extended the domain of "consciousness" beyond the apprehension of one's own individual existence, together with the apprehension of whatever additional data might be comprised in the latter; the development of ordinary usage has been even more gradual. From antiquity through the 1700s, a more outward-looking notion was, to be sure, current as well. But it applied at most to one's (co-) awareness of facts or of states of affairs, not to one's awareness of objects or of the world.[9] The earliest Oxford English Dictionary entry that concerns "external objects" is from Pope's *Rape of the Lock* (1712-14), although there may be earlier candidates in Dryden.[10] Neither Bailey[11] nor Johnson[12] recognizes the usage.

Though troubling to say it implies that the view was contested in his day, Reid puts it bluntly: "It is improper to say, I am conscious of the table which is before me. I perceive it, I see it, but I do not say I am conscious of it."[13] The Oxford English Dictionary classifies the usage as poetic. French, or at least academic French, simply ignores the option. Into the 1930s, it regards even the notion of *conscience* of oneself, and *conscience* of one's inner states, as purely philosophical.[14] Coste, in translating Locke, had to coin a term for the purpose, as did Leibniz in his commentary on Locke[15] The earliest citation that I have found of an extension of the term to the apprehension of "external phenomena" dates from 1864 in French.[16]

These facts should lead one to wonder whether something might not be involved in the notion of a "consciousness" of objects that is not easily capturable in less "poetic" talk about cognition or perception of objects—merely supplemented by the apparently *additional* fact that one needs to have a "consciousness" (a higher-order cognition or perception?) of that very cognition or perception.[17] In any case, Wolff had, by 1719, already established the notion of *Bewusstsein* as readily applicable to the consciousness "of ourselves and of other things [*Dinge*]."[18] In the light of this, it may be all the more notable that Kant himself remains disinclined to speak of one's *Bewusstsein* of objects (whether of *Dinge* in general, of *Gegenstände*, or of *Objekte*). He tends to do so only in contexts that emphasize that the objects in question are appearances or "representations."[19] As we have already seen, Kant even appears to offer a definition, according to which the proper objects of consciousness are one's own internal states. All of this may seem to provide difficulty for my reading. But as I have also noted, it is hard to know what to make of Kant's official "definition," in the light of his own view as to the role of consciousness in the constitution of cognition. Indeed, in the very passage in which he proposes it, and in which he claims that one's cognition of objects is constituted through some mode of consciousness of internal states, Kant illustrates what is supposed to be thereby constituted by referring to one's *Bewusstsein that something is a house*.[20] (That Kant in general insists on favoring self-consciousness, when he speaks of *Bewusstsein*, may of course be explained in a number of ways. As suggested earlier, it might simply reflect his fear of being taken to espouse the view of Leibniz and Wolff, that the difference between a mere intuition and a true cognition of objects lies in an irreducible difference with respect to one's clarity of consciousness of the latter.)

At least in particular cases, there seem to be readily available alternatives to talk about the consciousness of objects or appearances. Kant himself simply speaks of the cognition (*Erkenntnis*) of such things. Apart from that, where he is specifically concerned with *Bewusstsein*, he seems to be concerned with one's consciousness, not of objects or appearances as such, but of the synthesis *of* objects or appearances (or else with one's consciousness of the unity of such synthesis). But the difficulty is that there are a number of things that might be meant by the latter.

The following passage makes it clear that, whatever kind of consciousness, and of unity of consciousness, is essential to Kant's account of cognition in the *Critique*, it can only be comprehended in terms of an account of imaginative anticipation and retention in experience, that is, in terms of an account of *Reproduktion*. The passage is from the third of the sections that the first-edition Deduction devotes to the problem of synthesis, "Synthesis of Recognition in a Concept":

> If we were not conscious that what we think is the same as we thought a moment before, all reproduction in the series of representations would be useless. For it would in its present state be a new representation which would not in any way belong to the act whereby it was to have been successively generated [*zu dem Aktus, wodurch sie nach und nach hat erzeugt werden sollen*]. The manifold of the representation(s) would never, therefore, form a whole, since it would lack that unity which only consciousness can impart to it. . . . The word 'concept' might of itself suggest this remark. For this unitary consciousness is what combines the manifold, successively intuited, and thereupon also [*dann auch*] reproduced, into one representation. This consciousness may often be only faint, so that we do not connect

it with the act itself, that is, not in any direct manner with the generation of the representation, but only with the outcome. But notwithstanding these variations, such consciousness, however indistinct, must always be present; without it, concepts, and therewith knowledge of objects, are altogether impossible. (A103-4)

This passage may appear to deal with the problem of unity of consciousness solely in terms of a problem concerning the ascribability of representational states to subjects. In these terms, the relevant "manifold of representations" will presumably just be all such states, considered in relation to single subjects.[21] Alternatively, it might be all of the possible appearances that correspond, as correlates, to those states. In either case, the "one" to which the "many" of the manifold is supposed to relate is simply a single subject of self-ascribable states. Unlike the first-edition Deduction, the second may appear to deal exclusively with this aspect of the problem of "unity of consciousness." But there, as we have seen, this was not in fact Kant's primary concern. As I hope to show, it is different in the present case as well. Kant's argument is of course meant to bear on the problem of self-ascription. But the crux of the argument is that a concept of self-consciousness defined solely in terms of this notion can at best be derivative from a more basic concept of self-consciousness.[22]

Kant does not, in the present passage, raise a general question concerning the possibility of the self-ascription of representational states. He raises a question concerning a more fundamental ability. The latter is the ability to *anticipate*, as an integral part of the conceptualization of appearances, states that may eventually *be* self-ascribable states. (Alternatively, he raises a question concerning the anticipability of the correlative appearances.) From the context, it is also reasonable to suppose that the role of "retention" is to be interpreted in this light. The discussion of retention must, of course, be relevant to the problem of one's ability to self-ascribe past states.[23] But it cannot in the first instance merely bear on that question. As the quoted passage suggests, the primary question concerning "retention" is just as much a question concerning the notion of anticipation, so far as it is relevant to conception. Of course, as I have been reading Kant, the primary question concerning both must bear, not merely on a subject's ability to anticipate and retain, but on the way in which conceptual states *themselves* anticipate and retain.

With this distinction in mind, Kant's suggestion might be deeper than it first appears to be. For example, he might be suggesting the necessity of *states that anticipate states* that in their own turn embody, beyond their apprehension of a given appearance or appearances, a self-representation *as having been anticipated in the first place*: in other words, states that anticipate the possibility of their own retention. We shall see later that something like this—together with even more complex modes of "higher-order" anticipating—will in fact be required for a full elaboration of Kant's view.

In any case, we shall be concerned only with a particular manifold of eventually self-ascribable representations. We shall be concerned only with those that are anticipated and retained by any given representation in its own right, insofar as the latter is regarded as subject to conceptualization. Given this, the most natural suggestion regarding the relevant "unity of consciousness" is that it is not in fact a unity that bears on representations simply by virtue of their being all (at least in principle) ascribable to a single subject; rather, it must be whatever kind of unity is required for the forming of concepts *out of* representations. (It helps to recall that it is a question concerning the *nature* of concepts that provides the focus for Kant's formulations throughout this section. In line with this, Kant concludes his own elucidation of what the synthesis of "recognition" adds to that of "reproduction" with the conclusion that "the concept of [any] number *is* nothing but the consciousness of this unity of synthesis" (A103; emphasis added). At A107, similarly, he concludes that the transcendental unity of consciousness is the *a priori* ground of all *concepts*, not simply the ground of the knowledge to be gained with the help of concepts. I have commented on similar passages in the second-edition Deduction.)

The passage quoted above (from A103-4) clearly suggests an interplay between some kind of structure first introduced by means of a truly intellectual "consciousness" and some kind of structure already available through the purely imaginative capacity for *Reproduktion*. In that passage, Kant refers to the "act whereby" certain representations were "to have been successively generated." Presumably, this involves just the sort of anticipative capacity with which Kant had been earlier concerned: that is why Kant speaks of representations that were (already) *to have been* generated, i.e., were already anticipated as possible, independently of a contribution from the higher powers now to be examined. But Kant now says that this anticipative capacity is insufficient for the conceptualization of appearances. What is needed, he seems to say, is what can only be provided, not simply by one's ability to anticipate and retain, but by a certain mode of consciousness *of* whatever is anticipated or retained. To apprehend an appearance in a truly conceptual way, one must also have some kind of consciousness of those additional appearances, anticipated *in* the act of apprehension in question, precisely *as* appearances that are therein anticipated.

One may wish to attempt a simplification by reducing both of these elements in terms of the representational powers of already constituted conception. For example, one might take the "anticipations" ingredient in conceptualized apprehension simply to be *judgments*, implicit in such apprehension, bearing on the possibility of additional apprehension. And one might take whatever "consciousness" those acts essentially involve to be constituted by those *same* judgments, insofar as these are indeed implicit in the apprehension in question. But quite to the contrary of this, the proposed account calls for both a level of consciousness and a kind of anticipation and retention, ingredient in conceptual acts, that is (as it were) *not yet* conceptually judgmental at all. The full-blown act of conceptualization can only be what issues from the "application" of the former to the latter.

If we follow the proposed approach, then we will need, strictly speaking, to distinguish three possibilities, whereas we have so far recognized only two. We have, of course, the two possible cases: (a) where primitive imaginative anticipations and retentions are ingredient in intuitional states, but are "not yet" subjected to the forms of consciousness required for full-blown conceptualization, and (b) full-blown conceptualization in regard to imagined or perceived objects or appearances. (We may ignore the case of possible intuitions whose material is even more primitive than that of (a).) But to the extent that (b) is possible in the first place, a third and half-way case ought also to be possible: (c) where an intuitional state embodies the anticipation or retention *of the mere possibility* of states of type (b). That would be less primitive a phenomenon than (a), but would still fall short of an actual instance of (b). The question would then seem unanswerable: whether for a genuinely "conceptual" mode of consciousness we should strictly require (b), or at most something like (c). In any event, if states of type (b) are the paradigmatically "conceptual" ones, states of type (c) are presumably available only to creatures *capable* of the former states as well. I assume that Kant simply failed to distinguish between these two notions.

We might choose to regard instances of (c)-representation as involving a kind of "pre-predicative judgment." The title of *judgment* would of course associate them with states of type (b); the absence of appropriate intellectual form would associate them with (a). But then why not have felt free, *pace* Kant, to regard instances of (a)-representation as modes of "judgment" or even of "predication" in the first place—ones that are simply on a more primitive level than either (b) or (c)? What is important, in pursuing such issues of phenomenological taxonomy, is not to be misled by mere questions of terminology, and to remain clear about one thing: that whatever the relevant differences are, between the more and the less primitive levels, they could not merely involve differences, for example, in degree of *complexity* with regard to whatever type of anticipation and retention is already in question on the most primitive level. Some difference in "form" must also be involved.

With respect to the requisite notion of "form," it may in fact be possible to adopt an approach somewhat different from what I have so far suggested, consistently with the general line of this study. To do this, we might try to avoid the introduction of an irreducible form of *consciousness*, whose function it is to provide for the eventual formation of concepts. Instead, we might simply make use of our two notions of relatively primitive anticipation and retention, on the one hand, and of some function whereby this more primitive material gets embedded in sets of *higher-order* anticipations and retentions. By the latter, again, we can not mean sets of more complex anticipations and retentions. What we must mean is sets of anticipations and retentions that do not merely anticipate and retain correspondingly possible appearances (or correspondingly possible intuitions), but rather correspondingly possible appearances (or intuitions) *qua* appropriately relatable to *these* (actually given) appearances (or intuitions)—or perhaps even *qua* appropriately relatable to these (actually given) anticipations and retentions themselves. Here, the "forms" required for the constitution of full-blown conceptions, out of manifolds of primitive anticipations and retentions in intuition, would themselves simply be sets of appropriately higher-order anticipations and retentions. This is not quite the same as the account that I am proposing. But it is possible that, here too, Kant himself was not sufficiently clear as to the alternatives.

Once we have granted anticipation and retention on the more primitive (purely "animal") level, and introduced the possibility of their ingredience in intuition itself, then, in at least one respect, it would be a triviality to grant the possibility of "higher-order" anticipations and retentions in intuition. For example, it would be a triviality to grant the possibility, even on a purely "animal" level, of the anticipation or retention of the very satisfaction *of* some anticipation or retention. (In a sense, to anticipate something and to anticipate satisfaction of that very anticipation are just the same thing. That is presumably what constitutes the triviality in the case.) But that kind of "higher-order" anticipation and retention is not, of course, what I had in mind in the preceding paragraph. I pursue this point in more detail later. It should become clear, at least by then, why the proposed account would not in any case run afoul of Kant's own insistence that, with respect to consciousness, "there is no gradation leading from animals to men."[24]

The alternative still requires attention to the specific problem of "consciousness," but at a different point in our analysis. In particular, we would need to be careful not to think that the role of *self*-consciousness could be accounted for simply in terms of our recognition of the "higher-order" anticipations and retentions in question. In those terms, we could suppose ourselves to have done some justice to the problem of self-consciousness only to the extent that the ingredience in intuition of *any* kind of anticipation and retention was already conceded to involve some degree of "consciousness" to begin with (i.e., some degree of consciousness of possible objects or appearances, or at least of possible intuitions). After all, if the ingredience of those lower-level anticipations and retentions did not by itself amount to some level of consciousness in the first place, then how could the mere addition of "higher-order" anticipations and retentions just by itself imply that the subject was now self-"conscious"? By hypothesis, we would have to admit that the subject was now in some way self-*anticipative*. But why regard self-anticipation as a mode of self-*consciousness*—so long as anticipation was not by itself conceded to involve any mode of consciousness to begin with?

This second way of reading Kant—according to which the intellectual "form" required for the formation of concepts is merely a kind of higher-order anticipation and retention—would therefore require the supposition that the mere ingredience of such material in intuition already amounts to a genuine level of intuitional consciousness. In principle, I see no reason why Kant could not have conceded the point. In that case, however, it would be the mere form of intuition itself, at least as applied to a body of appropiate material, that constitutes "consciousness" as such. The (not necessarily chronologically subsequent) introduction of some higher form could then at most be constitutive of a higher *level* of consciousness, including, of course, *self*-consciousness, as Kant is concerned with that notion. As it happens, the *Critique* itself only occasionally suggests that the act of conceptualization, together with the self-consciousness from which it is inseparable, involves a different "level" of consciousness from what sensibility already involves. But it is a suggestion that Kant in fact repeats in many of his reflections outside the *Critique*.[25] Indeed, as we have already seen, he sometimes goes so far as to equate the peculiar quality of intellectual consciousness with nothing more than a difference in *clarity*, with respect to what is already available as material on lower levels.

With respect to his explicit comments on anticipation in judgment, Kant's own examples are in an additional way unclear or misleading as well. This is because they too specifically focus on the case of the eventual *satisfaction* of a subject's anticipations. Kant considers the case, for example, of a subject who is counting:

> If we were not conscious that what we think is the same as we thought a moment before, all reproduction in the series of representations would be useless. . . . If, in counting, I forget that the units, which now hover before me, have been added to one another in succession, I should never know that a total is being produced through this successive addition. . . . (A103)

Here, the emphasis is on the ability to recognize that a subsequently apprehended appearance, or a subsequently experienced representation, is related in a certain way to an earlier one. The problem with this is that our concern needs to be with the element of conceptualization that is directed toward given appearances, and with the structure of the anticipations necessarily involved in it, quite apart from whether those anticipations are ever in fact satisfied by subsequent apprehension. What is important is not the satisfaction, but the anticipation *of* it. So far, what I have argued is simply that the latter is provided by a capacity for *Reproduktion* that is incorporable into intuitions independently of a capacity for conceptual "recognition." The latter is then to be constituted by the (not necessarily chronologically subsequent) imposition of appropriate form on the "reproductive" material in question.

We might want to adopt a purely dispositional approach, or even some kind of functionalist approach, to the higher-order "consciousness" of potential satisfaction, supposed to be necessarily ingredient in the conceptualization of appearances. Doing so, at least, need not be incompatible with Kant's insistence on something more than purely animal anticipation. For this, we might simply regard the relevant dispositions (or the relevant functional states) as involving dispositions to *judge* in the full-blown sense (or as states that are apt to generate full-blown judgments, under the appropriate circumstances). It may also seem implausible to insist on anything more than this, by way of an actual "consciousness" of potential satisfaction, insofar as that consciousness is supposed to be ingredient in conception as such. In any case, Kant himself acknowledges that we ought not to connect the relevant consciousness "only with the outcome" of that act whereby some additional representation "was to have been successively generated"; we must rather connect it "with the act itself, that is . . . with the generation of the representation" in question (A103-4). In saying as much, he is presumably not making the trivial point that, in order to conceptualize an appearance as what one had all along anticipated, one must indeed have anticipated that appearance all along. His point must rather be that anticipations of the relevant sort—however otherwise construed—must involve the anticipation, not simply of appearances, but of the eventual apprehension *of* appearances. Indeed, as we shall see, they must involve the anticipation of the apprehension of appearances *qua* eventually apprehensible precisely *as* thus anticipated. Kant's point must be, further, that while this in turn needs to build upon animal anticipation (and "retention"), ingredient in intuitions themselves—*whatever* its nature—it needs also to involve a higher-order transformation of such material. It may have been Kant's uncertainty as to the nature of the foundational material that led him to blur the distinction between the problem of the structure of anticipation as such and that of the possibility of "recognizing" cases of its satisfaction or frustration.

Now we may return to our question concerning the distinction between two notions of unity of consciousness. It is obvious that such a distinction plays a role in the Deduction. What is less clear is what it amounts to. As we have already seen, Kant himself distinguishes a transcendental, and "original," unity of consciousness—or unity of "apperception"—from the merely empirical unity involved in the succession of representational states in a subject (A107; cf. B139-40). It is of course clear that the mere succession of states in a subject is not the same as the subject's consciousness of those states as its own. Hence it could not possibly account, for example, for the subject's consciousness of its own anticipations as eventually satisfied or satisfiable. So what more is needed?

We might be tempted to suppose that what is lacking needs to be directly supplied by one's capacity for judgment, namely, by one's capacity for judgment in regard to oneself as a subject of experiences, and by whatever additional judgments this in turn entails. What would be "transcendental" about the capacity in question, beyond the fact that it is a necessary condition of cognition, might then be taken to be that it involves the thought of a unifying center for experiences that is not itself an experienceable item in its own right. It is at best an object of judgment:

> This original and transcendental condition is no other than *transcendental appercep-tion*. Consciousness of self according to the determinations of our state in inner perception is merely empirical, and always changing. No fixed and abiding self can present itself in this flux of inner appearances. . . . What has *necessarily* to be represented as numerically identical cannot be thought as such through empirical data. (A107; cf. B133-4)

There is no doubt that Kant regards original, transcendental self-consciousness as something purely intellectual, somehow superadded to a body of more primitive (merely "empirical") material. The second edition seems to make the point more plainly than the first:

> It must be possible for the 'I think' to accompany all my representations; for otherwise something would be represented in me which could not be thought at all, and that is equivalent to saying that the representation would be impossible, or at least would be nothing to me. That representation which can be given prior to all thought is entitled intuition. All the manifold of intuition has, therefore, a necessary relation to the 'I think' in the same subject in which this manifold is found. But this representation is an act of *spontaneity*, that is, it cannot be regarded as belonging to sensibility. (B131-2).

The crucial question is what all of this is supposed to involve.

In the next section, we shall more fully explore the question of "intellectual" as opposed to "sensible" self-consciousness. For now, we need at least to be clear concerning the central problem in any purely judgmental approach to the "I think." The difficulty in the suggested approach is simply this: that to the extent that the "I think" involves purely judgmental "self-ascription"—whether or not

the subject in question is itself an experienceable item—the capacity for adding the "I think" to a manifold of given material could not possibly play the role
that Kant has in mind for it. That is, it could not play the role of a kind
of self-consciousness that is supposed to be an essential part of the constitution
of predicative consciousness in the first place. It could not do so precisely because the "self-consciousness" in question would already *be* a mode of predicative
consciousness.

We need to keep the distinction between "modes" of self-consciousness in
mind, when we consider the apparently bi-conditional structure of Kant's argument in the Deduction. As we have seen, Kant maintains that the act of conceptualizing any given intuition (whether sensory or merely imaginative) involves a kind
of self-consciousness that in some way rests on more primitive imaginative structures in intuition, but also goes beyond them by means of the "addition" of distinctively intellectual functions. In other words, any truly conceptualized instance of
the consciousness of objects entails an instance of self-consciousness. This is the
first part of the apparently bi-conditional claim. In it, the "consciousness" of objects in question is, of course, essentially predicative: it involves the "application"
of concepts to intuited objects. Kant's claim is then that this presupposes a kind
of self-consciousness that rests on intellectual functions. But it is important to be
clear that this is not at all the same as saying that it presupposes a kind of self-
consciousness that is predicative in nature.

The ambiguity is disguised by Kant's use of the term *apperception* and by his
use of the formula "I think." As we have seen, the former term might be employed
specifically in order to designate some kind of self-consciousness. But Kant also
uses it (though only when he regards apperception as "empirical") as nothing other
than one's recognition (or misrecognition) of *objects*:

> [A]pperception [represents appearances] in the *empirical consciousness* of the iden-
> tity of the reproduced representations with the appearances whereby they were
> given, that is, in recognition. (A115)

In these terms, we could put the first part of Kant's bi-conditional claim by saying
that "apperception" (of objects) presupposes "apperception" (of oneself).[26] This
may encourage the supposition that the latter, like the former, is predicative in
regard to its own "object," namely, the self. A similar point goes for Kant's use
of the formula "I think." That the formula must be able to accompany representations, so far as they are truly one's own, may mean that one must always be able
to conceptualize one's own intuitions in some way. But it may also mean something else, namely, that one must always be able to be "conscious" of oneself *as*
conceptualizing intuitions (or as able to). Both of these need to rest on intellectual
functions. But that does not imply that the latter is predicative (in regard to oneself) in anything like the way in which the former is (in regard to objects of possible
intuition).

Now for the completion of Kant's bi-conditional claim: including the part that
goes from self-consciousness to consciousness of objects. According to the latter
part, self-consciousness is not only necessary for, but also sufficient for, the consciousness of objects. But in fact, Kant appears to go even farther than this. For

he appears to have some kind of constitutive *identity* in mind, not simply a relation of condition to conditioned:

> Thus transcendental unity of apperception forms out of all possible appearances, which can stand alongside one another in one experience, a connection of all these representations according to laws. . . . The original and necessary consciousness of the identity of the self *is thus at the same time* a consciousness of an equally necessary unity of the synthesis of all appearances according to concepts, that is, according to rules, which not only make them necessarily reproducible but also in so doing determine an object for their intuition, that is, the concept of something wherein they are necessarily interconnected. (A108 [emphasis added]; cf. A122)

> The transcendental unity of apperception *is* that unity through which all the manifold given in an intuition is united in a concept of the object. (B139; emphasis added)

> This consciousness of my existence in time is bound up in the way of identity [*identisch verbunden*] with the consciousness of a relation to something outside me. (Bxln)

> In other words, the consciousness of my existence is at the same time an immediate consciousness [*zugleich ein unmittelbares Bewusstsein*] of the existence of other things outside me. (B276)

> [W]e can only determine ourselves in time, insofar as we stand in relation to things outside of ourselves and therein consider ourselves [*und uns darin betrachten*]. . . .[27]

There are at least two issues that might be raised by such claims. Most often, again, they seem to be taken as bearing on the possibility of self-ascription. This, in turn, might be taken in either a stronger or a weaker sense: either as concerning the possibility of self-ascription as such, or, more specifically, as concerning the possibility of knowing the truth of self-ascriptions. In either case, Kant's formulations in the quoted passages should appear to us extravagant. One might take the possibility of self-ascription, or at least of self-knowledge, in some way to presuppose a consciousness, or even a genuine knowledge, of objects (and *vice versa*). But it is difficult to see how either could be as intimately one, as Kant suggests they are, with the very *acts* whereby objects are known in the first place.

The situation appears considerably different, once we suppose that Kant is talking, not about self-ascription and the self-knowledge that can rest on it, but rather about the specific kind of self-consciousness that needs to have been in question to begin with—namely, the kind that needs to be regarded as formative of *any* kind of "ascription" in the first place. Kant's point would in that case be that this kind of self-consciousness is not merely presupposed by, nor does it merely presuppose, a consciousness of objects. It is rather what *constitutes* such consciousness.

This is not to say that Kant has no concern with the conditions of empirical self-ascription as such. The second-edition "Refutation of Idealism" is, for example, specifically concerned with it. But we need to see that there are two different ways in which one might try to show that self-ascription entails the consciousness of objects. One of them, apparently inspired by Wittgenstein, would differ from the one that I am attempting to elucidate. But it is perhaps more or less what Kant has in mind at some points, for example, in the "Refutation of Idealism." It attempts to discover necessary conditions of the possibility of self-ascription independently of the fact that self-ascriptive consciousness is a derivative mode of self-consciousness in the first place. In Kant's view, as I have proposed, self-ascriptive consciousness is derivative from a pre-predicative mode of self-consciousness. The latter in turn does not merely entail, but is one with, consciousness of objects.

III. Determinate and Indeterminate Self-Consciousness

I postpone to the next chapter further reflection on judgmental "form" as such. But before we attempt to do some justice to this notion of self-consciousness, as in some way "one" with the consciousness of objects, we need to consider the relationship between another pair of distinctions that are central to Kant's reflections. These are the distinctions between (relatively) indeterminate and determinate self-consciousness, on the one hand, and between purely intellectual and genuinely empirical self-consciousness, on the other. It will be important to see that, despite the empirical status of the latter, even empirical self-consciousness is, in its original structure, in a way "indeterminate" in nature. Apart from the problem of interpreting Kant, some reflection on these issues should help us to appreciate the bearing of Kant's theory on some issues of recent philosophical concern.

It is evident that there are various ways in which one might be "determinately" conscious of oneself as an individual distinguishable from others. But there also seem to be modes of self-consciousness that do not involve this determinacy. Under certain circumstances, it seems, one may be self-aware but unaware as to who (or even what) one is in particular; one's mode of self-consciousness is strangely indeterminate. This has suggested to some that one's true (or "absolute") self is really supra-individual. Certain aspects of Kant's thought have in fact been supposed to imply this, at least by some of his idealistic successors. Kant may in any case have been the first to appreciate the corresponding difficulties for any account of the consciousness of oneself as an individual.

Supposing that there is a distinct individual that one is, it remains a question what it could possibly be to be conscious of oneself as being that individual. Could there be, for example, some special way (say, α) in which one always perceives or describes oneself, such that correctly taking oneself to be a particular individual, as perceived or as described in any other way, simply amounts to correctly judging that the two modes of perception or description are modes of perception or description of a single individual? The problem with this seems obvious. It leaves us in the dark as to what could be involved in perceiving or describing oneself in the allegedly special way in the first place. After all, if to take the individual in question to be oneself to begin with were merely to take what is perceived or described in a certain way to be the individual that is also perceived or described as α, then we either begin an infinite regress or come close to making self-consciousness the consciousness of the truth of a mere tautology.[28] Thus the ability to identify oneself as a particular individual seems to demand the synthesis of two almost antithetical modes of self-consciousness; only one of them seems directly to involve the determinate consciousness of an individual that is either perceptually or descriptively distinguishable from others.

Kant's reflections on the problem of self-consciousness are not usually read as indicating any particular positive view regarding the solution to this problem: as I shall call it, the problem of "self-determination."[29] Clearly, it is not his primary aim to provide a solution. At most, as some have argued, Kant is trying to show that a certain condition—namely, consciousness of objects—is *necessary* for any kind of self-determination.

The question remains why Kant supposed the condition to be necessary. On some interpretations, its necessity is seen to lie in a purely negative consideration concerning self-determination. It is seen to lie in the fact that one is not really "given" any object in the first place, "identifiable" as oneself. What one is given, in the relevant sense, is simply a sequence of representations that are ascribable to oneself. This in turn seems to imply that awareness of oneself, as a subject of representations, could originally *consist* in nothing other than some mode of consciousness of those representations themselves, or least in some mode of consciousness of some connection or synthesis among them.[30]

This may suggest that Kant's conclusions concerning the necessity for a consciousness of objects indeed embody a positive doctrine concerning the nature of self-determination. However, the condition as so far stated, and the reasoning presumed to lead to it, are compatible with a number of different approaches to that question. For example, they are compatible with the view that one is originally aware of oneself, as the subject to which certain representations are ascribable, simply by means of a definite description: e.g., by means of the description *the subject that stands in relation R to these representations* or *the subject that stands in relation R to these objects* (for some unspecified relations). They are also compatible with a denial of that view. For example, they are compatible with the view that consciousness of oneself as the subject of representations simply *is* the consciousness of certain relations among those representations themselves.[31]

Whatever Kant's positive account of self-determination, it is important to see that he regards the latter as not only possible, but also as compatible with, and even as plainly requiring, that one be able to "identify" oneself as a particular spatiotemporal individual:

[T]he thinking being (as man) is itself likewise an object of the outer senses. (B415)

We are to *ourselves object of outer sense* from the start [*vorher*], because otherwise we would not perceive our *place* in the world and be able to intuit ourselves in relationship with other things. . . . I am myself an object of my outer intuition in space and without this could not know my place in the world.[32]

On the other hand, as already suggested, it is likewise Kant's view that, in some other sense, it is impossible to identify or "determine" oneself in any way at all.

One is at most conscious *that there is* an individual who one is; at worst, one is conscious of nothing more than a mere "synthesis of representations":

> I call them one and all *my* representations. . . . This amounts to saying that I am conscious to myself *a priori* of a necessary synthesis of representations. . . . (B135)

> [I]n the synthetic original unity of apperception, I am conscious of myself, not as I appear to myself, nor as I am in myself, but only that I am. (B157)

> I exist as an intelligence which is conscious solely of its power of combination. . . . (B158)

> The consciousness of myself in the representation 'I' is not an intuition, but a merely *intellectual* representation of the self-activity of a thinking subject. (B278)

> The I of apperception, and therefore the 'I' in every act of thought . . . [is] the poorest of all representations. (B408)

> The "I," the universal correlate of apperception and itself merely a thought, designates as a mere prefix a thing of indeterminate signification, namely, the subject of all predicates without any condition to distinguish this representation of the subject from that of a something in general, namely, substance; by the expression "substance," one has no concept as to what this substance is.[33]

In any case, there is at least some sense in which it is possible to "determine" oneself as a particular spatiotemporal individual. What's more, this possibility is a necessary upshot of whatever it is that requires a consciousness of objects in the first place, as a condition of "self-consciousness" for Kant.[34] So the original question remains: What can a self-determination of this sort possibly *amount* to? What can it possibly *be*, for Kant, to take some spatiotemporal individual as "oneself"? As powerful as it might be, the mere conclusion that a consciousness (or even full-blown knowledge) of objects is necessary for any kind of self-determination is neutral with respect to the question. At least, it is neutral so long as it amounts only to the demand that, since one is initially "given" nothing beyond representations, self-consciousness needs to rest on the awareness of relations among the latter, in particular on such as satisfy the conditions of a consciousness of objects.

It is perhaps arguable that Kant did not intend to shed more light than this on the problem of self-determination. Perhaps, that is, he was only concerned with a certain necessary condition of the latter. But it is difficult to believe that the question did not have a more substantial place in Kant's reflections. Obviously, Kant thought there was something problematic, even paradoxical, in the very idea that we are determinable as particular spatiotemporal objects.[35] (And this is so quite apart from commitment, grounded elsewhere in his thinking—for example, in his ethical theory—to the postulation of a personal identity on a purely noumenal level.) On the one hand, self-consciousness can only be, for Kant, the consciousness of a "synthesis of representations"—not the consciousness of any sort of object at all. On the other hand, the very reflections that lead Kant to this conclusion also lead him to the conclusion that one must be self-determinable as a spatiotemporal object. It would be incredible if, in the light of this, Kant did not regard his reflections as in some way clarifying what it is to be aware of an object as "oneself" in the first place.

Now I have so far been emphasizing a contrast between self-consciousness as the consciousness of some kind of "synthesis," on the one hand, and self-consciousness as the consciousness of oneself as a particular spatiotemporal individual, on the other hand. But the point is to see that we really need a threefold distinction. We can see this by noticing, first of all, that at least insofar as the former is the consciousness of synthesizing *activities*, it must be regarded by Kant as purely intellectual in nature. Sometimes, Kant says as much: "original" or "transcendental" self-consciousness is a purely intellectual sort of consciousness (cf. B157-8, B277n, B278). Obviously, whatever sort of consciousness this is, it must be distinguished from a determinate consciousness of oneself as a spatiotemporal individual. But the crux of the issue is precisely that Kant also sees the need for a consciousness of oneself that is *neither* purely intellectual in nature *nor* the determinate consciousness of a spatiotemporal individual:

> The 'I think' expresses an indeterminate empirical intuition, i.e. perception (and this shows that sensation, which as such belongs to sensibility, lies at the basis of this existential proposition). But the 'I think' precedes the experience which is re-quired to determine the object of perception. . . . An indeterminate perception here signifies only something real that is given, given indeed to thought in general, and so not as appearance, nor as thing in itself (*noumenon*), but as something which actually exists, and which in the proposition, 'I think,' is denoted as such. (B422n)

> The proposition 'I think,' or 'I exist thinking,' is an empirical proposition. But em-pirical intuition, and consequently the object thought as appearance, underlies [*liegt . . . zum Grunde*] such a proposition. . . . The proposition 'I think,' insofar as it amounts to the assertion, '*I exist thinking*,' is no mere logical function, but determines the subject (which is then at the same time object) in respect of exist-ence. . . . (B428-9)

On the one hand, as we can now see, Kant is prepared to acknowledge a form of self-consciousness that is not purely intellectual. Thus it does not, for example, merely contain the "completely undetermined concept of a thinking being in gen-eral," one where "all that I really have in thought is simply the unity of conscious-ness, on which, as the mere form of knowledge, all determination [of the subject in question] is based" (B426-7). To the contrary, the consciousness in question is a consciousness of oneself in particular, hence a "determinate" consciousness. Furthermore, insofar as it is specifically grounded in sense perception, it must be a consciousness of oneself as a phenomenally identifiable, if not already identi-fied, individual: the "real" that is given is not merely that of a noumenon. On the other hand, and despite all of this, the self-consciousness in question remains in a way "indeterminate." Presumably, this can only mean that it is not the con-sciousness of any particular *object*, identifiable as "oneself." Thus even ordinary empirical self-consciousness, of "oneself" as someone in particular, can be either a determinate or an indeterminate self-consciousness. Apparently, it can be a genuine empirical self-consciousness, of oneself in particular, but still not the consciousness of a determinate object identifiable as oneself.[36]

It is reasonable to conclude that this notion of an indeterminate but empirical self-consciousness—and neither that of a purely intellectual consciousness of some kind of "synthesis," nor that of empirical self-ascription—must be the focus of our attempt to clarify Kant's view. But at the same time, we must develop a sense in which self-consciousness, on its most basic level, is indeed nothing other than the consciousness of a "synthesis of representations":

> [T]his unity of consciousness would be impossible if the mind in knowledge of the manifold could not become conscious of the identity of function whereby it synthetically combines it in one cognition. . . . For the mind could never think this identity in the manifoldness of its representations, and indeed think this identity *a priori*, if it did not have before its eyes the identity of its act, whereby it subordinates all synthesis of apprehension (which is empirical) to a transcendental unity, thereby rendering possible their interconnections according to *a priori* rules. (A108; cf. B132-4)

We have, of course, already seen why self-consciousness needs to rest on, or even to be one with, the consciousness of a synthesis of representations. The reason is that nothing else is *available*, as a unitary object of immediate awareness, in all cases in which one is in fact self-conscious. In particular, "No fixed and abiding self can present itself in this flux of inner appearances" (A107; cf. B133). If anything unitary, and yet essentially self-like, is to be found in the flow of representations, it would thus apparently need to be something definable, not in terms of detectable components of that flow, but only in terms of unitary *activities*, necessarily directed or directable at such components. But how do we get from here to a correlative apprehension of objects?

The inference would seem to rest on Kant's theory concerning the nature of object-concepts. According to this theory, any truly conceptualized apprehension of objects is itself merely the apprehension of syntheses of representations:

> But it is clear that, since we have to deal only with the manifold of our representations, and since that x (the object) which corresponds to them is nothing to us— being, as it is, something that has to be distinct from all our representations—the unity which the object makes necessary can be nothing else than the formal unity of consciousness in the synthesis of the manifold of representations. It is only when we have thus effected [*bewirkt*] synthetic unity in the manifold of intuition that we are in a position to say that we cognize the object. (A105)

> This concept [of objective reference] cannot contain any determinate intuition, and therefore refers only to that unity which must be met with in any manifold of cognition which stands in relation to an object. This relation is nothing but the necessary unity of consciousness, and therefore also of the synthesis of the manifold, through a common function of the mind, which combines it in one representation. (A109; cf. B137)

But if this is Kant's approach, then he appears to be involved in a fallacy. For even if ("original") self-consciousness is no more than the consciousness of a synthesis of representations, and the consciousness of objects is no more than the consciousness of such synthesis as well, this does nothing to show that the unity in question in one of the two cases is in any way correlative with the kind of unity that is in question in the other. In the light of this difficulty, it might seem reasonable to return to a suggestion that I have already rejected. It might seem reasonable to return to the suggestion that, whenever Kant appears to equate self-consciousness with the consciousness of syntheses of representations, he only means to be saying, first, that self-consciousness rests on the ability to ascribe a manifold of states to a single enduring self and, second, that a necessary condition of such self-ascription is the ascription of predicates to objects, and *vice versa*. (And we might then regard such consciousness as purely "intellectual," simply in the sense that it rests, not on the consciousness of an intuitable object identifiable as oneself, but simply on that of the rules or criteria for the type of ascription in question.)[37]

IV. Self-Consciousness and the Imaginative Content of Perception

I want to elaborate an alternative reading. The alternative involves a very different approach to the "manifold" of representations and its "synthesis." I have partly prepared the way for it, by distinguishing between manifolds of representational states, anticipable and retainable as co-ascribable to single subjects, and manifolds of representational states anticipable and retainable *by other states* as co-ascribable to single subjects. But we now need to introduce an additional distinction. It is the distinction between the anticipation and retention of states by other states, appropriately related to the given ones, and the anticipation and retention of states anticipated and retained as states that the given ones might themselves actually *become* (or that might themselves actually have become the given ones).

This puts the point, as it were, in terms of the possible "stretching" of states of consciousness into the future (or from out of the past). But it will be crucial to see that the point might be put in terms of the possible stretching of the ("immediate") objects of consciousness themselves, that is, of "appearances." For this, what we require is simply the supposition that the immediate objects of intuitional consciousness are just as literally *stretches of time* (whether actual or possible stretches) as they are actual or possible regions of intuited space. To the extent that the objects are stretches of time and not only regions of space—and recalling the role of anticipation and retention as necessary, not simply in conception, but in the intuitive grasp of appearances themselves—the suggestion indeed allows us to consider, as genuine objects of consciousness, not simply manifolds of appearances that stand, or that might be conceptualized as standing, in possible relations with other ones, but the very stretches of possible *time* in which those appearances might be anticipated as stretching into other ones (or in which others might have been anticipated as stretching into them). What I shall argue, then, is that nothing but the essential correlation between these points of view is what assures us that the apprehension of such "syntheses of representations" always constitutes, on a pre-predicative but fully empirical level, the apprehension of possible futures or pasts as "one's own." Thereby, it both constitutes the most basic mode of self-consciousness, independently of the determination of oneself as an object, and at the same time provides the necessary basis *for* that determination.

That the notion in question has a useful bearing on the problem that concerns us I shall try to make more plausible with the following examples. I begin with a case that comes as close as possible to providing an instance of "selfless" absorption in some object or observed scene. If certain philosophers are correct, then there is at least one sense in which no state of consciousness is completely free of some kind of self-relation. According to Sartre, for example, all mental acts include an apprehension of themselves; this in turn is constitutive of a special kind of apprehension of "oneself."[38] So far considered, however, the latter still falls short of a conception of oneself as any kind of object, nor does it involve any kind of predicative ascription in regard to oneself. I want to begin with a case that is at least as (apparently) selfless as that.

It is useful to consider a certain sort of "scene," for example, a scene of a kind that might be a part of a movie. I choose this sort of example because, in many cases, one manages to get completely absorbed in such scenes, hence to be minimally or even, apparently, not at all self-aware. We may then imagine the effecting of a series of transformations. These will be of a kind that are often employed in such scenes. What I have in mind is any such series as will eventually issue in a case in which, independently of theoretical pre-dispositions, we can all agree that the viewer has become (at least imaginatively) conscious of being actually *involved* in the scene in question. In other words, whatever a particular theory—for example, Sartre's, or even Kant's own—might dictate regarding the viewer's antecedent condition, we would appear to have a case in which the viewer is at least subsequently "self-conscious." The relevant consideration will then be this: that, while the transformation that eventuated in the latter condition did indeed eventuate in a state of self-consciousness, it was effected precisely without any loss of one's complete and (relevantly) selfless absorption in the *objects* of consciousness.

Take the case of an automobile that is driven, in a scene in some movie, along a road that is at least in part visible to the viewer. Imagine that the camera is focused, for the duration of the scene, through the windshield of the car and onto the stretches of road. One may observe a scene of this sort in an apparently selfless way. One often does so while in fact driving. Now we are also familiar with scenes of a different sort. In these, the camera remains focused on the stretches of upcoming road, but various techniques produce a different effect in the viewing of them. The point is, of course, that they produce the effect of stretches of road that the viewer is actually *traveling*. That is, they produce an effect whereby upcoming objects, or upcoming stretches of road, are apprehended as successively closer to *oneself*, and not merely to the character who happens to be portrayed on the screen. (One does not need to imagine, though one may do so, that one is in fact that character.) In viewing a scene of this sort, one has become, in a way, particularly aware of *oneself*. But the point is this: One has not, for all this difference, become any less "selflessly" absorbed in the objects that are around or ahead of oneself: in this case, a movie screen.

Now it admittedly does not strictly follow from the fact that we can obtain this kind of effect, as the upshot of purely cinematographic adjustments, that in the final case one is as purely "object-directed" as before. One might, after all, hypothesize that, at some point in the process, a double state of consciousness had developed: one part of it is still the original, visual consciousness of the upcoming stretches of road as traveled by someone other than oneself (say, by James Bond); the other, somehow together with this, an at least imaginative state of consciousness of oneself as traveling those stretches. In a way, I am not suggesting that there would be anything wrong in putting the case in these terms. Whether we do so or not, the question remains: What is the point of appealing to a *double* mode of consciousness? A similar query must meet the suggestion, apparently equally truistic, that in such cases one is indeed merely "imagining that" one is traveling a stretch of road. It is clear that this can be said. The problem is that the "imagining," in such cases, seems indistinguishable from the *viewing*. (In other sorts of cases, one may be additionally led to the performance of distinct acts of reflection: explicitly taking note of certain feelings in one's stomach, for example, or wondering why one has come to the movie.)

The following consideration seems to me to constitute a reason for supposing that the apparently two components of such an experience are really inseparable aspects of a single experience. On the one hand, we should note that it is perfectly possible to imagine that one is traveling along the road in question (or along a road just like it), at just that speed, and under just the given circumstances, while viewing the scene in question, but *without* that scene at all appearing to one as it does in the case. (As to how, specifically, I am in fact supposing it to "appear" in the given case, my own suggestion would obviously be that this involves perceptible aspects—at least of objects as "appearances"—that, unlike one's speed and the objective road conditions, simply cannot be conceptualized in equally "objective" terms. But the point is that, despite this, we would still be directed toward no more than the appearances themselves.) On the other hand, it seems impossible for the scene in question to be appearing to one as it in fact does, yet without one thereby *imagining* that one is traveling along that road at just that speed, and so on. This seems to me a reason to suppose that whatever kind of imagining is in question, it does not occur as a series of distinct imaginative acts, merely externally (perhaps causally) connected with a series of acts of a purely perceptual nature.

My suggestion is that the case involves imaginative content, not in the form of acts of imagining alongside purely perceptual ones, but as material *through* which perceptual acts are constituted in the first place. Of course, there is no reason to suppose such material to be limited to what we might regard as merely passive "anticipation and retention." In the case at hand, it is reasonable to suppose one's apprehension to be effected, not simply through a manifold of anticipations and retentions, but through dispositions and tendencies of various sorts. Prominent among them might even be idiosyncratic tendencies, of a kind that becomes manifest when one actually drives a car. In any event, the suggestion is that the imaginative content that Kant takes to be *essentially* ingredient in any instance of objective apprehension is also what constitutes that special form of empirical self-consciousness—"indeterminate" but in principle determinable as the identification of a particular individual—that on his view is equally essentially embodied *in* such apprehension. The point of the example was simply to show that such a mode of self-consciousness *can* indeed be constituted by means of the mere ingredience of imaginative material in an experience, hence without any concept of oneself as subject of experience. (The content in question might even include, in this way, the anticipation and retention of a variety of upshots of "one's own" possible *actions*, without presupposing any actual concept of oneself as an agent.)[39]

Sometimes, Kant himself appears to go so far as to connect the mere "sensations" that are ingredient in perceptual states with a certain kind of self-consciousness as well, namely, with a consciousness of oneself as a being possessed of sense organs. Insofar as it functions as material in intuition, sensation is merely material "through which" an appearance is apprehended. Thereby, it is also reflected *in* any appearance as such. But even when it is ingredient in ordinary acts of perception, sensation, Kant holds, makes us aware of our own sense organs as well as of something in appearances.[40] It is hard to know how seriously to take this. Kant himself is not clear as to what is really involved in this allegedly dual character of mere sensations. In particular, it is not clear whether he does not shift between two different notions of "sensation." With one of them—the one that seems prominent in the Aesthetic—it would not be sensations as such that make us aware of our sense organs. It would rather be certain dispositions (or at least anticipations and retentions—which is the closest Kant himself ever *comes* to "dispositions") that are typically "associated" with sensations in that sense. On the other hand, those same dispositions might also be regarded as *constitutive* of "sensations," in a different sense of the term. Such a view is at least independently defensible. It is worth digressing to reflect on it.

Take the case of physical pains. No sensory states seem more apt than these to make a subject self-conscious. It might even seem to be "constitutive" of pains that they do so. Yet it has been argued that the supposedly essentially painful character of pains is not at all a function of their purely sensational aspect.[41] It is rather a function of dispositions of various sorts. This might be defended without any explicit appeal to my own analogy between the apprehension of perceptible qualities *through* sensations and their apprehension through whatever dispositions are in question. It is nevertheless useful for our purposes to extend the analogy as far as possible. So we may suppose, for a start, that the apprehension of a pain in a limb that actually feels painful does indeed involve apprehending that limb through particular pain-sensations of one's own; as a correlate of this, the limb (at least *qua* appearance) comes to exhibit a corresponding and phenomenologically unique *quality*.[42] Conceding this, the question will then be whether the bare apprehension of this quality—despite the fact that it is the objective correlate of one's own pain-sensations—needs to amount to the apprehension of what we would normally call *painful*. As suggested, the contrary is arguable.

Now in some sense, it seems, nothing can make one more self-aware, and necessarily so, than the awareness of something that is painful in a part of one's body. In general, however, it is not the case that, in becoming conscious of a part of one's body, one is thereby rendered self-conscious. In many cases, one can easily forget that some limb is in fact one's own, and selflessly contemplate the way that it happens to appear. Now why should we suppose that the case of pain is different? Why should a perceptible quality, just because it is perceptible only through pain-sensations of one's own, also be inevitably experienced as painful *to* oneself? Empirically, it does not seem to be the case that it is.[43]

The resolution of the apparent paradox may lie in the fact that there are really two qualities in question, each of them as immediately available to intuition as the other, and both of which one might be inclined to regard as the quality of phenomenal painfulness. One of them might be regarded as the correlate of mere pain-"sensations." But if it is, then there can be no *a priori* reason for supposing that the apprehension of that quality is ever in fact painful. That is, there can be no *a priori* reason for supposing that the apprehension of that quality is painful *to oneself* (or, for that matter, to anyone else). For the latter, what would need to be added? It is implausible to suppose that what needs to be added is just certain sorts of judgmental ascriptions in regard to oneself. That would be incompatible with the fact that the immediate experience of oneself as pained is as immediate and unreflective as the apprehension of any sensory quality in intuition.

It is this immediate and pre-predicative aspect of the painfulness of pains that suggests that their apprehension involves no more than the ingredience of a particular type of sensation in intuition. Were we prepared to broaden the notion of sensation to the purpose, we might even concede this point. But our question concerns what such a broadening would need to involve. Given the immediate and intuitive nature of the case, only one alternative seems open. One's "self" can have entered the picture in the first place, in the mere apprehension of a part of one's body, only to the extent that the quality of painfulness is apprehended in that part, not through mere sensations of pain at all, but through specific dispositions and tendencies as well—or, if through "sensations," then only to the extent that this notion has already been broadened to the purpose. What we usually regard as painfulness, as an immediately perceptible quality, would then be the correlate of this type of apprehension. And it is only *as* such a correlate that it could possibly be truistic to say that the apprehension of immediately perceived pain is the apprehension of something as painful to oneself.

Whether he should have done so or not, it seems clear that Kant himself did not regard sensations, insofar as they are supposed to convey a consciousness of one's own sense organs, as involving anything more than "sensations" in the sense that is more generally in question in the Aesthetic—where Kant merely considers them as corresponding to some "matter" in appearances. In particular, he does not appear to regard them as involving anything like the imaginative "dispositions" that need eventually to serve as material for conception. Nor do I have any reason for supposing that Kant considered extending to pains his more general approach to appearances and their qualities in the first place: regarding them, not as modes of consciousness, but as the intentional correlates of modes of consciousness. In any case, I chose the example of pain because it appears to involve, and essentially so, a consciousness of oneself as a specifically embodied being, but it also appears to involve a self-consciousness that is immediate and pre-predicative.

The supposition that, to the extent that pain does indeed involve an instance of self-consciousness of this kind, it must involve the apprehension of qualities "through" something more than sensations—or if only the latter, then only in a suitably broadened sense—is perfectly compatible with the immediate and pre-predicative aspect of such self-consciousness. For my purposes, then, the upshot is this: that just because, when so construed, the apprehension of pains *is* essentially self-conscious, we have an additional reason for concluding that the mere apprehension of objects through the right sort of material, and apart from the presence of concepts, is of itself *constitutive* of a basic and irreducible mode of self-consciousness. It is constitutive, that is, of a consciousness of oneself precisely in one's consciousness of certain perceptible dimensions of appearances (in this case, of parts of one's body as appearance). In the case of pains, we have a name for the quality in question, though we have seen it to be ambiguous. In other sorts of cases—for example, in the case of the "subjective" qualities of upcoming stretches of road, or in the case of Sartre's "streetcar-having-to-be-overtaken" [44] —language may come closer to failing us. [45]

It will be easier to appreciate this point, and in general to appreciate the significance of insisting, in the present context, on the notion of an object of awareness as an intentional correlate of the awareness of it, if we bear in mind my earlier suggestion concerning the general relation between our awareness of appearances and our awareness of space and time. Kant's notion (A22/B37) that time is the form of inner sense, while space is the form of outer sense, may generate the impression that we apprehend perceptible "material" only as filling regions of intuitively apprehended space, or portions thereof, and never as filling or even partially filling intuitively apprehended stretches of time. This is because we may think that what one immediately apprehends in intuitively apprehended time, as such, is never outer appearances—that is, never what we are free to take, or on occasion to refrain from taking, as actually existent matter in space—but only states or ingredients of states of the apprehending subject. But Kant maintains that it is outer appearances that constitute the material of inner sense (B67; cf. B154-6, B163, B220, B292; I have argued elsewhere against taking this claim as expressing the subjectivistic doctrine that outer appearances are made out of our own subjective states). We can recognize this point, while at the same time accommodating Kant's own distinction between the two "senses." The point will simply be that while outer appearances are perceptually *apprehended* as filling or as partially filling time as well as space, the temporal relations among them, construed as actual *existences* in space, are never themselves an object of perceptual apprehension; they are at most an object of judgment. (Strictly, what immediately "appears" in an intuitively apprehended stretch of time may of course then amount only to a temporal portion of the real material object judged to be in it.)

This finally frees us to recognize that, in the apprehension of outer appearances, one is indeed always apprehensive of a manifold of stretches of one's own possible future and past. For that future and past will always be presented (or at least "appresented") as a kind of intentional object in its own right. (More exactly, it will be presented as a possible future or past *portion* of the total intentional "object" apprehended.)

If one is likely to find a specific role for "anticipation and retention," in Kant's doctrine of synthesis, what one of course generally assumes to be anticipated or retained, in connection with a given experience, is just possible future or past experiences, or the correlative appearances, appropriately "connectible" with the given one. In turn, this might be thought to require the ability to conceive of oneself as a being capable of stretching into the future or past, in such a way as to serve as the possible subject of those experiences, or as the possible perceiver of those appearances. It might be thought to require this self-conception, because there is simply no purely intuitive *awareness* of stretchable selves, over and above the awareness of whatever experiences (or appearances) are in principle ascribable to (or perceivably by) them. But our new framework provides for a very different picture. For it accounts for a sense in which one is intuitively aware of a stretchable self precisely *by* providing a sense in which one is intuitively aware, not simply of given experiences, and of possible future and past experiences co-ascribable with them—but of the very (albeit possible) stretching *of this or that experience* (or, correlatively, of this or that "appearance") *itself* into the future and past.

Surely, to be immediately aware of this or that experience as stretching, or as having stretched, is a fundamental form of the awareness of *oneself* as stretching, or as having stretched. But it is not a form that needs to rest on any conception of a self to which experiences are ascribable. It needs to rest on no more than the awareness of experiences themselves. This intuitive character of such a self-experience is not, of course, incompatible with one's ability to conceptualize its object in various ways, for example, as a possible stretch of one's own experience. The point is simply that its intuitive character does not presuppose one's ability thus to conceptualize its object.

It should be clear what role is played in this account by the broadening of what may have been our initial grasp of Kant's theory of temporal intuition. It is crucial to be clear, as well, what role is played by our theory regarding the apprehension of intuited objects through imaginative anticipations and retentions. That one does not merely experience anticipations and retentions that are in some way externally connected with the apprehension of given appearances, but that given appearances are themselves apprehended *through* anticipations and retentions, is what allows us to say that, in the apprehension of those very appearances, one is in a special sense self-aware. That the appearances in question are apprehended through imaginative anticipations and retentions necessarily gives them a perceptible *dimension* that they would otherwise fail to exhibit. In particular, it gives them a perceptible dimension that is a correlate of one's own future and past (at least *qua* "anticipated" and "retained"). Ordinary language may lack the terms for a clear expression of this dimension of appearances (apart from those terms that already involve an explicit reference to "oneself" as anticipating and retaining in their regard). We have already seen that Kant had dealt with at least a part of this problem in his treatment of "transcendental affinity." What we are now encountering is another aspect of the same problem.

Thus Kant's point, I suggest, is simply that, however we conceptually *express* the relevant dimension, the spatiotemporal dimension that is correlative with the ingredience of the appropriate sort of anticipation and retention in intuition—as opposed to their external connection with intuitions—is constitutive of an original and transcendental self-awareness: one is aware of "one's own" experiences, as possibly stretching into the future and past, precisely *in the sense that* one is aware, not simply of given appearances, but of given appearances *through* a manifold of one's own anticipations and retentions. This mode of self-awareness is "transcendental," not simply because it is a necessary condition of the possiblity of knowledge, but because it is a form of self-awareness in which no self appears as an object. It is "original," because it is the necessary foundation for eventual *determination* of oneself as an object.

Kant may in fact have no "argument" that is meant to lead to this conclusion in a rigorous way, over and above his observation that nothing else is available, as material in intuition, for the original constitution of a self-concept.[46] In any event, once one reflects on the significance of the fact that, already below the level of conceptualization as such, appearances are not only apprehended through mere "sensations," but through manifolds of one's own anticipations and retentions, the claim in question may not appear to be far from the truth. To recall our previous examples, it at least seems to provide a plausible account of how, in merely traveling a road in the absence of self-reflection, or in merely experiencing a pain in some part of a body, one may *ipso facto* be aware of *oneself* as traveling that road, or as in pain. To account for this apparent identity of the consciousness of certain objects and the consciousness of oneself, we do not need to introduce any conceptual factors or criteria that are not already involved in the apprehension of the objects themselves: the road and some bodily part. By virtue of its own internal structure, the apprehension of those objects *is* at the same time self-apprehension.

Now apart from a genuine self-concept, one will, of course, be unable to *judge* of any intuitively apprehended future, in a way that is truly judgmental in Kant's sense, that it is indeed a stretch of "one's own" possible future. But we have only been attempting to account, so far, for a mode of self-apprehension that is the necessary *basis* for any self-determination—as of any object-determination—through concepts. Beyond this point, it is likely that Kant had few details in mind. But the basic view that is to be gathered from the materials now at hand seems to me to amount to a plausible view concerning the relation between original self-consciousness as Kant construes it—that is, the consciousness of oneself, not as an "object" of some description, but merely as a kind of "synthesis of representations"—and a self-ascriptively determinate consciousness of one's identity.

Kant's point may then simply be the following: In general, one's imaginative anticipations and retentions regarding appearances stamp the world of appearances with a unique and immediately experienced "orientation"; only relative to and derivatively from the intuitive apprehension of the latter is it then possible to form any genuine *concepts* of the various "points of view," or of the various possible alternative "centers" of orientation, from which a particular consciousness might be presumed to be active in the first place. The formation of a determinate self-concept may in turn be held to rest on a concept of just this sort, therefore to rest on precisely the kind of anticipational/retentional structure that is essential to the conceptualization of objects.[47]

Obviously, one may form a purely conceptual notion of various centers of orientation, in terms of purely general features determinative of those centers. The point of view from here or there may be defined in terms of such features. But our question concerns the possibility of regarding oneself as *occupying* such a center. Clearly, I do not simply mean by *myself* "whatever being is defined by such-and-such point of view." For, however that point of view is described, both temporally and spatially, I may always find it significant that I in particular happen to occupy it.[48] What more is needed? The suggestion is this: that one must not merely be able to locate the "center" in question, but that one constantly *live* it on a pre-conceptual level. The only available, non-circular, account of such "living," in turn, seems to me to be precisely what we have already discovered, in the notion of the sensible/imaginative material through which objects are apprehended. To apprehend the world *from* any point of view in the first place can only be to apprehend it *through* an appropriate body of material. As we have already seen, the world, *qua* appearance, necessarily reflects the material through which it is originally apprehended. That was the point of the account earlier proposed of transcendental affinity. It is now the same point that finally accounts for that special mode of apprehension that is involved in apprehending some particular point of view on that world as "one's own."[49] (In considering the plausibility of the suggestion, we need to bear in mind that the full range of imaginative material, ingredient as material in intuition, will stamp the world with an "orientation" that is much more than a matter of visual perspective. The orientation will also reflect, for example, one's anticipations concerning the possibility of *altering* any given perspective.)

However the notion is elaborated, it is not, after all, implausible to suggest that one's fundamental self-concept is simply that of *whatever* subject is in the appropriate way defined by some spatiotemporal "point of view" on the world. The point is simply to see that such concepts amount to "self"-concepts only because they originally derive from a more primitive and original mode of self-*consciousness* involved in the constitution of such points of view in the first place. The latter does not determine a subject through spatiotemporal concepts (though it does, of course, "determine" it in some other sense). Nonetheless, original self-consciousness guarantees that the subject is so determinable. At least, it guarantees that *some* subject is so determinable, namely, the subject precisely *qua* correlate of the "unity of objective experience."

I have added the final qualification, because all of this can only concern the so-called "empirical" subject. But Kant himself seems to take it to follow, from the fact that the conditions for the determination of any empirical subject are derivative from the original constitution of conceptual consciousness itself, that the empirical subject is not as such (i.e., *qua* empirical) the ultimate subject at all:

> The subject of the categories cannot by thinking the categories acquire a concept of itself as an object of the categories. For in order to think them, its pure self-consciousness, which is what was to be explained, must itself be presupposed. Similarly, the subject, in which the representation of time has its original ground, cannot thereby determine its own existence in time. (B422; cf. A401-2)

The empirical subject is a genuine "subject of consciousness." But it is, as we have seen, a subject of consciousness only so far as it is constituted *as* an empirical subject by the flow of consciousness itself, in the course of its own constitution of the experience of objects. Are we therefore required to conclude that the originally constituting—yet obviously empirical—activities of the consciousness in question are themselves ascribable to the empirical subject only to the extent that they are more truly ascribable, in some other sense, to some "other" subject as well (that is, to a noumenal one)? Is there, that is, one consciousness but two *subjects* of it?

> Dies macht nun ein Doppeltes ich aus, aber nicht des Bewustseyns (ich erscheine mir selbst, ich bin mir auch in diesem empirischen Bewustseyn doch der Beobachtete und zugleich Beobachter, der . . . [Kant's note breaks off at this point].[50]

This is a question that I propose to leave outside our present reflections.[51]

Despite all the foregoing, it should be clear that I have not attempted to construct a valid argument that in fact succeeds in linking self-consciousness with the consciousness of objects. I have at most presented the rudiments of a *theory* of the former that seems to me to link it with the latter in a way that best fits the overall "argument" of the Aesthetic and the Deduction. In so doing, my primary aim has been to improve on accounts that merely concern the conditions for the ascription of representations to oneself as a subject. The problem with those accounts is that they involve no serious reflection on what it *is* to be aware of oneself as a subject in the first place. As we have seen, it is Kant himself who seems to want to tell us something as to what self-consciousness really is, not merely as to certain of its necessary conditions. And it is in this context that he tells us that self-consciousness, in its transcendental structure, can be nothing more than the consciousness of a "synthesis of representations." At the same time, he also tells us, it must be a consciousness that is in some way *one* with a consciousness of objects. Commentators cannot, of course, fail to be sensitive to the first of these points. I have tried to be sensitive to both of them.

But there is a more serious shortcoming in the analysis as I have proposed it. Even if we accept the proposed theory of self-consciousness, it would at most be the case that object-consciousness entails transcendental self-consciousness (thus at least the possibility of a more determinate mode of self-consciousness). It would not be the case that the latter entails the former. For if the central idea is that transcendental self-consciousness is constituted through the ingredience of manifolds of anticipations and retentions in intuition, then it is not clear why it should require full-blown *conceptualization* of appearances. Presumably, there is nothing in principle preventing the ingredience of anticipations and retentions in intuition, independently of their serving as material for conceptions as well. In the absence of forms of the appropriately intellectual sort, the mere form of *intuition* might suffice for the ingredience in question. (I have already, at least, rejected the apparent difficulty that, as merely ingredient in intuition, the material in question could not constitute a kind of self-consciousness, simply because it could not amount to any "consciousness" whatsoever.)

It may be that Kant overlooked the possibility of the actual ingredience of anticipation and retention in intuition, apart from their serving as material for conception. As we have seen, he appears to have been sufficiently perplexed by their nature in the first place as to have been tempted, at points, even to regard their purely "imaginative" syntheses as, at bottom, intellectual. (But then, despite the mystery of it, Kant did know better.)[52] Quite apart from the obscurity of their intrinsic nature, Kant may also have been struck by the following fact: that there is only one *function* to be served by the ingredience of anticipation and retention in intuitions in the first place, namely, the making possible of the conceptualization of the latter.[53] Apart from that, anticipations and retentions might as well be merely externally connected with intuitions. Perhaps these factors led Kant to be insufficiently critical concerning the possibility of self-consciousness, apart from the conceptualization of appearances. But even if they did, they would of course still not explain Kant's even stronger conclusion, namely, that the constitution of orginal self-consciousness presupposes, not simply the conceptualization of appearances, but their conceptualization precisely as involving (what we would normally regard as) concrete *objects*.

It is in the "Refutation of Idealism" that Kant himself explicitly connects self-consciousness with the consciousness of concrete external existences. But for two reasons that text fails to help us. First, and without explanation, the so-called proof of the thesis supplements the perfectly reasonable claim—on which I shall have more to say in the next chapter—that self-consciousness presupposes consciousness of some kind of "permanence," with the hardly evident claim that self-consciousness presupposes the consciousness of something concretely *existing* as a permanent in intuition (B275-6). (Since no such permanent is available in "inner" intuition, Kant then simply concludes that it must involve matter in space.) Second, Kant in any case presents the issue as one that concerns the possibility of "empirically determined" self-consciousness from the start, whereas our question, in the Deduction, is one that concerns the possibility of a self-consciousness that is merely *determinable*. Indeed, Kant presents it as a question that does not concern mere self-"consciousness" at all, but rather full-blown *cognition* of oneself (B277).

It is not easy to be sure just what Kant has in mind in the "Refutation." One might easily presume that he is specifically concerned with the possibility of a conceptually determinate mode of self-identification. This, at least, would draw a distinction between the "Refutation" and the Deduction. But on the other hand, it is also arguable that Kant is concerned with the same question in both places. It may simply be that, in the later passage, he is implicitly admitting that the original Deduction (in both of its editions) has in fact failed to meet the objections in question. That at least would explain why Kant feels that he can conclude, in the "Refutation," that "empirically determinate" self-consciousness does not simply presuppose some *knowledge* concerning objects existing in space, but presupposes the "immediate consciousness" of them (B276, B277n). Still, it is difficult to see why the empirical determinable consciousness of oneself— not merely full-blown self-knowledge—needs to presuppose such consciousness.

I have only the following suggestion. It is a suggestion that relates to that element in any consciousness of concrete objects on which Kant himself places special emphasis in the first-edition Deduction, namely, the consciousness of some kind of "necessity" in the apprehension of appearances (A104ff). (Indeed, *necessity* seems to be the only one of the categories to which Kant gives particular attention in the first-edition Deduction. I shall have more to say about it in the next chapter.) On some level of clarity or other, Kant may have reasoned in the following way:

> (1) Original self-consciousness is constituted by the ingredience, in intuition, of anticipations and retentions concerning the course of possible experience. (Argument: There just isn't anything else available in intuition for the purpose.)

> (2) But original self-consciousness, if it is to be determinable as the consciousness of some identifiable individual, cannot merely involve the consciousness of *possible* experiences. (Argument: In a sense, anything is legitimately imaginable as possible. So if original self-consciousness merely involved the anticipation or retention of certain courses of experience as possible, it would fail to bear on the self-consciousness of any particular individual. So far as would be compatible with such consciousness, the "I" of which one was thereby conscious could be anyone: one could be imagining somebody *else's*, or even nobody's, possible future or past.)

> (3) Therefore, original self-consciousness must be constituted by the anticipation and retention of possible experiences, not simply as possible extensions of a given experience (or as experiences possibly having stretched to become a given experience), but as extensions of a given experience that are *necessary*, at least relative to certain antecedent conditions (or as experiences whose stretching to *become* a given experience was necessary, relative to certain antecedent conditions).

> (4) But the representation of experience in such terms as these simply *is* its representation in terms of objective concepts. (Argument: A104ff, concerning the concept of an "object.")

> (5) Therefore, original self-consciousness is impossible apart from the objective conceptualization of appearances.

The argument is, no doubt, far from conclusive. But on the basis of the materials that are to be found in the text itself, it seems to me likely to reflect Kant's own thinking. In any case, it seems to me better directed than attempts to formulate conditions for the possibility of self-consciousness simply in terms of the possibility of the self-ascription of predicates. Before we can see what is needed for the latter, purely *judgmental*, mode of self-consciousness, it is surely reasonable to suggest that we first need to have reflected on the latter's more basic ground in an original self-*consciousness*.

Chapter 7

Toward the Categories

I. Introduction

IT REMAINS to consider the possibility of applying this general approach to Kant's more specific specification of the "categories" of understanding. To be sure, the Deduction itself makes no effort in this regard, apart from its general argument that "forms of judgment" are required for the formation of concepts through the unification of manifolds in intuition. As to what the particular forms are, Kant simply appeals (B143) to a ready-made "table" alleged to display them (A70/B95). The categories are then supposed to be those very same forms. That is, they are supposed to be those same forms somehow functioning as concepts themselves, not merely as forms. Unfortunately, from our point of view, the table is a classification of the general forms involved in the uniting of already formed concepts into judgments. What we need to see is how the same functions might also, on a deeper level, be involved in the original formation of concepts from bodies of imaginative material. (This, it should be clear, would not be the same as showing that judgments involving the categories are logically entailed by, or presupposed by, judgments involving other concepts.)

It would be wrong to suppose that the Analytic of Principles provides the needed detail. Its arguments speak to the applicability of the categories to objects, in their role as concepts in their own right. It does not explicate their status as mere forms for the constitution of any concepts in the first place. A separate consideration is required for the problem of "application." For even if, as pure forms, all of the categories are indeed essential to the formation of empirical concepts, it would still not follow that, in their role as concepts, they are universally predicable of objects or events. At most it would follow that all empirical concepts in some way "contain" them. Though I shall have some more to say below, I am not, of course, concerned in the present study with a detailed account of the Analytic of Principles. Thus I shall not attempt to consider all of Kant's own arguments regarding the categories. In addition, I shall limit my attention to what seems to be the most problematic in Kant's theory, the concepts of causality, substance, and community of interaction.[1]

II. From Matter to Form: General Structures

As we have seen, Kant is especially attentive to the role of a clearly non-logical kind of "necessity"—thus at least of a proto-causality—in the first-edition Deduction's account of the concept of an "object." Obviously, what I propose to take very seriously in the account is the fact that Kant presents it in terms of what is needed in order that a "synthesis of recognition in a concept" may bear on, but also go beyond, a synthesis of imaginative "reproduction":

> The word 'concept' might of itself suggest this remark. For this unitary consciousness is what combines the manifold, successively intuited, and thereby also reproduced, into one representation. . . . At this point we must make clear to ourselves what we mean by the expression 'an object of representations'. . . . Now we find that our thought of the relation of all cognition to its object carries with it an element of necessity. . . . [T]he unity which the object makes necessary can be nothing else than the formal unity of consciousness in the synthesis of the manifold of representations. . . . But [a concept] can be a rule for intuitions only insofar as it represents in any given appearances the *necessary* reproduction of their manifold, and thereby the synthetic unity in our consciousness of them. The concept of body, in the perception of something outside us, necessitates the representation of extension, and therewith representations of impenetrability, shape, etc. (A103-6; my emphasis)

It should be clear that Kant is not merely concerned, in this passage, with the logical relation of necessity whereby the proposition that something is, say, a body entails the proposition that it is shaped or impenetrable. If he were, then only the sheerest confusion could explain why he formulates the issue in terms of the kind of necessity that concepts or predicates entail with respect to "reproduction," not merely with respect to other concepts or predicates. It should also be independently clear, from the context, that the relevant "unity of consciousness in the synthesis of the manifold of representations" is supposed to be some kind of unity with respect to immediately apprehensible appearances. The synthesis in question, Kant tells us, is "necessitated" by a concept *in the very perception* of an object as falling under it.

In this regard, the second-edition Deduction may seem less explicit than the first (B162-3). Kant considers there, as an instance of the "unity of the manifold," to be effected by means of the category of causality, a relationship that he represents as obtaining between two states of freezing water. In this case, it is appearances already conceptualized as material objects (quanta of water), or as their states (whether frozen or liquid), that are said to be brought to an appropriate sort of unity of consciousness through categories. (The same goes for Kant's discussion of "quantity" in the same passage.) But I have of course argued that the second edition, just as much as the first, requires an intellectual forming of materials on a level that is still "below" the level of conceptual representation. The passage does not speak to this point. At most, it can be intended to offer an example of a mode of conceptualizing appearances that is a necessary *upshot* of the more basic forming in question. The material for the latter cannot be concepts of objects and their states. It can only be a manifold of anticipations and retentions of possible appearances, in principle conceptualizable *as* objects and states. By the same token, any representation of "necessity" in regard to the (otherwise merely) anticipated and retained possible appearances cannot "yet" be the representation of causal relations as such.

In any case, in the first-edition Deduction, Kant proceeds to insist upon a "transcendental condition" for the relevant "necessity." All necessity, he claims, is grounded in such a condition (A106). The ground of this particular necessity is "transcendental apperception." Now we have already seen that Kant equates transcendental apperception with some kind of consciousness of oneself as an enduring self, and the latter of course in some way involves "necessity" in its own right. It does so at least in the sense that consciousness of oneself as an enduring self is a necessary condition of the conceptualization of appearances. But now Kant seems to make an implausibly stronger claim. For he seems to claim that original self-consciousness involves, beyond its role as a necessary condition of something, a special *consciousness of* the necessity of something. Specifically, we now seem to be dealing, not simply with a (relatively) necessary consciousness of something *identical*, but with a consciousness of something that is itself *necessarily* identical: with something that "has *necessarily* to be represented as numerically identical." This, in turn, is then held to require that we go beyond "empirical data" (A107). (In other passages as well, Kant seems to speak of the consciousness of one's identity as the consciousness of something that is "necessary," thus as an *a priori* mode of consciousness of some special matter of fact [e.g., A108, 109, 112, 113, 116].)

It has been argued, most ably by Guyer, that Kant indeed subscribes at this point to an implausibly strong view of self-identity.[2] But it is possible to offer a more plausible reading. (In making the point, I shall limit myself to the problem of anticipation in judgment. Later, I shall have more to say about the role of retention.) In conceptualizing an appearance as an object of a particular kind, I necessarily anticipate the possibility of additional appearances, relative to the satisfaction of certain conditions. This, I take it, is supposed to be evident directly from reflection on what concepts of objects are. But something else is now supposed to be evident from the nature of concepts. First of all, Kant now tells us that it is necessary, not simply that additional appearances be anticipated, conditional upon the satisfaction of particular conditions, but also that they be anticipated precisely as *necessary*, given satisfaction of those conditions. That is the first point. The second is one on which we have already touched in the preceding chapter.

In conceptualizing appearances, it is necessary, not simply that one anticipate additional appearances, conditional upon the satisfaction of certain conditions, but also that one (albeit pre-reflectively) anticipate those additional appearances precisely as ones that one might *oneself* eventually apprehend. (Indeed, we have seen that Kant seems to demand even more than this. He seems to demand, not simply the anticipation of appearances that one might oneself eventually apprehend, given the satisfaction of certain conditions, but of appearances whose very apprehension will contain a retention of *having been* anticipated in the first place. I shall have more to say about this point presently.) The conjunction of these points yields a harmless, but important, sense in which, in conceptualizing appearances, one necessarily represents, not simply one's own identity through a course of possible perceptions, but one's own "necessary identity" through such a course of perception. Obviously, this is not to say that one necessarily represents the necessity of one's own existence.

Now Kant may also have more than this in mind, when he says that one's identity is present to one "*a priori.*" But that is no cause for alarm either. If it means anything more than the truism that—like the representation of necessities in experience—we are dealing with something that can never be given "through empirical data" (since its representation involves necessity, and also because the transcendental self is not an intuitable object), then it may only be a way of indicating that one's original self-consciousness is indeed anticipational in nature. Kant himself acknowledges a sense of the *a priori* that comes to no more than this (B2). He makes it clear that he will not speak in that sense in the *Critique*, when he is considering cognition as such. But he does not rule out the possibility of speaking, in other contexts, of a mere thought, or of a mere consciousness, or of a mere representation of some matter of fact "*a priori,*" when he merely means a thought, or a consciousness, or a representation whose ground is a mere (though appropriately rule-governed) anticipation. For obvious reasons, Kant generally does not use the term in this way. But at A108, in particular, there is surely no reason to suppose that what is in question is the possibility of knowing or cognizing one's own continuing identity *a priori*, since Kant himself speaks merely of the possibility of *thinking* it *a priori*. I presume that Kant is simply intending to speak of a mode of thinking that is, in an important way, anticipational in nature. (Related uses of the term, in more explicit connection with causality, occur at A112 and B280.)

But why should Kant see a transcendental significance in the mere ability to *think* one's own identity *a priori*, if all that he means is the mere ability to anticipate its continuation? To see the answer, what we need to remember is that Kant is concerned with a special *way* of anticipating one's identity from the start, namely, with that mode of anticipation that is constituted in the very act of conceptualizing appearances. That indeed offers a puzzle demanding transcendental reflection: How can one manage to be engaged in the act of anticipating *oneself*, when one's attention is directed toward objects (appearances) distinct from oneself? It is, I suggest, precisely this puzzle that Kant is attempting to address in this context:

> For this unity of consciousness [i.e., transcendental unity of apperception] would be impossible if the mind *in cognition of the manifold* could not become conscious of the identity of function whereby it synthetically combines it in one cognition. The original and necessary consciousness of the identity of the self is thus *at the same time* [*zugleich*] a consciousness of an equally necessary unity of the synthesis of all appearances according to concepts, that is, according to rules, which not only make them necessarily reproducible but also in so doing determine an object for their intuition, that is, the concept of something wherein they are necessarily interconnected. For the mind could never think its identity *in the manifoldness of its representations*, and indeed think this identity *a priori*, if did not have before its eyes the identity of its act, whereby it subordinates all synthesis of apprehension (which is empirical) to a transcendental unity, thereby rendering possible their interconnection according to *a priori* rules. (A108; my emphases)

The trick is, of course, to see just how, in being conscious of nothing more than the manifold of representations, one may indeed at the same time be conscious of the unity of one's own "act"—that is, to see this without taking representations as states, in this context, potentially "ascribable" to oneself, as opposed to regarding them as the very *appearances* that are in principle conceptualizable as objects.

There is an additional difficulty to consider. It might seem that, on the proposed reading, Kant's position is inconsistent. This is because, it might be alleged, the position requires the postulation of judgmental form on what ought to be a pre-judgmental level. It is of course clear that judgmental form is needed in order to account for the difference between merely "sensibly" anticipating appearances and anticipating appearances as *necessary* (relative to certain conditions). The representation of anything as necessary, on Kant's view, rests on the capacity for differentiating between the modal forms of merely "problematic" or "assertoric" judgment, on the one hand, and "apodeictic" judgment, on the other (A74-6/B99-101). Since these distinctions are irreducibly "judgmental," they could not already have been available on the level of mere sensibility. But this, it appears, is no problem, since the representation of the necessity in question is introduced, in Kant's reasoning, only at the point at which imaginative material is finally transformed by judgment. Consider, however, the originally postulated material. Presumably, even purely "imaginative" anticipation is not merely the anticipation of appearances as forthcoming. Rather, it is the anticipation of appearances as *possibly* forthcoming, relative to the satisfaction of *conditions* (in their turn represented as possible). This seems to imply that we need to introduce "forms of judgment" after all, including at least the forms of hypothetical and problematic judgment, on a level that is altogether below what Kant himself recognizes as truly judgmental. If we do not, then we will be unable to find that body of material needed for judgmental form to transform in the first place.

It is important to see that, in effect, this difficulty is one that we have already considered. We disposed of it when we decided to avoid verbal quibbles as to whether or not "animal" anticipation involves concepts or judgments. It is merely a verbal quibble whether animals have concepts and judge or whether only more elevated beings are capable of such functions. The substantive question concerns the relation *between* purely animal and other modes of "judgment." We may concede that there is a sense in which animals engage in the representation of states of affairs as, say, "possible." Whether or not Kant himself was clear on it, there is no need for him to have denied it. Nor does consistency require that he provide an account of what "judgment" of the sort amounts to: whether it could be treated in purely dispositional terms or perhaps functionally, for example. To be consistent, all that Kant needs to hold is that whatever such judgment amounts to, it can at most serve as material in distinctively human judgments. (If it is not plausible to hold even this much, then Kant would end up on one of the horns of the dilemma that I have been trying to avoid: (a) ultimately regarding *both* human and animal judgment in purely dispositional or functional terms; (b) implausibly isolating the two sorts of judgment from one another, within the mental life of those human subjects in which both obviously play an important part.)

This line of response may seem to entail that it is impossible to draw any real line between "lower" and "higher" capacities. For example, if we concede that animals are capable of representing states of affairs as possible, then why *not* have conceded, in the first place, that they are capable of representing states of affairs as necessary, given the satisfaction of conditions that are possible? Consistently with this, after all, we might continue to hold that, whatever such representation amounts to, it could at most relate to the relevantly higher level by serving as the mere material in judgments on that level. But then the problem would remain: How could we specify the difference between such "levels" in the first place? Certainly, we will have deprived ourselves of the option of saying that the difference rests, even in part, on a capacity for the representation of "necessity."

So far as I can see, there are only two possible responses on the general account proposed. First, we might take the role of judgmental "form" to lie precisely in the fact that it does *not* merely serve to provide forms for "judgment," as the latter is normally understood, but rather that it serves equally for the incorporation of (possibly) "judgmental" material in *intuitions*. Apart from the latter function, and regardless of the internal articulation of the material in question (whether, for example, it involves a "representation" of possibility, necessity, or what have you) we might then have some kind of "judgment," but we would not have any kind of judgment that involves judgmental *form*. At the very least, this does not seem Kantian. It accords too great an importance to the form of intuition. In effect, it virtually equates the forms of judgment with the latter: what is needed for a full-blown (Kantian) judgment would simply be the incorporation of a certain sort of material by means of such form.

For a more promising approach, we need to take a closer look at the problem of self-consciousness. As it happens, this will eventually take us closer to seeing how the representation of objective nature, as subsumable under causal laws, is part of the constitution of empirical concepts. (We need to remember that the mere anticipation of appearances as necessary, relative to the satisfaction of certain conditions, does not suffice for the representation of causality involving objects or their states.) It is here that we finally need to return, as well, to my earlier suggestion concerning the role of "higher-order" modes of anticipation: anticipations not simply of appearances relative to conditions, nor even of appearances represented as necessary relative to conditions, but of appearances whose apprehension contains some kind of retention *of their very anticipation* in the first place.

In one respect, it should be clear that there is something lacking in any account of empirical concepts that takes the act of conceptualizing an appearance to consist in nothing more than a set of anticipations in regard to that appearance, or in regard to its apprehension—even when those anticipations are truly ingredient *in* the original apprehension in the first place. At the very least, what is lacking is the representation of the very *same* concept, as a potential ingredient in any number of additional apprehensions (or, alternatively, as "predicable" of any number of additional appearance), and of course in particular in those in fact anticipated.

This is not to deny that a particular set of anticipations, just like any concept, can be regarded as a repeatable "term," multiply tokenable or instantiable in any number of intuitions: any number of intuitions might contain this or that particular set of anticipations. But it is still impossible to suppose that any such set can by itself constitute a truly conceptual mode of representation. (In what follows, I continue to abstract, for a while, from the role of "retention." In addition, I also abstract from the normative dimension that Kant no doubt intended as part of his own notion of concepts as embodying "rules.")[3] If the intuition in question is to amount to genuine conceptualization, then it is plausible to suppose that at least the following is necessary: that I need to be doing more than merely anticipating whatever additional appearances are in question. Beyond this, I need to be anticipating those appearances precisely as appearances that are *subsumable under a particular concept.* It seems plausible to insist, in other words, that if I am not anticipating the additional appearances specifically as subsumable under whatever *concept* was supposed to have been applied in the first place, then my anticipation of those additional appearances will remain irrelevant to any would-be act of conceptualizing that appearance.

This may, of course, appear to imply that any account of conceptualization, in terms of the anticipation of appearances, is bound to be circular. I want to argue that it is not. As a first step, we need to see why the following suggestion is not a way out of the difficulty. It might seem that we can avoid circularity, simply by specifying that the anticipations peculiar to the conceptualization of appearances are to be regarded not merely as anticipatory of possible additional appearances, relative to certain conditions, but as anticipatory of additional appearances in whose very apprehension *the given set* of anticipations will *likewise* be an ingredient. The proposal simply appeals, as I have already suggested is necessary, to a second-order level of anticipational consciousness. At least one advantage of it will therefore be that it provides a criterion for distinguishing human from purely animal "judgment": even if there is a sense in which the latter involves the anticipation of possibilities, necessities, conditions, and the like, it does not, we might propose, involve higher-order anticipation of the sort suggested.

Whatever weakness the proposal may prove to have, it is important to be clear about one part of it. It is important to appreciate the sense in which the suggestion does not, although it may seem to, presuppose a conceptually determinate mode of self-awareness, as a necessary condition for the formation of any concept. If it presupposed such a mode of self-awareness, then the account would, of course, be circular. But it may seem in fact to be circular in just this way. For it presupposes the ability to represent sets of "one's own" anticipations, as a pre-condition of the formation of empirical concepts. However, we already have the materials to provide a response to this charge. The proposal, again, was this: that the anticipations peculiar to the conceptualization of appearances are simply anticipations of additional appearances, as appearances correlative with an apprehension that contains the very *same* anticipations as were originally in question. This was supposed to suffice, in a non-circular way, to meet the demand that conceptualization involves the anticipation, not simply of additional appearances, but of appearances that are in their own turn subsumable under the very same *concept* that subsumes the appearance originally in question. On the proposal, the role of the "same concept" is to be non-circularly filled by the set of original anticipations itself.

It should at least be possible to see, given our account of self-consciousness, that whatever "higher-order" awareness is required for this proposal cannot be presumed to rest on the possession of a self-concept. What we need to remember, for this point, is simply that an appearance that is apprehended *through* a set of anticipations is a different "object" for consciousness than an appearance that is apprehended through a different set of anticipations (or, if possible, through none at all). It is this fact, as I have suggested, that opens the door to recognition of the fact that the apprehension of appearances through sets of anticipations *already is*, by its very nature, a way of "apprehending" those anticipations themselves. But it is a way of apprehending them that does not presuppose any special kind of reflection on, not to mention a concept of, "oneself" as a subject of apprehension. The apprehension in question is directly constituted *in* the original apprehension of appearances.

This provides an important part of what we need to develop the Kantian theory of concepts. But it is not enough. It is insufficient, because it is plainly wrong to suppose that the conceptualization of a given appearance requires the anticipation of additional appearances as apprehensible through the very same anticipations as were ingredient in the apprehension of the given one. For example, in conceptualizing an appearance as a rose bush, I may be anticipating the possibility of additional appearances, each of which is likewise conceptualizable as a rose bush, and each of which is anticipable as the upshot of the satisfaction of certain equally anticipable conditions (that is, each of which is anticipable as the upshot of certain anticipable ways of "stretching" the given appearance). But I surely do not need to anticipate the apprehension of those additional appearances as *themselves* eventually apprehensible through these very same anticipations. That would in fact be incompatible with any reasonable conception of a perceivable objective reality. At most, what would be reasonable is that the additional appearances be anticipated as apprehensible through anticipations appropriately *related* to the given anticipations.

What is needed, therefore, is the notion of anticipating the apprehension of additional appearances as containing a suitable *transformation* of the anticipations ingredient in the apprehension of a given appearance. I need to anticipate appearances as ones in whose eventual apprehension will be contained the anticipation of additional appearances that are at most appropriately related to the ones that were anticipated in the apprehension of the given appearance—and that are obtainable upon the satisfaction of conditions that are at most correspondingly related to those originally in question. Among other things, for example, the additional appearances need to be anticipated as apprehensible through anticipations relating to the possibility of *getting back* to (or to the possibility of having been arrived at from) the starting point of the original appearance, whereas the original appearance was at most apprehended through anticipations relating to the possibility of getting from there to those (and, of course, to the possibility of having been arrived at from still others).

In general, what counts as a "suitable" transformation of an original set of anticipations may simply be expressive of what one takes to be the conditions of empirical objectivity. It must therefore be embodied, in general, in one's very *concept* of objective reality. But there is no circularity in conceding this: higher-order anticipations of just this sort are supposed to be *constitutive* of one's concept of empirical objectivity in the first place.

Obviously, this requires a degree of sophistication beyond anything that we have so far considered. (Remember: What is in question is not merely the capacity for a systematic transformation of one's own anticipations; it is the capacity for the anticipation of appearances as eventually apprehensible *through* such systematically transformed anticipations.) It is not implausible to suppose that this requires something beyond the capacity of most creatures. But while abilities of the sort require sophistication, they do not presuppose the capacity for any special kind of self-reflection on the part of anticipating subjects. Rather, the latter is supposed to be made possible through the former in the first place: on the present level of analysis, the anticipation of appropriately systematic transformations of "one's own" anticipations, in the eventual apprehension of additional appearances, simply *is* a way of anticipating additional appearances. It is just a more sophisticated (though not merely more "complex") way of anticipating appearances. Therefore, to whatever extent it may indeed be the case that distinctively human self-apprehension rests on the ability to conceptualize appearances—which is that part of Kant's theory to which commentators' attention is usually limited—this claim remains compatible with the suggestion that—in a sense that is usually overlooked—it is precisely through such conceptualization that distinctively human self-apprehension is originally constituted.

From here, it is a short distance to Kant's notion of concepts as, or serving as, "rules" in relation to appearances (cf. A106). But the present account is different from what that notion may be supposed to entail. It may be supposed to involve the idea that concepts, as mental "predicates," are quasi-linguistic items or terms, attachable to given perceptions or appearances (instantiable or "tokenable" by them), but only to be counted as *representations* to the extent that the subject is in command of the rules that "govern" those predicates. The metaphor suggests a notion that is very different from the one proposed. It suggests that the rules determinative of representational content function as part of a system of rules that govern would-be predicates in a purely external way, that is, by virtue of factors distinct from the way in which those predicates are actually constituted, as "terms," in the first place. So far as I can see, this yields a purely mechanical account of understanding.

The proposal has the advantage of regarding the rules that "govern" concepts as internal to concepts themselves. But it does so without abandoning the idea that concepts are indeed a kind of "term" to be governed in the first place—which they need to be in order to be sufficiently like *predicates*. What we need to see is that the terms in question are sets of anticipations. Once we see this, then we are free to suppose that one part of such sets is simply a set of higher-order anticipations. The latter bear on transformation *of those very sets*, as they move from intuition to intuition. The "rules" that define the identity of concepts are just higher-order anticipations that bear on sets that include lower-order anticipations as well. The conceptualization of appearances is their apprehension through sets of the latter, appropriately embedded in the former. No more than this, then, needs to be involved in Kant's notorious doctrine of the "imposition" of intellectual form on sensible material. What is noteworthy, as I see it, is simply that the forms in question are not merely externally related to the corresponding material.

Their relation is not analogous, for example, to that between a "functional role" and a term that happens to "play" it.

These suggestions provide, finally, for a more substantial role for the phenomenon of "retention" as well. In doing so, they explain Kant's suggestion, noted earlier, that experience requires, not simply the retention of earlier experiences, and not simply the retention of earlier experiences by experiences themselves, but the *anticipation* of experiences *as* themselves retaining the fact of their own anticipation. On one level, it might seem trivially obvious that something like this is required for experience. For if anticipations are going to be relevant to experience in the first place, then we need to be able to recall that anticipated appearances had in fact been anticipated. But while it may be essential that subjects retain their anticipations in this sense, it would not follow that such retentions are a part of the structure of conceptual *acts*. Nor would it follow that whatever *anticipations* are essential to conceptual acts are, at bottom, anticipations of acts that are in their own turn specifically retentional. (Here, I am ignoring the more primitive types of anticipation and retention that we considered in Chapter Three. That these more primitive types are also essential, not simply to experience in general, but to the structure of individual states or acts of consciousness, still falls short of entailing that they are specifically essential to the act of conceptualization. For the latter, we need to be concerned with the more "associational" type of anticipation and retention.)

III. Causality, Substance, and Community of Interaction

This take us at least significantly close to some of the full-blown categories that Kant claims to be counterparts of the purely "logical" forms of judgment. We may begin with the concept of causality. Kant's notion of concepts of objects as "rules," or as somehow serving as rules, is presumably supposed to be relevant to his view of the role of this concept in experience. In this respect, what we therefore need to recall is the way in which we have now expanded our account beyond an appeal to a notion of anticipational and retentional "rules" that bear merely on the anticipation and retention of appearances as possible upshots (or even as necessary upshots) of the possible advance of experience, given the satisfaction of certain conditions. Beyond this, we have in effect introduced the requirement that appearances, as potential subjects for conceptualization, must be regarded as subject to whole *systems* of rules, systematically correlated with all of the possible "points of view" from which any appearances are possibly obtainable in the first place.

It follows from this that *every* point of view from which appearances are anticipable as possible must be regarded as subsumable under an overarching system of rules. This is because the anticipation of any possible appearance, in connection with a given one, is necessarily correlative with the anticipation of the possibility of *returning*, *via* a rule-governed transformation of the originally anticipated path, from that appearance to the given one. This at least takes us well past the mere proto-causality with which we began. It is not implausible to suppose, it seems to me, that it takes us far enough past that notion to account for a concept of an objective "world of appearances," i.e., for an objective nature in Kant's sense:

> The unity of apperception is thus the transcendental ground of the necessary con-
> formity to law of all appearances in one experience. This same unity of apperception
> in respect to a manifold of representations (determining it out of a single one) acts
> as the rule, and the faculty of these rules is the understanding. All appearances,
> *as possible experiences*, thus lie *a priori* in the understanding, and receive from
> it their formal possibility, just as, insofar as they are mere intuitions, they lie in
> sensibility, and are, as regards their form, only possible through it. However exag-
> gerated and absurd it may sound, to say that the understanding is itself the source
> of the laws of nature, and so of its formal unity, such an assertion is nonetheless
> correct, and is in keeping with the object [*dem Gegenstande*] to which it refers,
> namely, *experience*. (A127; my emphases)

> That the *laws* of appearances in nature must agree with the understanding and its
> *a priori* form, that is, with its faculty of *combining* the manifold in general, is no
> more surprising than that appearances themselves must agree with the form of sen-
> sible intuition *a priori*. For just as appearances do not exist in themselves but only
> relatively to the subject in which, so far as it has senses, they inhere, so the laws
> do not exist in the appearances but only relatively to this same being, so far as it
> has understanding. . . . As mere representations, they are subject to no law of con-
> nection save that which the connecting faculty prescribes. Now it is imagination that
> connects the manifold of sensible intuition; and imagination is dependent for the
> unity of its intellectual synthesis upon the understanding, and for the manifoldness
> of its apprehension upon sensibility. All possible perception is thus dependent upon
> synthesis of apprehension, and this empirical synthesis in turn upon transcendental
> synthesis, and therefore upon the categories. (B164)

That something like the proposed reasoning is in fact Kant's own is also suggested by the following comparison, offered by Kant himself, between (a) the
ground of our knowledge that all matter has a degree of presence in space and
(b) the ground of our knowledge regarding universal causality:

> [a] This reveals the possibility of knowing *a priori* a law of alterations, in respect
> of their form. We are merely *anticipating our own apprehension*. . . . *In the same
> manner, therefore,* in which time contains the sensible *a priori* condition of the pos-
> sibility of a continuous advance of the existing to what follows, [b] the understand-
> ing, by virtue of the unity of apperception, is the *a priori* condition of the possibility
> of a continuous determination of all positions for the appearances in this time,
> through the series of causes and effects. . . . (A210-11/B255-6; my emphases).

Of course, none of this is meant to amount to a proof of the Second Analogy—
that all *events* are causally necessitated. At most it amounts to the conclusion that
all objects are subject to causal laws. And all that it additionally attempts to do,
with this conclusion, is to show how it can be grounded directly in reflection on
the original constitution of concepts of objects out of what would otherwise remain
purely imaginative anticipations and retentions. It seems obvious that the Second
Analogy attempts to do more than this. That is not my concern here, although
I have also argued elsewhere that, at least on a relatively sophisticated "phenome-

nalism" of the sort that I have ascribed to Kant, together with some additional (though false) assumptions that seem to be Kant's, even that stronger inference can be regarded as valid.[4]

It may not be possible to come even this close in regard to Kant's argument for a universal "community" of causal interaction in the Third Analogy, that is, with regard to the principle of reciprocal causality among all coexisting objects:

> Things are coexistent when in empirical intuition the perceptions of them can follow upon one another reciprocally. . . . Thus I can direct my perception first to the moon and then to the earth, or conversely, first to the earth and then to the moon; and because the perceptions of these objects can follow each other reciprocally, I say that they are coexistent. . . . [But] the synthesis of imagination in apprehension would only reveal that the one perception is in the subject when the other is not there, and reciprocally, but not that the objects are coexistent, *that is*, that if the one exists the other exists at the same time, *and that this is necessary, in order that* the perceptions can follow one another reciprocally. Consequently, in the case of things which coexist externally to one another, a pure concept of the reciprocal sequence of their determinations is required, if we are able to say that the reciprocal sequence of the perceptions is grounded in the object, and so to represent the coexistence as objective. (B256-7; my emphases)

I shall presume that we may take the liberty of supposing that Kant is putting his own point somewhat poorly in this passage. This would seem to be necessary in order to find a line of thinking that is in fact plausibly ascribable to someone of Kant's intelligence.

In the light of our results so far, it ought to be expected that we take very seriously Kant's claims about the "reversibility" of perceptions. On some readings, that notion is given a surprisingly minimal role in Kant's argument. In the argument as stated, Kant himself seems to suggest that judgments that conceptualize appearances as coexisting objects *are* just at bottom judgments about the possibility of certain in principle reversible perceptions, or at least—as I would prefer to put it—that they are judgments that contain, as their whole "material," nothing more than *anticipations* (and retentions) of possibilities regarding reversible perceptions. On some other accounts, the role of the reversibility of perception becomes purely negative. For example, one might suppose Kant's concern with that notion to be motivated simply by the need to show that the reversibility of perceptions is insufficient—as it obviously is—as a criterion for the determination of whether or not objects are in fact coexistent. Positively, one might argue, what is then required for the actual determination of such facts is not any sort of consideration that bears on "perceptions" at all, but rather an appeal to rules concerning "objects" directly.[5] In any case, I want to attempt to give a more positive role to perceptual reversibility.

Let us begin with Kant's reference to what mere "imagination" can give us in this passage. In particular, we need to take special care in regard to his claim that what imagination reveals (*angeben*) is, for example, merely that a certain perception is present, while some other is not. As we already now, Kant specifically connects the notion of imagination, in the Deduction, with the capacity for representing what is *not* present, not with the capacity for representing what is present while something else isn't. So it would seem reasonable to suppose that, in the present passage, Kant is in fact intending to ascribe to the imagination, not simply the indication that some perception is present at a moment while some other is absent, but, more specifically, the representation *of* the very absence of the latter, while the former is present. In addition, we cannot help but presume that the relevant type of imaginative representation, in this case, is meant to be none other than some type of *anticipation*, namely, anticipation of the very possibility *of the presence* of what is in fact absent.

With these as our initial presumptions, it is then reasonable to conclude that Kant's real point about what imagination can and cannot give us, in this passage, is not simply (and trivially) that a sequential *awareness* of perceptions is insufficient in order to account for the representation of objects as coexistent. The point must rather be, more informatively, that not even any number of additional (first-order) *anticipations* is sufficient to account for such representation. Someone, of course (for example, Hume), might well have supposed that it is sufficient. Kant wants to inform us that something more is needed.

Now obviously, one thing that is needed for the representation of objects as coexistent is the representation of a certain kind of "necessity." That, of course, is needed for any representation of objects. Kant, I take it, wants to make it clear that something else is needed as well. This is evident from the phrase that I emphasized in the passage that I quoted. The additional factor has something to do with a representation of "reciprocity." But what could be the *subject* of reciprocity in this case, if Kant is not to beg the question from the start, with respect to his establishment of the need for reciprocity among the states of *objects*? We can only suppose that Kant's formulation is unclear. What can be in question, at this point, cannot be the reciprocity of objective states. It can only be the reciprocity of possible perceptions.

If the reciprocity in question concerns the possibility of perception, then it presumably amounts to more than the trivial two-fold fact (i) that at a certain moment a certain perception, say B, may be anticipated (and even anticipated as necessary, under certain conditions) while some other, say A, is actually present to perception and, reciprocally, (ii) that at another moment A may be anticipated while B is actually present. That would yield no more than the weakly "reciprocal" anticipation with which we began: imagination informing us that some perception is present while some other, which might have been present, is not. What Kant might additionally be supposing, I therefore suggest, involves a rather more complex type of anticipation. It involves the anticipation, not simply of "reciprocally" *perceivable* (first A then B, or first B then A) perceptions, but of reciprocally *anticipable* perceptions. That is, it involves a structure in which A, while perceived, anticipates B, not simply as necessary under certain conditions, but precisely as *itself* in turn anticipating A; and, reciprocally, it involves a structure in which B, while perceived, anticipates A, not simply as likewise necessary under certain conditions, but precisely as itself anticipating B.

In the terms developed earlier, what we have is the following situation. In conceptualizing some appearance A as a real object, we must, as we have already discovered in the Transcendental Deduction, be anticipating various possible modes of "stretching" A (*qua* appearance), so as eventually to arrive at upshots that are necessary, given the way that the stretching in question is anticipated as occurring. Now suppose that A (*qua* object) is conceptualized as coexisting with B. This implies that, among the manifold of anticipated stretchings of A, there will be at least one that is the "reciprocal" of one that would also have been anticipated in the act of conceptualizing B as coexisting with A. This is necessarily so because there will be at least one such stretching that culminates in an appearance conceptualizable *as B itself*. But, as we have also already seen in the Deduction, a special feature of the anticipations ingredient in conceptual acts is this: that they anticipate not merely the possible stretching of given appearances, so as to arrive at necessary upshots, but they anticipate the necessity of upshots that in their own turn "retain" the very possibility of *reversing* that anticipation, so as to arrive back at the original appearance as a necessary upshot as well.

It follows from this that, considering A and B together—as appearances conceptualizable as coexisting objects—the conceptualization of either of the two *as* coexisting with the other necessarily involves the anticipation of possible perceptions of the two that are *connected by a single system of necessities*. These necessities will, of course, in the first instance, bear on the "possibility of perception" itself. But for Kant, as I have interpreted him, judgments concerning the existence of objects and their states simply *are* judgments concerning (or, much better: simply are judgments that contain, as their "material," nothing more than anticipations concerning) the possibility of perceptions. Therefore, judgments concerning the coexistence of objects entail that those objects are causally connected with one another.

Strictly, this reasoning cannot get us to the conclusion of the Third Analogy, as Kant appears to intend it. At most, it can get us to the conclusion that coexistent objects stand in a single causal system, that is, in a system to which a common set of causal laws applies. I do not see how to get from there to the stronger conclusion that coexistent objects, be it directly or indirectly, causally *effect* one another at every moment: "Each substance . . . must therefore contain in itself the causality of certain determinations in the other substance, and at the same time the effects of the causality of that other . . ." (A212/B259). On the other hand, it has been argued that Kant did not intend the stronger conclusion in the first place, or at least that he was merely careless in espousing it.[6]

It remains to attend briefly to the First Analogy, and to the category of substance or permanence as the "substratum" of all change. Here is a formulation of a part of the argument that is relevant to our purpose. It appears only in the "B"-edition:

> [B] All appearances are in time; and in it alone, as substratum (as permanent form of inner intuition), can either coexistence or succession be represented. Thus the time in which all change of appearances has to be thought, remains and does not change. For it is that *in* which, and as *determinations of* which, succession or coexistence can alone be represented. Now time cannot be perceived on its own account [*für sich*]. Consequently there must be found in the objects of perception, that is,

in appearances, the substratum which represents time in general; and all change or coexistence must, in being apprehended, be *perceived in* [*an*] this substratum, *and through relation of appearances to it*. (B224-5; my emphases)

The argument, added in the the second edition, seems to differ from a formulation that appears in both editions:

[AB] Our *apprehension* of the manifold of [the?] appearance is always successive, and is therefore always changing. Through it alone we can never *determine whether this manifold* [my emphasis], as object of experience, is coexistent or in sequence. For such determination we require an underlying ground which exists *at all times*, that is something *abiding* and *permanent*, of which all change and coexistence are only so many ways (modes of time) in which the permanent exists. And simultaneity and succession being the only relations in time, it follows that only in the permanent are relations of time possible. In other words, the permanent is the *substratum* of the empirical representation of time itself; in [*an*] it alone is any determination of time possible. . . . Now time cannot be perceived in itself [*an sich selbst*]; the permanent in the appearances is therefore the substratum of all determination of time. . . . (A182-3/B225-6)

Not surprisingly, there is a problem in all of this that is comparable to what we encountered regarding the "Refutation of Idealism." The formulation in [AB] seems to rests on a consideration that is specific to the problem of *knowing* whether or not apprehended succession amounts to a case of successively apprehending some number of coexistent objects or states. (In the latter case, of course, we might also be dealing with the apprehension of a single object from different points of view, or with respect to different of its aspects.) What is "given" is, in an important sense, a succession of appearances. But the possibility always exists that the successive appearances ("this manifold") really *are* a set of coexistent objects, or possibly even a single continuously enduring object. Passage [AB] then seems to focus on the problem of "determining"—in the sense of coming to *know*—whether or not this is the case. (We shall presently see a second respect in which the "determination" of time is necessarily involved in any "determination" of the objective status of appearances.) By contrast, [B] focuses on a problem that is supposedly involved in apprehending successions that are determinable in *either* way in the first place; this is clear from its initial premise, which simply rests on the fact that time is the form of "inner intuition." Of course, if something is already necessary for an intuitional apprehension of succession in appearances, then it is also necessary for "determining" the objective status of what is thereby apprehended. But if the basic ground of argument is this, then it is perplexing why Kant originally formulates it at one remove from the point.[7] I shall limit myself to arguing that the approach that I have adopted can at least explain two things. First, it can explain why, in its later and presumably clarified version, the argument gives priority to purely intuited succession. Second, it can explain why Kant's argument appears to conflate two very different questions. The key is to be clearer than Kant himself was regarding the notion of a succession "of appearance(es)."

As we have already noted, Kant's language is often suggestive of a misleading model, namely, one that involves the discrete apprehension of successive appearances. We may well be skeptical as to the sense in which, usefully to Kant's own argument, the latter might be held to presuppose the representation of time as a "substratum." Certainly, we may say that the discrete apprehension of successive appearances in some way presupposes the representation of a single time "in which" those successive representations are contained. Presumably, such a representation would then have to involve either (a) some kind of apprehension of representations as successive states of oneself (or as the intentional correlates thereof) or (b) some kind of apprehension of representations (or of their intentional correlates) as coexistent or successive objects (or as coexistent or successive states of some object or objects). In either case, we would need to presuppose a single time in which the items are apprehended as temporally related. But there is nothing in this that should incline us toward saying that time needs to be presupposed as the "substratum" of whatever coexistence or succession may be in question.[8]

If we like, we might of course always regard time as a substratum in which successive moments or stretches of time "inhere." Such a substratum might then be regarded as in its own turn necessary as a background for the representation of coexistence or change among appearances. But this would still be different from regarding time as a substratum with respect to appearances themselves, apprehended as occupying, or as possibly occupying, such moments or stretches in the first place. If Kant cannot justify the stronger formulation, then his jump to a correlative "substance" as the material of appearances seems arbitrary.

It is at this point that we simply need to recall that the intuitive apprehension of stretches of time is the very *material* of any objectively determinable apprehension in the first place. This, of course, stems from my interpretation of anticipation and retention in terms of the imaginative grasp of appearances as stretching, or at least as possibly stretching, into the future or the past. I have argued that such a notion is needed in order to support Kant's attempt to regard some kind of consciousness of a "synthesis of representations," as the original and pre-judgmental mode of one's own self-consciousness. That notion, I would now suggest, can also provide a single account both of Kant's formulation of the argument in [B], as an argument concerning the role of time in "inner intuition," and of his ease in sliding to the role of time, in [AB], as the substratum of appearances determined with respect to their status as full-blown objects.

In this way of looking at things, Kant would not merely be concerned, in [B], with our general ability to apprehend succession, in the sense of apprehending manifolds of distinct, successively apprehended representations that also happen to be "determinable" in principle (if they are not hallucinations) as either successive or coexistent objects or states of objects. Nor would he merely be concerned, in [AB], with the specific problem of such determination, over and above the mere fact of temporal apprehension. Rather, we would need to suppose that Kant is concerned with the specific *kind* of apprehension that is essentially involved in the apprehension of any objectively determinable object or state of affairs, that is, with the kind of apprehension that involves the anticipation of appearances themselves as *stretching* through time.

If we suppose that the manifold of representations that requires time as a substratum, not as a mere "background," is the manifold *qua* imaginatively contained in the apprehension of appearances, insofar as the latter are candidates for objective determination, then it is no longer arbitrary to regard time as indeed that manifold's substratum. For, at least in that specific case, *stretches of time are the very object* of such a mode of apprehension of the manifold in the first place. If we were only considering an isolated multiplicity of appearances, successively apprehended, then at most we would be entitled to say that the apprehension of those appearances is a way of apprehending (possible) regions of *space*, namely, a sensory way of apprehending them. The fact that the appearances in question were also apprehended successively would give no title to suppose, by analogy, that such apprehension is also a way of apprehending stretches of time. An awareness of time might be presupposed as a "background" for that apprehension. But there is no useful sense in which we would be entitled to insist that it is the very subject or substance of what is thereby apprehended.

It is important to see that this does not contradict Kant's assumption that time cannot be perceived *für sich* or *an sich selbst*. Kant is perfectly clear that time is an object of *intuition*. The only way it can be so, of course, is if *stretches* of time are an object of intuition. When Kant says that time cannot be "perceived by itself," he cannot possibly mean to deny such points. Presumably what he means is that, apprehended only as objects of intuition, stretches of time are not yet apprehended as objective states of affairs. For that, they need to be conceptualized *as* such states of affairs. Now at this point Kant assumes that, whatever is conceptualized, within the realm of appearance, as an objective state of affairs must, at least in that capacity, be regarded as in principle sensibly perceivable in its own right, in such a way that the perception in question will have an eventual bearing on the "determination" (in the sense of "knowing-that") of objectivity in the case. In this sense, intuitively apprehended time is not, as such, sensibly perceivable. Its apprehension is a necessary ingredient in the conceptualization of appearances as sensibly perceivable objects in space; indeed, the apprehension of manifolds of stretches of (possible) time is the *only* ingredient—in the sense of material—in the conceptualization of appearances as such objects. But that, we may suppose, is just Kant's point in denying that time can be perceived in itself. While the apprehension of stretches of time is the only ingredient in the conceptualization of appearances as concrete objects, in the sense of providing the *material* for the latter, such apprehension could not possibly constitute the latter in its own right. For that, we need something more than the intuitive apprehension of stretches of time. But this is also compatible with recognizing that, in another sense, the conceptualization of appearances involves nothing more. In another sense, it does not involve anything more than a way of conceptualizing *those very stretches of time*.[9]

Thus supposing that Kant is focusing, not merely on the subjective apprehension of time, as in [B], nor merely on the problem of the objective determination (in the sense of "knowing-that") of appearances, as in [AB], but precisely on the respect in which the latter *is* the former, objectively "determined,"[10] we can understand why both of these considerations are present in a single argument, and also why Kant slides from one to the other. The slide is legitimate on one assumption: that the objective determination of appearances is the determination of time itself; it is not merely determination against time as a "background." That it is not simply the latter follows from the proposed account of anticipation and retention as the matter of conceptualizing appearances. On that account, there is indeed an important sense in which time itself is always the "object" that one conceptualizes as matter in space. From this, it is at least not unreasonable to infer that *something*, if not time itself, must be the substratum for all appearances and their changes.

Of course, my interest in this study has in any case not been in arguments for specific categorial concepts, as Kant offers them in the Analytic of Principles. It is only in the more general claim that sensible material needs to be subjected to some kind of judgmental form, both as a necessary condition of the conceptualization of appearances as concrete objects and, precisely in that capacity, as constitutive of original self-consciousness. If, along the lines that I have sketched, a valid argument cannot be constructed for any of the Analogies of Experience, it is more important to assess the account I have offered as an attempt to shed some light, from a non-functionalist direction, on Kant's general theory of understanding and consciousness in the Deduction.

IV. Appendix: Judgments about the Past

It will be useful to conclude with some speculation regarding a somewhat more specialized problem. It concerns the role of anticipation and retention in judgments about the past. It may seem plainly impossible to account for such judgments on the general theory of judgment that I have proposed. There may be a temptation to say that judgments about the present are constituted out of anticipations in regard to possible experience. But judgments about the past are difficult to construe in such terms. In addition, to the extent that "retention" is understood, as it often seems to be, as itself already a kind of judgment about the past, one would not normally suppose it to provide a workable supplement in this regard. However, neither anticipation nor retention is, in a relevant sense, intrinsically judgmental. It is therefore worth considering whether we might not indeed have the materials, along the lines proposed, for dealing with judgments about the past.

Since we are limiting our concern to the problem of predication in intuition, the problem would seem to concern the possibility of judging with regard to imagined stretches of time. In particular, it would seem to concern the possibility of judging, of some imagined stretch of time, (a) that it is past, (b) that it has certain contents, and possibly also (c) that it extends back a certain distance from the present. But apart from that special case, there may, of course, also appear to be a prior question concerning the possiblity of intuitionally imaginative judgments of *any* kind. I shall simply assume that, to deal with this, Kant will already need to have postulated a specially "modalized" form of anticipation and retention. Such modalization will be needed in order to account for the obtaining of a general and non-formal "sameness" of concepts, insofar as they are supposed to be predicable both of imagined and of perceived objects.

Somehow, merely imagining a rose bush is an activity that needs to mobilize just the "same" anticipations and retentions as would have been involved in actually seeing one. The only difference could be, as we might put it, that in the former case those anticipations and retentions are present in a purely "problematic" mode. That is to say, they are not simply "imaginative" by virtue of being contained as material *in* an instance of imagining. They are "imaginative" in the way that might be involved in an actual, though purely imaginative, mode of *perception* of some object as well. In the latter case, one need not, in an important sense, actually "have" (not even conditionally) a certain set of anticipations regarding the perceived object. All the same, one somehow manages to perceive the object *through* those very anticipations that one does not actually have. Once again, this simply shows something that Kant himself no doubt failed to appreciate, namely, the need for various "forms of judgment" on the level of purely imaginative material. As I have argued, concession of the point is perfectly compatible with recognizing the need for distinctively "higher" forms of judgment, namely, those involved in the incorporation of such material into full-blown concepts and judgments.

Now the first feature that we need to attend to, regarding judgments of imagined stretches of past time, is this: that they must involve the imagining of stretches of time that stretch up to (or back from) the present. It is important to see that this is not a matter of actually *judging* that the stretches in question are ones that include, or even simply reach up to, the present (as when I judge abstractly that the present is included in the twentieth century). If it were, then our attempt to appeal to such imagining, as part of an account of judgments of the past, would be circular. We must rather be dealing with a strict analogue of what we have been considering under the heading of "anticipation." The latter involves the intuitional apprehension of a present appearance as (possibly) stretching into the future. We have already seen that this is not a matter of "judgment," in any sense that threatens circularity. What we first need to acknowledge, therefore, is a corresponding mode of intuitional awareness in which the present is nonjudgmentally apprehended as the continuation of something past. But we have already seen (Chapter Three, Section IV) that this general structure is any case necessary for any sort of experience whatsoever.

At least this much is already involved whenever one experiences—and, therefore, always—a state of consciousness as having had a past. As I took pains to note earlier, this can be regarded as a type of "retention," but it is very different from the associational phenomenon that Kant usually connects with that title. What is crucial is to recognize that this type of retention is not at all a matter of judging that one's current state of consciousness has a past. Nor is it a matter of apprehending some past state of affairs or object as somehow related to a second object or state of affairs that one identifies as the present moment. That would be no more plausible than regarding the anticipation of possible appearances, insofar as it functions as an ingredient in the intuitive apprehension of objects, as a matter of intuitively apprehending those appearances as objects as well. Nor need we, in either case, conclude that one is therefore committed to the recognition of some mysterious kind of immediate access to *truths* about the future or the past. To see this, we need simply remind ourself that the "objects" in question, at least as so far considered, are no more than the intentional correlates of consciousness: though they are intuitively apprehended, there is always the possibility that they did not, and that they never will, exist apart from the apprehension of them.

I take it to be independently evident that there is such a thing as non-judgmentally apprehending present appearances as termini of stretches of time. Again, we may simply regard the phenomenon as a counterpart of non-judgmentally apprehending those same appearances as in turn (possibly) stretching into the future. In the latter case, the total (intentional) object of consciousness will be the presently given appearances, presumably conceptualized in this way or that, and also experienced—though not necessarily conceptualized—as stretching in a manifold of ways into a manifold of possible futures. In the former case, the same appearances will be—however they are also conceptualized—non-conceptually experienced as stretching *from* a manifold of at least possible pasts. (In either case, their standard mode of "appearing," in those earlier or later portions of the whole, might, of course, be very different from their mode of appearing in the present. This is compatible with the whole being regarded as a single, intuitively apprehended "object," only one part of which is in fact presently appearing.)

Once we have recognized this, then we will have no reason to refuse recognition to a closely related structure of experience. In fact, the latter seems to be just as directly evident in experience as the former. What I have in mind is only the reverse of what we have already granted, namely, a case in which the focal object is no longer present appearances, hence a presently "appearing" object, apprehended as part of a whole that stretches beyond it into the past, but a completely *past* stretch, intuitively apprehended in imagination—though, again, not necessarily conceptualized—as part of a larger stretch, stretching beyond it up to the present. Its apprehension as part of a stretch of time that stretches beyond it up to the present is, of course, what guarantees that we are dealing with an intuition directed, not merely toward an imagined stretch of time, but toward a stretch of time imagined as *actually past*. So far, there is therefore no circularity in our account of judgments concerning stretches of past time: the "apprehension" in question, though pre-conceptual, is simply what *constitutes* one's (imaginative) "judgment" that the imagined stretch is a stretch imagined in the past. (But there is, of course, no guarantee that what one imagines to be *in* that stretch of time was actually in it. What one imaginatively places, or even takes to have been, in the year 1900 may not have been in it; one may nevertheless be imagining it as present in that very year.)

What remains is to consider how such a stretch of imagined past time is specifically *conceptualizable:* How do we account for its conceptualization with respect to its contents (what one imagines, or even takes, to have existed, or even merely possibly to have existed, during the imagined stretch of time), duration (a past day? year? century?), or actual distance from the present (*which* day, year, or century?)?

Now consider, again, the case of merely imagining a rose bush. We have so far considered that sort of case in an oversimplified way. We may now consider various sorts of cases. For example: (1) (If it is possible) The non-temporal case:

I imaginatively represent a region of space that I (purely "problematically") conceptualize as containing a rose bush. (2) The temporal but non-historical case: I imaginatively represent a stretch of time (but without necessarily conceptualizing it as of any particular duration) that I conceptualize as containing a rose bush, but without experiencing it as actually stretching back from the present, that is, without apprehending it as having been a stretch of actually past time. (3) The minimally historical case, introduced in the preceding paragraphs: I imaginatively represent a stretch of time (but without necessarily conceptualizing it as of any particular duration) that I may conceptualize as containing a rose bush, and I experience that stretch as stretching back from the present (but without necessarily conceptualizing it as at any particular distance from the present).

What I have so far argued is that nothing more is needed, for (3), than (a) the purely *general* ability to conceptualize, at least "problematically," in imaginative intuition, and (b) the ability to apprehend stretches of time as stretching back from the present. (Case (2), of course, only requires the first of these elements.) The second of these features is no more mysterious than the basic structure of anticipation and retention in the first place; the first seems to involve no more than the ability to incorporate anticipations and retentions, at least in a suitably "modalized" form, into purely imaginative intuitions. On the other hand, we still have not—not even with (3)—arrived at a judgment regarding the existence of an object in the past. We have at most made room for a case of merely imagining an object *as* existing in the past. It should also be clear that a case of (4), actually conceptualizing the stretch in question as of some particular duration, and conceptualizing its distance back from the present as of some particular length, would still not yield (5), a judgment regarding the existence of an object in the past. At most, it would yield a case of imagining an object *as* existing for some particular time in the past, at a particular distance from the present.

It may seem impossible to deal with this problem in the terms that are available to us. The only alternative would seem to be that our conceptualization of an object is no longer to be constituted through the incorporation of "problematically" modalized anticipations and retentions in imaginative intuition. For the latter would not appear to amount to the affirmation of any real *existence* in the past. Instead, it would appear that the judgment in question needs to be constituted through the incorporation, in imaginative intuition, of what we might call genuinely *assertoric* anticipations and retentions. This would seem to be demanded by the fact that the object is no longer merely imagined as occupying some imaginatively apprehended past, but is actually taken to have *been* in that past. But then this, though apparently required, seems impossible. If the anticipations and retentions in question are not merely "problematic" in mode, then we would seem to have a case of regarding an object as *present*, not merely as existing at some point in the past. Surely, one cannot apprehend an object "through" anticipations that one does not in fact have. But if one does in fact have them, and they are not problematically "modalized," then one would seem to be actually *anticipating* in the very manner in which one normally anticipates in regard to present reality.

This objection may appear to be telling against an attempt to deal with judgments about the past in terms of anticipations and retentions as material in imaginative intuition. But I am not convinced that it is. The difficulty seems to be that, according to the proposed account, judgments about the past would turn out to be indistinguishable from judgments about objects in the present. But the proposal does not seem to me to entail this. At most it implies that judgments about the past might involve the very same *anticipations* as the ones that we would ordinarily have in regard to certain present objects. But in the sense that concerns us, the anticipations in question are not themselves *judgments*. They are at most the material for judgments.

It may also help to remember that we are dealing only with intuitional judgments. Thus we are not dealing, for example, with everything that might come under the heading of "having a belief," or "thinking," about the existence of an object in the past. The latter might be construed in any number of ways, perhaps of interest in empirical psychology, but of no interest here. However the notion is construed, it is no doubt implausible to suppose that, so long as one "has the belief" or "thinks" that some object formerly existed, one must continue to have a particular set of (unmodalized) anticipations concerning possible perceptions of that object. But the present account carries no such implication. At most, it entails that, so long as one is actually *judging* (that is, actually predicating in intuition), to the effect that an object formerly existed, then one must be in a particular set of anticipational states bearing on possible perceptions of that object. In any case, it is crucial to remember that, even then, the states in question are not themselves judgments. They are not even states of "consciousness," in the full-blown Kantian sense. At most, they serve as material *through* which certain types of states of consciousness are constituted. In the present case, they serve as material through which a past stretch of time is imaginatively apprehended.

Strictly speaking, that an object is apprehended "through" some set of anticipations regarding the possibility of perceptions no doubt implies that one is, for the moment, indeed "anticipating" the possibilty of those very perceptions, at least given the satisfaction of certain conditions. But we need not take this to blur the distinction between judging that an object formerly existed and that it actually exists now. The distinction will not be blurred, so long as we remember that one's state of consciousness is never totally constituted by such anticipations in the first place. We may agree that, both in judging that an object formerly existed and in judging that the same object really exists now, one must be apprehending an intuitively (imaginatively or sensorily) apprehended object through the very same set of anticipations. But there may still be a crucial difference. In the one sort of case, one's state of consciousness may be constituted through those anticipations serving as material in the conceptualization *of given appearances*; in the other, it may be constituted only through their serving as material in the conceptualization of a past (and merely imagined) stretch of time. Since the anticipations are not themselves ways in which objects are judgmentally present or past, there is no danger that the judgments that contain them must really be the same.

Now we may consider a second feature of judgments about objects in the past. This is that they are conceptualized as occupying times that are at a more or less definite distance in the past. What could this involve? It must in any case involve more than apprehending imagined time as merely stretching back from the present, as in (3). For the latter, we may need no more than a very primitive mode of imaginative "retention," as an essential ingredient in imaginative intuition whose focus is a past stretch of time. For the former, we need a full-blown mode of conceptualization, namely, the conceptualization of an imagined past as at a certain distance from the present. Once again, our only recourse would appear to be to some special mode of "anticipation." For reasons that we have already seen, this cannot, of course, be a merely "problematic" mode of anticipation. If it were, we would not be dealing with anything that amounts to genuine affirmation regarding existing in the past. What we seem therefore to require is yet another appeal to a special *mode* of anticipation. We might call it: anticipation-*in-retention*. But to account for it, we need to capitalize on a special feature of anticipation in general.

Consider the case of ordinary anticipation, as an ingredient in perception. One anticipates certain possible extensions of a given perception, as upshots of certain conditions. Obviously, this does not mean that one anticipates those upshots as immediately forthcoming. The antecedent conditions are presumably anticipated as requiring a certain time for their own satisfaction. Therefore, ordinary anticipations must already involve, on a pre-conceptual level, an anticipation of "having to wait" some more or less determinate length of time, in order for a given experience to stretch to the point of its anticipated terminus. Now we are attempting to regard intuitive judgments about an object in the past in terms of the ingredience—in an imaginative intuition whose object is a past stretch of time—of the same, or at least the same sorts of, anticipations as would ordinarily provide the material for conceptualization of objects in ordinary perception. To do this, we may now simply make use of the facts: first, that, as already conceded, even a minimally historical case such as (3) already contains the apprehension of a phenomenal present from which an imagined stretch can be reached by stretching "back" (or of a phenomenal present which can be reached from that stretch by stretching "forward"); second, that ordinary anticipations already involve the anticipation of having to "wait" for certain upshots. Putting the points together, we have the basic materials required for a case in which some past is imaginatively apprehended (as in (3)) as stretching back from a present that in turn needs to be *awaited*, in more or less determinate respects, from the point of view of that past. To recognize this as possible, we need simply permit a modification of the kind of anticipation that is already involved in one's ordinary perceptions of objects. The modification must concern the fact that the merely imaginative apprehension of an object needs to apprehend it, not simply through anticipations of the same sorts of *upshots* as are ordinarily anticipable in perception, but also through the anticipation of upshots whose terminus would now be in the very *present*.

If sense can in fact be made of this modality of anticipation—where what is "anticipated" is anticipated as yet to come in the *present*—then it would follow that a "phenomenalistic" account of judgments about the past would not, as often supposed, need to rest on the conceivability of a subject's traveling back into the past from the present, in order to obtain the relevant "possible (and, under given circumstances, necessary) perceptions." It would only need to rest on the possibility of presently anticipating (*in* the apprehension of an imaginatively represented past) the possibility of arriving at the present *from that past*, in order to obtain certain possible perceptions. By the same token, the proposed account does not presume that past objects need to have left presently perceivable *traces*. At most it requires the "anticipation" of their having done so. (It should be clear, in other words, that the relevant anticipation of upshots to come in the present is not the same as the judgment that those upshots really are obtainable in the present. It is at most the "anticipation" of their obtainability, and even their necessary obtainability, given certain possible *ways* of stretching from past to present.)

What then remains to be explained is the representation of *how long* one would need to wait in order to arrive at the present, from an imaginatively apprehended past. But it seems to me that we now have at least the basic materials for dealing with this question as well. The materials are provided by two facts: first, that the present is already represented in any imaginative apprehension of the past (by virtue of the purely intuitive apprehension of the latter as stretched back from the former, or of the former as stretched forward from the latter); second, that anticipation already contains, in its basic structure, the anticipation of having to wait for anticipated upshots. The two together ought to allow for the construction of a mode of anticipation through which objects would be apprehensible, in imaginative intuition, not simply as in the past, but as at certain distances from the present. Once again, the relevant mode of anticipation will have to be what I have called "anticipation-in-retention." The rest will simply need to hinge on precisely *what* is anticipated in this mode. Consider, for example, the imaginative apprehension of a stretch of past time through a body of material containing, among other things, the following anticipation: the anticipation of eventually being able to apprehend the present, if one were only to wait for the earth to revolve around the sun ten thousand times. Though it may at first appear to be circular to do so, we might simply propose that apprehending a stretch of past in this way—or at least in some such way—amounts precisely to apprehending it as what we would ordinarily call "ten thousand years ago."

The reason the suggestion may seem to be circular is that we now appear to have introduced a particular set of *concepts* (*sun, revolution, ten thousand*, etc.), in order to specify what particular anticipations are in question. What we were trying to do, by contrast, was to explain how any conceptualization of the past is originally *constituted* in terms of certain sorts of anticipations in the first place. But the reason that this does not introduce circularity into the account is simply that we are not now dealing with the general problem of concept-formation. The account would be circular if the original material for the formation of concepts, as predicates in intuition, must always itself be something conceptually formed. Apparently contrary to Kant, I have granted that it must, in a sense, be "judgmentally" formed. But this is not the same as saying that it must already have been formed into concepts in the relevant sense. The latter involves a specific structure of judgmental forming, correlative with the constitution of original self-consciousness.

Nothing rules out the ingredience of concepts among the material for the formation of at least certain *additional* concepts in intuition. Thus, for example, the concept of "having to wait ten thousand years for the present" may simply not be an example of a concept that is formed out of anticipations of the sort that we have called purely "animal" in nature. Rather, it might be formed out of anticipations that are formed with the help of additional concepts that are only in their own turn formed out of such more primitive material. Many concepts are no doubt like this. (To be sure, in his discussion of analyticity, Kant himself gives the impression that concepts are, at least in many cases, directly formed out of other concepts; they are not merely formed out of material to which other concepts contribute [A6-7/B10-11]. But it should be evident that this formulation poses a problem of interpretation in its own right.) There will be no contradiction in admitting this, so long as the concepts that contribute to the formation of anticipations, out of which other concepts are then formed, are not—in the final "analysis"—themselves formed out of anticipations of that particular kind. In other words, there must eventually be a set of concepts that are directly formed out of anticipations (and retentions) to which concepts do not contribute. That this is the case does not seem implausible. (Again, this should not be confused with the implausible claim—apparently, and unfortunately, Kant's own—that there must be concepts that are formed out of anticipations that are totally devoid of "judgmental form.")

In these terms, it seems to me that it may be possible to account for the conceptualization of imagined times as stretches of real history, in terms of the general account of conceptualization as the incorporation of anticipations and retentions in intuition. To do it, we simply need to appreciate the following points: (1) The general possibility of imagining stretches of time in the first place is already conceded with the introduction of time as a "form of intuition." (2) The possibility of imagining past times as stretching from the actual *present* is simply a "retentional" counterpart of the basic structure of anticipation that has already been conceded, namely, of its structure as involving the non-judgmental apprehension of appearances as (possibly) stretching into the *future*. (3) The basic structure of anticipation, already conceded, also includes the capacity for anticipating upshots for which it is necessary to *wait* some length of time. (4) There is nothing incoherent in the idea that the conceptualization of past times involves their apprehension through manifolds of *anticipations*, appropriately comparable to those through which present appearances are apprehensible. (This yields the basic structure of "anticipation-in-retention," and it provides the basis for the representation of particular sorts of objects as occupying past times.) (5) In the light of (1)–(4), there is nothing incoherent in the idea of apprehending past times through the anticipations of upshots, where the latter would require waiting until the present for their obtainment. Finally, (6) there is nothing incoherent in the idea of apprehending past times through the anticipation of upshots, where the latter would require a conceptually determinate *length* of waiting. (This provides the basis for the representation of past times as at certain distances from the present. I assume that it also contains material sufficient to account for the representation of past times as of particular lengths.)

Conclusion

I CONCLUDE with a brief summary, and with an acknowledgment of certain limitations to what I have proposed in this book. I have tried in these chapters to provide a reading of the Transcendental Deduction that takes some aspects of Kant's view more seriously than has been customary. I have done this because it may help us in an understanding of Kant, but also for what I take to be the intrinsic significance of the ideas. The first of these concerns the distinction between matter and form in intuition. I have tried to show that it is foundational, in ways not generally recognized, to the theory of understanding that Kant develops in the Deduction. With respect to that distinction, I have resisted some common temptations. For example, I have resisted the temptation to suppose that the matter of intuition is merely whatever (possible) *objects* are objects of the possible experiences of subjects who are (relevantly) such as ourselves. I have also resisted the temptation to suppose that the form of intuition is either a simple place-holder, in the Aesthetic, for what the Deduction eventually proves to be a function of understanding or at best a function of limits on the latter, rightly or wrongly posited as necessary in the Aesthetic. The matter of intuition is, as Kant insists it is, some aspect of our own subjective condition: in the Aesthetic, what Kant calls *Empfindung*. The form is then an irreducible mode of (possible) intentional *directedness* toward (possible) objects *through* such material. I have tried to show that these distinctions allow for a more adequate view of the relationship between perceptual and imaginative consciousness than would otherwise be possible. With respect to some of the standard issues of Kant interpretation, I have also tried to show that, as I have drawn it, the distinction entails neither the absurd view that "appearances," as objects of intuition, are made out of sensations nor the view, absurd to the minds of some, that a full-blown consciousness of objects is impossible apart from concepts. However, while it does not entail the latter view, I have argued that there is no harm in supposing, with Kant himself, that the mere form of intuition does indeed constitute at least some *level* of consciousness.

Recognition of an ambiguity in the notion of a "concept," and in some related notions (such as "judgment"), might help with the latter point. It seems clear that Kant thinks, and reasonably so, that non-human animals, and human infants, are in some way conscious beings. Yet they do not exercise true conceptual abilities. At most, they have "intuitions" of various sorts. One is likely to conclude that Kant was simply closed-minded to the recognition of conceptual abilities in animals. In turn, this might be supposed to evidence an implausibly discontinuous picture of animal-to-human development. But I have argued that it is possible to regard animal conception as fundamentally different in "form" from the human, without supposing a radical discontinuity between the levels. The solution is to see that merely animal conception needs to serve as, but as no more than, "matter" *in* distinctively human conception.

This leads to the second leg of my reading of the Deduction. I have based my reading on the suggestion that Kant's distinction between matter and form in conception, understanding, or judgment builds precisely upon the corresponding distinction in the Aesthetic. Again, this is not simply to demand a distinction between some domain of possible objects, as "matter" for possible conception, and some "form," or set of forms, for the eventual conceptualization of such objects, that is, for judgments in their regard. Our lesson from the Aesthetic must remain: that directedness toward objects of any kind needs to be constituted as directedness *through* one's own subjective condition. Except on the most unpalatable readings of Kant, objects themselves are of course not part of one's own subjective condition. On the other hand, once we have eliminated unworkable pictures of mental fabrication (of objects out of material in intuition), the most natural supposition may appear to be this: that judgments refer to objects "through" intuitions simply in the sense that they refer one's intuitions *to* objects in the first place. This, at least, would permit supposing that intuitions are the "matter" of conception. And these are indeed a part of one's own subjective condition.

It is truistic that it is the essence of judgment, or at least of "judgments of experience," to "refer" intuitions to objects in Kant's view. But if we take this ability as basic, then we have presupposed what needs explaining: that judgments themselves are able to have objects. If judgments do not have objects, then they cannot refer intuitions *to* objects. But it would seem incredible if, having insisted that a distinction between matter and form, intrinsic to any intuitional state as such, is essential to an account of the latter's potential object-directedness, Kant could suppose that judgments, by contrast, are *simply* object-directed, without any need for a corresponding articulation in terms of matter and form. Nor should we suppose the difficulty met by appeal to a final, and equally truistic observation, namely, that the Kantian forms of judgment are forms for the forming of *concepts* into judgments. Apart from the fact that concepts themselves need to be formed, we have yet to be sufficiently serious in regard to the relation between the problematic of the Transcendental Deduction and the Aesthetic's original insistence upon form for the directionality of intuition—that is, for its directedness, or even potential directedness, toward any objects *of the very judgments* whose possibility is now in question in the Deduction. As I argued in Chapter One, if the task of judgment is to conceptualize *those* very objects, then the relevant judgments must simply be intuitions as well. In other words, the relevant forms of judgment can be nothing other than whatever is needed for the transformation of intuitions into intuitional judgments. In turn, the foundational "matter" of the latter must be matter in intuition. Clearly, this cannot be *Empfindung* as Kant conceives it. If it were, then there could be no such thing as conceptualization in mere imagination. But there is no difficulty in supposing that it is something "imaginative." (I have tried to show that recognition of this is compatible with Kant's own view that *Empfindung* is *the* "matter" of intuition *as such.*)

While some of Kant's explicit claims lend themselves to the supposition that imagination provides a kind of "matter" for conception, he does not very plainly suggest that it does so by virtue of providing matter for intuition as well. In this respect, my reading of the Deduction must be regarded as (re)constructive. But it remains an indisputable fact that Kant himself places weight on the fact that concepts need to be "formed." It is also clear that he is preoccupied, in both editions of the Deduction, with the establishment of a "middle" position for the faculty of imagination, between those of intuition and full-blown understanding. I hope in any case to have shown how the proposed reading is fruitful in regard to some of Kant's more puzzling doctrines—such as the doctrine of transcendental affinity, the distinction between judgments of "perception" and "experience," and the account of self-consciousness as "one" with the consciousness of objects—as well as in regard to a number of other unclarities in the Deduction, such as its division into "stages" as well as numerous apparent contradictions regarding the respective roles of the various faculties. In addition, I have suggested that attention to these notions should also shed some light on the very notion of "consciousness" as such—that is, on the notion of consciousness of *objects*—and on the question of its relative modernity.

It remains to add some brief comments concerning admitted limitations in the view that I have ascribed to Kant. First, I have deliberately limited my attention to judgments in intuition, that is, to judgments that conceptualize an object in either a sensory or a purely imaginative manner. But it may seem obvious that we need to allow for judgments of a much more abstract sort. I argued in Chapter One that it is not in fact clear that Kant himself is unequivocally prepared to allow non-intuitional judgments, at least as judgments of any sort that might constitute a genuine *Erkenntnis*. (Any other sort of judgment would apparently be one that somehow involves mere "forms" of judgment, or perhaps "unschematized" categories. I have not been concerned with the intelligibility of that notion in this study.) But as also noted earlier, such disallowal would seem disastrous for any attempt, such as Kant appears to offer, to recognize at least some "analytic" judgments as instances of *Erkenntnis*.

Perhaps the following distinction can avoid the difficulty, without abandoning the supposition that *Erkenntnisse* are, or at least always contain, intuitional judgments. First, let us note that the view of judgment, hence of concepts, that I have defended in this study is, in a certain sense, restricted to what we might call "basic" or "simple" judgments and concepts. But we need to be careful about this notion of simplicity. According to the proposed view, all judgments and concepts contain some material, structured in some way. They must therefore be, in some sense, "analyzable" with respect to that material. But as I argued in Chapter One, in rejecting the possibility of phenomenalistic "analyses," this is perfectly compatible with denying that the analyses in question involve analysis of judgments or concepts in terms of other concepts that a given concept contains (although, of course, such analysis must at least employ *some* concepts, in its exposition of given concepts). Judgments or concepts that are unanalyzable in terms of other judgments or concepts may be regarded as simple. I have offered no hypothesis as to which are in fact simple in this sense.

We might continue to suppose, then, that all "simple" judgments are intuitional judgments in Kant's view. It should be clear that this leaves room not only for a kind of analytic judgment, but for a notion of concepts as "containing" other concepts. In fact, Kant himself suggests how the latter notion might be elaborated. As I observed in note 6 to Chapter One, for example, Kant proposes that the concept *black man* (or the concept *the black man*) is really a kind of *judgment*, namely, a "problematic" judgment. Presumably, Kant's point is this: that the concept in question is nothing distinct from a multiply instantiable feature of a certain possible *conception*, namely, the conception of some (possible) man as (possibly) black. Any such conception, Kant must presumably suppose, is somehow "compounded" out of two distinct conceptions, of a man and of something black (in the way that a man might be). Correspondingly, the "concept" in question is really a complex one, not simply in the sense that it contains some body of material, but that it contains other *concepts* within itself. On account of this, we might therefore regard the judgment that a black man is black, or that he is a man, as an "analytic" judgment, even though it *contains* judgments that are, at least imaginatively, intuitional. And we might insist that such a judgment is a genuine *Erkenntnis* precisely because it contains such material.

It should be clear that I have not tried to show precisely how such compounding of concepts might take place. At most, I have tried to show that something like this sort of view must be Kant's. Kant himself, of course, supposes that judgmental "form" is needed for the purpose. What I have tried to show is that he thereby blurred the distinction between two different roles for judgmental form, namely, as responsible for the compounding of concepts and judgments into more complex ones, and as responsible for the original formation of any concepts in the first place, out of a material that is not yet conceptual at all. It is the latter notion that I have argued to be central to Kant's theory in the Transcendental Deduction. Whether he was then simply misguided, in the Metaphysical Deduction, in supposing there in fact to be a single set of forms, able to perform this double function, is a question from which I have abstracted. But I have tried to show that considerations internal to the problem of concept-formation can plausibly be seen as grounding an appeal to at least some of the concepts in question in the Analytic of Principles, namely, those of substance, causality, and community of interaction.

In any case, it is important to remind ourselves that there is a second sense in which the proposed view is after all compatible with the recognition of nonintuitional judgments. According to the proposed view, a judgment, at least in the sense that concerns us, involves the ingredient of a body of anticipations and retentions in an intuitional state. Namely, it involves the ingredient of the sort of body of anticipations and retentions that is sufficient to constitute, in constituting the awareness of an object or possible object, a mode of self-consciousness sufficient for grounding the eventual formation of a genuine self-concept. Correlatively, it involves the ingredient of material sufficient to constitute an awareness of a world of re-identifiable objects. But bodies of such material may also be present in a subject, yet without providing any material for apprehension in intuition—that is, without providing material for the apprehension of appearances *through* that material. Considered in itself, it is difficult to know how to regard such material. One might regard it in purely dispositional terms, for example (or in terms of the physiological underpinning of dispositions), or perhaps purely "functionally," in terms of the typical causes and effects of certain subjective state-types. In any case, considered in itself, the material in question is presumably what accounts for a great deal of any subject's behavior in regard to objects that surround it.

It is not, in fact, implausible to identify the occurrence of such bodies of material in a subject—either just by themselves or as causally "connected" with occurrences of sensation—with instances of "belief," "judgment," and even of "knowledge." The proposed view allows for this concession. All that it excludes is the extension of such an approach to the elucidation of belief or judgment or knowledge, when these latter are supposed to involve genuine modes of *consciousness*. Indeed, though I have not argued it, it seems to me reasonable to insist that any purely dispositional or functional approach can be supposed to illuminate *any* notion of "belief," "judgment," or "knowledge" only to the extent that the corresponding behavioral or functional material is regarded as at least potential material for genuinely intuitional judgment as well.

It is also necessary to recognize a certain role for language. I have, of course, concentrated on the notion of anticipation and retention of possible "appearances," as a kind of possible "stretching" (backward or forward) of a given appearance. But even when what one ordinarily regards as the "conceptualization" of appearances in fact involves anticipation and retention in intuition, it no doubt often involves the ingredient of a certain sort of purely *linguistic* anticipation and retention. When I "see" an appearance "as" some kind of object, the primarily operative body of anticipations and retentions is surely one that often simply involves anticipation and retention of the possibility, not of the "stretching" of the conceptualized appearance itself, but merely of the *saying* of (or the permissibility of the saying of) certain possible things in regard to that appearance.

This indeed might be thought to be Kant's own main point: that concepts as "rules" are primarily rules for the occurrence of "judgment," in the sense of rules for the permissible *saying* of certain things. I do not believe that Kant had any such view in mind. But the view that I have proposed can at least tolerate the point as first stated, namely, that much of what passes for the conceptualization of appearances in intuition involves no more than a certain sort of linguistic anticipation and retention. It is difficult to know how to account for the latter notion. But such an account must at the very least be undertaken, in order to provide a phenomenologically adequate account of that special mode of "talking to oneself" that passes, in many cases, for conceptualization.

A second limitation concerns the proposed notion of a "concept." Concepts are anticipations and retentions of an appropriately structured sort, potentially ingredient in intuitional states. Now it should at least be clear that this proposal does not open the way to a certain charge of psychologism. In particular, it is not guilty of psychologizing concepts in the sense of failing to recognize their status as logical "predicates," potentially instantiable in any number of distinct psychological acts, and whose existence does not depend upon the actual occurrence of psychological phenomena. That apparent difficulty is avoided by noting that the claim that concepts "are" bodies of anticipations and retentions is merely short for saying that acts of conceptualization are constituted by nothing more than the ingredience of appropriately structured anticipations and retentions in intuition. That a particular concept is multiply or repeatedly instantiable, or that it exists at all (in whatever sense a concept might be thought to "exist" in the first place), is presumably nothing more than a matter of the (logical) *possibility* of the appropriate sort of ingredience of anticipations and retentions in intuition.

But a different sort of difficulty may appear to obtain, and to be a product of too "psychologistic" an approach to concepts. It concerns the conditions for saying that multiple instances of judgment do or do not involve instantiation of one and the same concept. It may appear that any minimal difference in the anticipations and retentions ingredient in intuitional states would suffice to exclude the possibility that we are dealing with a single instantiated concept. But it is extremely unlikely that precisely the same anticipations and retentions are ever ingredient in distinct intuitions. The implausible conclusion would therefore seem to follow that, whether or not it is logically possible, it is extremely unlikely that the same concept is ever in fact multiply instantiated or repeated in intuitional judgment.

In meeting this difficulty, we need to recall that what is not in question is merely the unlikelihood of the very same anticipations and retentions being *connected* with distinct intuitions. What is relevant is only the question of what sets of anticipations and retentions are "connected" to intuitions by virtue of constituting a body of material *in* those intuitions, as opposed to being merely externally, perhaps causally, attached to them (and are in their own turn embedded in appropriate sets of *higher-order* anticipations and retentions). In addition, we have already noted a respect in which the proposed account does not in fact require ingredience of precisely the same anticipations and retentions, as a condition for the sameness of a concept. As we saw in Chapter Seven, whether the ingredience of distinct bodies of anticipations and retentions constitutes the multiple instantiation of a single concept hinges rather on whether or not they satisfy appropriate rules for the *tranformability* of the one into the other.

Apart from these points, it may also help to bear the following in mind. The proposed account has assumed no obligation to provide an account of the identity conditions of concepts, in the sense of providing conditions for the identity of linguistic *meanings*. Kant's interest, and my own, has been in certain special aspects of mental activity. What conditions are involved in the judgment that two different *words*, for example, express the same "concept" may therefore well involve conditions beyond what we have been exploring. In any case, our concern has been with certain necessary conditions. For various purposes—for example, for an analysis of language—one may well introduce additional requirements for the sameness and difference of concepts.

Finally, an observation concerning the notion of the "synthetic *a priori*." Obviously, I have not been particularly concerned to show how my reading of the Deduction could explain how its "conclusion" could possibly involve synthetic *a priori* knowledge, and precisely what sort of *argument* could possibly have been used to arrive at it. The latter neglect is primarily because, as I have already noted, I have found it more profitable not to assume that the "Deduction" is in the first instance a deductive argument at all. It is better to read it, I think, as attempting to elaborate a theory, able to account, among other things, for our possession of certain instances of synthetic *a priori* knowledge. As for the possibility of any such judgments in the first place, whether or not Kant offers any valid argument for them, at least the following should be clear: insofar as the Deduction reflects on concepts, in order to yield its results, it cannot possibly reflect on purely analytic relations involving those concepts. For the theory it offers is a theory concerning the original *formation* of any concepts whatsoever. For the same reason, we must, of course, at least acknowledge a respect in which the alleged new "knowledge" is knowledge *about* what is *a priori*. In any event, to whatever extent Kant's reflection on the problem of concept-formation succeeds in providing an adequate account of original *self-consciousness*, and to whatever extent the latter proves to be "necessary for experience" (as Kant assumed it was for distinctively human experience), the basic argument of the Deduction is simply this: that since original self-consciousness is equivalent to original concept-formation, the application of the original "forms of judgment," in the conceptualization of objects, is likewise necessary for experience.

Notes

Preface

1. *Reflexionen zur Metaphysik*, 5927 (18.388-9). Cf. *Reflexionen zur Anthropologie*, 212 (15.81): "Sensibility is the affectibility of the capacity for representations. Understanding is the spontaneity of our capacity for representations. . . . Consciousness relates to [*geht auf*] both. Consciousness of the manifold in the former representations (coordination) or intuitions is aesthetic clarity, in concepts it is logical clarity. Both [modes of consciousness] are mere form." A110: "This thoroughgoing synthetic unity of perceptions is indeed the form of experience; it is nothing else than the synthetic unity of appearances in accordance with concepts." A129: ". . . this unity of possible consciousness also constitutes the form of all cognition of objects; through it the manifold is thought as belonging to a single object. Thus the mode in which the manifold of sensible representation (intuition) belongs to one consciousness precedes all cognition of the object as the intellectual form of such cognition. . . ." A346/B404: ". . . consciousness in itself is not a representation distinguishing a particular object, but a form of representation in general, so far as it is to be entitled cognition. . . ."

2. *Wiener Logik* (24.807):

> Empfindungen, z.E. Reiz, Rührungen sind die Materie der Sinnlichkeit, die Anschauung ist ihre Form. Einbildungskraft gilt also nur von der Form der Sinnlichkeit, aber nicht von der Materie.

3. Cf. *Logik*, I, §2 (9.91): "Die Materie der Begriffe ist der *Gegenstand*, die Form derselben die *Allgemeinheit*."

4. See my *Representational Mind* (Bloomington: Indiana University Press, 1983).

Chapter One: The Framework

1. Cf. Norman Kemp Smith, *A Commentary to Kant's 'Critique of Pure Reason'* (New York: Humanities Press, 1962; reprint of 2nd edition of 1923), pp. 270ff. Kemp Smith takes Kant to waver between a subjectivistic reading, where the "appearances" given to sensible intuition are made out of sensory states of the individual, and a phenomenalistic position, where they are objective relative to the individual. However, even the latter approach seems to take appearances to be made out of some special sort of material—just not states of the individual subject (pp. 276-77). Cf. T. E. Wilkerson, *Kant's Critique of Pure Reason* (Oxford: Oxford University Press, 1976), p. 190: "[W]e should not be confused by Kant's distinction between 'formal' and 'material' idealism, for his own 'formal' idealism is indistinguishable from the 'material' idealism of Berkeley."

2. This seems to apply, for example, to Arthur Melnick, *Kant's Analogies of Experience* (Chicago: University of Chicago Press, 1973), pp. 7-14, and to Henry E. Allison, *Kant's Transcendental Idealism* (New Haven: Yale University Press, 1983), pp. 94-98. Of course, the tendency to reduce the forms of intuition to irreducible limitations or presuppositions with respect to intuitable objects is still compatible with a number of positions on the role

of sensation. But the claim that the latter is matter for "forming" in intuition gets downplayed.

3. I assume, for the purpose of our interest in this study, that ordinary perception involves sensations. It is, of course, arguable that "perception" through sense organs does not always do this.

4. See *Representational Mind* (Bloomington: Indiana University Press, 1983), Chapter Two.

5. Cf. Ermanno Bencivenga, "Knowledge as a Relation and Knowledge as an Experience in the Critique of Pure Reason," *Canadian Journal of Philosophy*, 15 (1985), p. 596n6; Rolf George, "Kant's Sensationism," *Synthese*, 47 (1981), 241–42. George suggests that, on many occasions, "reference" would be the most suitable term. In any case, Kant seems always to intend the conceptualization of intuitions.

6. A related stumbling block, or the same put differently, lies in Kant's claim that "judgment" always combines at least two concepts. This seems to be the drift of the Metaphysical Deduction (A70/B95–A80/B106). Cf. also the early (1770–72?) *Reflexionen zur Metaphysik*, 4634 (17.616-7). In the latter, Kant argues that a concept is required, in order to constitute the cognition of a potential subject of judgment in the first place, out of the representations that provide the mere "material" for such cognition. Then a second concept will be able to predicate something of it. It is unclear why the first action does not already amount to a kind of judgment: at the very least to the *problematic* judgment that a certain sort of object *might* be present as subject for (further) judgment. I conclude that Kant's insistence on the combining of concepts is a holdover from an approach that he is in the process of rejecting. Elsewhere, he cites the representation *this black man* as an example of a "problematic" representation that one ought to call a concept, in order to distinguish it from the judgment that the man is in fact black. Obviously, the representation is as full-blown a judgment, albeit problematic in form, as would be required by the Metaphysical Deduction. It involves two concepts. But Kant could as easily have illustrated his point with the simpler representation, *this man*, distinguishing the latter from the judgment that the object is indeed a man. See Letter to Beck, July 3, 1792, trans. Arnulf Zweig, in *Kant: Philosophical Correspondence* (Chicago: University of Chicago Press, 1967), pp. 192–93. For the distinction between the two approaches to judgment in Kant, see Moltke S. Gram, *Kant, Ontology, and the A Priori* (Evanston: Northwestern University Press, 1968), esp. Chapter Two.

7. For an interpretation of the analytic/synthetic distinction in terms of the distinction between "referential" and non-"referential" judgments, see Gram, Chapter Three.

8. Strictly, the suggestion requires regarding intuitions, and their forms, as repeatables—as when we say that one is in "the same" intuitional state as previously, or as some other person is. Throughout, the point should be clear in context. The same ambiguity, of course, arises for the "material" of intuitions. But when regarded as material of *concepts*, as well as of intuitions, this must, of course, always be regarded as repeatable. As material of conceptual *acts*, they may be regarded either way, depending on how the latter are regarded.

9. Cf. *Metaphysical First Principles of Natural Science*, tr. James Ellington (Indianapolis: Bobbs-Merrill, 1970), Preface, p. 12, note (4.474): ". . . categories, which are thought, are nothing but mere forms of judgments insofar as these forms are applied to intuitions." B288: ". . . the categories are not in themselves *cognitions*, but are merely *forms of thought* for the making of cognitions out of given intuitions." Cf. A147/B187, A239/B298, A248/B305. On the other hand, on the categories as forms of judgment somehow converted into concepts in their own right, see B143, A321/B378.

10. I do not want to suggest that the mere embodiment of sensations in intuitional states suffices for a truly cognitive apprehension of the corresponding correlate in appearances, for example, for apprehension of colors as "qualities" of possible objects. On the other hand, I do not hold that full-blown conceptualization is required for some reasonable *level of consciousness* of such qualities. The role of anticipations and retentions, as material for conceptualization, offers what seems to me a happy compromise: we may concede that a

certain level of apprehension of sensory qualities involves more than bare "sensation," but less than fully constituted concepts of such qualities. We might also note, as I emphasize in Chapter Three, that there are in any case important analogies between anticipations and retentions, as material for concepts, and mere sensations in the Kantian sense.

11. Throughout, I use the term *conceptualize* ambiguously: sometimes for predications with respect to objects or appearances, other times for the corresponding operations in cognitive states themselves, *through* which such predications are effected. Context should make the point clear. It should also be clear why it is not inappropriate to use a single term in these ways.

12. I have argued in more detail elsewhere for the general approach to intuition, and its forms and objects, with specific attention to the interpretation of the Aesthetic. In the present study, my case rests primarily on the utility of the approach with respect to the account of conceptualization that I base on it. In any event, I return to this issue in the next section. For now I would simply forestall an objection to the quoted passage, when it is read as making a point about "imagining." The objection is that impenetrability, hardness, and color are no less imaginable than extension and figure. The reply is that, in Kantian terms, these would be mere abstractions of a certain sort. Extension and figure, by contrast, are presumably intended as (possible) particulars, namely, as possible regions of space. Given this distinction, it is not implausible to claim that one imagines colors, and the like, simply in that one imagines, of some extension or figure, *that it is colored*, etc.

13. This may seem to be contradicted at B276n. To the question "whether we have an inner sense only, and no outer sense, but merely an outer imagination," Kant replies that the latter always presupposes the former. This may seem to imply that mere imagining possesses no intrinsic object-directedness, but merely derives that character from an external relation with sensory intuition. But we need to remember that the question here is that of the very possibility of outer sense in the first place. It is specifically this, Kant says, that amounts to the above question. His reply to the question (that "in order even to imagine something as outer, that is, to present it to sense in intuition, we must already have an outer sense") does indeed grant that imagination already involves the "form of intuition." In other words, the mere ability to imagine objects as realities in space, as opposed to merely imagining that there are such things, demonstrates the possibility in question. It does this, not because it presupposes the actual occurrence of corresponding sensory intuitions (which, as a purely empirical matter, Kant did assume: A715/B743), but because it already contains in itself whatever is required for that possibility (apart from mere "sensation," the possibility of which all parties to the argument already concede). To some extent this construction seems contrary to Gendlin's recent comment on the passage. See Eugene T. Gendlin, "Time's Dependence on Space: Kant's Statements and Their Misconstrual by Heidegger," in *Kant and Phenomenology: Current Continental Research*, ed. Thomas M. Seebohm and Joseph J. Kockelmans (Washington: University Press of America, 1984), 147–60. Gendlin takes Kant to be holding that imagining always rests on the subject's being "affected passively by something we can know only in its results" (p. 154). Since imagination does not involve actual sensations, this may seem to imply the merely external view, rejected above. However, imagining always involves some "taking" of what is imagined, even if it is not always full-blown conceptual taking. This can be accounted for in terms of the ingredience of anticipations and retentions that, contrary to some of Kant's own claims, are not themselves intuitions, but a kind of quasi-sensory "material" in intuition. In any case, I am very much in agreement with Gendlin's claims concerning the radical dependence of time on space, which constitute his main point of interpretation. Cf. *Representational Mind*, pp. 158–71.

14. This seems to be implied by the definition of sensation as "the effect of an object upon the faculty of representation, *so far as we are affected by it*," i.e., by the object (A19/B34). Cf. also Bxln: "For outer sense is already in itself a relation of intuition to something actual outside me." It may also lie behind Kant's insistence that the mere apprehension of "appearances" implies the real existence of something thereby appearing (A252-3, B306), although Kant elsewhere includes mere hallucinations as instances of outer intuition

(B278). At *Anthropologie*, §24 (7.161), he says that some people who suffer from delusions mistake the appearances of inner sense for genuine sensations. But in the same passage, he seems to characterize the former in terms of how *der Mensch sich innerlich empfindet*. His most official definition simply states that "sensation relates solely to the subject as the modification of its state" (A320/B376). Even more strongly against a relational approach, cf. Letter to Beck, January 20, 1792 (Zweig, p. 183):

> Perhaps right at the outset you can avoid defining "sensibility" in terms of "receptivity," that is, the manner of representations in the subject insofar as he is affected by objects; perhaps you can locate it in that which, in a cognition, concerns merely the relation of the representation to a subject, so that the form of sensibility, in this relation to the object of intuition, makes knowable no more than the appearance of this object. That this subjective thing constitutes only the manner in which the subject is affected *by representations* [emphasis added], and consequently nothing more than the receptivity of the subject, is already implied by its being merely the determination of the subject.

15. Cf. A19-20/B34: "so far as we are affected by it [the object]." Also *Anthropologie*, §§15ff (7.153ff).

16. I use the term *reality*, and cognates, not for Kant's *Realität* (as a kind of intentional correlate of sensation in appearances: A166/B207ff), but for *Wirklichkeit, Sein*, or *Dasein* (A218/B266, A225/B272ff). However, the notions are connected: "Reality [*Realität*], in the pure concept of understanding, is that which corresponds to a sensation in general; it is that, therefore, the concept of which in itself points to being [*ein Sein . . . anzeigt*] (in time)" (A143/B182). Also A175/B217: "But the real, which corresponds to sensations in general . . . represents only that something the very concept of which includes a being. . . ."

17. There may seem to be an obvious alternative to supposing that the sensations involved in a sensory intuition are states out of which that intuition is at least in part formed. The alternative might suppose that the sensational aspect of an intuition is not a function of distinct "states" ingredient in it, but of special properties or features of it; or if a function of distinct states, then of states merely externally (e.g., causally) *connected* to an intuition. The latter suggestion could not explain how sensations could make a difference in how an object is intuitively *apprehended*. One would have to suppose that, considered in itself, the "apprehension" in question was not intuitive at all, but a purely conceptual affair. On the other hand, as properties or features of an intuition, sensations could make the difference in question only if they were determinate forms of the determinable quality of intuitional directedness. But in that case, purely imaginative intuition would be unintelligible. For we would have to say that the latter, apart from whatever conceptual elements it contains, is characterized by nothing *but* a purely determinable quality (intuitional "form") that does not occur in any determinate mode. (Below, I extend this point to argue for intuitional material even beyond mere sensations.)

18. In *Representational Mind* (pp. 33–34), I defended the neutrality thesis against an objection based on the "Refutation of Idealism." Kant's claim, as I there formulated it, was that the very *conception* of oneself as a subject of intuitional states presupposes a conception of oneself as living in a world in which, at least in general, one's intuitions are directed toward real things. One reviewer seems to have taken it from this that I hold Kant to be claiming that it is at most necessary to *conceive* of (i.e., not to *take?*) the objects of one's intuitions as at least in general real. But I said that this was "at the very least" what Kant's position amounts to. My argument, in that context, only concerned the conceptions as such. It was that the fact that (a) a conception of oneself as an experiencer of intuitions entails (b) the necessity of conceptualizing objects in a generally non-neutral way is perfectly compatible with (c) the claim that every intuition as such possesses a neutral object-directedness (in addition to whatever other kind of directedness it might possess). The en-

tailment, that is, is compatible with the fact that every intuition presents an "object" that one is free to take or not to take as real.

19. For a similar approach to the concept of an object in Kant, and a defense of its ontological neutrality, though in terms different from my own, cf. Bencivenga, "Knowledge as a Relation . . .", as well as "Understanding and Reason in the First Critique," *History of Philosophy Quarterly*, 3 (1986), 195–205. In the latter, Bencivenga argues that it is ultimately Reason that provides the standard required for judgments of reality. See also Bencivenga's *Kant's Copernican Revolution* (Oxford: Oxford University Press, 1987).

20. Cf. Wilfrid Sellars, "Notes on Intentionality," *Journal of Philosophy*, 61 (1964), 655–65, reprinted in *Philosophical Perspectives* (Springfield: Charles C. Thomas, 1967).

21. A related objection is raised against Brentano's (later) approach to the intentionality of consciousness in Roderick M. Chisholm, "Brentano on Descriptive Psychology and the Intentional," in *Phenomenology and Existentialism*, ed. Edward N. Lee and Maurice Mandelbaum (Baltimore: Johns Hopkins University Press, 1967).

22. For a criticism of this sort of approach, see Stephen Stich, *From Folk Psychology to Cognitive Science* (Cambridge, Mass.: MIT Press/Bradford Books, 1983), Chapter Four. With particular reference to Kant, I return to the issue in the next chapter.

23. Cf. Eddy Zemach's appeal to "display sentences" (e.g., "Unsafe," posted on a bridge): "De Se and Descartes: A New Semantics for Indexicals," *Noûs*, XIX (1985), 195.

24. Though he does not do so in the particular case of imagination, Searle, for example, appeals to "feelings" as essential to certain states of consciousness, over and above whatever "intentional content" and "direction of fit" are in them: John Searle, *Intentionality* (Cambridge: Cambridge University Press, 1983), p. 35.

25. The suggestion, however, has been defended by Moreland Perkins, in *Sensing the World* (Indianapolis: Hackett, 1983). He suggests that the qualities in question get taken, not as objects, but as qualities *of* objects.

26. Christopher Peacocke, *Sense and Content: Experience, Thought, and their Relations* (Oxford: Clarendon Press, 1983), esp. pp. 113–116. In any case, Peacocke himself does not show how to apply his proposal to cases, as one might call them, of *purely* imagining that "this" is such-and-such (as opposed, for example, to thinking such thoughts in regard to some actually, past or present, existing thing or place).

27. The same difficulty appears to apply to the alternative Peacocke offers in *Thoughts: An Essay on Content* (Aristotelian Society Series, 4 [Oxford: Basil Blackwell, 1986]). Although, unlike the earlier book, it considers only perceptually demonstrative content, the view seems to be, in general, that the notion is to be explicated in terms of the pattern of "canonical grounds and commitments" of a content.

28. Cf. Norman Malcolm, "Thoughtless Brutes," Presidential Address to the American Philosophical Association, Boston, December 28, 1972; D. Davidson, "Thought and Talk," in *Mind and Language: Wolfson College Lectures 1974*, ed. Samuel Guttenplan (Oxford: Oxford University Press, 1975).

29. Cf. Stich, pp. 104–6.

30. The threefold distinction between sensory, imaginative, and conceptual content might be useful in dealing with the sort of case considered by Peacocke, concerning the problem of "switches" in the perception of groups and aspects (*Sense and Content*, pp. 24–26). Peacocke operates with a twofold distinction between sensory and representational content.

31. I shall view concepts, apart from anticipations and retentions regarding the possible course of future and past experience, as mere "forms of judgment," hence not really concepts at all. This may seem to rule out the thinkability of a reality other than appearances. Nevertheless, the forms of judgment, for Kant, do possess some representational function of their own. It might be argued that this provides the basis for abstract "thought" of a non-conceptual kind. Cf. *Representational Mind*, pp. 141–46.

32. Strictly speaking, of course, one does not "conceptualize" an appearance as objectively real in Kant's view, in the sense that one conceptualizes an appearance as, say,

roughly circular in shape. The latter involves application of a concept (*circularity*), in a way that the former does not. Instead, the former merely involves a special form of judgment, through which some concept (*other* than that of existence) is in its own turn applied to an object (cf. A226/B272-3). This, it should become clear, is still compatible with my contention that all "application" of concepts is in the end reducible to an operation of the pure forms of judgment on the material ingredient in intuition.

33. If the suggestion is correct, then despite the apparent reduction of objects to "possible appearances," Kant's phenomenalism at most concerns the sense in which objects might be supposed to *exist*, when they are objectively real. This does not contradict Kant's claim, in the *Prolegomena*, that his "idealism concerns not the existence of things (the doubting of which, however, constitutes idealism in the ordinary sense) . . .": tr. Lewis White Beck (Indianapolis: Bobbs-Merrill), p. 41 (4.293). It is clear from the context that Kant's point is that his view does not *deny* that material objects really exist. As for the objection that Kant could in any case not be concerned with the *sense* in which material objects exist, since that would make his project merely explicative of the meaning of certain sorts of *statements:* it should be clear that I take the point to concern what it *is to judge* appearances to be real objects.

34. I hope that this attempt to reconcile the fact (a) that the relevant "truth conditions" concern the satisfaction of anticipations regarding possible perceptions with the fact (b) that the *judgment* for which they are conditions is a judgment about something *other* than mere perceptions, namely, about material objects, may meet the objection raised against my approach by Ralf Meerbote, in a review of my earlier book (*Kant-Studien*, LXXVI [1985], 466). There, Meerbote also suggested the possibility of appealing to something like Carl Posy's approach in terms of "assertability" conditions as conditions of truth, as opposed to "referential" ones, in order to avoid the apparent contradiction. (See, for example, Posy's "Brittanic and Kantian Objects," in *New Essays on Kant*, ed. Bernard den Ouden [New York: Peter Lang, 1987], pp. 29–46.) Posy's own emphasis (p. 35) is on conditions that are sufficient to *justify* (an assertion), as opposed to eventual *satisfaction* (of certain anticipations). As he points out (p. 40), the demand for bivalence in truth conditions might be met, in that case, by appealing to a Peircian notion of *eventual* assertability. In any case, the same advantage that Posy seeks for his approach ought presumably to come to mine:

> The assertabilist can be quite receptive to our natural inclination to anchor what we say and think in a non-linguistic (indeed non-epistemic) world. And he can perfectly well speak of the anchoring relation as "referential." But, in that case he simply will not use that notion of reference to found his semantics, his conception of truth. (P. 37)

Apart from this, I don't know whether either Meerbote or Posy would regard the present account as a useful counterpart in the philosophy of mind of what would otherwise be purely semantical distinctions.

Chapter Two: Extending the Framework

1. Cf. Patricia Kitcher, "Kant on Self-Identity," *Philosophical Review*, 91 (1982), esp. pp. 65ff.

2. A similar objection is raised by Daniel Dennett against the attempt to account for psychological states by appeal to the tokening of "mental sentences": *Brainstorms* (Cambridge, Mass.: MIT/Bradford Books, 1979), p. 49.

3. For a cogent discussion, see also Robert B. Pippin, "Kant on the Spontaneity of Mind," *Canadian Journal of Philosophy*, 17 (1987), 449–76.

4. Immanuel Kant, *Foundations of the Metaphysics of Morals*, tr. Lewis White Beck (Indianapolis: Bobbs-Merrill, 1959), pp. 70–71 (4.452), translation slightly modified. Cf. *Reflexionen zur Logik*, 2476 (16.386):

Verstand und Vernunft sind frey: subiective Ursachen afficiren zwar, aber determinieren nicht den Verstand.

For a detailed and convincing argument for subsuming the two instances of freedom under the common heading of "autonomy," see Gerold Prauss, *Kant Über Freiheit als Autonomie* (Frankfurt: Vittorio Klostermann, 1983).

5. *Reflexionen zur Metaphysik*, 5611 (18.252).

6. Stephen Stich, *From Folk Psychology to Cognitive Science* (Cambridge, Mass.: MIT Press/Bradford Books, 1983), pp. 55–56.

7. John R. Searle, *Intentionality* (Cambridge: Cambridge University Press, 1983). Generally, Searle himself speaks of the Background as co-determining, along with intentional content—and possibly also along with a Network of other intentional states—a state's "conditions of satisfaction." But as should become clear, it seems equally legitimate to say, in Searle's view, that the Background helps to determine intentional content itself. In any case, Searle also speaks (p. 54) of the Network and Background as "affecting" a state's content. (Unless I note otherwise, the following points are all to be found in Chapter One of this work. The point about irreducibility is also confirmed in Chapter Ten.)

8. In Searle's view, a part of any such description will always be a "clause" to the effect that a certain sort of object is causally responsible for the production of that very experience (pp. 47ff).

9. It may seem obvious that there is non-intuitional intentional content. One may consider, for example, the content of a mere belief. As suggested in Chapter One, Kant's own "judgments" and "cognitions" are at least very different from what one often calls "beliefs," precisely by virtue of being essentially intuitional (though also, of course, conceptual) in form. As for those beliefs that are *non*-intuitional, my inclination is to hold that these could be regarded as *contentful* only in a sense of no concern to Kant. In light of my treatment of consciousness in Chapter Six, the same will go for any type of "mental" state, insofar as its possession of content is supposed to be independent of its status as occurrent consciousness. The latter might be regarded as essentially conceptual in form. In any case, it is essentially *intuitional*.

10. "[I]n general the Intentionality of a perceptual experience is realized in quite specific phenomenal properties of conscious mental events" (p. 45).

11. "Perhaps there might be more biologically primitive Intentional states [i.e., more primitive than the human—at least in any real life situation: p. 140] which do not require a Network, or perhaps not even a Background" (p. 140n). It is also important to remember that, for Searle, it is always intentional content that determines conditions of satisfaction; they are not, as it were, "directly" determined by material in the Network or Background. The latter may at most determine certain *aspects* of the conditions of satisfaction (cf. p. 66). Or, as Searle seems to prefer to say, intentional content determines a state's conditions of satisfaction, given its position "in" a Network and "against" a certain Background (p. 19). Perhaps the strongest formulation is this: "It would, therefore, be incorrect to think of the Background as forming a bridge between Intentional content and the determination of conditions of satisfaction, as if the Intentional content itself could not reach up to the conditions of satisfaction" (p. 158). (On at least one other occasion, Searle uses "Intentional content" so as precisely to *include* elements of the Network and Background: p. 232.)

12. Hubert L. Dreyfus, "Dasein's Revenge: Methodological Solipsism as an Unsuccessful Escape Strategy in Psychology" (A Comment on Fodor's *Methodological Solipsism*), *Behavioral and Brain Sciences*, 3 (1980), 79; see also p. 79n1.

13. Searle does argue, convincingly I think, against any *a priori* rejection of the claim that intentional content—despite its irreducible status—is both *caused* by, and also "realized in," neurophysiological structures. His argument appeals to the plausibility of saying such things as, for example, that the liquidity of water is both caused by the molecular behavior of molecules and realized in the very collection of molecules that is in question (p. 265). The general solution, in other words, "is that there can be causal relations between

phenomena at different levels in the very same underlying stuff" (p. 266). Since this solution is meant to concern causally determining conditions, not merely enabling ones, it is not meant to bear on the question of causal relations between Background material and the instantiation of intentional content by mental states, and of course it could not do so, since the latter is not realized in the former. So despite the enabling/determining distinction, the relation in question remains at least as problematic as Descartes' postulation of causal relations between material and mental properties.

14. For a thorough study of Husserl's own understanding of his relationship to Kant, see Iso Kern, *Husserl und Kant*, Phaenomenologica 16 (The Hague: Martinus Nijhoff, 1964).

15. Edmund Husserl, *Ideas Pertaining to a Pure Phenomenology and to a Phenomenological Philosophy: First Book*, tr. F. Kersten (The Hague: Martinus Nijhoff, 1983), §35, p. 72; cf. §§36-37. (Husserl, at this point, has already made clear that the "something" need not be taken as anything real. In the same section, he also distinguishes the "consciousness" in question from full-blown *attention* to some object.)

16. *Ibid.*, §84, p. 200.

17. *Ibid.*, §§35-37, §84: Husserl's term for the "actional" or "wakeful" is *aktuell*. The suggestion of "wakeful" is that of the W. R. Boyce Gibson translation (New York: Collier Books, 1962). Incidentally, the actional/non-actional distinction is particularly difficult, or perhaps ambiguous. In any case, it does not, or at least not always, mean directedness that is specifically *attentive* vs. inattentive directedness. The latter distinction involves, or at least can involve, a distinction between attention and inattention to features or aspects of objects in the foreground.

18. This suggestion will be especially relevant to my discussion of affinity in Chapter Four and of self-consciousness in Chapter Six. (On the relationship between awareness of regions of space and of space as a "whole," see my *Representational Mind* [Bloomington: Indiana University Press, 1983], Chapter Three.) As to possible comparison with Searle, it is also worth noting that, while Searle insists upon the influence of Background on intentional content, not only does he not try to *explain* this by reference to what is in the background of consciousness, he also does not appear to regard the Background as in fact *in* the background of consciousness in Husserl's sense. In any case, it can be in the background of consciousness for Searle only in the *sense* that it has an influence on intentional content.

19. Husserl, *Ideas: First Book*, §§88ff.

20. The main proponents of this approach are Dagfinn Føllesdal ("Husserl's Notion of Noema," *Journal of Philosophy*, 66 [1969], 680–87) and Hubert Dreyfus ("The Perceptual Noema: Gurwitsch's Crucial Contribution," in *Life-World and Consciousness: Essays for Aron Gurwitsch*, ed. Lester Embree [Evanston: Northwestern University Press, 1972], pp. 135–70]). Both of these essays have been reprinted in *Husserl, Intentionality, and Cognitive Science*, ed. Hubert Dreyfus (Cambridge, Mass.: MIT Press/Bradford Books, 1982).

21. Perhaps the most recent critique of this approach (with which I am familiar) may serve as a guide to some of the recent literature: Mary Jeanne Larrabee, "The Noema in Husserl's Phenomenology," *Husserl Studies*, 3 (1986), 209–30. Cf. Robert Sokolowski, "Intentional Analysis and the Noema" (esp. sec. 6), *Dialectica*, 38 (1984), 113–29; Lenore Langsdorf, "The Noema as Intentional Entity: A Critique of Føllesdal," *Review of Metaphysics*, 37 (1984), 757–84. An attempt to steer what appears to me to be something of a middle course may also be seen in J. N. Mohanty, *Husserl and Frege* (Bloomington: Indiana University Press, 1982); cf. my review of it in *Husserl Studies*, 1 (1984), 320–30. In an earlier study, I also criticized the Føllesdal/Dreyfus approach (although, in a still earlier study, I had defended it), in terms that still appear to me to be sound: "On Intensionalizing Husserl's Intentions," *Noûs*, XVI [1982], 209–26). However, my own positive suggestion was there at best misleading, and even certainly wrong in Husserl's own terms. I suggested that the noema, in relation to ordinary "objects," is a total intended (but not *ipso facto* attended-to) complex of "possible states of affairs" involving the latter, precisely as the latter is intended by consciousness. This is un-Husserlian in that, for Husserl, the appre-

hension of "states of affairs" involves a level of categorial form that is not essential to object-directedness as such. What I meant to suggest is rather that the noema is what consciousness is always free to take *as* a complex of states of affairs in regard to some object, given both appropriately focused attention *and* appropriately categorialized apprehension. (As an additional argument against the Dreyfus/Føllesdal approach, incidentally, I would mention that it does not sit well with the fact that, while Husserl assigns "meaning-*bestowing*" to the noetic act, he regards the concrete [noematic] *meaning* in question as a correlate, not simply of that act, but of that act's "apprehension" of the noema *through* a body of hyletic Data. It is difficult, given that, to regard the original "apprehension" of such meanings as at all analogous to the apprehension of Fregean *Sinne*. Why should the latter ever need to be apprehended *through* any particular body of "material"?)

22. Husserl, *Ideas: First Book*, §§130-131, pp. 312–13.

23. Kern points out that, on Husserl's reading of Kant, the latter in general (though not exclusively) considered *Anschauung* in the "objective" sense and for the most part neglected the structure of intuitional consciousness as such—or even tended to confuse the one with the other (*Husserl und Kant*, pp. 65–67). As I suggested in Chapter One, this impression of Kant may be more an artifact of the obscurity of Kant's terminology.

24. The apparent incompatibility of taking Husserl's suggestion in perfectly general terms, on the one hand, and as concerned with "*definite* intentions directed toward *individuals*," on the other, is offered by David Woodruff Smith and Ronald McIntyre as a serious deficiency in Husserl's own presentation of the notion in question: *Husserl and Intentionality* (Dordrecht: D. Reidel, 1982), p. 203.

25. Edmund Husserl, *Ideen zu einer reinen Phänomenologie und phänomenologischen Philosophie: Zweites Buch*, ed. Marly Biemel (The Hague: Martinus Nijhoff, 1952), esp. §10 and §§15–18.

26. This point ought to make it clear why it would be wrong to regard the *X*-structure in a Husserlian noema as the correlate of what has recently been called "rigid designation" or "reference"—the latter notion being understood in terms of reference to re-identifiable objects in the more familiar sense. For a similar point delivered against an attempt to extend the Føllesdal/Dreyfus to the special case of temporal awareness, see William McKenna's review (*Husserl Studies*, 2 [1985], 291–99) of Izchak Miller's *Husserl, Perception, and Temporal Awareness* (Cambridge, Mass.: MIT Press/Bradford Books, 1984). See also Smith and McIntyre, pp. 203ff, for an attempt to compare the two notions.

27. However, I shall be arguing in Chapters Four and Six that Kant's own doctrines of affinity and self-consciousness involve a broadening of his view precisely with regard to this point. Throughout, it should also be clear, I have abstracted from the question of "intuition" of *essences* in Husserl. As Kern points out (pp. 54ff), Husserl regarded Kant's neglect of this notion as a serious weakness, but at the same time regarded his own understanding of it as a "phenomenologically clarified" version of Kant's notion of pure intuition (p. 59).

28. "[W]e find those sensuous moments overlaid by a stratum which, as it were,"

"animates," which *bestows sense* (or essentially involves a bestowing of sense)—a stratum by which precisely the concrete intentive mental process arises from the *sensuous, which has in itself nothing pertaining to intentionality* (*Ideas: First Book*, §85, p. 203).

[W]ith respect to intentionality we immediately confront a wholly fundamental distinction, namely the distinction between the *components proper* of intentive mental processes and their *intentional correlates* and their components. . . . On the one side, therefore, we have to discriminate the parts and moments which we find by an *analysis of the really inherent* pertaining to mental processes . . . on the other side, the intentive mental process is consciousness of something . . . and we can therefore inquire into what is to be declared as a matter of essential necessity about the side of this "of something". . . . Corresponding in every case to the multiplicity of Data pertaining to the really inherent noetic content, there is a multiplicity of Data, demonstrable in actual pure intuition, in a correlative "*noematic content*" or, in short, in the "*noema*." . . . (Ibid., §88, pp. 213–14; cf. §97)

On the other hand, Kern points out that Eugen Fink, for example, objects to regarding Kantian sensations as an instance of Husserlian "matter." The objection is on the ground that, for Husserl, even the apprehension of "sense data" is eventually regarded as constituted *via* some kind of "intentionality." Kern's response (p. 274) is that the comparison is legitimate, since on any such deeper level of constitution, the very *notions* of constitution and of intentionality take on a new meaning. (We might also note that, at least on occasion, Husserl himself speaks of the material in question as having a *kind* of "intentionality"—but in scare-quotes: see note 30, below.)

29. Ibid., §85, p. 203.

30. Cf. ibid., §47, pp. 106–7:

Experienceableness never means a mere logical possibility, but rather a possibility *motivated* in the concatenation of [rationally motivated] experience. This concatenation itself is, through and through, one of [purely immanental] "motivation." . . . (The bracketed phrases are Husserl's marginal notes. See Kersten's footnotes to the passage and Karl Schuhmann's volume of supplementary materials: Husserliana, III.2 [The Hague: Martinus Nijhoff, 1976], p. 497)

In a footnote to this passage, Husserl then adds: "It should be noted that this fundamental phenomenological concept of motivation . . . is a *universalization* of that concept of motivation in accordance with which we can say, e.g., that the willing of the end motivates the willing of the means." See also *Ideen: Zweites Buch, Beilage* XII, p. 337. There Husserl speaks of "sensations" and "reproductions" as:

. . . behaftet mit Tendenzen, "Intentionen auf," die sich erfüllen im Kommen der "intendierten" Impressionen oder Reproduktionen. Diese Triebe [*n.b.*] oder Tendenzen sind zum Sinnlichen selbst gehörig. . . . [In these sensory tendencies, the] "intentionale Objekt," das worauf die reproduktive Tendenz gerichtet ist, fungiert "motivierend," wirkt als Reiz.

On the relevant concept of motivation, see also *Ideas: First Book*, §52, §§136ff (esp. p. 337), §140.

31. Edmund Husserl, *Analysen zur passiven Synthesis* (1918-26), ed. Margot Fleischer (The Hague: Martinus Nijhoff, 1966), p. 14.

32. Ibid., p. 13.

33. Ibid., *Beilage* XXV, p. 428. Regarding kinaesthetic "motivation," see also *Ideen: Zweites Buch*, §9, §10, pp. 21–22, and §18, pp. 57–58.

34. Shaun Gallagher ("Hyletic Experience and the Lived Body," *Husserl Studies*, 3 [1986], 131–66) argues that, because the material in question is already "object"-directed (it is "already ensouled or animated" [p. 148; cf. pp. 152–53]), Husserl himself ought not to have seen it as mere material for intentional forming. But there is no inconsistency, so long as we are prepared to distinguish *kinds* of directedness. In fact, Husserl took Kant's notion of imagination in the Deduction to have, at least implicitly, embodied the recognition of a pre-conceptual *judgment*. Cf. Kern:

Husserl war sich wohl bewusst, dass in Kants Begriff der Einbildungskraft, die sowohl sinnlich als auch verstandesmässig (spontan) ist, und deren Synthesis die phänomenale Welt anschaulich bildet, die schroffe Scheidung von Sinnlichkeit und Verstand überwunden ist. (P. 64)

Kern himself concludes that Husserl is too generous on the point. However, his argument presupposes that Kant's distinction between sensibility and understanding ultimately rests on that between the "sensible and intelligible worlds." Kern is similarly ungenerous in commenting on Husserl's concession that, despite the apparently contrary stance of the Aesthetic, Kant recognized the need for a special sort of "aesthetic synthesis"; Kern's reasoning is the same here too (p. 252).

35. Croce himself says that, while "Kant and Hegel say the same thing . . . the latter does so with greater awareness and clarity, that is, much better": *Logica come scienza del concetto puro*, 9th ed. (Bari: Editori Laterza, 1964), p. 349. Italian scholars do not, at least, unanimously succumb to the apparent slighting of Kant. Precisely with respect to the question of a theory of *consciousness*, Francesco Valentini insists that Croce's thought must indeed be regarded as "a form of Kantianism" (*La controriforma della dialettica* [Roma: Editori Riuniti, 1966], p. 17); Eugenio Garin insists on the appreciation of its significance as a "return to Kant" (*Cronache di filosofia italiana* [Bari: Editori Laterza, 1975], p. 265). With particular attention to the question of matter and form, but with less inclination toward phenomenological and more toward Hegelian formulations, Gennaro Sasso devotes considerable attention to the Kantian background in *Benedetto Croce: La ricerca della dialettica* (Napoli: Casa Editrice A. Morano, 1975), pp. 237–76. I would note that my acquaintance with Croce's thought, and the happy discovery of his "Kantianism," was made possible by a Professional Leave Award from the University of Tennessee for the academic year 1982–83, permitting independent study at the University of Rome and the National Library of Rome.

36. Croce makes it clear that this was Hegel's primary shortcoming: *Logica*, pp. 350–51, and "Ciò che è vivo e ciò che è morto della filosofia di Hegel," in *Saggio sullo Hegel seguito da altri scritti di storia della filosofia*, 5th ed. (Bari: Editori Laterza, 1967), p. 65.

37. "[T]he distinction between reality and non-reality is extraneous to the inner character of intuition": *Estetica come scienza dell'espressione e linguistica generale*, 11th ed. (Bari: Editori Laterza, 1965), p. 5. Regarding understanding, Croce concedes that "reality" is always presupposed by thought—but the reality in question is not, in this, "realistically" conceived:

> [E]very individual judgment presupposes the existence of that of which one speaks . . . even when this thing consists in an act of imagination, so long as this act is recognized as such and as such existentialized. And therefore judgments of that sort are subject to the concept of a reality that bifurcates into actual reality and possible reality, into existence and non-existence or mere representability. (*Logica*, p. 109)

Cf. *Estetica*, p. 32, distinguishing the "real imaginary" [*la fantastica reale*] from the "purely imaginary" [*dalla fantastica pura*].

38. Rejecting mere sensation: "Il mito della sensazione," in *Discorsi di Varia Filosofia*, II, 2nd ed. (Bari: Editori Laterza, 1959), p. 4. On material other than mere sensations, Croce includes feelings, impulses, emotions, states of passion, desire, suffering, problems and questions, habits and capacities, practical intentions, appetites, tendencies, volitions, even "actions"; in short, the whole "personality" of the subject: cf. *Estetica*, pp. 14, 105, 111–12; *Logica*, pp. 133–34, 141, 189; "L'intuizione pura e il carattere lirico dell'arte," in *Problemi di estetica*, 6th ed. (Bari: Editori Laterza, 1966), p. 23.

39. These are, beyond the intuitional and conceptual, the "practical," "economical," or "volitional" as such and, finally, the distinctively moral: cf. *Filosofia della practica*, 8th ed. (Bari: Editori Laterza, 1963), p. 226; "Ciò che è vivo . . . ," pp. 86–88; *Logica*, pp. 54, 65–66. For a thorough study of Croce on this point, see Sasso, especially Part II.

40. " . . . I have still not managed to find in that school anything that enriches or so much as stimulates my mind . . . seems superfluous and sterile and vain . . . and therefore to treat as if it did not exist": *Discorsi di Varia Filosofia*, II, p. 33. However, the specific object of Croce's scorn was Husserl's ambition that philosophy be "scientific."

41. Cf. *Logica*, pp. 133, 140–43, 236. So far as I can tell, Croce's denial of purely "analytic" judgments does not, strictly speaking, apply to (what he regards as) mere *pseudo-judgments*, that is, to judgments involving empirical (pseudo-)concepts; see note 42, below. As for Kant himself, we already noted in Chapter One that genuine "cognitions" always appear to involve the conceptualization of intuitions. But, of course, well-known aspects of his thought require that Kant leave room for "thoughts" that are not cognitions at all (Bxxvff). These presumably involve a "use" of the mere forms of judgment, apart from corresponding material. However we deal with this, the question in any case remains of allegedly nonintuitional "judgments" in which ordinary *empirical concepts* are employed. According to my own approach, this would most naturally be understood in terms of some notion of identity with respect to manifolds of anticipations and retentions, potentially ingredient in intuitions, but also in principle capable of ingredience in non-intuitional representational states. If we can make sense of that notion, then I presume we ought to be able to make some sense of the notion of a purely analytic judgment. However, it would be misleading to say, as Kant does, that such "judgments" express relations among "concepts" (A6/B10ff). Strictly, they would seem at most to express relations of potential inclusion/exclusion among various sets of anticipations and retentions, of the sort that in turn provide *material* for formation into genuine concepts. Naturally, one is free to speak of such sets of anticipations and retentions as themselves "concepts." But to do so would involve a sense of the term different from what Kant himself is centrally concerned with in the *Critique*. On the analytic/synthetic in Croce, more immediately below.

42. Ibid., pp. 15, 24.

43. Ibid., pp. 121, 221, 225–26.

44. The point must lie behind Croce's insistence, for example, that all intuition is a form of "expression": cf. *Estetica*, pp. 11ff, 153ff. It must also lie behind Croce's insistence that all (genuinely) historical study is the study of something "contemporary"—indeed, that all true understanding is a form of self-understanding: cf. *Teoria e storia della storiografia*, 11th ed. (Bari: Editori Laterza, 1976), pp. 4ff, 46, 123–24. But perhaps the most forceful expression of the point is to be found in the statement of Croce's closest follower:

> Indeed those affects or feelings that ignite and spread into passions, and, reawakening and stimulating the will, translate it into action, are *identified with* the corresponding objects; for a love is not other than the woman loved, and the pleasure of travel, as one can read somewhere in Croce, is not such as follows upon the travel as its result but is inseparable from the travel, and one could say indeed that it is the travel itself. And such-and-such object (such-and-such a woman), such-and-such love (or hate). (Alfredo Parente, *Croce per lumi sparsi* [Firenze: La Nuova Italia Editrice, 1975], p. 6.)

Similarly, " . . . on the epistemological level the contemporaneity of the past means . . . the very sameness [*medesimezza*] of past and present"—sameness, that is, precisely in the sense that "the image of a flower is nothing other than the flower itself" (Alfredo Parente, "Sul concetto di 'contemporaneità' della storia. L'aspetto pratico e il teoretico del problema," *Rivista di studi crociani*, XVIII [Oct.-Dec., 1981], 364).

Chapter Three: Synthesis

1. In anticipation of what follows, we may presume at least three factors to be sources of Kant's own unclarity: (1) the radical character of the view in question; (2) a felt tension with the Aesthetic, in that the latter identifies only sensation as material of intuition; (3) the possible fear that if (empirical) concepts are "made out of" something comparable to the material of intuitions, then concepts would become a kind of particular. As suggested already, *ad* (2), the proposed view is still compatible with holding that sensation alone (in a suitably narrow sense) is the material of intuition *qua* intuition. It is simply that conceptu-

alization of the latter requires the ingredience of specifically imaginative material. *Ad* (3): while the proposed extension of the matter/form distinction may raise the fear in question, it is resistible by focusing on the proposal's own harmlessly reductive character. The suggestion that concepts are "made" out of this or that material is to be analyzed merely in terms of claims about what conceptual *acts or processes* are made out of. It is unsurprising that Kant was not always clear in this regard.

2. Jonathan Bennett, *Kant's Analytic* (Cambridge: Cambridge University Press, 1966), p. 138.

3. See Raymund Schmidt's note to the passage in his edition in the *Philosophische Bibliothek* series (Hamburg: Felix Meiner, 1956; reprint of edition of 1930).

4. There is occasion for unclarity here. For example, at some points Paton says (a) that the concepts employed in ordinary judgments must actually *guide* the imaginative syntheses at work in those judgments; elsewhere, (b) he describes understanding's role merely in terms of its ability "to conceive the various principles upon which imagination synthetizes [*sic*] the given manifold." In the latter case, concepts are merely concepts *of* imaginative syntheses. See H. J. Paton, *Kant's Metaphysic of Experience* (London: George Allen and Unwin, 1936), I, p. 264, for (a); p. 487 (cf. pp. 273ff), for (b).

5. Most famously, at least with regard to the first edition, cf. Martin Heidegger, *Kant and the Problem of Metaphysics*, tr. James S. Churchill (Bloomington: Indiana University Press, 1962): "[E]verything in the essence of pure knowledge that has a synthetic structure is brought about by the imagination" (p. 66); "This means nothing less than reducing pure intuition and pure thought to the transcendental imagination" (p. 145). Cf. George Schrader, "Kant's Theory of Concepts," in *Kant: A Collection of Critical Essays*, ed. Robert Paul Wolff (Garden City: Doubleday Anchor Books, 1967), p. 148: "In fact, understanding itself may be viewed as a function of imagination operative at the conscious level and in accordance with explicitly formulated rules and laws." The issue, of course, turns on the crucial transformation to the conscious level. Heidegger and Schrader aside, this must be accomplished, so far as I can see, precisely *via* an operation of "pure understanding." In any case, any so-called application of empirical *concepts* would merely be what *emerges* out of such pure operations. (Schrader is not perfectly clear, immediately adding that imagination also needs to "follow the laws of understanding" [p. 148].)

6. *Logik Dohna-Wundlacken* (24.710).

7. For brevity, I speak of empirical concepts throughout, whenever I mean non-*categorial* concepts. In other words, the general approach is also intended to apply to mathematical concepts.

8. Though short on details, Gilles Deleuze has perhaps been most insistent on the two factors to which I try to do justice in this chapter, namely, the original and autonomous contribution of the faculties and also, under the determination of one of them, elevation of the "lower" to a special higher status: Gilles Deleuze, *Kant's Critical Philosophy: The Doctrine of the Faculties*, tr. Hugh Tomlinson and Barbara Habberjam (Minneapolis: University of Minnesota Press, 1983), esp. pp. 22–23, 34.

9. Heidegger, pp. 167, 169, respectively.

10. Cf. *Logik*, I, §2 (9.91): "Die Materie der Begriffe ist der *Gegenstand*, die Form derselben die *Allgemeinheit.*"

11. It is sometimes suggested that empirical concepts are themselves the intellectual "forms" that come to be embedded in the fabric of intuitions. Cf. Schrader, p. 150. However, Schrader leans toward a kind of "imposition" model as well (pp. 138, 149). By contrast, he regards the *a priori* forms of understanding merely as forms for the ordering of empirical concepts (p. 138), or for their formation (p. 140); they do not themselves seem to undergo a process of embedding in intuition.

12. *Wiener Logik* (24.907). Cf. *Anthropologie*, §3 (7.131): " . . . von etwas, d.i. einer Bestimmung des Gegenstandes meiner Vorstellung, abstrahiren, wodurch diese die Allgemeinheit eines Begriffs erhält und so in den Verstand aufgenommen wird." *Reflexionen zur Anthropologie*, 207 (15.79–80): "Verstand macht aus Erscheinungen Anschauungen der Gegenstände und aus diesen Begriffe." Also, *Logik Pölitz* (24.566), *Logik Busolt* (24.654),

Reflexionen zur Logik, 2839, 2942, 2947, 3057, *Logik*, §5 (9.93-4). In related but somewhat different terms: "Anschauungen . . . zuvor zu Begriffen erhoben werden, um zum Erkenntnisse des Objects zu dienen" (*Erste Einleitung in die Kritik der Urteilskraft*, XI [20.247]); "[T]he categories are not in themselves *cognitions*, but are merely *forms of thought* for the making of cognitions out of given intuitions" (B288); "[T]he categories, which are thought, are nothing but mere forms of judgments insofar as these forms are applied to intuitions . . . by such application our intuitions first of all obtain objects and become cognitions" (*Metaphysical First Principles of Natural Science*, tr. James Ellington [Indianapolis: Bobbs-Merrill, 1970], Preface, p. 12 [4.474]).

13. The second edition devotes minimal attention to what Kant had earlier described (Axvi-xvii) as the "subjective" side of the Deduction, the side that "seeks to investigate the pure understanding itself, its possibility and the cognitive faculties upon which it rests," but is not essential to the *Critique*'s aim of establishing that experience is necessarily subject to understanding in the first place. My primary concern is precisely with the "subjective" question. As Kant himself makes a point to say, it is in any case not a question of mere causal origins for the understanding and its operations (Axvii). He also says, in both editions, that Transcendental Logic would "treat of the origin of our cognitions of objects [*auf den Ursprung unserer Erkenntnisse von Gegenständen gehen*], so far as it cannot be attributed to the objects" (A55-6/B80). (One might note the presence of both notions of the *Ursprung* of concepts—the causal and, as we might put it, the "constitutive" notions—in the last of the passages quoted at the end of the present paragraph.) As to questions concerning the "mere" *how* of concept application, Kant also says that this "can be solved almost by a single conclusion from the precisely determined definition of a judgment in general (an act by which given representations *first become cognitions* of an object)" (*Metaphysical First Principles*, p. 13 [4.475]; my emphasis).

14. *Reflexionen zur Metaphysik*, 5932 (18.391).

15. *Reflexionen zur Logik*, 2839 (16.540).

16. Paton, pp. 201-3. Cf. Henry E. Allison, "Analytic and Synthetic Judgments," in *The Philosophy of Immanuel Kant*, ed. Richard Kennington (Washington: The Catholic University of America Press, 1985), p. 18:

> By the content of an empirical concept, Kant means the sensible *features* that are thought in it as marks. . . . The main point is that simply having a set of sensible *impressions* that are associated with one another is not the same as having a concept. The latter requires the thought of the applicability of this set of sensible *impressions* to a plurality of possible objects. With this thought these impressions become transformed into "marks," i.e., partial conceptions. (Emphasis added)

Cf. Manfred Baum, *Deduktion und Beweis in Kants Transzendentalphilosophie* (Königstein/Ts.: Athenäum Verlag, 1986), pp. 100–101, 106, 119.

17. Cf. *Logik*, Introduction, VIII (9.58):

> Ein Merkmal ist dasjenige an einem Dinge, was einen Theil der Erkenntniss desselben ausmacht. . . . Alle unsre Begriffe sind demnach Merkmale und alles Denken ist nichts anders als ein Vorstellen durch Merkmale. Ein jedes Merkmal lässt sich von zwei Zeiten betrachten: Erstlich, als Vorstellung an sich selbst; Zweitens, als gehörig wie ein Theilbegriff zu der ganzen Vorstellung eines Dinges und dadurch als Erkenntnissgrund dieses Dinges selbst.

Reflexionen zur Logik, 3057 (16.634):

> Eine Vorstellung, die durch das Bewusstsein als Merkmals allgemein wird, heisst (klarer) Begriff.

18. *Logik*, §6, Anm. 2 (9.95):

Abstracte Begriffe sollte man daher eigentlich abstrahierende (conceptus abstrahentes) nennen, d.h. solche, in denen mehrere Abstractionen vorkommen. So ist z.b. der Begriff Körper eigentlich kein abstracter Begriff, denn vom Körper selbst kann ich ja nicht abstrahiren, ich würde sonst nicht den Begriff von ihm haben.

This might be taken to say, in effect, that (except insofar as they are mere dispositions to form them) concepts are indeed nothing other than the "acts" of conception themselves. But without *Merkmale* as literal components of such acts, any specificity in them must then be provided precisely by whatever material is independently incorporable within intuitions to which they are "applied." In themselves, they would be mere forms of conception. Cf. *Anthropologie*, §3 (7.131): by abstracting from certain features, an intuition "receives" the *Allgemeinheit* of a concept, *und so in den Verstand aufgenommen wird*.

19. See *Representational Mind* (Bloomington: Indiana University Press, 1983), Chapter One.

20. On at least *pure* concepts as *Handlungen* of the understanding, cf. A57/B81. Also *Reflexionen zur Logik*, 2856 (16.548) and *Logik*, §5 (9.93), on actions of the understanding that *einen Begriff ausmachen*.

21. Cf. *Reflexionen zur Metaphysik*, 5927 (18.388-9):

Category is the representation of the relation of the manifold of intuition to a universal consciousness (to the universality of consciousness, which is properly objective). The relation of representations to the universality of consciousness, consequently the transformation [*Verwandlung*] of the empirical and particular unity of consciousness, which is only subjective, into a consciousness that is universal and objective, belongs to Logic. . . . Two components of cognition take place *a priori*. 1. Intuitions, 2. Unity of consciousness of the manifold of intuitions (even of empirical intuitions). This unity of consciousness constitutes the form of experience as objective empirical cognition.

Cf. *Reflexionen zur Anthropologie*, 212 (15.81): "Sensibility is the affectibility of our representational power. Understanding is the spontaneity of our representational power. . . . Both [consciousness] are mere form." Also B305-6: Categories "are nothing but forms of thought, which contain the merely logical faculty of uniting *a priori* in one consciousness the manifold given in intuition." Cf. B148-9.

22. Regarding the flexibility of the term *sensation*, though without any commitment to the present account, cf. Paton, p. 487: "the synthesis of imagination is always sensuous, even when it is a pure synthesis as in the construction of a mathematical figure." Paton simply elaborates by observing that by itself imagination "could give us only pictures or images." I might also remind the reader of Husserl's extension of the term *Empfindung*, discussed in Chapter Two.

23. Similar points are made, for example, by Robert B. Pippin: *Kant's Theory of Form* (New Haven: Yale University Press, 1982), esp. Chapters 2–5, 8. Pippin concludes that Kant sees the need for a gap-bridging "schematism," to mediate between the demands for imposition of concepts on indeterminate manifolds and some reasonable sense in which the "given" provides a degree of determinate guidance; see esp. pp. 112–23, 143–50, 222–28. But this way out is closed to Kant, short of breaking down his own rigid distinction between sensibility and understanding (pp. 227–28). Cf. Malte Hossenfelder, *Kants Konstitutionstheorie und die Transzendentale Deduktion* (Berlin: Walter de Gruyter, 1978), pp. 107–8: If a concept's job is to serve as a "rule" for the reproduction and anticipation of representations, then something else must be assigned the task of accounting for our ability to recognize the latter as in fact falling under any given concept. It is tempting to suppose it to be Kant's futile endeavor precisely to account for the second of these tasks in terms of the first. I am suggesting that it is rather a question of focus on two distinct aspects of concepts: on their conceptual form as such and on the imaginative material that is animated by but no less ingredient in them.

24. Cf. Paton, pp. 264ff. Also Robert Paul Wolff, *Kant's Theory of Mental Activity* (Cam-

bridge, Mass.: Harvard University Press, 1963), pp. 133–34. Bennett suggests something analogous, at least with respect to one's grasp of the "synthesis" required for self-knowledge (pp. 111ff). He also makes it clear that the synthesis in question is of an intellectual sort. It is simply whatever is involved in one's grasp of the "criteria" for application of the relevant concepts (pp. 108ff).

25. Paton, pp. 487–88.

26. Ibid., pp. 264ff.

27. Wolff identifies concepts with rules (pp. 130–34). But he continues to speak of the rules as rules for imaginative synthesis. It is unclear why he regards the synthesis in the case as imaginative rather than intellectual. In addition, Wolff speaks of concepts themselves as "forms of mental activity" (p. 70). It is unclear what sort of activity is supposed to be in question. Bennett (p. 54) also identifies concepts with rules, but apparently not in Wolff's sense. At least in Kant's more considered moments, a concept is merely an ability or skill (i.e., to *have* a concept is simply to have certain instances of the latter). What it is an ability to *do* appears to be something primarily linguistic.

28. P. F. Strawson, "Imagination and Perception," in *Experience and Theory*, ed. Lawrence Foster and J. W. Swanson (Amherst: University of Massachusetts Press, 1970), p. 41.

29. Henry Allison, *Kant's Transcendental Idealism* (New Haven: Yale University Press, 1983), pp. 161–64. Allison has maintained in discussion that his aim is definitely to preserve a notion of imaginative synthesis on a pre-intellectual level. The reference to "inner sense," apparently meant to accomplish this, seems to me too vague for the purpose. As stated, it remains compatible with regarding the need to anticipate and retain in regard to possible future and past moments as nothing more than a necessary *limitation* on human conceptualization, as opposed to an actual *function* that is pre-conceptual in nature.

30. With emphasis on the history of Kant's usage, Oswaldo Market argues that Kant in general regards the manifold in terms of his own notion of sensation as the material of intuitions: "Das Mannigfaltige und die Einbildungskraft," in *Akten des 5. Internationalen Kant-Kongresses*, ed. Gerhard Funke et al. (Bonn: Bouvier Verlag Herbert Grundmann, 1981), I.1, pp. 255–67. However, Market formulates the primary problem in terms of the "noematic" question as to how that material is to be formed into a distinctly apprehensible image (cf. pp. 264-67), as opposed to a "noetic" question concerning the original formation of cognitive states through which an image is to be apprehensible in the first place. In this respect, Market's approach resembles that of Hoke Robinson, who also emphasizes that the Kantian manifold is in the first instance a manifold in any given intuition: "Anschauung und Mannigfaltiges in der Transzendentalen Deduktion," *Kant-Studien*, 72 (1981), 140–48.

31. Apart from the duality of intentionally correlative manifolds, Kant may, of course, also seem to embrace another duality, namely, between a manifold of empirical and a manifold of *a priori* or pure intuition (A76-7/B102-3, A99-102). But it is not impossible that these are really the same distinction. We need to remember that it is precisely the *a priori* forms of intuition that, in a sense, *provide* the relevant manifold of anticipations and retentions. They provide it, at least, in the sense of needing to *incorporate* that material in empirical intuitions in the first place, in order for it to be relevant to conceptualization. To some extent, this may suggest Kemp Smith's distinction between an empirical manifold, synthesized by the understanding, and a pre-conscious manifold out of which (productive) imagination synthetically generates material for the understanding in the first place. This is on what Kemp Smith calls the "phenomenalist" reading of Kant. On the "subjectivist" reading, by contrast, imagination simply is understanding at work, either transcendentally or empirically, upon a manifold of material provided by states of the individual subject. Cf. Norman Kemp Smith, *A Commentary to Kant's 'Critique of Pure Reason'* (New York: Humanities Press, 1962; reprint of 2nd edition of 1923), pp. 224–27, 264ff. However, the material that Kemp Smith seems to have in mind is more like a manifold of mere sensations than a set of imaginative anticipations and retentions.

32. Cf. *Anthropologie*, §1 (7.127-8), Letter to Herz, 26 May, 1789 (11.520). Also

Reflexionen zur Anthropologie, 212 (15.81):

> Die Sinnlichkeit ist die affectibilitaet der Vorstellungskraft. Verstand ist die sponta-
> neitaet der Vorstellungskraft. . . . Das Bewusstseyn geht auf beyde. Das Bewusst-
> seyn des Mannigfaltigen in den ersten Vorstellungen oder Anschauungen ist aesthe-
> tische Deutlichkeit, in Begriffen logische Deutlichkeit.

See also Paton, pp. 332–34, for a criticism of the claim that Kant regarded the conceptualization of experience as necessary for "consciousness" *simpliciter*. One might note that, in
the *Critique* itself, even mere sensation is regarded as a species of "representation with
consciousness" (A320/B376). I shall have more to say in Chapter Six about the problem
of consciousness.

33. Note the departure from Kemp Smith's translation: "in the manifold of *these* representations." My own reading emphasizes a distinction that Kemp Smith consistently blurs,
namely, between appearances, and whatever manifold they contain, and our representations *of* appearances, and their own internal manifolds (of anticipations, retentions, or what
have you).

34. *Erste Einleitung in die Kritik der Urteilskraft*, V (20.211). I have added the emphasis
to suggest the affinity between animal "inclinations" and animal "anticipations."

35. In general, "Imagination is the faculty of representing in intuition an object that is
not itself present" (B151). Cf. B278-9, on dreams and illusions as imaginative intuitions.
Also A713/B741, *Anthropologie*, §28 (7.167), and *Critique of Judgment*, Introduction, VII
(5.190), on imagination as faculty of intuitions *a priori*. In fact, Kant seems to regard imagination in general as a kind of *pure* intuition:

> Empfindungen, z.E. Reitz, Rührungen sind die Materie der Sinnlichkeit, die An-
> schauung ist ihre Form. Einbildungskraft gilt also nur von der Form der Sinnlich-
> keit, aber nicht von der Materie. (*Wiener Logik* [24.807])

It should be clear from Chapter One why even empirical imagination may be said to involve
mere intuitional form. It is empirical on account of the concepts that are in it; sensations
(at least in the normal sense) are absent.

36. Just the opposite reaction seems to be Kemp Smith's. After commenting on the problem of retention in "serial consciousness" at A102, he notes that "Kant renders his argument needlessly complex and dimishes its force" precisely by considering in the same context the case of anticipable orderliness in nature (p. 247). One should in any case note that
orientation toward the immediately forthcoming or receding, insofar as it is part of the ingredient "material" of any given act of consciousness, is just the case of what Husserl has
called *protention* and *retention*. Though it may be a bit misleading to Husserlians, I retain
the latter of these terms to designate the other case as well, because the only natural alternative would be Kant's own choice, *Reproduktion*, and that is still more misleading.

37. Heidegger, p. 94.

38. Cf. G. J. Warnock, "Concepts and Schematism," *Analysis*, 9 (1949), 77–82. See also
Bennett, p. 46, though Bennett takes Kant to do better, in more considered moments,
by at least inclining to identify concepts with rules of some sort. For a defense of Kant
against the charge, though in very different terms from my own, see Lauchlan Chipman,
"Kant's Categories and Their Schematism," *Kant-Studien*, 63 (1972), 36–50; Ralph C. S.
Walker, *Kant* (Routledge and Kegan Paul, 1978), p. 90; Graham Bird, *Kant's Theory of Knowledge* (Routledge and Kegan Paul, 1962), p. 63. Hubert Schwyzer ("How Are Concepts
of Objects Possible?" *Kant-Studien*, 74 [1983], 22–44) recognizes the application problem
as a genuine one, but solvable only once Kant's purely logical conception of the forms of
judgment is replaced by something more like Wittgenstein's conception of "forms of life"
(pp. 40ff). Daniel O. Dahlstrohm ("'Knowing How' and Kant's Theory of Schematism," in
Kennington, pp. 71–85) concedes that possession of a concept and the ability to apply a
concept may be distinguishable for empirical concepts, but that their indistinguishability

for *a priori* concepts poses a problem that Kant could solve, if at all, only by appeal to a special philosophical hermeneutic. In my own view, the distinction ought to be equally problematic for empirical concepts, given Kant's understanding of their nature. Apparent counter-examples, drawn from intuitions concerning concept identity under various circumstances of their "possession," may simply rest on a different notion of a concept. Kant himself generally thinks of concepts, not as possessions, but as (aspects of) cognitive activities. The solution to the difficulty, for both pure and empirical concepts, ought to rest squarely on a distinction between aspects of those activities themselves.

39. Cf. Paton, pp. 35–37 (though Paton himself suggests, not that concepts are rules, but rather concepts of rules). Kemp Smith (pp. 334ff) sees the "rule" approach as embodying a vaccilation between the third-thing approach and a straightforward identification of concepts with their schemata. The latter in any case at least leans toward a more adequate form/matter conception of concepts, as opposed to a "predicative" or "class-theory" approach (p. 338). Gram argues that, beneath the two approaches, a third is hidden (apparently also, at least partly, from Kant himself), identifying schemata with intuitions, but he considers only the problem of pure concepts in this context: Moltke S. Gram, *Kant, Ontology, And the A Priori* (Evanston: Northwestern University Press, 1968), pp. 91ff. Bennett (p. 144) observes that, ironically, Kant himself presents a perfectly convincing refutation of the third-thing approach at A133/B172, in arguing that there can be no general solution to the problem of concept-application, i.e., of "judgment." Swing argues that Kant simply shifted back and forth between the two approaches: Thomas Kaehao Swing, *Kant's Transcendental Logic* (New Haven: Yale University Press, 1969), p. 57. Cf. Pippin, pp. 145–48.

40. Pippin, pp. 146–47. Pippin sees the only hope to lie in a breakdown of the very distinction between sensibility and understanding (pp. 227–28). For a similar objection, cf. Hossenfelder, pp. 107–8: if a concept's (or a schema's) job is simply to serve as a "rule" for the reproduction and anticipation of particular representations, then something else (presumably already conceptual) must account for our ability to recognize the latter as subsumable under that rule, in any relevant sense, in the first place.

41. Pippin, pp. 112–23, 143–50, 222–28.

42. Dahlstrom suggests that the remark is meant to apply only to empirical concepts (p. 75). Cf. "Transzendentale Schemata, Kategorien und Erkenntnisarten," *Kant-Studien*, 75 (1984), 40.

43. Commentators also find some difficulty in the way Kant distinguishes schemata from images. He attributes the latter to the "empirical faculty of productive imagination":

> This much only we can assert: the *image* is a product of the empirical faculty of productive imagination; the *schema* of sensible concepts, such as of figures in space, is a product . . . of pure *a priori* imagination. (A141-2/B181)

Kemp Smith, following Vaihinger, takes this to be a slip: Kant means to attribute images to reproductive imagination. But the first-edition Deduction also appears to attribute the apprehension of "images" to productive imagination (A120-1). Though Kant does not explicitly call it productive at that point, he says that "active" imagination is responsible for the apprehension of images. It is said to rest upon reproductive imagination as upon a subjective "ground." I discuss these issues in the next chapter.

44. By contrast, Patricia Kitcher ("Kant on Self-Identity," *Philosophical Review*, 91 [1982], 41–72), takes Kant to be talking here, not about relations by virtue of which intuitions are "generable," and to which some mode of conceptualization would then be applicable, but about (causal) relations by virtue of which a mode of conceptualization is itself "generable" (pp. 65ff).

45. Ibid., p. 106; emphasis added.

46. Gram, pp. 100ff.

47. Allison, *Kant's Transcendental Idealism*, pp. 181ff.

48. Ibid., p. 184.

49. It is important to bear in mind that, in doing this, we need to be talking about intui-

tions as multiply instantiable *types* of representational states, rather than as particulars: as when we say that the "same intuition" is determined in this or that manner on two different occasions.

50. Allison himself is skeptical about the attempt to distinguish schematized from unschematized categories, as two distinct sets of concepts (*Kant's Transcendental Idealism*, p. 188, and note 36 to that page).

51. Ibid., p. 188. Sometimes by a schema Kant no doubt means some particular element or aspect of pure intuition, regarded noematically. That is, he means some aspect of spatio-temporal form itself. Although one could never *refer* to such elements in pre-categorial terms, they must, of course, be distinct from the corresponding category: a necessary aspect of spatiotemporal reality is obviously not the same thing as a necessary aspect of our *representation* of spatiotemporal reality. But in other cases, transcendental schemata are regarded by Kant as representations themselves. It is, of course, only in the latter sense that I identify them with the schematized categories. As for the "unschematized" catego-ries, these could only be the pure forms of judgment, regarded as the functions required (a) in application to pure intuition, for the constitution of categories/schemata, as modes of representation, and (b) in application to manifolds of anticipation and retention, for the production of all other concepts. Naturally, to the extent that the relevant anticipations and retentions are themselves spatiotemporal in "form," the categories, hence the tran-scendental schemata, may be said to be "included" in all other concepts, hence in all other schemata.

52. Cf. Heidegger, p. 114: "The use of pure concepts *as* [emphasis added] transcenden-tal determinations of time *a priori*, i.e., the achievement of pure knowledge, is what takes place in schematism."

Chapter Four: Production, Reproduction, and Affinity

1. Even so charitable a commentator as Paton, and despite his own rejection of the "patchwork thesis" (cf. "Is the Transcendental Deduction a Patchwork?" *Proceedings of the Aristotelian Society* [1929–30], reprinted in *Disputed Questions*, ed. M. S. Gram, [Atascadero, Calif.: Ridgeview, 1984], pp. 64–93), comments: "It is this striking fact [of Kant's inconsistency regarding productive and reproductive imagination] which (along with some others of less importance) inclines me to the belief that the provisional exposition may represent an earlier level of reflexion . . . " (*Kant's Metaphysic of Experience* [London: George Allen and Unwin, 1936), I, p. 364).

2. Cf. Robert Paul Wolff, *Kant's Theory of Mental Activity* (Cambridge, Mass.: Harvard University Press, 1963), p. 141: The cause of Kant's indecision as to whether there is a single capacity for reproduction, exhibiting both a transcendental and an empirical dimen-sion, or whether rather only productive imagination is transcendental, "is Kant's desire to do justice to the scientific world of real empirical objects, while yet preserving his belief that those objects are products of the activity of the mind." The most extreme attribution of the doctrine of such transcendental manufacture is Kemp Smith's; see Chapter Three, note 31. A somewhat more sympathetic approach is Henry Allison's, "Transcendental Affinity—Kant's Answer to Hume," in *Kant's Theory of Knowledge*, ed. L. W. Beck (Dordrecht: D. Reidel, 1974), pp. 119–27. Allison distinguishes two lines of argument in Kant, both attempting to move from our capacity for merely empirical association to the awareness of an objective order internal to the world of appearances. The cruder of these arguments rests on a viewpoint "close in spirit to Berkeley" and according to which appear-ances are "nothing apart from consciousness." However, even from that viewpoint, it is fallacious. By contrast, the more sophisticated argument translates claims about appear-ances into claims about our possible experiences (of public objects), and then inquires con-cerning necessary conditions of these.

3. Cf. Paton, *Kant's Metaphysic of Experience*, I, p. 481: the weaker conclusion is "obvi-ous enough" from the start. Cf. also Paul Guyer, "Kant's Tactics in the Transcendental Deduction," *Philosophical Topics*, 12 (1981), 173: The argument here is " . . . clearly

fallacious. For, even if we concede that to be able to reproduce representations requires being aware of a regularity among these representations, Kant's argument still requires . . . [not just necessity of awareness of regularity, but awareness of a necessary regularity]."

4. By contrast with this reading, Kemp Smith takes Kant's point in the argument precisely to be that "all apprehension is an act of judgment"(*A Commentary to Kant's 'Critique of Pure Reason'* [New York: Humanities Press, 1962; reprint of 2nd edition of 1923], p. 257.)

5. Wolff suggests that Kant has shifted from progressive to regressive argument, that is, to "assuming what he hopes to prove" (p. 153). Cf. Kemp Smith (p. 255) on the corresponding passage at A121-2.

6. One might take Kant to be arguing that an anticipable order among objects is a necessary condition of association simply because the latter is a form of consciousness, consciousness presupposes self-consciousness, and the latter presupposes that order. Thus Kemp Smith, commenting on the passage at A121-2: Kant may seem to be arguing that worldy regularity is necessary for full-blown "experience," and then begging the question as to whether associations need to be full-blown experiences in the first place; but in fact he needed no such assumption regarding association, since it would have worked equally well to have begun with an arbitarily subjective notion of the latter (so long as we presume it to involve consciousness of any sort: pp. 255–56). Cf. Wolff, p. 156: "Kant claims to prove that the validity of the categories is a necessary condition of consciousness itself." Of course, if this were Kant's point, then there would have been no reason in the first place to consider *association*. Any form of consciousness would be equally relevant to the argument.

7. This formulation of the second line of reasoning has the advantage of showing how it essentially refers to, while remaining distinct from, the first. The dual aspect may thus help explain Kant's apparent self-contradiction at A122-4.

8. Cf. *Erste Einleitung in die Kritik der Urteilskraft,* VII (20.220). Here Kant attributes the capacity for *Auffassung,* or for *apprehensio,* of the manifold of (the) appearance to the faculty of imagination. This distinguishes such apprehension from the understanding's *Zusammenfassung* of the manifold in the concept of an object. It also seems clear from the context that the manifold is indeed a manifold that is contained within the very intuition to which the concept in question is thereby applied.

9. Paton, *Kant's Metaphysic of Experience,* I, pp. 445ff.

10. Ibid., p. 450.

11. The passage is worth some discussion. In it, Kant distinguishes between a "principle of affinity, which has its seat in the understanding and expresses necessary connection," and a mere "rule of association." The latter is always empirical and to be found only in reproductive imagination. This may seem to run counter to my own apparent interposition of a third term between the two, that is, of an objective yet productively imaginative affinity between the levels of mere reproduction and understanding. But we need to remember, first of all, that in the view that I am proposing there is an important sense in which the particular, and conceptually representable, lawfulness of nature is one and the same as the affinity that I am ascribing to imagination. It simply is the latter, regarded no longer as a necessary condition of conceptual representation, but insofar as it has itself *become* conceptual representation. Second, while what Kant is here calling a "principle of affinity" is indeed something transcendental, it is nonetheless not what Paton (see above) regards as "transcendental affinity." It is not the mere transcendental *requirement* of some order of nature or other. It rather already involves a *representation,* at least on some level, of some particular order or other. It involves whatever kind of representation of such an "order of nature" needs to be ingredient in concepts of objects, in order to constitute their very possibility as concepts in the first place. As Kant puts it, it involves the *Herausgehen aus dem Begriffe eines Dinges auf mögliche Erfahrung, welches a priori geschieht und die objektive Realität desselben ausmacht.* Insofar as the *Herausgehen* in question is a presupposition of the conceptual representation of a nature that is so much as *possible* in the first place, it of course cannot itself rest on already established empirical concepts. But insofar as it nonetheless involves representation of a particular order of things, neither can it be

a product of the mere operation of understanding in general—that is, a product of what the categories alone require. (On the connection between the representation of "possibile" objects and the "objective reality" of concepts, see A220/B268ff.) Finally, that Kant is indeed concerned with a kind of representation, not merely with a transcendental requirement, is evident from his specific criticism of Hume. Hume is said to have confused a transcendental *Herausgehen* with a merely empirical and associational "synthesis of objects." But Hume could hardly have been guilty of confusing anything so abstract as the mere *requirement* of particular "syntheses of objects," or of particular instances of *Herausgehen*, with particular syntheses themselves.

12. It is at least evident that, however related, the usage is not quite the same. At A572/B600 Kant's point is simply that, if all possible predicates were contained in a single *Inbegriff*— as a kind of supreme being—then we could conclude that all possible things have a real "affinity" among themselves. Though the suggestion involved in the supposition is, of course, an extraordinary one, the notion of affinity in the consequent is simply our everyday notion, not any of the philosophical ones so far in question. The consequent itself is, of course, in a way extraordinary. But this is only because of the extraordinary character of the *reason* offered on behalf of a possible "affinity" among things in the first place. There seems to be nothing special in the latter notion as such. The passage at A657/B685 is rather different. This is not only because it attaches a special meaning to the term in question (namely, to designate a certain sort of continuity among possible species), but more importantly because it regards affinity as the counterpart of a perfectly legitimate, and even in some sense necessary, demand of transcendental reason. In this respect, it relates more closely to Kant's concerns in the *Critique of Judgment*.

13. Günter Wohlfart, "Zum Problem der transcendentalen Affinität in der Philosophie Kants," in *Akten des 5. Internationalen Kant-Kongresses* (Bonn: Bouvier Verlag Herbert Grundmann, 1981), I.1, p. 314. Though he regards both of the passages discussed in the preceding note as relevant, Wohlfart regards only the second as decisive with respect to his identification of the problems of affinity in the first and in the third *Critique* (p. 316).

14. Wohlfart observes (and cites other authorities: p. 318, n. 30) that the treatment of affinity in Section IV of the "First Introduction" "is as it were the link between the treatment of affinity and the Deduction of the Ideas in the Dialectic of Pure Reason and the Deduction of Purposiveness" in Section V of the ("second") Introduction to the third *Critique*. In a sense, I do not disagree. But Kant points out in the following section that he has so far only been considering a *conceived* (*gedachte*) harmony or purposiveness in nature. Then he turns, in Section VI, to what seems to me more centrally at issue in this context, namely, to the case of our actual ability to perceive any kind of purposiveness in nature. (Cf. the transition from Section VI to Section VII in the "First Introduction.") Wohlfart himself considers aesthetic judgment as central to any discussion of affinity in Kant (pp. 321–22). I presume that our difference on this must stem from a difference regarding the nature of aesthetic "judgments" in the first place.

15. *Critique of Judgment*, §5 (5.209); cf. Introduction, Section VII, *passim*. (The provision of references to Kant's relatively brief sections should be sufficient to facilitate consultation of the available translations.)

16. "First Introduction," Sections VII–VIII (20.221, 224); *CJ*, Introduction, Section VII (5.190) and §39 (5.292).

17. Cf. *CJ*, Introduction, Sections VII–VIII (5.189, 192).

18. "First Introduction," Section VIII (20.224); *CJ*, Introduction, Section VII (5.190), §9 (5.217).

19. Cf. *CJ*, Introduction, Section VII (5.189): "Hence the object is called purposive only in virtue of the fact that its representation is immediately connected with the feeling of pleasure; and *this representation itself is* [emphasis added] a representation of the purposiveness."

20. "A New Look at Kant's Aesthetic Judgments," in *Essays in Kant's Aesthetics*, ed. Ted Cohen and Paul Guyer (Chicago: University of Chicago Press, 1982), pp. 87–114.

21. Cf. the passage quoted, in note 19, from *CJ*, Introduction, Section VII (5.189). In that same section, Kant also speaks of judging *durch* the feeling of pleasure (5.190), and of the latter *gleich als ob* it was a predicate combined with the object itself (5.191). And he plainly speaks of the pleasure itself as the very aesthetic judgment (*dieses Urteil:* 5.191). Cf. "First Introduction," Section VIII, 20.228 (the representation of subjective purposiveness in an object is, in aesthetic apprehension, *so gar einerley* with the feeling of pleasure it contains) and 20.230 (the concept of formal but subjective purposiveness is *mit dem Gefühle der Lust im Grunde einerley*); cf. also Section XII (20.249). At 20.224, in Section VIII, Kant speaks of the pleasurable sensation as the *Bestimmungsgrund* in the judgment. In *CJ*, §1, he speaks of being conscious of a representation *mit* the sensation of satisfaction (5.204). This Bernard translates merely as "as connected with the sensation of satisfaction": *Critique of Judgment*, tr. J. H. Bernard (New York: Hafner 1968), p. 38. In §9, Kant says that a contradiction is involved in supposing that the pleasure in question might precede the corresponding judgment (5.216-7). On pleasure as a "predicate," see also §§36–37 (5.287-8, 289).

22. In "First Introduction," Section VIII, Kant speaks of the predicate of the judgment both as a sensation and yet also as containing "the subjective conditions of a cognition in general" (20.224). Cf. *CJ*, §9 (5.219): "The excitement of both faculties (imagination and understanding) *is* [emphasis added] the sensation whose universal communicability is postulated by the judgment of taste."

23. "First Introduction," Section VIII (20.230-1). In the case of distinctively "ethical" feeling, for example, Kant says that the cognitive faculty is not connected with the faculty of desire (to do one's duty) *by means of* (*vermittelst:* Kant's emphasis) that feeling, since the latter itself would seem to be, as the sensation "of" the rational determinability of the will, *gar kein besonderes Gefühl*, over and above the very determination of that faculty. By analogy, one might presume that distinctively aesthetic feeling would be equally one with the corresponding determination of the cognitive faculties in question. Cf. Lewis W. Beck's discussion of Kant's notion of pleasure in *A Commentary on Kant's Critique of Practical Reason* (Chicago: University of Chicago Press, 1960), p. 93. Some kind of identification of pleasure taken in an activity with that activity itself is, of course, a familiar Aristotelian notion. Without explicitly conceding that Kant identifies the two as well, in the particular case of "acts" of apprehension and pleasure in them, Beck himself is uncomfortable with Kant's own way of putting things. He makes a point of adding, to his formulation of Kant's claim that pleasure *is* the "idea" of the self-supporting aspect of certain activities, hence of their "agreement" with the subject's internal condition, that "it would perhaps be clearer to say that pleasure is the feeling produced by such agreement."

24. *CJ*, Introduction, Sections IV–V.

25. "First Introduction," Section IV (20.209-10).

26. In whatever respect we judge it to be new, we need not in any case accept Buchdal's claim that it is only with the systematic demands of reflective judgment that we first encounter the demand that particular events in fact be subject to laws. So far as I can see, the textual evidence that Buchdal cites is perfectly compatible with the following reading instead: The first *Critique* has established that the conceptualization of any intuition necessarily involves the representation of certain courses of experience as necessary, under certain anticipable and retainable conditions, in relation to that intuition. But this still leaves open the question as to what the particular laws are, with *respect* to which the necessities in question obtain. The latter problem is the one that requires a transcendental principle that had not been enunciated in the earlier work. What is new is not the principle that nature is subject to causal necessities. That was already established by reflection on the problem of conceptualizing particular intuitions. It was established through an analysis of that special mode of consciousness by which an intuition's imaginatively anticipated and retained content actually comes to serve as material in the *conceptualization* of that intuition. That is something we have not yet considered. It may, of course, be described, though Kant does not do so, as itself a kind of principle of "reflective judgment," not merely as a principle of "understanding." It in any case bears on a different problem from what Kant

himself calls the problem of reflective judgment in the third *Critique*. The latter does not concern the constitution of a particular concept, out of the material possibly available within any particular intuition. Rather, it concerns the constitution of concepts (in the plural) out of the material (actually) available among *numerous* intuitions. (In this respect, we may then say, only the former is indeed a "constitutive" principle of experience.) Cf. Gerd Buchdal, *Metaphysics and the Philosophy of Science* (Cambridge,Mass.: The MIT Press, 1969), esp. pp. 500–505, 516–19, 641–45.

27. To make this point, it might help to distinguish, with a consistency not found in Kant himself, between knowledge in the sense of *Erkenntnis*, which is Kant's main concern in the Transcendental Deduction (and which I have tended to translate as "cognition"), and knowledge in the sense of *Wissen*. It seems clear, though, that Kant himself often uses the former term for both purposes. Cf. Chapter One, note 5.

28. Cf. *CJ*, Introduction, Section V (5.183):

> We find in the grounds of the possibility of an experience in the very first place something necessary, viz. the universal laws without which nature in general (as an object of sense) cannot be thought; and these rest upon the categories, applied to the formal conditions of all intuition possible for us, so far as it is also given *a priori* . . . . But now the objects of empirical cognition are determined in many other ways than by that formal time condition. . . . We must therefore think in nature, in respect of its merely empirical laws, a possibility of infinitely various empirical laws which are, as far as our *insight* [*Einsicht*: emphasis added] goes, contingent. . . . (Bernard translation, pp. 19–20)

It is precisely the problem of dealing with the latter, in turn, that requires postulation of the transcendental principle of judgment. Cf., similarly, "First Introduction," Section V (20.212, note):

> To be sure pure understanding (and indeed through synthetic principles) teaches us to *think* [*denken*: emphasis added] of all things of nature as contained in a transcendental *system according to concepts a priori* (the categories); but the faculty of (reflective) judgment, that *also* [emphasis added] seeks concepts for empirical representations as such, must assume beyond this for its own purpose that nature, in its boundless manifold, has hit upon such a division of the latter into genera and species that it makes it possible for our judgment to achieve *insight* [*Einhelligkeit*: emphasis added] in the comparison of natural forms and to arrive at empirical concepts and their mutual interconnection, by means of rising to ever more universal, though still empirical concepts; that is, judgment *also* [emphasis added] presupposes a system in accordance with empirical laws, and this *a priori*, consequently through a transcendental principle.

Chapter Five: The Second-Edition Deduction

1. Obviously, categorial synthesis provides the general form of one's "consciousness" of appearances, in the sense that it provides the general form of any (non-categorial) *conceptualization* of appearances. Nobody denies that. To anticipate, the point is simply to argue that noncategorial concepts, hence the conceptualization of appearances, are themselves constituted by an irreducible consciousness of synthesis in the first place. So the latter, in its role as what constitutes concepts, cannot itself be understood in terms of application of concepts to appearances.

2. Cf. Hans Wagner, "Der Argumentationsgang in Kants Deduktion der Kategorien," *Kant-Studien*, 71 (1980), 361; Viktor Nowotny, "Die Struktur der Deduktion bei Kant," *Kant-Studien*, 72 (1981), 275–76; Bernhard Thöle, "Die Beweisstruktur der transzendentalen Deduktion in der zweiten Auflage der 'Kritik der reinen Vernunft'," *Akten des 5. Internationalen Kant-Kongresses*, ed. Gerhard Funke *et al.* (Bonn: Bouvier Verlag Herbert

Grundmann, 1981), pp. 309-11; Henry Allison, *Kant's Transcendental Idealism* (New Haven: Yale University Press, 1983), pp. 161ff.

3. Nowotny (p. 278) holds that the issue could not possibly be resolved apart from the schematism chapter; cf. Thöle (p. 310). Pippin emphasizes the connection with the problem of schematism as well: Robert B. Pippin, *Kant's Theory of Form* (New Haven: Yale University Press, 1982), p. 182. He eventually concludes (pp. 226–28) that the problem is insoluble apart from an undermining of Kant's own rigid distinction between sensibility and understanding. Allison (pp. 167ff) also judges the second stage a failure, on account of Kant's inability to make the transition from a mere synthesis in our *apprehension* of things to conditions that are applicable to objects themselves.

4. Thöle (p. 309) emphasizes Kant's claim, at B147, that the objects we are given in space and time are themselves perceptions. Allison (p. 167) only concedes as a premise that objects in the order of spatiotemporal *apprehension* are "modifications of inner sense." That premise, in his view, is simply insufficient to carry Kant's conclusions into the order of ordinary objects of experience. Wagner's formulations seem to remain neutral as between the two orders. He speaks alternately of the need for a unity in space and time themselves and in our perceptions of space (p. 361). He does not indicate what sort of manifold, in either case, that unity is to be presumed relative to.

5. Cf. Gerold Prauss, *Erscheinung bei Kant* (Berlin: Walter de Gruyter, 1971) and *Kant und das Problem der Dinge an sich* (Bonn: Bouvier Verlag Herbert Grundmann). In the latter (p. 100), Prauss postulates a conceptual *Vorleistung* responsible for the promotion of *Anschauung* to the level of truly "judgmental" *Deutbarkeit*. But he seems to equate *Anschauung* with *Empfindung* (cf. pp. 63ff, 210). My own account is otherwise similar to Prauss's, insofar as the relevant *Vorleistung* is non-judgmental. But I would not want to call it "conceptual" either. Hoke Robinson, in "Anschauung und Mannigfaltiges in der Transzendentalen Deduktion," *Kant-Studien*, 72 (1981), 140–48, speaks instead of the transformation of *Proto-Anschauung* into *Anschauung*, by means of the forms of judgment (p. 146), but it is unclear how the *transformandum* relates to Kantian *Empfindung*. In any case, his demand for something sub-intuitional rests on the fact that intuition is already —because essentially *einzeln*—"unified." In my own view, the intrinsic *Einzelnheit* of intuitions is simply that aspect by virtue of which the "application" of concepts *to* them gives those concepts "directedness" in the sense explicated in Chapter One. Whatever sort of "unity" *this* requires is not what concerns us now. What concerns us now is a unity involved in the constitution of concepts themselves.

6. It should be clear that the manifold in question could be regarded as "unorganized" only with respect to the sort of unity that intellect provides. As a set of imaginative associations on the part of a normally functioning being, the manifold may be presumed organized at least according to whatever structures are in fact operative among anticipations and retentions as such (that is, on a level below the sort of conceptualization that Kant himself regards as distinctively human).

7. Allison, p. 165.

8. For this way of formulating the issue in Leibniz, see *Representational Mind* (Bloomington: Indiana University Press, 1983), pp. 18ff.

9. Kemp Smith attributes much of the confusion to Kant's tendency to waver between conceptualization as predication, or concept-"application," or "subsumption" under concepts, and conceptualization as involving a more literal imposition of some kind of *form*. Kant regards the *categories* in the latter way, but only occasionally does he seem so to regard concepts in general—for example, when he identifies them with what would otherwise be their mere schemata: Norman Kemp Smith, *A Commentary to Kant's 'Critique of Pure Reason'* (New York: Humanities Press, 1962; reprint of 2nd edition of 1923), pp. 335–38. As I see it, the source of confusion is more often Kant's tendency to equate the "noetic" and "noematic" perspectives. Kemp Smith simply leaves all questions in terms of the ambiguous imposition of form on "intuitions." Perhaps much of the unclarity in his own approach stems from a consequent failure to distinguish between views of concepts

that do away with their predicative status altogether and those that attempt to *account* for that status in terms of the internal structure of cognitive states. In contrast to both approaches, Paton regards all talk about the imposition of form, outside of the Aesthetic itself, as out of order from the start: "Nor is the problem solved by saying that the category is the form and the intuition the matter, and that these have no existence apart from one another. The forms of intuition are space and time, and the categories are forms, not of intuition, but of thought" (H. J. Paton, *Kant's Metaphysic of Experience* [London: George Allen and Unwin, 1936], II, p. 27). In any event, for Paton all concepts including the categories are "predicable" (p. 25).

10. Paton insists that, despite apparent assertions to the contrary, imagination consistently functions as an essential "element in" every empirical synthesis (II, pp. 397, 403n1, 413–14). But what that appears to come to is simply that a concept is always "a concept both of the object and *of* [emphasis added] the particular synthesis through which ideas successively given are combined in the object" (p. 402). Kemp Smith attributes the ambiguity to yet another tension in Kant, namely, to that between two forms of idealism. On the "subjectivisitic" variant, imagination is understanding operating as a faculty of individual subjects, upon those subjects' mental states (p. 227); on the "phenomenalistic" variant, it is—or at least "productive" imagination is—responsible for the working up of noumenal sensations, on a preconscious, hence pre-individual, level, into the appearances upon which an individual's faculties will then first be able to operate (pp. 264-70, 274).

11. Kant adds the following note:

> Whether the representations are in themselves identical, and whether, therefore, one can be analytically thought through the other, is not a question that here arises. The *consciousness* of the one, when the manifold is under consideration, has always to be distinguished from the consciousness of the other. . . . (B131n)

Kant should not be taken as suggesting that the concepts of synthesis and of unity of synthesis might after all be a single concept. Given his approach to the identity of concepts, in terms of identity of "consciousness" (A7/B11), that would of course be impossible. What Kant is suggesting is possible, despite the non-identity of the concepts of synthesis and of unity of synthesis, must rather be that the concepts may be *correlative* in a certain way: just as one considers the relevant "unity" only in relation to a certain kind of synthesis, one considers a synthesis *qua* synthesis only in relation to a corresponding unity *of* it. This may imply, but only in an uninteresting sense, that the synthesis is itself intellectual.

12. "[W]ir erkennen den Gegenstand, wenn wir in dem Mannigfaltigen der Anschauung synthethische Einheit bewirkt [n.b.] haben" (A105).

13. In *Reflexionenen zur Logik*, 1790 (16.116), Kant even refers to *Erscheinung* as "eine wirkliche Handlung der Erkenntniskraft . . . die auf das obiect geht"; sensation, by contrast, is a mere "theil vom eignen Zustande des Subiekts."

14. Cf. A79/B104: "The concepts which give *unity* [Kant's emphasis] to this pure synthesis"; A94: " . . . (2) the *synthesis* of this manifold through imagination; finally (3) the *unity* of this synthesis through original apperception [Kant's emphases]"; A118: "This synthetic unity presupposes or includes [*schliesst sie ein*] a synthesis"; A130: "The synthesis of the manifold through pure imagination, the unity of all representations in relation to original apperception, precede [n.b.: Kant's plural] all empirical cognition"; A155/B194: "The synthesis of representations rests on imagination; and their synthetic unity, which is required for judgment, on the unity of apperception"; A158/B197: " . . . the formal conditions of *a priori* intuition, the synthesis of imagination, and the necessary unity of the latter in a transcendental apperception"; cf. also A115-6.

15. Obviously, I take "analytic unity of consciousness," in this passage, to be the sort of unity that a concept, as a *Merkmal* or as representative of one, confers upon a manifold of intuitions of which it is predicable. The passage may be read differently. For example, Allison (pp. 143–44) takes analytic unity to be the unity of *Merkmale* within concepts them-

selves (or in judgments). Manfred Baum rejects this reading and adopts one similar to my own: *Deduktion und Beweis in Kants Transzendentalphilosophie* (Königstein/Ts.: Athenäum Verlag, 1986), pp. 22–23, 99–100. On the other hand, as I observed in a note to Chapter Three, Baum and Allison agree that the formation of any empirical concept involves the conversion of intuitional representations *into* the very *Merkmale* that are contained in it.

16. The general point applies whether *Merkmale* are regarded as (possible) "marks" of objects or as representations *of* possible marks. Kant himself is often ambiguous as between the two: "Every concept, as a partial concept, is contained in the representation of things as the ground of their cognition, that is, these things are contained under it as a *Merkmal*" (*Logik*, I, §7 [9.95]).

17. This notion of "expression" must of course be a special one. As suggested in Chapter Two, we may relate it to Croce's claim that all intuitions are expressive acts, hence in their own nature "linguistic."

18. Parenthetical references to the *Prolegomena* are to the fourth volume of the *Akademie-Ausgabe*. I utilize, with modification, Lewis White Beck's revision of the Carus translation (Indianapolis: Bobbs-Merrill, 1950). Beck's pages also carry the *Akademie* pagination.

19. Beck points out that while the *Prolegomena* (p. 299n) says that "The room is warm" could never become a judgment of experience, the *Logik* (§40) classifies "The stone is warm" as just such a judgment: "Did the Sage of Königsberg Have No Dreams?" in *Essays on Kant and Hume* (New Haven: Yale University Press, 1978), p. 52n. For a recent discussion of Kant on primary and secondary qualities, see Margaret D. Wilson, "The 'Phenomenalisms' of Berkeley and Kant," and (in reply to Wilson) Elizabeth Potter, "Kant's Scientific Rationalism," in Allen W. Wood, ed., *Self and Nature in Kant's Philosophy* (Ithaca: Cornell University Press, 1984), pp. 157–73 and 174–84, respectively.

20. Allison suggests (p. 152) one possible reading of this: "By such a judgment, Kant means perceptual awareness itself, not a reflective judgment about this awareness" (as Allison takes it to be: p. 150). On such a reading, Allison holds, the perceptions in question would be "modes of consciousness with their own peculiar 'subjective objects' (appearances)." Depending on how this was taken, it might or might not accord with my own approach. As he indicates (p. 152n47), such a view is defended by Prauss, with the exception that Prauss regards such judgments as judgments of "inner sense": Gerold Prauss, *Erscheinung bei Kant* (Berlin: Walter de Gruyter, 1971), pp. 150ff. Both Prauss and Allison object, against Kant, that judgments of perception must in any case contain categories.

21. According to Beck (p. 53), judgments of perception are judgments about either associations of ideas or particular subjective episodes. He also cites Prauss, pp. 120, 215–16, 137, 145. (As I indicated in the preceding note, Allison shares the view.)

22. Allison considers this suggestion in regard to Kant's distinction between subjective and objective unity in §§18–19 of the *Critique*, a distinction that can in fact "be seen as a reversion to the standpoint of the *Prolegomena*" (p. 156). His objection (pp. 157–58) is twofold: Kant's suggestion that such associations might then *become* objective judgments in their own right is confused; equally confused is his illustration (B142) of a would-be subjective unity by reference to what is already an objective judgment, namely, a judgment *about* some particular association ("If I support a body, I feel an impression of weight"). I return to the *Critique* itself shortly.

23. Cf. A765/B793: Regarding *a priori* principles, Hume "concluded that they are [emphasis added] nothing but a custom-bred habit." The imaginative faculty that generates such habits is merely "imitative" (A766-7/B794-5).

24. Beck, p. 58.

25. Ibid., p. 60.

26. Dieter Henrich, "The Proof-Structure of Kant's Transcendental Deduction," *Review of Metaphysics*, 22 (1969), pp. 647–48.

27. Wagner, p. 358: Kant's use of *insofern* in §20 is not restrictive at all, but merely indicates the respect in which the categories are necessary for sensible intuitions generally.

Cf. Robinson, p. 142; Nowotny, p. 272; Thöle, p. 306. Eckart Förster makes the same point, in his review of Allison's book (*Journal of Philosophy*, 82 [1985], 734–38). As Förster points out (a) B144n (to §21) says that the ground of the first stage of proof consists in "the represented *unity of intuition* [my emphasis] by which an object [*ein Gegenstand*] is given"; (b) in addition to several passages that indicate that the unity in question in the first stage is necessary for "the relation of representations to an object [*Gegenstand*], and therefore their objective validity" (B137), Kant makes it clear that the object (at this point, the *Objekt*) to which reference is thereby constituted is already "a determinate space" (B138); (c) §26 says that the first stage already demonstrates the applicability of the categories "as cognitions *a priori* of objects [*Gegenstände*] of an intuition in general." Regarding (c), one might, of course, try to enforce a distinction between a demonstration of applica*bility* (that is, of the mere possibility of application) and a demonstration that the categories actually do apply to objects.

28. Cf. Wagner, p. 356. As Wagner notes, the point is also made by Raymond Brouillet, "Dieter Henrich et 'The Proof-Structure of Kant's Transcendental Deduction'" *Dialogue*, 14 (1975), 639–48.

29. Henrich, p. 653.

30. Ibid., p. 649.

31. Cf. Robinson, pp. 144–46; Nowotny, p. 275.

32. It is a difference with respect to the question of the unity of space and time that may constitute the main difference between my own approach and Baum's. For Baum, the Deduction's second stage is defined by the need for a synthesis, below the level of judg-mental forming but necessarily in conformity with it, that is constitutive of the unity of space and time as such, not simply of appearances as objects of possible intuition (pp. 12ff, 80–81, 109ff, 153ff). Regarding the first stage, if I understand him, I agree with Baum that the point is to prove the applicability of the categories to appearances, in abstraction from the question of the latter's ingredience in a real world of nature. Where I differ is over his view that, only with removal of that abstraction, do we see the need for a synthesis applicable to space and time themselves. Removing the abstraction in the second stage, we will simply have moved from space and time, and any appearances in them, as corre-lates of sensible apprehension as such, to the actual space and time of the natural world, and the objects in it. *Both* stages require a synthesis generative of spatiotemporal unity.

33. Allison, though judging the second stage a failure, offers what is probably the most elaborate form of this reading. Thöle's approach is similar, in that he takes the distinction of stages to rest on the distinction between *Denken* and *Erkennen* (p. 307). He describes objects as the intuitive "correlates" of the otherwise purely logical forms of *Verbindung* (p. 309). On the other hand, he also criticizes the suggestion that the argument was not already concerned with spatiotemporal representation in its first stage. It might be that Thöle's is ambiguous as between a position like my own and one like Allison's.

34. Cf. Nowotny, pp. 274–75—although he *also* describes the first stage as involving purely *formale Denkeinheiten* and a purely formal notion of synthesis (p. 276). In any case, he sees the needed completion, involving application to objects, as calling for a doctrine of "schematism" (p. 278). Wagner (p. 365n, in criticism of Brouillet) rejects the approach, on the ground that the need for unity in spatiotemporal representation had already been in question prior to §26. The objection, of course, applies against Allison's approach as well. According to Wagner's approach, the crucial move is from sensible intuition to *Wahrnehmung* in particular (pp. 360–61), but I have not been able to get clear what that move is supposed to involve. If I understand him, Robinson (p. 146) takes the transition from a general determination of conditions of experience to the specifically human case simply to rest on *unseren tatsächlichen Besitz von Erfahrungserkenntnis*. On the other hand, his account is comparable to my own, insofar as it rests, even in its first stage, on the need for unification of a manifold within any single intuition, not simply of a manifold of distinct or distinguishable intuitions (p. 142). As for the question of the Deduction's in-completeness, Kant himself seems to say that the second-edition Deduction provides a suf-ficient explanation as to "how" the categories apply to objects, in terms of the account of

judgment offered in §19: *Metaphysical First Principles of Natural Science*, tr. James Ellington (Indianapolis: Bobbs-Merrill, 1970), Preface, note, pp. 13–14n (4.475-6).

35. Cf. Thöle (p. 307).

36. Cf. Chapter Three, note 16.

37. It may be useful to compare the analysis to follow with some aspects of Baum's approach, in particular with his approach to the Deduction's first two sections (§§15-16). Baum has argued, for example, that §15 already makes two things evident. First, it makes it evident that Kant's overall argument is meant to consist in the uncovering of a *single* factor capable of resolving *both* of the questions that require the Deduction's distinction into two stages in the first place. Second, it makes it evident that the role of this factor is prior to any problem concerning the "ascribability" of representations to subjects of consciousness. The latter problem does not arise until §16. The following analysis should show that I agree with Baum on both of these points and with his assessment of their importance, if not with the details of his account. See Baum, pp. 82ff. For my differences with Baum, see notes 15, 32, 37, above.

38. This formulation should indicate why, though I have continued to use the term, it may be misleading. What is represented, in regard to the past, is not intuitions formerly apprehended and now "retained." It is rather intuitions that one *might* have apprehended, and out of which the present intuition might in turn have evolved. I shall have much more to say about this issue in the next chapter.

39. For a defense of taking Kant at his word, see Baum, p. 84. Kemp Smith follows Mellin's substitution of "empirical or non-empirical" for Kant's *sinnlichen oder nicht sinnlichen*.

40. As I have indicated (Chapter Three, note 16), both Baum and Allison take the notion seriously in their readings. But they take too seriously the suggestion that what this involves, in turn, is the conversion of sensible impressions into *Merkmale*.

41. Cf. Allison, p. 158.

42. *Reflexionen zur Logik*, 3145 (16.678-9). Cf. A95: Apart from "elements of a possible experience," we are left merely with the "logical form *for* [*zu*] [my emphasis] a concept, not the concept itself through which something is thought." See Chapter Three, Section II, for further references regarding the transformation of representations *into* concepts. Kant himself, I would note, applies the matter/form distinction ambiguously in relation to concepts. It is a notion entirely different from the one that concerns us here, when Kant says that "the matter of concepts is the *object*, their form *universality*" (*Logik*, I, §2 [9.92]).

43. *Metaphysical First Principles*, Preface, pp. 12–13, note (4.474-5). Cf. B288: "the categories are not in themselves *cognitions*, but are merely *forms of thought* for the making of cognitions out of given intuitions." On the categories as forms "converted" into concepts in their own right, see also B143, A321/B378. On the categories as forms *for* (the formation of?) concepts, A147/B187: "The categories, therefore, without schemata, are merely functions of the understanding for concepts [*zu Begriffen*]." Also *Reflexionen zur Metaphysik*, 5932 (18.391): "This unity of consciousness (of the connection of our representations is as much *in us a priori* as the foundation of all concepts, as the form of appearance is as the foundation of intuitions."

Chapter Six: Self-Consciousness

1. One might note that Kant speaks of operations *in* concepts, not merely of operations among or connecting them. (Cf. B143: "[T]hat act of understanding by which the manifold of given representations (be they intuitions or concepts) is brought under one apperception, is the logical function of judgment.")

2. We need to recall that it is not a question of temporal priority; it is not that the material in question must actually be in an intuition before the act of conceptualizing it, although it might be, or a significant portion of it might be.

3. *Reflexionen zur Metaphysik*, 5932 (18.391).

4. *Logik*, I, §17 (9.101; emphasis added).

5. Cf. *Logik*, §§5–6 (9.93-4). If what is in question is, as Kant seems to claim, a matter of "abstracting" from certain *Merkmale*, so as to bring others more clearly to a unity of consciousness, then it is difficult to see how this could be done prior to an already operative work of conceptualization. But we may suppose that Kant has at least vaguely in mind a different process, whereby a subject "abstracts" from certain of its own anticipations and retentions, ingredient in intuition, so as to bring others to a special sort of unity of consciousness—thereby first *constituting* any apprehension of *Merkmale*. (Cf. *Reflexionen zur Logik*, 3057 [16.634]: "Eine Vorstellung, die *durch das Bewusstsein als Merkmals* allgemein wird, heisst (klarer) Begriff." Adickes takes the emphasized portion to mean: "through the fact that one has become conscious of one's own representation *as of a Merkmal.*" But we might simply take Kant to be saying that "A (clear) concept is a representation that, *through consciousness*, becomes general—as the consciousness of a *Merkmal.*") We might in any case note that Kant emphasizes, as conditions of abstraction, both "comparison" of and "reflection" upon one's own *representations*, and that at least the former he concedes to be within the capacity of animals: *Logik*, "Introduction," VIII (9.64). We might also recall the connection between "comparison," in Kant's terminology, and Humean association.

6. *Logik*, Introduction, V (9.33). Jäsche seems to have drawn the material for this passage from the Pölitz set of Kant's lecture notes, dating possibly from 1789 or 1790 (24pt2.510). But the same point is to be found in the Dohna-Wundlacken (24pt2.701) and the *Wiener* versions.

7. Cf. *Metaphysical First Principles of Natural Science*, tr. James Ellington (Indianapolis: Bobbs-Merrill, 1970), Chapter III, Proposition 2, "Observation," p. 103 (4.543): "Das Bewusstsein, mithin die Klarheit der Vorstellungen meiner Seele. . . ." (However, Ellington's translation somewhat obscures the equivalence in question.)

8. For a consideration of various attempts to read Kant along such lines, see Paul Guyer, "Kant's Tactics in the Transcendental Deduction," *Philosophical Topics*, 12 (1981), 157–99. See also "Kant on Apperception and *A Priori* Synthesis," *American Philosophical Quarterly*, 17 (1980), 205–12, and "Kant's Intentions in the Refutation of Idealism," *Philosophical Review*, 92 (1983), 329–83.

9. C. S. Lewis, *Studies in Words* (Cambridge: Cambridge University Press, 1960), Chapter 8.

10. On Pope, see OED entry 6c under *conscious*: "Some o'er her lap their careful plumes display'd/Trembling, and conscious of the rich brocade" (*Rape of the Lock*, 3.116). Earlier—and no less ambiguous—candidates seem to me to be Dryden's reference to "hunted *Castors*, conscious of their store" in *Annus Mirabilis*, line 97 (1667), and the following from *All For Love*, IV, 1 (1677): "You are of Cleopatra's private counsel,/Of her bedcounsel, her lascivious hours;/Are conscious of each nightly change she makes,/And watch her, as Chaldeans do the moon. . . ." Incidentally, Dryden also seems to be slighted with respect to entry 6d, regarding usage with a subordinate clause. The OED lists the phrase "conscious he did see it" from Burthogge (1694). But consider *The Hind and the Panther*, Part 2.1, line 1068 (1687): "But strive t'evade [promises], and fear to find 'em true,/As conscious they were never meant to you."

11. Nathan Bailey, *Dictionarum Brittanicum* (Hildesheim: Georg Olms, 1969; reprint of edition of 1730).

12. Samuel Johnson, *A Dictionary of the English Language* (New York: AMS Press, 1967; reprint of edition of 1755).

13. Thomas Reid, *Essays on the Intellectual Powers of Man* (1785), Essay I, Chapter 1 (Cambridge, Mass.: M.I.T. Press, 1969), p. 10. (A passage added to the third [1734] edition of Berkeley's *Third Dialogue* speaks, in order to deny it on philosophical—not linguistic—grounds, of the consciousness of the existence or essence of matter.)

14. *Dictionnaire de l'Academie Française*, 8th ed. (1932).

15. Peter Remnant and Jonathan Bennett, "Notes" to Leibniz's *New Essays on Human Understanding* (Cambridge: Cambridge University Press, 1981), p. xxxvi.

16. *Trésor de la Langue Française* (Paris: *Centre National de la Recherche Scientifique*,

1977).

17. This very common approach to consciousness is espoused, for example, by D. M. Armstrong in *A Materialist Theory of the Mind* (London: Routledge and Kegan Paul), pp. 323ff.)

18. Gertrud Jung, "Suneidesis, Conscientia, Bewusstsein," *Archiv für die gesamte Psychologie*, 89 (1933), pp. 535ff. Cf. Hans Amrhein, "Kant's Lehre vom 'Bewusstsein überhaupt,'" *Kantstudien Ergänzungshefte*, 10 (Würzburg: jal-reprint, 1973; reprint of edition of 1909), p. 6.

19. A120: perception is appearances "combined with consciousness"; A190: insofar as, being mere representations, they are inseparable from the apprehension of them, appearances are *Gegenstände des Bewusstseins*; A371: outer *Gegenstände* are "nothing but representations, the immediate perception (consciousness) of which is at the same time a sufficient proof of their reality"; A404: the Fourth Paralogism wrongly concludes that the soul's consciousness "is not the consciousness of many things [*mehrerer Dinge*] outside of it, but *of the existence of itself only*, and of other things merely as its *representations*."

20. *Logik*, Introduction, V (9.34); cf. Pölitz (24pt2.510), Dohna-Wundlacken (24pt2.702). Cf. also Blomberg's reference to the consciousness of "objects" or "things" *durch Bewusstsein* (24pt1.40); Philippi speaks of becoming conscious of the material contained in an *Objekt* (24pt1.341), and of such facts as that a perceived object is a group of stars (24pt1.410).

21. Cf. Patricia Kitcher, "Kant's Real Self," in *Self and Nature in Kant's Philosophy*, ed. Allen Wood (Ithaca: Cornell University Press, 1984), p. 140: ". . . to be self-conscious, for Kant, is to attribute mental states to one's (thinking) self . . . .Thus, Kant would understand the doctrine that consciousness requires self-consciousness as maintaining that any being which makes judgments about its own mental states must be able to attribute those states to its own thinking self." Cf. Patricia Kitcher, "Kant on Self-Identity," *Philosophical Review*, XCI (1982), 41–72. Also, Graham Bird, *Kant's Theory of Knowledge* (London: Routledge and Kegan Paul, 1962), pp. 137–38: "His argument is, then, that just as such categorial rules are required for objective discriminations in general, so this same condition holds for our discrimination of persons." Cf. also Guyer, *op. cit.*; Jonathan Bennett, *Kant's Analytic* (Cambridge: Cambridge University Press, 1966), pp. 113ff. For a criticism of Guyer's general approach, with a focus on "Kant on Apperception . . . ," see Karl Ameriks, "Kant and Guyer on Apperception," *Archiv für Geschichte der Philosophie*, 65 (1983), 175–86. Ameriks opposes Guyer's view that the capacity for mere representation demands unity of apperception; what demands it is rather the capacity for a relatively low-level "awareness" *of* one's representations. So far as I can tell, Ameriks does not say how the latter in turn relates to one's capacity for the "self-ascription" of representations, though he does explicitly distinguish it from the "reflexive" ascription of representations that provide "objective knowledge" (pp. 183-84).

22. Cf. Jay F. Rosenberg, "'I Think': Some Reflections on Kant's Paralogisms," in *Midwest Studies in Philosophy*, X (1986), p. 524–25: "[T]he logical function of ascribing many thoughts to one subject is distinct from the logical function of attributing many properties to one object. . . . The 'I' which is the subject *of experiences* (E-subject) is not, as such, a subject *of predicates* (P-subject). Despite the formal parallelism of the one-versus-many pattern, the way in which one 'I' "collects" many thoughts or experiences ("its" thoughts and experiences, those which it "has") is nevertheless functionally, and thus logically, radically different from the way in which one object "collects" many properties. . . . " As should soon become clearer, I also share Rosenberg's view concerning the comparison of Kant and Sartre. See p. 516, and also Rosenberg's "Apperception and Sartre's 'Pre-Reflective Cogito,'" *American Philosophical Quarterly*, 18 (1981), 255–60. Rosenberg's views have since been developed in detail in *The Thinking Self* (Philadelphia: Temple University Press, 1986). The approach is "functionalistic" to an extent that I am not inclined to follow, although Rosenberg combines it with a version of ("logical") phenomenology that allows him to elaborate the functionalist perspective in a manner that far surpasses the more usual nods in that direction.

23. Cf. Bennett, pp. 113ff.

24. *Logik Dohna-Wundlacken* (24pt2.702).

25. In the *Critique*, see A320/B376. Cf. Letter to Herz, 26 May, 1789 (11.520): "[Apart from categories, representations] . . . would still (I imagine myself to be an animal) carry on their play in an orderly fashion . . . in me, though I am unconscious of my existence (granting that I would still be conscious of every single representation, but not of their relation to the unity of representation of their object, by means of the synthetic unity of apperception) . . . without in the least cognizing anything thereby, not even this condition of myself'; *Reflexionen zur Anthropologie*, 206 (15.79): "Consciousness makes nothing intellectual, rather it presents things [*bietet es das Ding*] to the understanding." Cf. also *Anthropologie*, §1 (7.127-8), and *Reflexionen zur Anthropologie*, 212 (15.81). In the *Logik* (Introduction, VIII [9.64-5])—and the same point, or variation upon it, is to be found throughout Kant's reflections and lectures on logic—Kant distinguishes a mere level (*Grad*) of representation *mit Bewusstsein*, available to mere animals, from the level of true cognition (*Erkennen*). In this context, Kant even grants animals the capacity to "compare" the representations of which they are conscious; what he denies them is the capacity to do so *mit Bewusstsein*.

26. An interesting article by Mark Kulstad ("Leibniz on Consciousness and Reflection," *Spindel Conference 1982, Southern Journal of Philosophy*, XXI [1983], 39-66) makes it clear how unclear Leibniz had been, regarding the sense in which the transition from unconscious to conscious perception might involve a special mode of "apperception" of the *objects* of perception, or rather only of one's own original perceptual state (or perhaps both in a sense, but with the former in effect reducible to the latter).

27. *Reflexionen zur Metaphysik*, 5654 (18.313).

28. Cf. Hector-Neri Castañeda, "He: A Study in the Logic of Self-Consciousness," *Ratio*, 8 (1966), 130-57; "On the Phenomeno-Logic of the I," *Akten des XIV. Internationalen Kongresses für Philosophie* (1968), 260–66.

29. The term may, of course, be misleading; but cf. B426-7, B157, B157n, B277. Marta Ujvari ("Personal Identity Reconsidered," *Kant-Studien*, 75 [1984], 328–39) argues, in criticism of an earlier paper of mine, that it makes no sense to identify the "self" of "indeterminate" self-consciousness with any individual. It is merely a kind of function or form. The threefold distinction that I make below allows me to grant this, but only with respect to one of the two senses in which self-consciousness might be supposed to be "indeterminate." I would also note how my own approach differs from Strawson's, with which Ujvari associates mine in her article. Strawson's attempt is to show that certain modes of awareness of objects are necessary for forming the concept of a subject of experience *in general*. My own is to show their necessity as a condition for something both more and less "determinate" than this: less, in that the self-consciousness of which such object-consciousness is to be a condition is not, as such, conceptual at all; more, in that it is a mode of self-consciousness that is nonetheless sufficiently rich to provide "material" for the *formation* of a determinate self-concept. Cf. P. F. Strawson, *The Bounds of Sense* (London: Methuen and Co., 1966), pp. 93ff. (Regrettably too late for more elaborate comment, I have now also noticed that a similar distinction between transcendental, indeterminate empirical, and determinate empirical self-consciousness is drawn by Wolfgang Becker in *Selbstbewusstsein und Erfahrung* [Freiburg: Verlag Karl Alber, 1984], pp. 184, 238ff.)

30. Cf. Norman Kemp Smith, *A Commentary to Kant's 'Critique of Pure Reason'* (New York: Humanities Press, 1962; reprint of edition of 1923), pp. 251–52; Robert Paul Wolff, *Kant's Theory of Mental Activity* (Cambridge, Mass.: Harvard University Press, 1963), pp. 116, 119, 132, 161, 187. H. J. Paton (*Kant's Metaphysic of Experience* [London: Allen and Unwin, 1936]) appears to interpret the argument this way at times (I, pp. 512–13); other times, to rest it more directly on the claim that self-consciousness requires distinguishing oneself from other things (pp. 398n6, 405, 464, 548).

31. Kant would presumably only be specifying the relations held necessarily to obtain among the *objects* of representations supposed ascribable to oneself. These, of course, at most *correlate* with the relevant relations among those representations themselves.

32. *Reflexionen zur Metaphysik*, 6315 (18.619-20); cf. 5461 and 6317. Kant also argues (5621, 6315) that while the soul is not in, or at least cannot perceive its location in, the body, it must nevertheless be *where* the body is.

33. *Metaphysical First Principles of Natural Science*, Chapter Three, Proposition 2, "Observation" (4.542-3; tr. Ellington, pp. 103–4). In this passage, Kant also says that, while the "I" expresses a "thought," it does not express any concept. Cf. A108, B132, B137, B153.

34. Cf. *Reflexionen zur Metaphysik*, 6315.

35. Cf. ibid., 5654 (18.313): "One can indeed posit time in oneself, but not posit oneself in time and therein determine oneself, and yet it is in this that empirical self-consciousness consists. . . ."

36. Cf. B422n: While "I exist thinking" is grounded in the apprehension of appearances, the "I" *in* that proposition "is purely intellectual, because belonging to thought in general."

37. Cf. Bennett, pp. 107ff.

38. Jean-Paul Sartre, *Being and Nothingness*, tr. Hazel E. Barnes (New York: Washington Square Press, 1943), Introduction, III, and Part Two, Chapter One, Section I.

39. "Concept" is, of course, a vague term. A dog, anticipating the upshot of certain actions of its own, perhaps possesses a "concept" of itself as acting. At least part of my point is simply that what Kant himself regards as "conceptualization" is supposed to be something beyond the capacity of dogs. Presumably, Kant does not deny the latter's ability to anticipate possible upshots of their actions. The point is then that it is out of such merely "animal" material that Kant regards (empirical) concepts as constituted in the first place.

40. *Anthropologie*, §§15ff (7.153ff).

41. Cf. Norton Nelkin, "Pains and Pain Sensations," *Journal of Philosophy*, 83 (1986), 129–48; G. Lynn Stephens and George Graham, "Minding Your P's and Q's: Pain and Sensible Qualities," *Noûs*, XXI (1987), 395–405.

42. Through an interesting interplay between ontological and phenomenological reflection, but without the matter/form apparatus as I attempt to employ it, Laird Addis has also defended the idea of pains as intentional objects, namely, as objects of a mode of "direct awareness": "Pains and Other Secondary Mental Entities," *Philosophy and Phenomenological Research*, XLVII (1986), 59–73. As such, pains are—unless they happen to be, as is (onto-)logically possible, unreal objects (p. 68)—particulars that exemplify "the property that makes [them] a pain" (p. 69). This property is not (onto-)logically connected with one's attitude of liking or disliking the object, or the feeling, in question (p. 65). However, since Addis apparently allows only one "mode" *per* instance of awareness (p. 60; but cf. p. 64), I take it that he would not be inclined to recognize a distinct property—exemplifiable by the same particulars that exemplify the property of "painfulness" in the first sense—that would make the objects in question also painful in a second sense, namely, as correlates of a certain mode of disliking.

43. See references included in the articles cited in note 41, above.

44. Jean-Paul Sartre, *The Transcendence of the Ego*, tr. Forrest Williams and Robert Kirkpatrick (New York: Noonday Press, 1936), p. 49.

45. I don't mean to suggest that one is aware of oneself as pained *only* in such cases; cf. Sartre's discussion of the consciousness of pain in one's eyes, as constituted through certain modes of consciousness of a book that one happens to be reading: *Being and Nothingness*, pp. 436ff.

46. Despite my opposition to Kitcher's functionalistic reconstruction, I am very much in sympathy with her view that the Deduction should be read, not so much as an argument to establish Kant's positive position regarding self-consciousness, but as the presentation of a *theory* of the latter, meant to be more adequate than any other available, and sufficient in turn for a deduction of the categories from it. "Kant's Real Self," p. 116: "While Kant offers some explicit argumentation in favor of this claim, the crucial support for it does not come from arguments, but from his improved understanding of mental states."

47. On oneself as "center of orientation," cf. Husserl, *Ideen zu einer reinen Phänomenologie und Phänomenologischen Philosophie: Zweites Buch*, ed. Marley Biemel (Den Haag: Martinus Nijhoff, 1952), §18, pp. 56–57, 65, and §41. Naturally, I am also very much in

sympathy with the following statement by Rosenberg, "'I Think: Some Reflections . . . ,'" p. 528: "What is needed [for transcendental self-consciousness] is not some unique and mysterious form of nonempirical or nonintentional consciousness but a proper appreciation of the global structures of our *ordinary* empirical awareness and the diverse modes of our *actual* intentional representations, an appreciation of the *sort* of 'unity of consciousness' which is ours."

48. Cf. Thomas Nagel, *The View From Nowhere* (Oxford: Oxford University Press, 1986), pp. 54ff.

49. This approach has some similarities to G. E. M. Anscombe's in "The First Person," in *Mind and Language*, ed. Samuel Guttenplan (Oxford: Oxford University Press, 1975), but also an advantage over it. Anscombe gives as the sense of "I am this thing here": "This thing here is the thing . . . of whose action *this* idea of action . . . of whose movements *these* ideas of movement . . . of whose posture *this* idea of posture . . . [a]nd also, of which *these* intended actions, if carried out, will be the actions" (p. 61). We agree on the centrality of "ideas" of such things as movements, posture, and actions in particular, as opposed to accounts that define the *I*, from occasion to occasion, as the subject of this or that experience (supposedly picked out on each occasion), regardless of its content. But Anscombe is subject to the objection that individuation of "ideas," at least as mental occurrences, is parasitical upon individuating the subject: Anthony Kenny "The First Person," in *Intention and Intentionality: Essays in Honor of G. E. M. Anscombe*, ed. Cora Diamond and Jenny Teichman (Ithaca: Cornell University Press, 1979), pp. 3–13. On the suggested alternative, the "ideas" in question are simply one's own (anticipated or retained) movements, postures, and actions themselves, insofar as these are reflected in the appearances that are the *objects* of the corresponding mental occurrences.

50. *Reflexionen zur Metaphysik*, 6354 (18.680).

51. I have a bit to say on the matter in *Representational Mind* (Bloomington: Indiana University Press, 1983), pp. 180–81.

52. Cf. B151: "*Imagination* is the faculty of representing in intuition an object that is *not itself present*"; *Logik Dohna-Wundlacken* (24pt2.701-2):

Die Sinnlichkeit enthält zwei Vermögen, den Sinn und die Einbildungskraft [dies ist die Zauberkraft des menschlichen Geistes] oder das Anschauungsvermögen eines Gegenstandes, sofern er nicht da ist, der Sinn aber das, sofern der Gegenstand da ist.

53. Cf. A123: "[Productive imagination] . . . aims at nothing but necessary unity in the synthesis . . ."; B151: "[Figurative synthesis] . . . directed merely to the original synthetic unity. . . . "

Chapter Seven: Toward the Categories

1. An interesting discussion of the categories of quantity and quality, that also seems to me to have some affinity with my own approach, is offered by Gordon Nagel in *The Structure of Experience: Kant's System of Principles* (Chicago: University of Chicago Press, 1983), pp. 84ff.

2. Paul Guyer, "Kant's Tactics in the Transcendental Deduction," *Philosophical Topics*, 12 (1981), 157–99.

3. What concerns me, in what follows, is the need to represent possible appearances, not simply "through" given sets of anticipations, but precisely as subsumable under the very concepts that are *formed* out of anticipations. This, I argue, requires the anticipation of possible appearances as the intentional correlates of (possible) apprehension through *suitably modified* sets of the original anticipations. It may be that the relevant notion of "suitability" is all that Kant himself intended by way of the essentially normative in conception. But the notion of normativity enters at another point as well. Beyond the requirement that appearances be apprehended through the anticipation of appearances that are in their

own turn to be apprehended through suitable modifications of the original anticipations, we also require some sense of the relative *(prima facie) reasonableness* or *unreasonableness* of apprehending a given appearance through particular anticipations rather than others in the first place. In the first case, I presume, the criteria of "suitability" are simply part of the very *conception* of objectivity. No irreducibly "normative" element is really in question. But it may be in question in the second case. In any event, Kant offers no account of whatever sort of normative "consciousness" then needs to be in question.

4. See "Necessity and Irreversibility in the Second Analogy," *History of Philosophy Quarterly,* 2 (1983), 203–15.

5. Cf. Arthur Melnick, *Kant's Analogies of Experience* (Chicago: University of Chicago Press, 1973), pp. 94ff. Admittedly, Melnick's reconstruction of the Third Analogy comes validly closer to Kant's conclusion than I do. On the other hand, in application to the Second Analogy, that same general approach to Kant's concern with the reversibility of perceptions leads Melnick nowhere close to Kant's own conclusion that all events are causally determined.

6. Cf. Norman Kemp Smith, *A Commentary to Kant's 'Critique of Pure Reason'* (New York: Humanities Press, 1962; reprint of edition of 1923), pp. 387ff. The point, according to Kemp Smith, is simply that judgments of coexistence involve "reference of each existence to the totality of systematic relations within which it is found" (p. 389).

7. If the argument is in fact to be read, as I do not myself read it, with the emphasis on "determination" in the sense of knowing-that, in regard to the occurrence of certain sorts of changes, then I would agree with Henry Allison (*Kant's Transcendental Idealism* [New Haven: Yale University Press, 1983], p. 206) that D. P. Dryer's reconstruction is the most plausible one: *Kant's Solution for Verification in Metaphysics* (Toronto: University of Toronto Press, 1966), pp. 353ff.

8. Allison (p. 201) calls this stage of the argument the "Backdrop Thesis." However, while he concedes that it falls short of Kant's conclusion that phenomenal change is change in the state of an underlying substratum, he seems too easily to grant that, because time is imperceptible, there must at least *be* something (or things) permanent in appearances, as a perceptible "model" of the imperceptible Backdrop (p. 203). So far as I can see, it is not so easy to get to this apparently weaker thesis without first establishing the stronger one.

9. For a more detailed discussion of temporal stretches, as an object of spatial, not merely of temporal, intuition, see *Representational Mind*, Chapter Six.

10. It should be clear that a double notion of "determination" must be in question, namely, one that includes both (a) conceptualization of appearances as concrete objects and (b) empirical "determination" (in the sense of knowing-that) of the grounds for actually doing so.

Index